Communications in Computer and Information Science   **1233**

Commenced Publication in 2007
Founding and Former Series Editors:
Simone Diniz Junqueira Barbosa, Phoebe Chen, Alfredo Cuzzocrea,
Xiaoyong Du, Orhun Kara, Ting Liu, Krishna M. Sivalingam,
Dominik Ślęzak, Takashi Washio, Xiaokang Yang, and Junsong Yuan

More information about this series at http://www.springer.com/series/7899

Fernando De La Prieta et al. (Eds.)

Highlights in Practical Applications of Agents, Multi-Agent Systems, and Trust-worthiness

The PAAMS Collection

International Workshops of PAAMS 2020
L'Aquila, Italy, October 7–9, 2020
Proceedings

 Springer

Editors

see next page

ISSN 1865-0929   ISSN 1865-0937   (electronic)
Communications in Computer and Information Science
ISBN 978-3-030-51998-8   ISBN 978-3-030-51999-5   (eBook)
https://doi.org/10.1007/978-3-030-51999-5

This Springer imprint is published by the registered company Springer Nature Switzerland AG
The registered company address is: Gewerbestrasse 11, 6330 Cham, Switzerland

Volume Editors

Fernando De La Prieta 🆔
University of Salamanca
Salamanca, Spain

Jaime Andrés Rincón Arango
Polytechnic University of Valencia
Valencia, Spain

Elena Del Val
Polytechnic University of Valencia
Valencia, Spain

João Carneiro
Instituto Superior de Engenharia do Port
Porto, Portugal

Fernando Lopes
National Laboratory for Energy and Geology
Amadora, Portugal

Philippe Mathieu
University of Lille
Villeneuve d'Ascq, France

Alia El Bolock
German University in Cairo
New Cairo City, Egypt

Jaume Jordán Prunera
University of Valencia
Valencia, Spain

Rubén Fuentes
Complutense University of Madrid
Madrid, Spain

Vicente Julian
Polytechnic University of Valencia
Valencia, Spain

Preface

The PAAMS Workshops complemented the regular program with new or emerging trends of particular interest connected to multi-agent systems. PAAMS, the International Conference on Practical Applications of Agents and Multi-Agent Systems, is an evolution of the International Workshop on Practical Applications of Agents and Multi-Agent Systems. PAAMS is an international yearly tribune for presenting, discussing, and disseminating the latest developments and the most important outcomes related to real-world applications. It provides a unique opportunity to bring multi-disciplinary experts, academics, and practitioners together to exchange their experience in the development of agents and multi-agent systems.

This volume presents the papers that were accepted in the workshops during the 2020 edition of PAAMS: Workshop on Agent-Based Artificial Markets Computational Economics (ABAM), Workshop on Agents and Edge-AI (AgEdAI), Workshop on Character Computing (C2), Workshop on MAS for Complex Networks and Social Computation (CNSC), Workshop on Decision Support, Recommendation, and Persuasion in Artificial Intelligence (DeRePAI), Workshop on Multi-Agent Systems and Simulation (MAS&S), Workshop on Multi-agent based Applications for Energy Markets, Smart Grids and Sustainable Energy Systems (MASGES), and Workshop on Smart Cities and Intelligent Agents (SCIA). Each paper submitted to PAAMS went through a stringent peer-review process by three members of the International Program Committee of each track. From the 57 submissions received, 34 were selected for presentation at the conference.

We would like to thank all the contributing authors, the members of the Program Committees, the sponsors (IBM, Armundia Group, EurAI, AEPIA, AFIA, APPIA, FBKI, CINI, CNRS, KUL, AIR Institute, and UNIVAQ), and the Organizing Committee for their hard and highly valuable work. We are thankful for the financial support received from the project "Virtual Ledgers" (Id. SA267P18) by the Regional Government of Castilla y León and FEDER funds.

Thanks for your help – PAAMS 2020 would not exist without your contribution.

May 2020

Fernando De La Prieta
Philippe Mathieu
Jaime Andrés Rincón Arango
Alia El Bolock
Elena Del Val
Jaume Jordán Prunera
João Carneiro
Rubén Fuentes
Fernando Lopes
Vicente Julian

Organization

General Co-chairs

Yves Demazeau   National Center for Scientific Research, France
Tom Holvoet   Catholic University of Leuven, Belgium
Stefania Costantini   University of L'Aquila, Italy
Juan Manuel Corchado   University of Salamanca and AIR Institute, Spain

Workshop Chair

Fernando De la Prieta   University of Salamanca, Spain

Advisory Board

Bo An   Nanyang Technological University, Singapore
Paul Davidsson   Malmö University, Sweden
Keith Decker   University of Delaware, USA
Frank Dignum   Utrecht University, The Netherlands
Toru Ishida   University of Kyoto, Japan
Takayuki Ito   Nagoya Institute of Technology, Japan
Eric Matson   Purdue University, USA
Jörg P. Müller   Clausthal Technical University, Germany
Michal Pĕchouček   Technical University in Prague, Czech Republic
Franco Zambonelli   University of Modena and Reggio Emilia, Italy

Organizing Committee

Juan M. Corchado Rodríguez   University of Salamanca and AIR Institute, Spain
Fernando De la Prieta   University of Salamanca, Spain
Sara Rodríguez González   University of Salamanca, Spain
Javier Prieto Tejedor   University of Salamanca and AIR Institute, Spain
Pablo Chamoso Santos   University of Salamanca, Spain
Belén Pérez Lancho   University of Salamanca, Spain
Ana Belén Gil González   University of Salamanca, Spain
Ana De Luis Reboredo   University of Salamanca, Spain
Angélica González Arrieta   University of Salamanca, Spain
Emilio S. Corchado Rodríguez   University of Salamanca, Spain
Angel Luis Sánchez Lázaro   University of Salamanca, Spain
Alfonso González Briones   University Complutense of Madrid, Spain
Yeray Mezquita Martín   University of Salamanca, Spain

Enrique Goyenechea	University of Salamanca and AIR Institute, Spain
Javier J. Martín Limorti	University of Salamanca, Spain
Alberto Rivas Camacho	University of Salamanca, Spain
Ines Sitton Candanedo	University of Salamanca, Spain
Elena Hernández Nieves	University of Salamanca, Spain
Beatriz Bellido	University of Salamanca, Spain
María Alonso	University of Salamanca, Spain
Diego Valdeolmillos	AIR institute, Spain
Roberto Casado Vara	University of Salamanca, Spain
Sergio Marquez	University of Salamanca, Spain
Jorge Herrera	University of Salamanca, Spain
Marta Plaza Hernández	University of Salamanca, Spain
Guillermo Hernández González	AIR Institute, Spain
Luis Carlos Martínez de Iturrate	University of Salamanca and AIR Institute, Spain
Ricardo S. Alonso Rincón	University of Salamanca, Spain
Javier Parra	University of Salamanca, Spain
Niloufar Shoeibi	University of Salamanca, Spain
Zakieh Alizadeh-Sani	University of Salamanca, Spain

Local Organizing Committee

Pierpaolo Vittorini	University of L'Aquila, Italy
Tania Di Mascio	University of L'Aquila, Italy
Giovanni De Gasperis	University of L'Aquila, Italy
Federica Caruso	University of L'Aquila, Italy
Alessandra Galassi	University of L'Aquila, Italy

Contents

Workshop on MAS for Complex Networks and Social Computation (CNSC)

Workshop on Decision Support, Recommendation, and Persuasion in Artificial Intelligence (DeRePAI)

Workshop on Multi-agent Systems and Simulation (MAS&S)

**Workshop on Multi-agent based Applications for Energy Markets,
Smart Grids and Sustainable Energy Systems (MASGES)**

Workshop on Smart Cities and Intelligent Agents (SCIA)

Workshop on Agent-Based Artificial Markets Computational Economics (ABAM)

Workshop on Agent-Based Artificial Markets Computational Economics (ABAM)

In recent years, the worlds of economy and finance have benefited from a tremendous stream of innovations coming from the computer science community. Among others, simulation techniques have allowed for the testing of new methods in algorithmic trading while new regulation or market innovations are imposed to optimize the automation of trade execution, in an increasingly complex financial system. Artificial intelligence, in this context, finds a new field of amazing applications.

This workshop of the PAAMS conference focuses on the application of agents and all artificial intelligence techniques applied to the fields of economics or finance. Areas of special interest include but are not limited to simulation, ACE, algorithmic trading, agent-based artificial markets, high-performance trading, smart grids, design of artificial traders, market and policy design, auctions, matching mechanism designs, and economics education with ABM.

Organization

Organizing Committee

Philippe Mathieu   University of Lille, France

Program Committee

Frederic Amblard   University of Toulouse 1, France
Javier Arroyo   University Complutense Madrid, Spain
Hugues Bersini   Université libre de Bruxelles, Belgium
Olivier Brandouy   University of Bordeaux IV, France
Florian Hauser   University of Innsbruck, Austria
Philippe Mathieu   University of Lille, France
Paolo Pellizzari   Ca'Foscari University of Venice, Italy
Ragupathy Venkatachalam   Goldsmiths, University of London, UK
Tiago Pinto   Polytechnic of Porto, Portugal
Marta Posada   University of Valladolid, Spain
Marco Raberto   University of Genoa, Italy
Roger Waldeck   Télécom Bretagne, France

Murat Yildizoglu	University of Bordeaux IV, France
Freiderike Wall	Alpen-Adria Universität, Austria
Segismundo Izquierdo	University of Valladolid, Spain

Ethical Concerns and Opportunities in Binding Intelligent Systems and Blockchain Technology

Davide Calvaresi[1]([✉])(iD), Jean-Gabriel Piguet[1], Jean-Paul Calbimonte[1](iD),
Timotheus Kampik[2](iD), Amro Najjar[3](iD), Guillaume Gadek[4],
and Michael Schumacher[1](iD)

[1] University of Applied Sciences and Arts Western Switzerland,
Delémont, Switzerland
davide.calvaresi@hevs.ch
[2] Umeå University, Umeå, Sweden
tkampik@cs.umu.se
[3] University of Luxembourg, Luxembourg City, Luxembourg
amro.najjar@uni.lu
[4] Airbus Defence and Space, Toulouse, France
guillaume.gadek@airbus.com

Abstract. Intelligent systems are becoming increasingly complex and pervade a broad range of application domains, including safety-critical systems such as e-health, finance, and energy management. Traditional approaches are no longer capable of addressing the demand for trust and transparency in these applications. Hence, the current decade is demanding intelligent systems to be autonomous, and in particular explainable, transparent, and trustworthy. To satisfy such requirements, and therefore to comply with the recent EU regulations in the matter (e.g., GDPR), intelligent systems (e.g., Multi-Agent Systems - MAS) and technologies enabling tamper-proof and distributed consensus (e.g., Blockchain Technology - BCT) are conveying into reconciling solutions. Recently, the empowerment of MAS with BCT (and the use of BCT themselves) has gained considerable momentum, raising challenges, and unveiling opportunities. However, several ethical concerns have yet to be faced. This paper elaborates on the entanglement among ethical and technological challenges while proposing and discussing approaches that address these emerging research opportunities.

Keywords: Blockchain · Multi-Agent Systems · Ethics · Transparency · Trust

1 Introduction

After years spent in trying to delegate *automatable* tasks (e.g., mass-production industry), our contemporary societies are experiencing machine delegation of a

© Springer Nature Switzerland AG 2020
F. De La Prieta et al. (Eds.): PAAMS 2020 Workshops, CCIS 1233, pp. 5–16, 2020.
https://doi.org/10.1007/978-3-030-51999-5_1

growing amount of *strategic/intelligent* tasks [9], for which transparency and trustworthiness of the intelligent entities (e.g., agents) and their behaviors must be ensured. For example, in the healthcare domain (eHealth in particular), any actor (e.g., caregiver, insurance, pharmacy, and smart-devices) can be modeled as an agent with specific behaviors [11,12,17]. Usually, actors such as medical doctors and nurses are traditionally considered cooperative and trustworthy. Nevertheless, in many settings, they can have conflicting or competing interests (e.g., insurance companies and privately owned healthcare organizations). Thus, the demand for transparent reputation management to promote (and possibly ensure) *correct* behaviors is imperative.

To enforce basic coordination rules among agents, the usage of ledgers-based technologies (e.g., blockchain) has been proposed as a relevant solution [5]. At first glance, the systems reconciling BCT and MAS offer new perspectives for the empowerment of the individuals.

Currently, the users have to interact with Trusted Third Parties (TTP) unavoidably (e.g., platforms such as Airbnb and Uber), which are far from being egalitarian. Conversely, it is broadly accepted that BCT eradicates the monopoly on the information and ensures a certain degree of equality in control of the contracts' implementation. Thanks to the use of BCTs in MAS, the informational and executive asymmetry that underpins the business model of many platforms could come to an end. However, can the BCT actually deliver this massive societal promise? For systems that are based both on Multi-Agent Systems (MAS) and BlockChain Technology (BCT), and are operating in safety- and information-critical domains, a range of challenges and related opportunities is emerging. In particular, four fundamental questions should find an answer: *(i)* How can we prevent the ecosystem of technologies like BitCoins from being dominated by the wealthy few? *(ii)* In a MAS, when a "bad" decision is made, who is liable for it? *(iii)* Can we truly get rid of every intermediary, especially in the case of smart-contracts? and *(iv)* How to construct a fair reputation-building system through BCT and MAS, which could avoid setting a user's undue reputation in stone?

This article *(i)* reviews recent trans-disciplinary work across computer science, legislation, and ethics; and *(ii)* proposes a structured synthesis of the current technological and ethical challenges of BCT and MAS, detailing the corresponding research opportunities. Solving these challenges may help BCT to comply with its promises and effectively empower multi-agent systems and their users.

The rest of the paper is organized as follow: Sect. 2 introduces background on blockchain and its intersection with MAS, Sect. 3 identifies challenges in this scope, and Sect. 4 discusses research opportunities to explore in this domain. Finally, Sect. 5 concludes the paper.

2   Blockchain and MAS: Transparency, Trust, and Ethics

To cope with the increasingly sophisticated AI systems deployed in our everyday lives, many recent initiatives called for explainable [21], transparent [3], and responsible AI systems [15]. Moreover, works such as [30] advocated the integration of implicit or explicit reasoning about ethics for such intelligent systems.

In MAS, which include complex, numerous, and fast negotiations, the complete visibility of the secured history of the transactions can be crucial (e.g., in the context of legal disputes). For these reasons, *trust* and *reputation* have been highlighted as two key factors in artificial agent societies [34, 35]. Nevertheless, very few works go beyond theoretical models to actually deploy trust and reputation-based mechanisms in agent societies. With the emergence of BCT, trust and reputation of different agents can be intertwined with distributed ledger technologies, thus accessible by all the stakeholders. Moreover, several works have recently underlined the need for **accountability** in MAS organizations [6]. Thanks to the use of BCTs in MAS, the informational and executive asymmetry that underpins the business model of many platforms can come to an end.

BCT eradicates the monopoly on the information and ensures a certain degree of equality on the control of the contracts' implementation. Nevertheless, recent studies allowed the conclusion that such features offered by BCT are "necessary" but not "satisfactory" conditions to meet the collective empowerment of users fully. Indeed, two limits to the empowerment strategy can be mentioned: *(i)* how should a user know that another would be ready to pass a contract with the need for a reminder (e.g., a virtual assistant)? An intermediary might still be needed to match supply and demand. Thus, the end of informational asymmetries and monopolies cannot be expected only from BCT. Possible inequalities can be overcome once users (people or agents) have achieved an agreement; *(ii)* although smart-contract-based technologies prevent malicious and erroneous agreements' implementations, they do not *eliminate the risks of mistakes*. Indeed, users are demanding that the decisions involving them or taken on their behalf (as a contracting party) have to be explainable. Henceforth, transparency without explainability is no longer acceptable [4, 13].

Among the various blockchain applications deployed in the market, their use as a monetary platform turned out to be problematic [14]. Focusing mainly on BitCoin, renowned economists are doubtful of the contributions of BCT to social good [26, 37]. From a practical point of view, money laundering and illegal transactions (drugs, murders, human trafficking) may use BCT to realize the payments [16]. From a more theoretical point of view, if BitCoin (or similar) were to be really used at a large scale, the role of the regulatory authorities could not be ensured anymore, which let a clear path to generalized fraud (and risk for the services provided by the states).

Finally, before the ethic stands the law: some popular uses of BCT represent an infraction. The most latent contravenes the European General Data Protection Regulation (GDPR), even though the complex nature of distributed fund transfer networks makes it hard to identify the actors, responsibilities, and acts[1]. Beyond the specific features of BitCoin, the unique identifiers of every wallet *is*

---

[1] https://medium.com/@kkarnapp/what-does-the-gdpr-mean-for-bitcoin-9b57ebdd8766.

to be considered as personal data; and so it should be stored and protected as such (which is incompatible with the nature of the network) [10].

3   Challenges

Since its inception, blockchain has been typically associated with norms and values like democracy, transparency, and decentralization of power. However, the socio-technical properties of blockchain technologies as an economic system bring with them a set of ethical challenges that are diametrical to the idealistic moral propositions associated with blockchain [7].

C1 - *Erosion of the socio-cultural blockchain ecosystem*
While blockchain was initially an ideology-driven technology, mostly supported by left-leaning or libertarian technology enthusiasts, the current domination of the ecosystem by "Bitcoin millionaires" has turned the blockchain community in a highly unequal society (Estimated Gini coefficients consider North Korea as the country with the most unequal distribution in the world[2] [25]). The dominance of the ecosystem by a wealthy few, who can easily take control of emerging cryptocurrencies has rendered the vision of an egalitarian ecosystem impossible.

C2 - *Technical immutability of smart contracts in enterprise software contexts*
Usually, the roll-out of new enterprise software solutions is associated with organizational stress that negatively influences the well-being of employees. However, the possibility of a controlled "roll-back" of updates and new implementations is typically possible and hence provides a safety net for worst-case scenarios. Moreover, in modern continuous integration scenarios, small improvements and ad-hoc bug fixing (so-called "hot fixing" can be deployed in production systems almost instantaneously. Given the technical immutability of smart contracts, and the socio-technical fact that finding cross-organizational consensus for new smart contract deployments is laborious. This becomes clear when looking at the prevalence of organizational conflicts and communication issues that hamper the *intra-organizational* implementation and adoption of IT systems [39], as well as at the slow pace at which multi-organizational technology-oriented negotiations in standardization processes move forward. These safety nets are weaker in BCT-based (typically consortium blockchain-based) enterprise system deployments, which can facilitate intra-organizational stress, inefficiencies, and operational mismanagement. New solution approaches are required to address this shortcoming of blockchain-based systems.

C3 - *Smart contract complexity as Blockchain Fraud*
Fraud, overstated capabilities, and unfulfilled promises are obstacles hindering the evolution of public blockchains from being a niche phenomenon to a broadly applicable technology. Moreover, the advent of highly complex smart contracts (e.g., executing machine learning models and agent-based simulations) can exacerbate even more the already challenging path of BCT [24]. The deployment of

---

[2] https://bitcointalk.org/index.php?topic=51011.0.

such smart contracts will further increase the power imbalance between smart contract developers/providers and users. In particular, malicious smart contract providers can use complex models with *hard-to-foresee* emergent properties to perform behaviors that their users do not expect when they commit stakes (money or goods) to a blockchain-based system [23]. Finally, although the initial intention and functionality of a smart contract are beneficial for society, complex chain code can learn or evolves in unintended/unexpected directions (given the employment of BCT in fast-paced evolving environments). Unintended side-effects can facilitate system exploitation by malicious third parties (both at design- and run-time). Thus, to deliver an actual societal benefit, requirements elicitation, rules enforcement, norms definition, and laws revision have to face crucial changes.

C4 - *Theoretical and effective empowerment: from accessibility to workability*
Merging BCT and MAS showed the possibility to implement *secure* behaviors and to provide the availability of *shared data* among the participating agents. Nevertheless, the dynamics in these environments are quite complex and sometimes relying on workarounds—thus, hindering an effective utilization of these data. Indeed, current prototypes and proofs-of-concept require extensive knowledge and support regarding legal aspects and data science. This limitation constitutes a barrier for the adoption of BCT-based agent systems as a viable means for user empowerment.

C5 - *The persistent need for intermediaries to implement smart contracts*
The hope of getting rid of intermediaries through the use of smart contracts is associated with the specific challenge "to adapt the system and the contracting parties' liability accordingly". Such a challenge is not solely related to BCT. Indeed, it also extends to those MAS relying on smart contract technologies, where part of the implementation of a contract is delegated to agents or AI algorithms in general.

The possible risks connected with such a delegation are *(i)* lousy implementation of a contract through AI and *(ii)* even if no glaring mistake seems to have occurred, the terms of a contract may leave room for interpretations, i.e., requiring further consensus procedures between the contracting parties.

In both cases, there will be no platform liable for possible mistakes. Moreover, can we truly believe that the two contractual parties are liable for a decision that has been delegated?

C6 - *Liability in AI delegation*
The advancements in AI-based decision-making engines allowed an increased degree of machine-delegation. However, in domains such as stock-negotiations and forensics analysis, to outline the liability boundaries amount the parties is increasingly complex. Assuming that human contracting parties let their virtual assistants (agents) interact on their behalf, how can *trust* and *liability* be unequivocally determined and associated with the actors? (e.g., single virtual agent, overall system, the system designer, and the human user).

C7 - *Constructing a fair reputation-building system through BCT and MAS*
Several MAS rely on the ability to establish a mutual trust achieved via secure
reputation building mechanisms and to ensure that no one has been over- or
under-evaluated. Mutual trust demands at least for *(i)* the authenticity of the
reputation's origin, *(ii)* its traceability, and *(iii)* accuracy. Thanks to *(i)* and
(ii), a given agent A should assume the correctness of B's remarks about C.

Certainly, BCT supports the satisfaction of *(i)* and *(ii)* [22]. The public
storage of information ensures traceability and the possibility for each user to see
if and about what precisely two actors agree or disagree with. The authenticity of
an assessment is better warranted by the possibility of identifying the contributor
(when using a non-anonymous permissioned BCT). In addition, it allows building
a two-level assessment in a MAS: the evaluation of a given transaction, and a
more general assessment of someone's reputation, resulting in the previous local
evaluations provided by his peers.

Ethical concerns arise concerning *(iii)*. Does the advocated reputation management strengthen, in the absence of guarantees, the overall accuracy of the
assessments? The epistemological principle that underlies the model is that
transparency goes hand in hand with a deeper sense of responsibility for truth
and accuracy. Unfair and malicious behaviors are supposed to be detected over
time, leading to the exclusion of the non-objective member from the group.

Nevertheless, to what extent is this principle *fair*? Abramova et al. [1] proposed a study based on Airbnb showing that people read the comments and try
to distinguish between fair and unfair criticisms, while Mayzlin et al. [29] proved
that fraud is not a big matter in peer-to-peer platforms. Nevertheless, other
studies mitigated the "collective wisdom" hypothesis. According to Origgi and
Pais [32], whenever the cover of anonymity is removed, users might be reluctant
to give negative evaluations. Such a behavior can be due to fear of retalia-
tion [2,33], to avoid conducts [20], and due to concerns regarding legal consequences [20]. Nevertheless, literature shows a certain number of biased reporting:
herding behavior, self-selection [38], and strategic manipulation of reviewing [27].
Such social aspects can remarkably impact the accuracy and trustworthiness of
the data stored on the shared ledgers.

Moreover, if an actor debuts in a community with a bad reputation rating (either if deserved, unfortunate, or undeserved), its near and possibly entire
future might be affected (possibly creating unjust harms). Although these concerns are not solely and explicitly linked to bridging BCT and MAS, to elaborate
on the ethics of rating dynamics is unavoidable.

C8 - *Right to be forgotten*
To pursue the principle of data minimization and limit potential abuses of personal data, GDPR aims at creating the right for the erasure of personal data
that are "no longer necessary in relation to the purposes for which they were collected or otherwise processed" and if the data subject withdraws the consent for
processing them (art. 17). In the case of BCT, compliance with article 17 raises
at least two main issues. Above all, "since blockchain is a form of decentralized
transactions, it is questionable to whom the GDPR's requirements of upholding

a standard for personal data usage is addressed (...)". Clearly, the GDPR has set a legal framework primarily intended for centralized personal data collectors. Thus, to scale it to distributed ledger technologies based on the concept of a completely decentralized environment (especially public BCT) is having unpredictable consequences and interpretations [40]. Moreover, data persistence is a fundamental feature of BCT. It seems almost impossible to guarantee the right to be forgotten without losing all the benefits inherited by this underlying technology (transparency, authenticity, and security). As indicated by the Open Data Institute, "the irreversibility and transparency of public BCT mean they are probably unsuitable for personal data" [36]. Finally, besides the general hype, the suitability of certain application domains for distributed ledger technologies should be adequately reassessed.

4   Research Opportunities

This section elaborates on the research opportunities standing beyond the challenges discussed above. Concerning **C1**, there is an emerging third era of blockchain that tangibly links the digital world with the physical world. Nevertheless, measuring the wealth distribution in cryptocurrency is quite challenging, mainly due to the anonymous nature of transactions (sender and receiver data are inaccessible). The New Bitcoin Distribution [8] models the sharing of Bitcoin Wealth in such a way that Wallet and Address data are entirely disregarded, assuming that the Power Law applies to Bitcoin Wealth Distribution and Bitcoin Wealth Distribution exactly mirrors the Global Wealth. Another solution is GoodDollar [31], designed with a mission to end economic inequality for developing a new cryptocurrency on a global scale and an open-source to distribute money through the principles of a Universal Basic Income (UBI).

Concerning **C2**, there are two possible approaches. One the one hand, in specific circumstances, being able to switch between blockchain-based and non-blockchain mechanism dynamically can improve the system flexibility. In particular, when organizational dynamicity becomes predominant (w.r.t. the need for following specific procedures specified in the chain code/smart contract), allowing a (semi)autonomous switch can be crucial. On the other hand, smart contracts can be designed to be autonomous, possibly adjusting and evolving their behavior over time. Kampik and Najjar [24] proposed a conceptual framework relying on agent-based simulations and/or machine learning algorithms to determine which and whether a process variant should be allowed to be executed under given circumstances. Nevertheless, more research (in particular, implementing and empirically evaluating the proposed approaches) is necessary.

Concerning **C3**, an essential approach would be to enable ethical and normative reasoning as an inherent capability of the blockchain protocol. Works in the literature distinguish between *implicit* and *explicit* ethical agency [18,30]. On the one hand, current agents have no understanding of what is ethically "good" and what is "bad" since they implicitly respect their designer's assessment of the ethical implication of each action (if any). On the other hand, agents might be empowered with unbiased (possibly BCT-based) explicit moral knowledge. Thus decoupling artificial autonomous systems distinguish from the (possibly biased) moral perception of the designer, thus avoiding immoral behavior with or without human intervention [18,30]. Nevertheless, in a multi-stakeholder scenario, integrating and reflecting the moral values and views of all stakeholders in the moral behavior of the autonomous system is more challenging. A possible solution is proposing an artificial moral agent architecture that uses normative systems' techniques and formal argumentation to reach a moral agreement among stakeholders [28]. Using this technique, it is possible to abstract how a particular stakeholder can reach a particular decision concerning the morality of an action. Each stakeholder can be modeled as a source of arguments where an argument can be a statement about whether an action is moral or a reason for considering a particular action as moral. Therefore, the final decision will be the outcome of a consensus-making process involving the normative systems of all the stakeholders.

Concerning **C4**, a key aspect is to equip virtual or human agents with mechanisms and technologies to control both *data* and *behaviors* governed by BCT. To do so, we envision the development of new methodologies for co-constructing BCT solutions, in which MAS help bridging the gap between human interactions and the definition of smart contracts-based behaviors.

Concerning **C5**, intermediaries can play crucial roles in "interpreting" will and commands of its human user, detecting possible procedural or contextual mistakes, and in solving possible problems between the contracting parts. These scenarios demand that MAS leverage on smart contract technologies to enhance trust in their behaviors. Therefore, BCT-enabled MAS must provide internal procedures to assess and review possibly defective AI.

As described in **C6**, to assess delegation and correctness of the ledger requires considering the authenticity of information leading to reputation assessment, as well as its subjectivity. Possible approaches may include the study of decentralized regulation mechanisms where agents can use traceability analysis to determine the accuracy and/or correctness of the ledger's contents. Moreover, the agents may be equipped with mechanisms for evaluating which data or interaction they are willing to make publicly visible through the ledger. The agents' internal knowledge and their goals will play a fundamental role in the decision-making process that will evaluate potential trade-offs.

Concerning **C7**, the biases characterizing the human judgment are linked more to human psychology and nature rather than to BCT and MAS. For instance, the fact that prior ratings impact the evaluations of subsequent reviewers or that some users may artificially enhance the trustworthiness of others when writing reviews because they might be friends is not a technical matter.

However, the fact that the BCT "sets things in stone" raises the responsibility of the system's designers to elaborate on the ethics of rating dynamics beyond the existing procedures of conciliation. Thus, we suggest undertaking two significant improvements that would enable to counter-balance the potential harm of an under-rating. First, the rights of human agents would benefit from a culture of pseudonymization in MAS. Indeed, the systematic pseudonymization could help to mitigate the bias of under-reporting of negative ratings and to avoid that under-assessment have further consequences outside a MAS. Second, the designers might need to implement a "right to a second chance" either in MAS, BCT, or both. Differently from the "right to be forgotten", the "right to a second chance" does not requite deleting data at the end of a contractual commitment. Although it is ethically debatable, an individual can have the right to create a new account when his reputation is worsening. MAS, where the accounts are linked to transparent identities, would not be affected (even if a person wants to provide the same service that had been previously undermined).

Concerning **C8**, the right to be forgotten brings us back to the question of liability for which no concrete solution has been identified yet. Indeed, propositions such as removing the access to a given piece of data (e.g., impeding the execution of a smart contract or destroying its key—if encrypted) are still debated. Nevertheless, as Ward points out, the main data at hand when analyzing blockchains is transactional information and public keys, and only transactional data can be considered as personal data [40]. Henceforth, the only viable trend currently envisioned is to limit transactional information in a blockchain environment, by storing the personal data in a database without affecting the blockchain itself – off-chain – which would allow complying with data regulation while still keeping some advantages of the BCT [3,19]

5   Conclusion

BCT-enabled MAS can boost next-generation systems yielding many societal advancements. Bridging MAS and BCT envisions stimulating opportunities and exciting challenges. Nevertheless, several ethical concerns (mostly implicated by the early stage of the involved technologies) will need to be carefully taken into consideration. This paper aimed at providing a first elicitation and mapping of the ethical challenges and research opportunities in the field of BCT-enabled MAS. In particular, we elaborated on the current ethical concerns entangled with the growing technological challenges. Although the systems' complexity and the sophistication of their AI engines are growing at a fast pace, compliance with ethical standards will play a crucial role in future designs. However, the current research is still far from undertaking most of the challenges identified in this study. The solutions suggested in this paper are intended to provide credible paths for future research and to foster the recent initiatives for explainable, transparent, and responsible AI within full compliance with ethical regulations.

References

1. Abramova, O., Shavanova, T., Fuhrer, A., Krasnova, H., Buxmann, P., et al.: Understanding the sharing economy: the role of response to negative reviews in the peer-to-peer accommodation sharing network. In: ECIS 2015 Completed Research Papers, Paper 1. ECIS AISel, IL, USA (2015)

2. Adamic, L.A., Lauterbach, D., Teng, C.Y., Ackerman, M.: Rating friends without making enemies. In: Fifth International AAAI Conference on Weblogs and Social Media (2011)
3. Albanese, G., Calbimonte, J.P., Schumacher, M., Calvaresi, D.: Dynamic consent management for clinical trials via private blockchain technology. J. Ambient Intell. Hum. Comput. 1–18 (2020).
4. Anjomshoae, S., Najjar, A., Calvaresi, D., Främling, K.: Explainable agents and robots: results from a systematic literature review. In: Proceedings of the 18th International Conference on Autonomous Agents and MultiAgent Systems, pp. 1078–1088. International Foundation for Autonomous Agents and Multiagent Systems (2019)
5. Aste, T., Tasca, P., Di Matteo, T.: Blockchain technologies: the foreseeable impact on society and industry. Computer **50**(9), 18–28 (2017)
6. Baldoni, M., Baroglio, C., Boissier, O., Micalizio, R., Tedeschi, S.: Engineering business processes through accountability and agents. In: Proceedings of the 18th International Conference on Autonomous Agents and MultiAgent Systems, pp. 1796–1798. International Foundation for Autonomous Agents and Multiagent Systems (2019)
7. Baldwin, T.: George Edward Moore. In: Zalta, E.N. (ed.) The Stanford Encyclopedia of Philosophy. Metaphysics Research Lab, Stanford University, Summer 2010 edn. (2010)
8. BambouClub: Are you in the Bitcoin 1%? A New Model of the Distribution of Bitcoin Wealth (2017). https://medium.com/@BambouClub/are-you-in-the-bitcoin-1-a-new-model-of-the-distribution-of-bitcoin-wealth-6adb0d4a6a95. Accessed 04 Nov 2019
9. Bruckner, M., LaFleur, M., Pitterle, I.: Frontier issues: the impact of the technological revolution on labour markets and income distribution. Department of Economic & Social Affairs, UN (2017). Accessed 24
10. Buocz, T., Ehrke-Rabel, T., Hödl, E., Eisenberger, I.: Bitcoin and the GDPR: allocating responsibility in distributed networks. Comput. Law Secur. Rev. **35**(2), 182–198 (2019)
11. Calvaresi, D., Cesarini, D., Sernani, P., Marinoni, M., Dragoni, A., Sturm, A.: Exploring the ambient assisted living domain: a systematic review. J. Ambient Intell. Hum. Comput. **8**, 1–19 (2016)
12. Calvaresi, D., Marinoni, M., Dragoni, A.F., Hilfiker, R., Schumacher, M.: Real-time multi-agent systems for telerehabilitation scenarios. Artif. Intell. Med. **96**, 217–231 (2019)
13. Calvaresi, D., Mualla, Y., Najjar, A., Galland, S., Schumacher, M.: Explainable multi-agent systems through blockchain technology. In: Calvaresi, D., Najjar, A., Schumacher, M., Främling, K. (eds.) EXTRAAMAS 2019. LNCS (LNAI), vol. 11763, pp. 41–58. Springer, Cham (2019). https://doi.org/10.1007/978-3-030-30391-4_3
14. Dierksmeier, C., Seele, P.: Cryptocurrencies and business ethics. J. Bus. Ethics **152**(1), 1–14 (2018)
15. Dignum, V.: Responsible autonomy. In: Proceedings of the 26th International Joint Conference on Artificial Intelligence, pp. 4698–4704. AAAI Press (2017)
16. Dostov, V., Shust, P.: Cryptocurrencies: an unconventional challenge to the AML/CFT regulators? J. Finan. Crime **21**(3), 249–263 (2014)
17. Dubovitskaya, A., Urovi, V., Barba, I., Aberer, K., Schumacher, M.I.: A multiagent system for dynamic data aggregation in medical research. BioMed Res. Int. (2016)

18. Dyrkolbotn, S., Pedersen, T., Slavkovik, M.: On the distinction between implicit and explicit ethical agency. In: Proceedings of the 2018 AAAI/ACM Conference on AI, Ethics, and Society, pp. 74–80. ACM (2018)
19. Finck, M.: Blockchains and data protection in the European union. Eur. Data Prot. L. Rev. **4**, 17 (2018)
20. Fradkin, A., Grewal, E., Holtz, D., Pearson, M.: Bias and reciprocity in online reviews: evidence from field experiments on Airbnb. In: Proceedings of the Sixteenth ACM Conference on Economics and Computation, pp. 641–641. ACM (2015)
21. Gunning, D.: Explainable artificial intelligence (XAI). Defense Advanced Research Projects Agency (DARPA), Web 2nd (2017)
22. Gürcan, Ö.: Multi-agent modelling of fairness for users and miners in blockchains. In: De La Prieta, F., et al. (eds.) PAAMS 2019. CCIS, vol. 1047, pp. 92–99. Springer, Cham (2019). https://doi.org/10.1007/978-3-030-24299-2_8
23. Kampik, T., Najjar, A., Calvaresi, D.: MAS-aided approval for bypassing decentralized processes: an architecture. In: 2018 IEEE/WIC/ACM International Conference on Web Intelligence (WI), pp. 713–718, December 2018. https://doi.org/10.1109/WI.2018.000-6
24. Kampik, T., Najjar, A.: Simulating, off-chain and on-chain: agent-based simulations in cross-organizational business processes. Information **11**(1), 34 (2020). https://doi.org/10.3390/info11010034
25. Kim, J.H., Kim, T.: Economic assimilation of North Korean refugees in South Korea: survey evidence. KDI School of Pub Policy & Management Paper (06–19) (2006)
26. Krugman, P.: Bitcoin is evil. The New York Times **28**, 2013 (2013)
27. Lauterbach, D., Truong, H., Shah, T., Adamic, L.: Surfing a web of trust: reputation and reciprocity on couchsurfing.com. In: 2009 International Conference on Computational Science and Engineering, vol. 4, pp. 346–353. IEEE (2009)
28. Liao, B., Slavkovik, M., van der Torre, L.: Building Jiminy cricket: an architecture for moral agreements among stakeholders. In: Proceedings of the 2019 AAAI/ACM Conference on AI, Ethics, and Society, AIES 2019, pp. 147–153. ACM, New York (2019). https://doi.org/10.1145/3306618.3314257. http://doi.acm.org/10.1145/3306618.3314257
29. Mayzlin, D., Dover, Y., Chevalier, J.: Promotional reviews: an empirical investigation of online review manipulation. Am. Econ. Rev. **104**(8), 2421–55 (2014)
30. Moor, J.H.: The nature, importance, and difficulty of machine ethics. IEEE Intell. Syst. **21**(4), 18–21 (2006)
31. Moya, V.: GoodDollar: cryptocurrencies would end inequality (2019). https://latinamericanpost.com/24800-gooddollar-cryptocurrencies-would-end-inequality. Accessed 04 Nov 2019
32. Origgi, G., Pais, I.: Digital reputation in the mutual admiration society. Studi di Sociologia **2**(2), 175–193 (2018)
33. Overgoor, J., Wulczyn, E., Potts, C.: Trust propagation with mixed-effects models. In: Sixth International AAAI Conference on Weblogs and Social Media. AAAI (2012)
34. Ramchurn, S.D., Huynh, D., Jennings, N.R.: Trust in multi-agent systems. Knowl. Eng. Rev. **19**(1), 1–25 (2004)
35. Sabater-Mir, J., Vercouter, L.: Trust and reputation in multiagent systems. Multiagent Systems, p. 381 (2013)

36. Smith, J., Tennison, J., Wells, P., Fawcett, J., Harrison, S.: Applying blockchain technology in global data infrastructure (2016). https://theodi.org/article/applying-blockchain-technology-in-global-data-infrastructure/. Open Data Institute

37. Stross, C.: Why i want bitcoin to die in a fire (2013). http://www.antipope.org/charlie/blog-static/2013/12/why-i-want-bitcoin-to-die-in-a.html

38. Tussyadiah, I.P.: Strategic self-presentation in the sharing economy: implications for host branding. In: Inversini, A., Schegg, R. (eds.) Information and Communication Technologies in Tourism 2016, pp. 695–708. Springer, Cham (2016). https://doi.org/10.1007/978-3-319-28231-2_50

39. Ward, J., Hemingway, C., Daniel, E.: A framework for addressing the organisational issues of enterprise systems implementation. J. Strateg. Inf. Syst. **14**(2), 97–119 (2005)

40. Ward, Y., et al.: An analysis of the applicatibility of gdpr to blockchain technologies. L'Europe Unie **13**(13), 86–90 (2018)

What an Experimental Limit Order Book Can Tell Us About Real Markets?

Annalisa Fabretti[(⊠)]

Department of Economics and Finance,
University of Rome Tor Vergata, Rome, Italy
annalisa.fabretti@uniroma2.it

Abstract. Limit order book are widespread in markets. A vast literature study their properties and stylized facts with the aim of getting insights about the trading process and the order placement. In this paper an experimental order book is studied with the same aim. Since laboratory experiments offer a controlled environment in which causes and effect can be much better identified with respect to the field, the study of experimental data can give valuable insights even when results mismatch with theory or empirical findings. The analysis shows some similarities but also differences and understanding why is also a valuable goal faced and discussed here and not yet totally accomplished.

Keywords: Limit order book · Stylized facts · Laboratory experiment

1 Introduction

Many financial markets use limit order book mechanism to trade. In the last decades a very large stream of literature takes care of understanding the empirical findings coming from the analysis of limit order book data (see Gould et al. (2013) for a comprehensive survey). Not surprisingly, it emerges that traders are highly conditioned by the state of the book. Indeed traders submit more limit orders and less market orders when spreads are large, they tend to place orders at relative prices close to the majority of active orders and this suggests that they look more at the top of the order book when deciding whether submit a market or a limit order (Cao et al. 2008). Biais et al. (1995) observed a clustering of events that might be explained either by the splitting of large orders, by mimicking behavior or by similar reactions of traders to new pieces of information arriving on the market. Many authors (see Bouchaud et al. (2002) among many) successfully fit the distribution of relative prices with power law and argue that traders submit also orders deep in the book with an optimistic belief of a possible large change in price to exploit. Among limit and market orders also cancellations take a large space in traders' decisions, indeed in some market the majority of limit orders ends in cancellation and the mechanism of cancellation is not yet completely clear (Gould et al. 2013). Given this picture, data coming from limit order book give a wide opportunity to understand in deep the trading

© Springer Nature Switzerland AG 2020
F. De La Prieta et al. (Eds.): PAAMS 2020 Workshops, CCIS 1233, pp. 17–28, 2020.
https://doi.org/10.1007/978-3-030-51999-5_2

process and, despite a large number of correlated studies and models, the puzzle about how the order placement works has not yet been solved.

Laboratory experiments offer a controlled environment in which the causes and effects can be much better identified with respect to the field. Laboratory experiments allow more easily to observe agents' behavior or attitude and to understand how individuals use the available information or form expectations. For this reason experimentation is a suitable ground to develop and test models and theory. Indeed many researches used laboratory experiments to investigate price formation, expectation and learning (Anufriev and Hommes 2012; Assenza et al. 2014; Hommes 2011) or to verify theories (Asparouhova et al. 2016) and even when laboratory findings do not match with the theory or the field we can get new insights.

Experimentation in finance is not largely implemented; despite a large set of laboratory experiments on auction market rules (Plott and Smith 2008), the empirical properties of experimental order books compared to those of real markets have not yet been investigated. In the present research an investigation of an experimental order book is performed with several aims: a) comparing the experimental order book with findings of real markets; b) facing the challenge of understanding the trading process adopted by human subjects in the lab; c) testing in what extent the experimental order book behaves as a real one. To do so some stylized facts, relative prices and the consistency with some models have been considered.

The experimental limit order book under analysis comes from a laboratory experiment designed to investigate the impact of tournament incentives on investment strategies and market efficiency (Fang et al. 2017)[1]. Data consists of 17520 records each containing 49 fields (period, market, buyer, seller, maker, ask price, bid price, quantity, submission and execution time...). First, a preliminary analysis has been performed to reveal heterogeneity in markets and no evident impact of incentives on market dynamics and subjects' behavior. Second, some stylized facts and the distribution of relative prices have been investigated. Finally, the consistency of subjects' choice with some classical models has been considered.

It is worthy to say that the possible investigations are limited for several reasons. Indeed some features or stylized facts could not appear given the small dimension of the system (few agents trading in few periods) or can not be investigated for the small number of observations. An example is the hump-shaped depth profile that it cannot be found in a statistically significant way given few data. Another example is the event clustering that has been investigated in these data and not found; this is not surprising since event clustering can occur when traders split large orders or when traders react similarly to the same event, but it is not here the case since traders have not so large endowments and no external information arrive to motivate reactions by traders. Biais et al. (1995) studied

---

[1] I must stress that the experiment has been designed and performed by D. Fang, M. Holmen, D. Kleinlercher, M. Kirchler and results are published in Fang et al. (2017). I have got data by courtesy of authors.

conditional probabilities in real markets finding that the probability to submit a limit order is higher when the spread is high, when few limit orders are in the book and when the volatility is high. One third of markets shows this stylized fact, while no diagonal effect significantly emerges. Moreover, the relative prices have been considered and a distribution with a power law behavior emerges in line with empirical literature (Bouchaud et al. 2002). Coherently with empirical findings subjects submit orders deep in the book far away from the best bid and the best ask with the belief that large movements in prices can occur.

Two models have been selected and the consistency of data with these models studied. To address the model consistency, a rate of compliance, that compares real actions with model forecasted actions, has been defined. The selected models are the theoretical model by Fang et al. (2017)[2] and a cut off strategy model coming from an adapted version of Foucault (1999) with reservation prices as Hommes et al. (2005). In both cases it results that some individuals are highly compliant and some others are lowly compliant and no evidence emerges that an investment manager or an ordinary trader follows a strategy according to her compensation structure. Both models present some drawbacks, the former is too simplified while the latter does not admit the possibility to submit limit orders outside the spread, while the empirical investigation shows that roughly 20% of limit orders is placed outside the spread.

In conclusion, results show some similarities with real market but also some (expected) mismatches, indeed, for example the absence of stylized facts could be attributed to a limited time of trading and homogeneity of agents in terms of information and endowments. Despite subjects are homogenous in some respects, their heterogeneity of behavior emerges clearly both between and within agents (Conte et al. 2011) and it can be motivated just in term of different decision processes or beliefs. However this heterogeneity can produce noise that hinders the investigation.

The rest of the paper is organized as follows: Sect. 2 provides a statistical analysis of limit orders and stylized facts; Sect. 3 presents models and tackles the model compliance; Sect. 4 concludes.

2   Data Analysis

Data consists of 17520 records each containing 49 fields (period, market, buyer, seller, maker, ask price, bid price, quantity, submission and execution time...). Participants for each experimental market trade in a continuous double auction market in 12 rounds each lasting 150 s. There are 3 tournament treatments and one control: winner takes all (WTA), beat the market (BTM), elimination contest (EC) and all ordinary traders (OT) as control. In each run of the experiment 8 subjects are equally divided into investment manager (IM), paid according the tournament structure, and ordinary traders (OT), that receives the final wealth. At the end of each period a buy back value from a uniform distribution between 0 and 100 is realized and payoff are assigned. An investment manager is winner in

---

[2] According with the experiment has been designed.

each period if her/his wealth is the best of four in WTA, at least the second best in BTM and not the worst in EC. At the end, a period is selected randomly and rewards of that period are assigned to participants. For a complete description of the laboratory experiment the reader can refer to Fang et al. (2017).

A preliminary qualitative analysis of data has been performed. Figure 1 shows two markets (5 and 7) for the WTA (treatment 1); the best bids and asks are plotted for the twelve periods, the realization of the buy back value (distributed as a uniform between 0 and 100) is reported at the end of each period; moreover for any period the number of limit orders, market orders and deleted orders are reported above the specific sub plot. It is worthy to note that markets 5 shows high prices (bids and asks above the expected value of the buy back value that is 50) with a quite large spread and an apparent tendency to narrow through the periods. By contrast market 7 of the same treatment shows a narrow spread with prices very close to the expected value. Similar observations hold for all treatments and markets, here not reported for the sake of brevity. Looking at the number of orders we can observe that some markets are more lively in terms of the quantities and deletion. Even though we discuss only two markets of one treatment, as example, the conclusion is that markets differ for spreads and initial prices without significant differences among treatments; data show also that the initial submitted prices have a big influence on the rest of the dynamics (as in Heemeijer et al. (2009)). From the individual point of view, difference in subjects' behavior among treatments do not clearly emerge and, indeed, subjects' different behaviors cannot be mostly attributed to the treatment and show a high heterogeneity between agents and within agents (Conte et al. 2011).'

In Fig. 2 the networks obtained considering individuals as the nodes and trades as the edges are reported to give an overview of all the markets and treatments. A green node is an investment manager, magenta is an ordinary trader; edges are trades between individuals and thicker the edge greater the number of trades between the two individuals. In Fig. 2, no significant differences emerge between treatments. A high heterogeneity emerges, individuals within the same market and having the same incentives can be highly active or totally inactive (see for example individual 1 and 2 in market 8 of treatment WTA or individuals 7 and 8 in market 9 of treatment BTM). There are markets with a lot of trades and all the individuals almost equally active and markets more uneven (compare for example markets 8 and 9 in WTA).

The high heterogeneity that can be seen in these few examples is a common denominator of all the treatments and markets. The treatment has no relevant effect on the individual behavior and also on the aggregate outcomes. This finding comes partially in contrast with the theoretical and empirical findings of Fang et al. (2017) that say that at the individual level Investment Managers are more aggressive than Ordinary Traders, while treatments have little impact on the aggregate market outcome.

In the following analysis data were processed in two ways, one respecting the division in treatments and markets and another without considering it. The former wants to save and verify the aim of the original research question for which the experiment has been built; the latter comes natural after the finding of no apparent differences in treatments and it is motivated by the need of having a large set of data for studying some features of the distribution of the relative prices or the cancellations.

2.1 Limit Orders and Stylized Facts

Theoretically limit orders should mostly be within the spread if the individual wants to compete with present orders or at the best prices (bid or ask) if the individual is just willing to buy or sell (see Rosu (2009), Hollifield et al. (2004), Foucault (1999)). However the empirical observations in real markets and also in lab experiments reveal that many individuals submit orders outside the spread; the humped shape of the order book says also us that the market automatically selects a distance from the spread in which the majority tends to crowd orders (Bouchaud et al. 2002). In Table 1 mean values (with standard deviation in parenthesis) of the percentage of limit order inside, outside or at the spread are reported. The mean is obtained calculating the rate for each period in each market, then the mean across the period and finally the mean across the markets in each treatment. In line with theory, the percentage of limit orders inside the spread is much higher than those outside and the difference is statistically significant. There is a significant tendency in the majority of markets to submit more sell orders than buy orders. In Table 2 results of the t-test on the difference between the number of limit orders in sell side and buy side are reported; "Y" means that the difference is significant. It is worth to note that treatment WTA, OT and EC are in the majority of the cases (8 over 9 or 7 over 9) significantly unbalanced, while treatment 2 is unbalanced only in 4 cases over 9. However in the majority of cases (with just few exceptions) this unbalance is motivated by trading prices over the stock expected value. This suggests that traders are aware that the stock is overvalued and notwithstanding they trade it.

Table 1. Mean and standard deviation (in parenthesis) of LO percentage in buy and sell side inside, outside the spread or at the best prices of the spread.

Treatment	In LOB	Out LOB	At LOB	In LOS	Out LOS	At LOS
WTA	0.1838	0.0843	0.0708	0.3102	0.1686	0.1823
	(0.0902)	(0.0392)	(0.0286)	(0.0718)	(0.0580)	(0.0794)
BTM	0.2100	0.1099	0.1074	0.2938	0.1196	0.1593
	(0.0948)	(0.0602)	(0.0629)	(0.0879)	(0.0547)	(0.0686)
EC	0.2038	0.0737	0.0852	0.3183	0.1562	0.1628
	(0.0796)	(0.0315)	(0.0388)	(0.1159)	(0.0521)	(0.0665)
OT	0.1912	0.1024	0.0875	0.3137	0.1774	0.1278
	(0.0462)	(0.0386)	(0.0406)	(0.1037)	(0.0763)	(0.0369)

Table 2. Results of unbalanced markets between sell and buy limit orders. "Y" means that the market showed a significant unbalance in sell side

Treat/Market	1	2	3	4	5	6	7	8	9
WTA	Y	Y	Y	Y	Y	Y	Y	N	Y
BTM	N	N	Y	Y	N	Y	N	Y	N
EC	N	Y	N	Y	Y	Y	Y	Y	Y
OT	Y	Y	Y	Y	N	Y	Y	Y	Y

Event Clustering. It is observed that the conditional probability of a certain market event, given that the previous one belongs to the same class, is higher than the unconditional probability of that market event, this is known as the diagonal effect (Biais et al. 1995). Formally, denoting by $\{m_t\}$ the sequence of markets event, with $t = 1, ..., T$, and Ψ the space of types (limit order, market order or cancellation) the hypothesis to be verified is

$$P(m_t = \psi \mid m_{t-1} = \psi) > P(m_t = \psi) \qquad \psi \in \Psi$$

Biais et al. (1995) classify market events in 7 types[3] for each side (buy or sell) according aggressiveness as in Harris and Hasbrouck (1996). Here the same classification complies a too strong fragmentation of data, hence we reduce to three simple types: limit order (LO), market order (MO) or cancellation (Del).

After computed the conditional and unconditional probability for limit order in both sides and marker order in both sides (no cancellations because data are too few) a t-test has been applied to verify if any significant difference in the two probabilities occurs; only market 5 in treatment EC gives significant results. This is not so surprising since event clustering can occur when trader split large orders to avoid to impact the market, or when traders react similarly to the same event or for imitation. The former two cases (order splitting and news reaction) do not apply here because traders have not large endowments (they start with the same endowments) and no external information or change in fundamentals occur to motivate reactions by traders. By another hand the imitation could applies here but the small quantity of data could constitute a hurdle to detecting it.

Conditional Probability of Limit Orders Given the Spread. Biais et al. (1995) found on Paris Bourse that the probability to submit a limit order is higher when the spread is high, when few limit orders are in the book and when the volatility is high. According Biais et al. (1995) the spread is high if it is higher than the mean, hence we want to verify

$$P(m_t = LO \mid s_t > \bar{s}) > P(m_t = LO \mid s_t \leq \bar{s})$$

---

[3] 3 types of market orders (large, market and small), 3 types of limit orders (with price within the spread, at the best bid or ask, at a price outside the spread).

where s_t is the spread at time t and $\bar{s}$ is the mean spread in the period. Results of a t-test at 5% level performed for each market and each treatment are reported in Table 3 where Y means that the difference is significant (the stylized facts appears) and N it is not. Less than half of markets for each treatment shows the stylized fact with the exception of OT, where only one market does.

Table 3. Results of conditional probability of limit orders given the spread. "Y" means that the conditional probability of arriving a limit order when the spread is over the mean is statistically greater than the conditional probability of arriving a limit order when the spread is down the mean

Treat/Market	1	2	3	4	5	6	7	8	9
WTA	Y	N	N	N	N	Y	N	Y	N
BTM	N	Y	N	Y	Y	N	Y	N	N
EC	Y	N	N	Y	N	Y	N	N	Y
OT	N	N	N	N	N	N	N	Y	N

Relative Prices. Relative bid prices are defined as the difference between the best bid and the bid of the incoming order, similarly the relative ask prices are the difference between the ask and the best ask. The distribution of relative prices presents a power law with $\mu = 1.269$ for the buy side and $\mu = 1.072$ for the sell side. Bouchaud et al. (2002) argue that traders place limit order far away

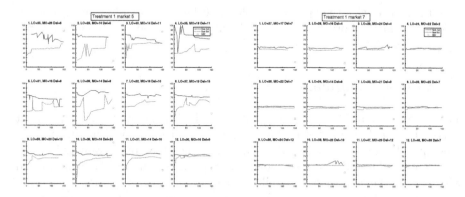

Fig. 1. The bid and ask in the 12 periods (150 s of trading) are reported for treatment Winner Takes All (treatment 1); two markets, 5 and 7, that differ for spread behavior; in market 5 the spread is quite wide with prices higher than the expected buy back value while in market 7 the spread is narrow and close to the expected buy back value. For each period the number of limit market and deleted orders are reported as additional information. The light blue circle at the end of each periods is the realized buy back value. (Color figure online)

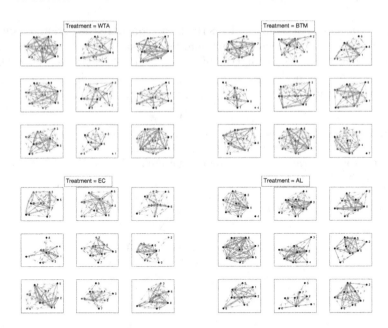

Fig. 2. All 9 markets of treatment WTA (top on the left), BTM (top on the right), EC (bottom on the left) and the controll AL (bottom on the right) are reported as networks; each nodes is an individual, while edges are trades that occur between the two nodes, the network is weighted with respect the number of trades. Magenta nodes are individuals with linear payoff while green ones are the investment managers with tournament incentives. (Color figure online)

from the spread with the optimistic belief that large changes in price can occur, indeed placement of orders with prices highly far from the best bid or ask is not so rare in the data.

3   Models Compliance

The issue of testing the consistency of a model with respect to the data is not trivial. Hollifield et al. (2004), for instance, tested theoretical implications of their model. Indeed their model implies that the thresholds evaluated at the orders chosen by traders form a monotone sequence when the orders are ranked with respect the execution probability. Hence, they tested this monotone property to verify the consistency of the model with respect to the empirical data. Their results are not so encouraging and, indeed, they found that the model is consistent just assuming extreme traders' valuation.

In the following we define the rate of compliance. Let $a_t^{(i)}$ be the real action of subject i at time t and $\hat{a}_t^{(i)}$ the forecasted action by the model $\mathcal{M}$. The compliance is defined

$$c(a_t^{(i)}, \hat{a}_t^{(i)}) = \begin{cases} 1 \ if & a_t^{(i)} \ and \ \hat{a}_t^{(i)} \ same \ type \\ 0 \ otherwise \end{cases}$$

then

$$RoC = \frac{\sum_{k=1}^{N_a} c(a_{t_k}^{(i)}, \hat{a}_{t_k}^{(i)})}{N_a}$$

where $\{t_k\}_{k=1,..,N_a}$ is the time sequence in which actions take places and N_a the number of actions.

In the following two models are considered: Fang et al. (2017) theoretical model and a cut-off strategy model coming from an adaptation of Foucault (1999) model to the laboratory data.

3.1 Fang et al. (2017)

According to Fang et al. (2017) investment managers compete in a constant sum game and their strategies depend on the proportion θ of winners. Given F the distribution of the buy back value (the fundamental value), the best strategies in Winner Takes All (WTA) is given by lemma A8 and holds if $\theta < 1/2$

- if $p < F^{-1}(\theta)$ all managers maximize demand, hence they buy as much as they can;
- if $p = F^{-1}(\theta)$ a $1 - \theta$ proportion of managers buy as much as they can and θ proportion of managers sells everything;
- if $p \in (F^{-1}(\theta), F^{-1}(1 - \theta))$ a proportion $F(p)$ minimizes demand selling everything they have and $1 - F(p)$ buy as much as they can;
- if $p = F^{-1}(1 - \theta)$ a $1 - \theta$ proportion of managers sells everything and θ proportion of managers buy as much as they can;
- if $p > F^{-1}(1 - \theta)$ all managers sell.

The best strategies in Elimination Contest (EC) is given by lemma A9 and holds if $\theta > 1/2$

- if $p < F^{-1}(1 - \theta)$ all managers maximize demand, hence they buy as much as they can;
- if $p \in [F^{-1}(1 - \theta), F^{-1}(\theta)]$ managers demand an amount between the maximum to sell and the maximum to buy;
- if $p > F^{-1}(\theta)$ all managers sell.

The best strategies in Beat the Market (BTM) is given by the following statement and holds if $\theta = 1/2$, hence $F^{-1}(1 - \theta) = F^{-1}(\theta) = v^*$ that is the median value of the buy back value

- if $p < v^*$ all managers maximize demand, hence they buy as much as they can;
- if $p = v^*$ any demand is optimal;
- if $p > v^*$ all managers sell.

Ordinary traders behave as investment managers under the BTM treatment.

Note that according to the theory most of managers take corner positions: sell everything or buy as much as they can. This does not happen in reality where rarely individuals take such extreme decisions. Having the compliance of orders both on the side and quantities is almost unattainable; hence we assume an action to be compliant if the model is able to predict the side.

It is not surprising that some individuals (that keep a constant strategy) are high compliant and some others (that switch between buy and sell given no changes in fundamentals) are scarcely compliant. Indeed this analysis does not produce any relevant result. There is no evidence that an investment manager or an ordinary trader follows a strategy according to her compensation structure.

The model does not distinguish between market and limit order neither it considers the possibility to delete an order, hence the compliance comes to be too rough and not informative enough.

3.2   A Cut Off Strategy Model

Some perfect rationality models address the agent's choice problem via a cut-off strategy. An agent that must select between decision D_1 or D_2, using a statistics $Z(t)$ and a cut off value z adopts a strategy

$$D_1 \ if \ \ Z(t) \leq z$$
$$D_2 \quad otherwise$$

One of the first models to adopt this type of strategy in limit order book framework is Chakravarty and Holden (1995), that finds an extension in Foucault (1999). Adapting Foucault model[4] here gives a simple model but theoretically consistent. The forecasted action of trader i at time t is

$$\hat{a}_t^{(i)} = \begin{cases} MOB & if & A_t^m \leq R_t^{(i)} \\ MOS & if & B_t^m \geq R_t^{(i)} \\ LOB \ or \ LOS \ if \ B_t^m \leq R_t^{(i)} \leq A_t^m \end{cases}$$

where $R_t^{(i)}$ is the reservation price of individual i that gives the cut off price. The reservation price is modeled by two heuristics: trend following and anchoring and adjustment according to Hommes et al. (2005). The Trend Following (TR) heuristic sets

$$R_t = p_{t-1} + g(p_{t-1} - p_{t-2})$$

where $g = 0.4$ (weak TR) or $g = 1.3$ (strong TR) as in Anufriev and Hommes (2012) while the Anchoring and Adjustment (A&A)

$$R_t = (1 - m)\bar{p}_{t-1} + mp_{t-1} + l(p_{t-1} - p_{t-2})$$

---

[4] Details of adaptation are here omitted but given on request.

where p_{t-1} is the last traded price, p_{t-2} is the second last traded price and $\bar{p}_{t-1}$ is the sample average of all past prices; $m = 0.5$ and $l = 1$ are set as experimentally estimated in Hommes et al. (2005).

Actions differ by order (limit or market) and side (buy or sell) only in the market order case, hence the compliance is considered only with respect market order buy (MOB), market order sell (MOS) and limit order (LO).

The results of the compliance tests are summarized in Table 4. There are very compliant subjects and others very low compliant, no much differences between treatments, investment managers and ordinary traders, also verified by specific hypothesis tests that are not so relevant to report here. There are also small differences between TR and A&A in setting the reservation price, thus the statistics of the rates of compliance in Table 4 are done on the maximum values between the two heuristics.

Note that according to this cut off strategy model no limit orders outside the spread are expected, however the empirical evidence showed that more than 20% of orders are outside the spread, this fact is not yet well investigated in literature.

Table 4. Results of rate of compliance Cut Off Strategy Foucault model readapted

Treatment	Mean	Std	Min	Max	N
IM WTA	0.5210	0.2644	0.2139	0.7852	36
IM EC	0.5339	0.2726	0	0.8403	36
IM BTM	0.4885	0.2996	0	0.8025	36
OT	0.5208	0.2707	0	0.9132	72

4 Conclusion

In this research, data coming from an experimental order book have been studied with the main aim of understanding the decision process of the individuals. Some stylized facts and some similarity in dynamics with real market emerge for a few number of markets. On the one hand, the dissimilarity between real data and laboratory data are not surprising and confirm some conjectures on the nature of stylized facts, on the second hand many aspects are still to be interpreted. Differently by Fang et al. (2017) few differences emerged between treatments. Some individuals may take decisions even in opposite direction without apparent rationality, while others are high compliant with theory, hence a high heterogeneity and noise are present that contaminate results. Future research will face the challenge of investigating the mechanism of order placement with a specific focus on why individuals submit orders outside the spread and why individuals cancel orders.

References

Anufriev, M., Hommes, C.: Evolutionary selection of individual expectations and aggregate outcomes in asset pricing experiments. Am. Econ. J. Microecon. **4**, 35–64 (2012)

Asparouhova, E., Bossaerts, P., Roy, N., Zame, W.: Lucas in the laboratory. J. Finan. **71**, 2727–2780 (2016)

Assenza, T., Grazzini, J., Hommes, C., Massaro, D.: PQ strategies in monopolistic competition: some insights from the lab. J. Econ. Dyn. Control **50**, 62–77 (2015)

Biais, B., Hillion, P., Spatt, C.: An empirical analysis of the limit order book and the order flow in the Paris Bourse. J. Finan. **50**(5), 1655–1689 (1995)

Bouchaud, J.P., Mzard, M., Marc, P.M.: Statistical properties of stock order books: empirical results and models. Quant. Finan. **2**(4), 251–256 (2002)

Cao, C., Hansch, O., Wang, X.: Optimal placement strategies in a pure limit order book market. J. Finan. Res. **31**(2), 113–140 (2008)

Chakravarty, S., Craig, W.H.: An integrated model of market and limit orders. J. Finan. Intermed. **4**(3), 213–241 (1995)

Conte, A., Hey, J.D., Moffatt, P.G.: Mixture models of choice under risk. J. Econom. **162**(1), 79–88 (2011)

Fang, D., Holmen, M., Kleinlercher, D., Kirchler, M.: How tournament incentives affect asset markets: a comparison between winner-take-all tournaments and elimination contests. J. Econ. Dyn. Control **75**, 1–27 (2017)

Foucault, T.: Order flow composition and trading costs in a dynamic limit order market. J. Finan. Markets **2**(2), 99–134 (1999)

Gould, M.D., Porter, M.A., Williams, S., McDonald, M., Fenn, D.J., Howison, S.D.: Limit order books. Quant. Finan. **13**, 11 (2013)

Harris, L., Hasbrouck, J.: Market vs. limit orders: the SuperDOT evidence on order submission strategy. J. Finan. Quant. Anal. **31**(2), 213–231 (1996)

Heemeijer, P., Hommes, C., Sonnemans, J., Tuinstra, J.: Price stability and volatility in markets with positive and negative expectations feedback: an experimental investigation. J. Econ. Dyn. Control **33**(5), 1052–1072 (2009)

Hollifield, B., Miller, R.A., Sandas, P.: Empirical analysis of limit order markets. Rev. Econ. Stud. **71**, 1027–1063 (2004)

Hommes, C.H., Huang, H., Wang, D.: A robust rational route to randomness in a simple asset pricing model. J. Econ. Dyn. Control **29**(6), 1043–1072 (2005)

Hommes, C.: The heterogeneous expectations hypothesis: some evidence from the lab. J. Econ. Dyn. Control **35**(1), 1–24 (2011)

Plott, C.R., Smith, V.L. (eds.): Handbook of Experimental Economics Results, vol. 1. Elsevier, Amsterdam (2008)

Rosu, I.: A dynamic model of the limit order book. Rev. Finan. Stud. **22**, 4601–4641 (2009)

Workshop on Agents and Edge-AI
(AgEdAI)

Workshop on Agents and Edge-AI (AgEdAI)

Artificial intelligence (AI) has been integrated into our daily activity. We can find it in our smartphones, computers, voice assistants, cities, etc. However, most of these devices use the cloud to process and apply different AI techniques. This massive sending of information makes obvious the limitations of working in the cloud, such as latency, excessive energy consumption, security, and the cost of having a series of dedicated servers for this purpose. These limitations have created a bottleneck for implementing AI products and services in environments close to data sources. It is for these reasons that in recent years the idea of lowering AI has spread, coining the concept of EDGE AI.

This workshop focuses on the challenges of disaggregating AI processing through the use of agents and the EDGE AI paradigm, from devices located at the end of the network (IoT, Embedded Systems) to the cloud. Incorporating small machine learning models in battery-powered devices, the use of AI for network outage, the application of machine learning for data transmission, and the implementation of a cohesive infrastructure that allows developers to create AI software for the periphery.

The objective of this workshop is to bring together researchers and professionals who conduct research related to AI techniques in energy-efficient devices. We welcome any article on experiences related to the use of agents in edge devices.

The AgEdAI workshop is a forum to share ideas, projects, research results, applications, experiences, etc. associated with EDGE AI-based solutions and multi-agent systems within the framework of the International Conference on Practical Applications of Agents and Multiagent Systems 2020 (PAAMS 2020).

Organization

Organizing Committee

Jaime Andres Rincon Arango   Universitat Politècnica de València, Spain
Vicente Julián   Universitat Politècnica de València, Spain
Carlos Carrascosa   Universitat Politècnica de València, Spain

Towards the Edge Intelligence: Robot Assistant for the Detection and Classification of Human Emotions

Jaime Andres Rincon$^{(\boxtimes)}$, Vicente Julian$^{(\boxtimes)}$, and Carlos Carrascosa$^{(\boxtimes)}$

VRAIN, Valencian Research Institute for Artificial Intelligence,
Universitat Politècnica de València, Valencia, Spain
{jrincon,vinglada,carrasco}@dsic.upv.es

Abstract. Deep learning is being introduced more and more in our society. Nowadays, there are very few applications that do not use deep learning as a classification tool. One of the main application areas is focused on improving people's life quality, allowing to create personal assistants with canned benefits. More recently, with the proliferation of mobile computing and the emergence of the Internet of Things (IoT), billions of mobile and IoT devices are connected to the Internet. This allows the generation of millions of bytes of information about sensors, images, sounds, etc. Driven by this trend, there is an urgent need to push the IoT frontiers to the edge of the network, in order to decrease this massive sending of information to large exchanges for analysis. As a result of this trend, a new discipline has emerged: edge intelligence or edge AI, a widely recognised and promising solution that attracts with special interest to the community of researchers in artificial intelligence. We adapted edge AI to classify human emotions. Results show how edge AI-based emotion classification can greatly benefit in the field of cognitive assistants for the elderly or people living alone.

Keywords: EDGE AI · Assistant robot · Emotions · Elderly

1 Introduction

Recent developments in artificial intelligent (AI) technologies have played an important role in several areas of knowledge such as medicine [1], robotics [2] or autonomous cars [3]. One of this late developments is the remote use of large computing units with high-performance servers, capable of executing millions of calculations per second (this is what we know today as *Cloud*). Among the recognised cloud services we can find Amazon Web Services (AWS)[1], which introduced its Elastic Compute Cloud; Microsoft Azure[2], announced as *Azure*,

---

[1] https://aws.amazon.com/es/.
[2] https://azure.microsoft.com/es-es/.

© Springer Nature Switzerland AG 2020
F. De La Prieta et al. (Eds.): PAAMS 2020 Workshops, CCIS 1233, pp. 31–41, 2020.
https://doi.org/10.1007/978-3-030-51999-5_3

and Google Cloud Platform[3]. However, so much computing power has some drawbacks, such as the space they need and their high energy consumption.

In this regard, evolution of electronics and microelectronics has made it possible to create smaller, energy-efficient devices that are capable of accessing sensors or actuators, and with an internet connection, in other words, the Internet of Things (IoT) [4].

Using IoT devices we can connect everyday objects such as kitchen appliances, vehicles, thermostats, baby monitors, of the Internet through integrated devices. In this way, we can achieve a fluid communication between people, processes and things. However, sometimes, it is necessary to make a more intelligent interaction between the devices we have counted and the users. Nowadays, this is done by sending massively the data to the servers, which process, learn and classify these data. According to Cisco, about 50 billion IoT devices will be connected by 2020, but all these volumes of data are passive if they cannot be analysed or interpreted.

This high volume of data handling generates a series of problems such as latency in the reception of the results of the analysed data, the high energy consumption that these processing centers require and the space that they occupy. For these reasons, in the last few years a change in the IoT paradigm has been initiated, where it is no longer necessary to send data to servers for analysis, but it is now possible to perform an analysis or classification within these devices. This represents a great advance since these new devices have a low power consumption, are smaller and are equipped with structures capable of supporting deep learning models. These new elements are known as Edge AI devices, and they are being used in a massive way in applications of wearable devices such as [5], cyber-threats [6], implementation of machine learning algorithms in low memory devices [7], and assistant robot [8].

Personal assistants are perhaps some of the most interesting applications in which Deep Learning is used. This is mainly because they are in continuous interaction with humans. Allowing these assistants to learn their tastes, needs, perceiving how these needs affect their emotional states.

This data processing in most cases, is used to perform simple actions in the systems. However, some of these actions could be performed within each of the devices, for this it is necessary that these devices have the ability to use AI techniques as automatic learning models. These models would help to detect patterns in the lower layers of the system, thus avoiding the massive sending of information to the upper layers. This would reduce response times, as well as the massive sending of information to the same point.

These devices capable of performing these actions at a low level, is what we know today as Edge-AI. Edge-AI enables the creation of intelligent solutions in real-time using deep learning techniques. These solutions must have a number of key features, such as energy efficiency, low cost and a balance between precision and energy consumption. Currently, deep learning techniques are conventionally deployed in centralised computing environments. However, these applications

---

[3] https://cloud.google.com/.

have some limitations such as costs generated by energy consumption, or latency in the network due to massive data sending. To address these limitations, edge computing, often referred to as *Artificial Edge Intelligence*, has been introduced, in which calculations are performed locally from data acquired from various devices or sensors.

The challenges of meeting the requirements for implementing Edge-AI are to ensure high accuracy of the algorithms while having low power consumption. However, this would not be possible without the latest hardware innovations, including central processing units (CPUs), graphics processing units (GPUs), application-specific integrated circuits (ASICs) and system-on-a-chip (SoC) accelerators, which have made edge AI possible. Thanks to these advances there are applications such as the one presented by [9], in which they detect apples in real-time using Edge-AI or Smart Parking using Edge-AI [10].

This paper presents an assistant robot based on Edge-AI technology, which incorporates two devices capable of classifying emotional states and classifying the physical activities performed by the user.

2   Proposed Robot Assistant

The proposed edge AI-based IoT application is a low-cost assistant robot with the ability to classify emotions and recommend physical activities to improve the quality of life of users. The Fig. 1 shows the diagram of our proposal, which is divided into two parts: detection of emotions and classification of physical activities.

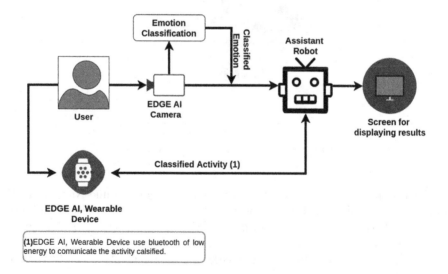

Fig. 1. Diagram of the proposed system.

The first one is in charge of classifying emotions and interaction with the user and the second one is in charge of detecting physical activity. The processes for the classification of emotions and physical activities are carried out using EDGE-AI devices. Deep learning models are embedded in each device for classification process. The hardware and software used are described below.

To classify the emotions we use a M5StickV K210 A Idevelopment system (Fig. 2) which uses AI technologies embedded on a K210 chip[4]. The Kendryte K210 is a chip system (SoC) with integrated machine vision and machine learning. This chip system employs advanced ultra-low processing with the help of a 64-bit dual-core processor. Also, it is equipped with a high performance hardware accelerator of the convolutional neural network (CNN) or KPU. The integrated machine vision function allows to create applications for object detection, image classification or face detection and recognition, providing the size and coordinates of the target in real time. With the K210's built-in microphone, it is possible to detect the orientation of the sound source, sound field images, voice alarm and voice recognition. All these features make this chip the ideal system for creating low-cost personal assistants.

Fig. 2. Development system M5StickV.

The classification of physical activity is based on an Arduino Nano 33 BLE (Fig. 3) with an embedded 9-axis inertial sensor, suitable for assisted mobility devices (such as canes or walkers), or physical therapy devices (such as dumbbells or medicine balls).

The Fig. 4 shows the prototype in charge of carrying out the classification of physical activities.

---

[4] https://kendryte.com/.

Fig. 3. Arduino Nano 33 Ble developer board.

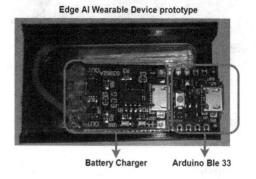

Fig. 4. Prototype Physical Activity Classifier.

Furthermore, this board can work with deep learning to use light tensorflow models in order to classify the activities performed by the user. This way the robot tracks the activity and checks if the user has completed the exercise. The classification of the exercises is supported by a database built with exercises for boosting balance, posture, and core strength for elderly population. The database was built with 30 people, 15 men and 15 women between 35 and 50 years old. Each participant was asked to perform a total of 10 sets of 5 repetitions for each exercise. The robot was designed to fit into the environment of an elderly person in a lonely condition, meaning a small robot that can be placed on a desk. The robot has a camera that enables it to detect and identify the face in order to classify the user's emotional state. To increase the acceptability of the assistant by the user, the robot was given a pleasant appearance with a neutral look, ensuring that its physical appearance does not interfere with the human-assitant interaction. In addition, an information display device was added, which has an LCD screen using a M5Stack[5] on which the face of the assistant can be shown, as well as the activities to be performed and relevant messages.

---

[5] https://m5stack.com.

The Fig. 5 shows the prototype of the assistant robot, with the different parts.

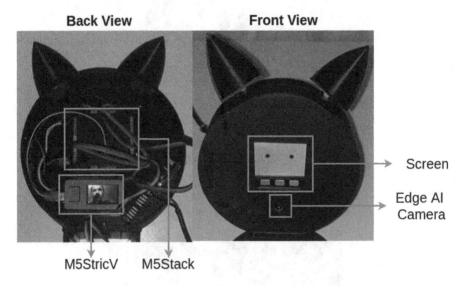

Fig. 5. Prototype of the assistant robot.

2.1 Software Description

This section describes each of the different steps carried out for the classification of emotions and the classification of activities. It describes the different tools used to carry out these tasks, as well as the division of the database and the different parameters that make up each of the networks used.

2.2 Emotion Classification

We propose an assistant robot with the ability to recognize emotional states. This ability provides the robot with information to interact more naturally with the user's and make some kind of recommendation based on their emotional state. To classify the emotions, a dataset was built in which the images were separated by classes, with each class representing an emotion. Seven emotions were taken into account to classify: fear, angry, disgust, happy, neutral, sad and surprised. We use the Karolinska Directed Emotional Faces (KDEF) database, containing 4900 images of human facial expression, as a source to build our dataset. The images show the faces of 70 amateur actors (35 men and 35 women) showing 7 different emotional expressions. Each expression is seen from 5 different angles. The selection criteria for the actors were: Age between 20 and 30 years and no beard or moustache. During the photo session participants were asked to use some or no makeup and no earrings or glasses. To perform the experiments we divided the data set into three parts, 80% for training, 10% for testing and 10% for validation.

In order to carry out the qualification of emotions using EDGE devices, it is necessary to carry out a series of steps. These steps are necessary, since, the models obtained after the training using Keras [11] are not compatible with the K210 chip. These steps are divided into, (i) obtaining the H5 model, (ii) transformation to tersorflow lite and finally (iii) obtaining the Kmodel modal. The network used to obtain the H5 model is a *Mobilenet* network [12]. This network was designed for mobile and integrated vision applications. MobileNets are based on a streamlined architecture that uses deep-separable convolutions to build deep and lightweight neural networks. We present two simple global hyperparameters that efficiently exchange between latency and accuracy. The Fig. 6 shows the normalized confusion matrix of our experiments.

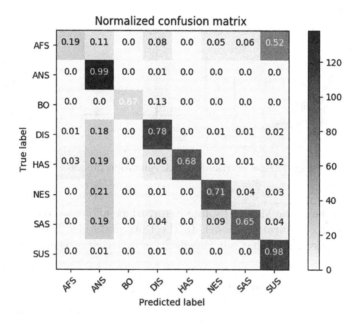

Fig. 6. Normalized confusion matrix of Emotion detection.

Once obtained from the trained model of this network, the next step is to transform it into Tensorflow Lite[6]. TensorFlow Lite has a set of tools that allows the develop to run TensorFlow models on mobile, embedded and IoT devices. The last step is the conversion of the tensorflow lite to K-Model, this transformation is performed using Sipeed tools[7].

2.3   Activity Classification

To carry out the classification of physical activities, a sequential network was used. To perform the classification of physical activities, a sequential network

---

[6] https://www.tensorflow.org/lite.

[7] https://www.sipeed.com.

was used. The model configuration parameters are shown in the next JASON code (1), which specifies the density per layer and the activation rule for that layer.

Training results using this configuration can be seen below, in Fig. 7 can be seen the Loss of the training and validation process.

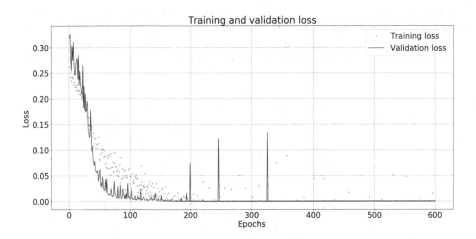

Fig. 7. Loss of Training and Validation process.

The Fig. 8 shows the Mean Absolute Error, which allows us to determine the accuracy of our classification model. In the tests performed this error is very low, so we can determine that our classification of activities is correct.

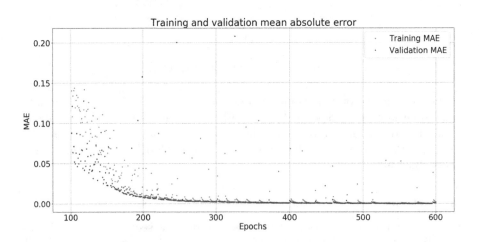

Fig. 8. Training and validation absolute error.

```
{
    'build_input_shape': (None, 714),
      'layers': [{'class_name': 'Dense',
          'config': {'activation': 'relu',
                     'activity_regularizer': None,
                     'bias_constraint': None,
                     'bias_initializer': {'class_name': 'Zeros',
                                          'config': {}},
                     'bias_regularizer': None,
                     'dtype': 'float32',
                     'kernel_constraint': None,
                     'kernel_initializer': {'class_name': 'GlorotUniform',
                                            'config': {'seed': None}},
                     'kernel_regularizer': None,
                     'name': 'dense',
                     'trainable': True,
                     'units': 50,
                     'use_bias': True}},
         {'class_name': 'Dense',
          'config': {'activation': 'relu',
                     'activity_regularizer': None,
                     'bias_constraint': None,
                     'bias_initializer': {'class_name': 'Zeros',
                                          'config': {}},
                     'bias_regularizer': None,
                     'dtype': 'float32',
                     'kernel_constraint': None,
                     'kernel_initializer': {'class_name': 'GlorotUniform',
                                            'config': {'seed': None}},
                     'kernel_regularizer': None,
                     'name': 'dense_1',
                     'trainable': True,
                     'units': 15,
                     'use_bias': True}},
         {'class_name': 'Dense',
          'config': {'activation': 'softmax',
                     'activity_regularizer': None,
                     'bias_constraint': None,
                     'bias_initializer': {'class_name': 'Zeros',
                                          'config': {}},
                     'bias_regularizer': None,
                     'dtype': 'float32',
                     'kernel_constraint': None,
                     'kernel_initializer': {'class_name': 'GlorotUniform',
                                            'config': {'seed': None}},
                     'kernel_regularizer': None,
                     'name': 'dense_2',
                     'trainable': True,
                     'units': 2,
                     'use_bias': True}}],
    'name': 'sequential'
}
```

Listing 1: Structure of the model for the classification of activities.

3   Conclusions and Future Work

This paper presents the integration of two Edge AI technologies for the classification of emotions and the classification of physical activities for humans. The proposed system uses low-cost, low-power sensor systems. In this way, the system developed does not need to send the information obtained to servers for analysis, thus decreasing the latency in obtaining responses. This represents a breakthrough in the state of the art and tools used to make applications using Edge AI. Due to the combination of several deep learning models and the use of different low cost hardware devices. Future work will focus on the development of new tests with a larger number of users. These new tests will allow us to use the information obtained to improve our learning models for better recognition of different activities and emotions. We also focus our future research on the integration of speech recognition with these devices (Edge), so that users can use voice to control the robot.

Acknowledgements. This work was partly supported by the Generalitat Valenciana (PROMETEO/2018/002) and by the Spanish Government (RTI2018-095390-B-C31). Universitat Politecnica de Valencia Research Grant PAID-10-19.

References

1. Chang, A.: The role of artificial intelligence in digital health. In: Wulfovich, S., Meyers, A. (eds.) Digital Health Entrepreneurship. HI, pp. 71–81. Springer, Cham (2020). https://doi.org/10.1007/978-3-030-12719-0_7
2. Yang, L., Henthorne, T.L., George, B.: Artificial intelligence and robotics technology in the hospitality industry: current applications and future trends. In: George, B., Paul, J. (eds.) Digital Transformation in Business and Society, pp. 211–228. Springer, Cham (2020). https://doi.org/10.1007/978-3-030-08277-2_13
3. Khayyam, H., Javadi, B., Jalili, M., Jazar, R.N.: Artificial intelligence and Internet of Things for autonomous vehicles. In: Jazar, R.N., Dai, L. (eds.) Nonlinear Approaches in Engineering Applications, pp. 39–68. Springer, Cham (2020). https://doi.org/10.1007/978-3-030-18963-1_2
4. Liang, F., Yu, W., Liu, X., Griffith, D., Golmie, N.: Towards edge-based deep learning in industrial Internet of Things. IEEE Internet of Things J. **7**, 4329–4341 (2020)
5. Nagaraju, P.B., Oliner, A.J., Gilmore, B.M., Dean, E.A., Wang, J.: Data analytics in edge devices. US Patent App. 16/573,745, 9 January 2020
6. Eskandari, M., Janjua, Z.H., Vecchio, M., Antonelli, F.: Passban IDS: an intelligent anomaly based intrusion detection system for IoT edge devices. IEEE Internet of Things J. (2020)
7. Harish, A., Jhawar, S., Anisha, B.S., Ramakanth Kumar, P.: Implementing machine learning on edge devices with limited working memory. In: Ranganathan, G., Chen, J., Rocha, Á. (eds.) Inventive Communication and Computational Technologies. LNNS, vol. 89, pp. 1255–1261. Springer, Singapore (2020). https://doi.org/10.1007/978-981-15-0146-3_123
8. Rincon, J.A., Martin, A., Costa, Â., Novais, P., Julián, V., Carrascosa, C.: EmIR: an emotional intelligent robot assistant. In: AfCAI (2018)

9. Ke, R., Zhuang, Y., Pu, Z., Wang, Y.: A smart, efficient, and reliable parking surveillance system with edge artificial intelligence on IoT devices. arXiv preprint arXiv:2001.00269 (2020)

10. Mazzia, V., Khaliq, A., Salvetti, F., Chiaberge, M.: Real-time apple detection system using embedded systems with hardware accelerators: an edge AI application. IEEE Access **8**, 9102–9114 (2020)

11. Chollet, F., et al.: Keras (2015). https://github.com/fchollet/keras

12. Howard, A.G., et al.: MobileNets: efficient convolutional neural networks for mobile vision applications. arXiv preprint arXiv:1704.04861 (2017)

Industrial Federated Learning – Requirements and System Design

Thomas Hiessl[1,2](✉)(ID), Daniel Schall[1](ID), Jana Kemnitz[1](ID),
and Stefan Schulte[2](ID)

[1] Siemens Corporate Technology, 1210 Vienna, Austria
{hiessl.thomas,daniel.schall,jana.kemnitz}@siemens.com
[2] Vienna University of Technology, Karlsplatz 13, 1040 Vienna, Austria
s.schulte@dsg.tuwien.ac.at

Abstract. Federated Learning (FL) is a very promising approach for improving decentralized Machine Learning (ML) models by exchanging knowledge between participating clients without revealing private data. Nevertheless, FL is still not tailored to the industrial context as strong data similarity is assumed for all FL tasks. This is rarely the case in industrial machine data with variations in machine type, operational- and environmental conditions. Therefore, we introduce an Industrial Federated Learning (IFL) system supporting knowledge exchange in continuously evaluated and updated FL cohorts of learning tasks with sufficient data similarity. This enables optimal collaboration of business partners in common ML problems, prevents negative knowledge transfer, and ensures resource optimization of involved edge devices.

Keywords: Federated Learning · Industrial AI · Edge computing

1 Introduction

Industrial manufacturing systems often consist of various operating machines and automation systems. High availability and fast reconfiguration of each operating machine is key to frictionless production resulting in competitive product pricing [15]. To ensure high availability of each machine, often condition monitoring is realized based on Machine Learning (ML) models deployed to edge devices, e.g., indicating anomalies in production [5]. The performance of these ML models clearly depends on available training data, which is often only available to a limited degree for individual machines. Increasing training data might be realized by sharing data within the company or with an external industry partner [3]. The latter approach is often critical as vulnerable business or private information might be contained.

The recently emerged Federated Learning FL method enables to train a ML model on multiple local datasets contained in local edge devices without exchanging data samples [13]. In this privacy-preserving approach, typically a server receives parameters (e.g., gradients or weights of neural networks) from local

© Springer Nature Switzerland AG 2020
F. De La Prieta et al. (Eds.): PAAMS 2020 Workshops, CCIS 1233, pp. 42–53, 2020.
https://doi.org/10.1007/978-3-030-51999-5_4

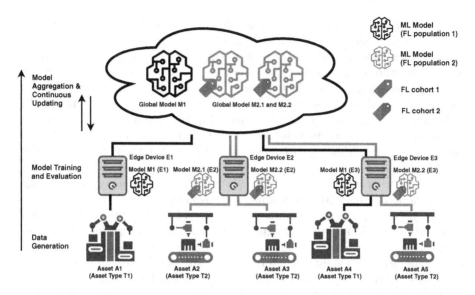

Fig. 1. Federated Learning (FL) with industrial assets; Assets generate data that are used in learning tasks for ML models executed on edge devices; Learning tasks for ML models based on the same asset type are part of a FL population; Learning tasks for ML models with similar data are part of a FL population subset named FL cohort; Knowledge transfer in continuously evaluated and updated FL cohorts ensures optimal collaboration with respect to model performance and business partner criteria

models trained on decentralized edge devices and averages these parameters to build a global model [11]. After that, the averaged global model parameters are forwarded to edge devices to update local models. This process is repeatedly executed until the global model converges or a defined break-up condition is met.

However, to solve the discussed challenges of successfully applying ML models in industrial domains, FL needs to be adapted. Therefore, the integration of operating machines and its digital representations named *assets*[1] need to be considered as depicted in Fig. 1. Assets generate data on the shop floor during operation. Edge devices record this data to enable training of ML models e.g., in the field of anomaly detection aiming to identify abnormal behavior of machines in production. To improve the model quality, FL is applied by aggregating model parameters centrally in a global model, e.g., in the cloud, and sending out updates to other edge devices. Typically, all models of local learning tasks corresponding to the same ML problem are updated. This set of tasks is called a FL population. In the depicted industry scenario, a FL population corresponds to all learning tasks for models trained on asset data with same data scheme, which is typically ensured if assets are of the same asset type,

---

[1] https://documentation.mindsphere.io/resources/html/asset-manager/en-US/ 113537583883.html.

e.g., learning tasks of models *M2.1 (E2)*, *M2.2 (E2)*, and *M2.2 (E3)* belong to *FL population 2*, since they are based on assets of *Asset Type T2*. In contrast, learning tasks of models *M1 (E1)* and *M1 (E3)* belong to *FL population 1*. However, assets even of same asset type could face heterogenous environmental and operation conditions which affect recorded data. Due to these potential dissimilarities in asset data, negative knowledge transfer can be caused by the model updates which decreases model performance [14]. For this, industrial FL systems need to consider FL cohorts as subsets of a FL population. This enables knowledge sharing only within e.g., *FL cohort 2* including *M2.2* models using similar asset data.

For this, we propose to establish FL system support for knowledge exchange in FL cohorts involving ML models based on asset data from industry. Furthermore, it needs support for continuous adaption of FL cohorts as ML models evolve over time. To additionally support efficient FL with high quality of asset data, we aim for resource optimization of involved edge devices and appropriate consideration of Quality of Information (QoI) metrics [8]. Hence, our contribution comprises requirements and a system design for Industrial Federated Learning (IFL) which we introduce in this paper. IFL aims to improve collaboration on training and evaluating ML models in industrial environments. For this, we consider current FL systems and approaches [1,2,10,11,13] and incorporate industry concepts as well as experience from industrial projects. The design of the IFL system is presented with respect to supported workflows, domain model, and architecture.

In Sect. 2 we refer to the basic notation of FL. We review related work in Sect. 3 and subsequently present requirements of IFL in Sect. 4. The design of the IFL system is presented in Sect. 5 with respect to supported workflows, domain models, and architectures. We conclude in Sect. 6 and provide an outline to future work.

2   IFL Notation

To introduce the basic notation of an IFL systems, we extend the FL notation by Bonawitz et al. [1] that define *device*, *FL server*, *FL task*, *FL population* and *FL plan*. Devices are hardware platforms as e.g., industrial edge devices or mobile phones, running *FL clients* to execute the computation necessary for training and evaluating ML models. To use FL, a FL client communicates to the FL server to run FL tasks for a given FL population. The latter one is a globally unique name that identifies a learning problem which multiple FL tasks have in common. The FL server aggregates results (i.e., model updates), persists the global model, and provides it to FL clients of a given FL population. A FL plan corresponds to a FL task and represents its federated execution instructions for the FL server and involved FL clients. It consists of sequences of ML steps as e.g., data pre-processing, training, and evaluation to be executed by FL clients and instructions for aggregating ML models on the FL server. Furthermore, we define *FL cohorts* that group multiple FL tasks within the same FL population and with similarities in their underlying asset data.

3   Related Work

3.1   FL Systems

Most of the current FL studies focus on federated algorithm design and efficiency improvement [9]. Besides that, Bonawitz et al. [1] built a scalable production system for FL aiming to facilitate learning tasks on mobile devices using *Tensor-Flow*[2]. Furthermore, *NVIDIA Clara*[3] provided an SDK to integrate custom ML models in a FL environment. This system has been evaluated with data from the medical domain, considering a scenario with decentralized image datasets located in hospitals. However, no aspects of dynamically changing data patterns in learning tasks of FL cohorts have been considered in literature so far.

3.2   Client Selection

Nishio et al. [12] optimize model training duration in FL by selecting only a subset of FL clients. Since they face heterogeneous conditions and are provisioned with diverse resource capabilities, not all FL clients will manage to deliver results in decent time. For this, only those who deliver before a deadline are selected in the current training round. To achieve the best accuracy for the global model, the FL server may select FL clients based on their model evaluation results on held out validation data [1]. This allows to optimize the configuration of FL tasks such as centrally setting hyperparameters for model training or defining optimal number of involved FL clients. Although, in IFL these client selection approaches need to be considered, the IFL system further selects FL clients based on collaboration criteria with respect to potential FL business partners.

3.3   Continuous Federated Learning

Liu et al. [10] propose a cloud-based FL system for reinforcement tasks of robots navigating around obstacles. Since there exist robots that train much and therefore update ML models continuously, the authors identify the need for sharing these updates with other federated robots. These updates are asynchronously incorporated in the global model to eventually enhance navigation skills of all involved robots. Based on that, in IFL the continuous updates are used to re-evaluate data similarity that is needed to ensure high model quality within a FL cohort organization.

4   Requirements

In this section we now present requirements that should be covered by an IFL system. Based on FL system features discussed in [9], we add requirements with respect to industrial data processing and continuous adaptation of the system.

---

[2] https://www.tensorflow.org/.
[3] https://devblogs.nvidia.com/federated-learning-clara/.

4.1   Industrial Metadata Management

To support collaboration of FL clients, we identify the requirement of publishing metadata describing the organization and its devices. Based on this, FL clients can provide criteria for collaborating with other selected FL clients. Although actual raw data is not shared in FL, it enables to adhere to company policies for interacting with potential partners. Asset models as provided by Siemens MindSphere (See footnote 1) describes the data scheme for industrial Internet of Things (IoT) data. Since industrial FL clients target to improve machine learning models using asset data, metadata describing the assets builds the basis for collaborating in suitable FL populations.

4.2   FL Cohorts

As discussed in Sect. 3.2, FL client selection plays a role in FL to reduce duration of e.g., training or evaluation [12]. Furthermore, client selection based on evaluation using held-out validation data, can improve accuracy of the global model [1]. In our experience, these approaches do not sufficiently address data generated by industrial assets and processed by FL clients. For this, our approach aims for considering asset data characteristics for achieving optimal accuracy and performance for all individual client models. To this end, we identify the requirement of evaluating models in regards to similarities of asset data influenced by operating and environmental conditions. This is the basis for building FL cohorts of FL tasks using asset data with similar characteristics. FL cohorts enable that FL clients only share updates within a subset of FL clients, whose submitted FL tasks belong to the same FL cohort. These updates probably improve their individual model accuracy better, as if updates would be shared between FL clients that face very heterogeneous data due to e.g., different environmental or operating conditions of involved assets. In manufacturing industries there are situations where assets are placed in sites with similar conditions, as, e.g., placing production machines into shop floors with similar temperature, noise and other features considered in the model prediction. In such cases, the IFL system needs to build FL cohorts.

4.3   Quality of Information

Since each FL client trains and evaluates on its local data set, aggregated global models result from data sets with diverse QoI. Furthermore, due to different agents operating in the industry as e.g., fully autonomous control systems as well as semi-autonomous ones with human interaction [6], different data recording approaches can influence QoI of asset data sets. Lee et al. [8] discuss different dimensions of QoI as e.g., *free-of-error, relevancy, reputation, appropriate amount, believability, consistent representation* and *security*. Based on that, we derive that there is the need to evaluate QoI on FL clients and use resulting metrics on the FL server to decide on the extent of contribution of an individual FL client in the parameter aggregation process. Storing QoI metrics next to existing industrial metadata of participating organizations further enhances building and updating suitable FL cohorts.

4.4 Continuous Learning

Artificial Intelligence (AI) increasingly enables operation of industrial processes to realize flexibility, efficiency, and sustainability. For this, often domain experts have to repeatedly understand new data with respect to its physical behavior and the meaning of parameters of the underlying process [7]. Moreover, continuously involving domain experts and data scientists in updating ML models by e.g., providing labels to recently recorded time series data, is a resource-intensive process, that can be faciliated by continuously collaborating in FL. Based on that, we identify the need of supporting continuously re-starting FL learning processes and cohort reorganization over time to consider major changes in asset time series data.

4.5 Scheduling and Optimization

Executing FL plans can cause heavy loads on edge devices, as e.g., training of ML models on large data sets [1]. Bonawitz et al. [1] identified the need for device scheduling. This involves that, e.g., multiple FL plans are not executed in parallel on single devices with little capacities, or that repeated training on older data sets is avoided while training on FL clients with new data is promoted. For industry purposes, it further needs optimization of cohorts communication. This means, that FL tasks linked to a FL cohort, can be transferred to other cohorts if this improves communication between involved FL clients with respect to e.g., latency minimization [4]. We believe, this decreases model quality due to preferring communication metrics over model quality metrics. However, IFL systems need to consider this trade-off in an optimization problem and solve it to maximize overall utility. Furthermore, collaboration restrictions of FL clients needs to be considered in the optimization problem. This ensures that no organization joins FL cohorts with other organizations that they do not want to collaborate with.

5 System Design

5.1 Domain Model

To establish a domain model for IFL, we consider FL terminology [1] as well as concepts from industrial asset models as discussed in Sect. 4.1. For this, Fig. 2 depicts *FL Population*, *FL Server*, *FL Client*, *FL Task* and *FL Plan* as discussed in Sect. 2. Herein, we consider to deploy and run the FL server either in the *Cloud*

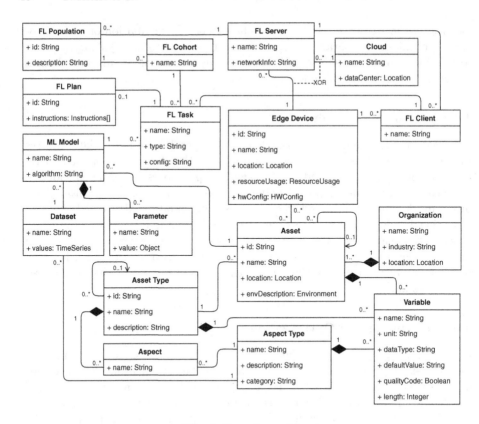

Fig. 2. Domain model

or on an *Edge Device*. The FL client is hosted on an industrial edge device, that is a hardware device on a given *location*. To support scheduling and optimization decisions of the FL server, the edge device contains *resource usage* metrics and hardware specifications (*hwConfig*). A FL task refers to a *ML Model* that needs to be trained with an *algorithm* on a given *Dataset* consisting of time series *values*. The scheme of the Dataset is defined by an *Aspect Type*, which contains a set of *Variables*. Each Variable has *name, unit, dataType, defaultValue* and *length* attributes to define the content of the corresponding time series values. The *qualityCode* indicates whether a variable supports *OPC Quality Codes*[4]. This enables to record and evaluate QoI metrics on the FL client as discussed in Sect. 4.3. Since industrial ML tasks typically consider data from industrial assets, we define an *Asset* (e.g., a concrete engine) operating on a given *location* facing environmental conditions (*envDescription*). The asset is an instance of an *Asset Type* (e.g., an engine) that collects multiple *aspects* (e.g., surface vibrations) of corresponding aspect types (e.g., vibration) again collecting variables (e.g., vibrations in x, y, z dimensions). The asset is connected to an edge device

---

[4] https://www.opcsupport.com/s/article/What-are-the-OPC-Quality-Codes.

which is recording data for it. To express the complexity of industrial organizations, hierarchical asset structures can be built as it is depicted with recursive associations of assets and related asset types, considering nesting of, e.g., overall shop floors, their assembly lines, involved machines and its parts. Finally, we introduce FL cohorts as groups of FL tasks. A FL cohort is built with respect to similarities of assets considered in the attached ML model. So, creating FL tasks intents to typically solve ML problems based on asset data, whereas the aspect type referred in the Dataset of the ML model are used in the linked asset.

5.2   Workflows

To regard the requirements of Sect. 4, we propose several workflows to be supported by the IFL system.

FL Client Registration. Assuming the FL server to be in place, the FL client starts participation in the IFL system by registering itself. For this, the FL client has to submit a request including organization and edge device information. Furthermore, aspect types are handed in, describing the data scheme based on which the organization is willing to collaborate in FL processes with other organizations. Additionally, the assets enabled for FL are posted to the FL server, to provide an overview to other organizations and to ensure that IFL can build FL cohorts based on respective environmental conditions.

Cohort Search Criteria Posting. After FL client registration, other FL clients can request a catalog of edge devices, organizations and connected assets. Based on this, cohort search criteria can be created potentially including organizations, industries, and asset types as well as aspect types. This enables to match submitted FL tasks to FL cohorts based on client restrictions for collaboration and their ML models.

Submit and Run FL Tasks. The FL client creates a FL task including references to the ML model without revealing the actual data set and submits it to the FL server. If FL tasks target the same problems, i.e., reference to the same aspect types and corresponding ML model, the provided FL task is attached to an existing FL population, otherwise a new FL population is created. IFL then builds FL cohorts of FL tasks based on metadata provided during registration and posted cohort search criteria. If no cohort search criteria is provided by the FL client, the submitted FL Tasks are initially considered in the *default* FL cohort of the given FL population. To actually start FL, a FL plan is created including server and client instructions to realize e.g., *Federated Averaging* [11] on the server and training of ML models on every involved FL client. The *configuration* of FL tasks allows for defining parameters for supported algorithms of IFL for, e.g., setting break-up conditions for FL or defining the number of repeated executions over time. Since FL tasks are either realized as training or evaluation plan, the exchanged data between FL client and FL Server are different. While training plans typically include the sharing of model parameters as, e.g., gradients or weights of neural networks, evaluation plan execution results in metrics that are stored by IFL to further enable FL cohort reconfiguration and optimization.

Update FL Cohorts. Collected metrics in the FL process enable to update FL cohorts with respect to splitting and merging FL cohorts. Furthermore, moving FL tasks between cohorts is considered in IFL. The respective metrics include information like the environmental changes of assets and model accuracy. Furthermore, similarity measures of ML models are computed based on possible server-provided data. If such evaluation data is present, a strategy for updating FL cohorts includes to put FL tasks in the same FL cohort, where its ML model predicts ideally the same output based on provided input samples.

Evaluate QoI. The QoI of raw data used by each FL client is computed on edge devices and mapped to OPC Quality Codes as defined in Sect. 5.1. Besides using submitted QoI for e.g., updating FL cohorts, IFL considers QoI in the contribution weights of FL clients when it comes to weighted averaging of model parameters as defined in [11].

Continuous Learning. After time series data is updated and if needed properly labelled, FL tasks are submitted. For this, either synchronous [11] or asynchronous [2] FL processes are triggered. In the asynchronous case, IFL determines the timing for notifying FL clients to update ML models according to recent improvements of one FL client.

Optimize Computation and Communication. First, the FL server loads resource usage from edge devices to determine the load caused by executed processes. Second, network statistics (e.g., latency) are identified as recorded for model update sharings between FL clients and the FL Server. Third, statistics of past FL plan executions, e.g., duration of processing is loaded to be incorporated in an optimization model. Finally, this model optimizes future FL plan executions considering QoS criteria [4] as processing cost, network latency, and cohort reconfiguration cost.

5.3   Architecture

To realize the workflows presented in the previous section, we propose the IFL architecture depicted in Fig. 3.

Considering two types of parties involved in IFL, we present the *FL Application* and the *FL Server*, whereas the former is a container for a *Client Application* that is a domain-dependent consumer of IFL. Furthermore, the FL Application contains the *FL Client* that interacts with the FL server.

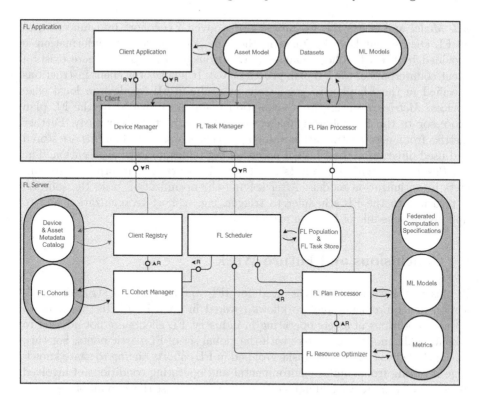

Fig. 3. FL client and server architecture

We now discuss the main components of the IFL system and its responsibilities. First, the FL client registration workflow involves the *Device Manager* of the FL client. It provides an API to the client application to register for FL. The client application provides a list of participating edge devices and general information of the organization. Forwarding this to the *Client Registry* allows persistence in the *Device & Asset Metadata Catalog* stored on the FL server. cohort search criteria posting is supported by device manager and client registry too, with additionally exposing an interface to the *FL Cohort Manager* to provide the device & asset metadata catalog and the FL cohort search criteria for creating FL cohorts.

Submitting new FL tasks is initiated by invoking the *FL Task Manager* which is in charge of enriching the information provided by the FL task with information of the associated ML model and targeted asset. After forwarding the FL task to the server-side *FL Scheduler*, it is mapped to the corresponding FL population and persisted. Furthermore, the FL Scheduler attaches scheduling information to timely trigger execution of all FL tasks of a FL population. To actually run a FL task, the FL Scheduler hands it over to the *FL Plan Processor*. It translates the FL task to a FL plan and corresponding instructions as defined in *Federated Computation Specifications*. Subsequently, it creates the corresponding global

ML Model and starts the FL process for a given FL cohort by connecting to all FL clients that have FL tasks in the same FL cohort. This information is provided by the FL cohort manager. Analogously to FL plans, there exists a client counterpart of the FL plan processor too. It invokes the client instructions specified in the FL plan to, e.g., train or evaluate ML models on local edge devices. *Metrics* resulting from evaluation plans are provided by the FL plan processor to the FL cohort manager to update cohorts continuously. Further metrics from, e.g., continuous learning approaches or QoI evaluations are stored and used directly by the FL plan processor e.g., during model aggregation. The *FL Resource Optimizer* connects to the metrics storage to incorporate parameters in optimization models. After solving the optimization task, the solution is returned to the FL scheduler to trigger, e.g., cohort reorganization and to update the schedule of FL plan executions.

6 Conclusions and Future Work

In this work, we identified the need for IFL and provided a structured collection of requirements and workflows covered in an IFL architecture. Due to diverse conditions of assets operating in industry, FL clients are not advised to exchange ML model parameters with the global set of FL participants. For this, we concluded to consider FL tasks grouped in FL cohorts aiming to share knowledge resulting from similar environmental and operating conditions of involved assets. Furthermore, we highlighted that FL can decrease the amount of resource-intensive work of domain experts considering less continuous updates of datasets and labelling to be done. Additionally, making use of metrics resulting from QoI and ML model evaluations can be used for FL cohort reorganizations and weighting in the FL process.

As future work, we consider evaluation of a pilot implementation of the IFL system in industrial labs. Furthermore, the incorporation of FL open source frameworks as *PySyft*[5], *TensorFlow Federated (TFF)*[6], and *FATE*[7] needs to be evaluated with respect to production readiness and support for concurrent communication and computation needed for FL cohorts. Additionally, efficient asynchronous and decentralized FL for industrial edge devices without involving a server is an interesting future research direction. Finally, forecasting of potentially negative knowledge transfer that decreases model quality could complement the idea of dynamically reorganizing FL cohorts.

---

[5] https://github.com/OpenMined/PySyft.

[6] https://www.tensorflow.org/federated.

[7] https://fate.fedai.org/.

References

1. Bonawitz, K., et al.: Towards federated learning at scale: system design. CoRR abs/1902.01046 (2019). http://arxiv.org/abs/1902.01046
2. Chen, Y., Ning, Y., Rangwala, H.: Asynchronous online federated learning for edge devices (2019)
3. Clifton, C., et al.: Privacy-preserving data integration and sharing. In: Proceedings of the 9th ACM SIGMOD Workshop on Research Issues in Data Mining and Knowledge Discovery, DMKD 2004, pp. 19–26. Association for Computing Machinery, New York (2004). https://doi.org/10.1145/1008694.1008698
4. Hiessl, T., Karagiannis, V., Hochreiner, C., Schulte, S., Nardelli, M.: Optimal placement of stream processing operators in the fog. In: 2019 IEEE 3rd International Conference on Fog and Edge Computing (ICFEC), pp. 1–10, May 2019. https://doi.org/10.1109/CFEC.2019.8733147
5. Husaković, A., Pfann, E., Huemer, M.: Robust machine learning based acoustic classification of a material transport process. In: 2018 14th Symposium on Neural Networks and Applications (NEUREL), pp. 1–4, November 2018. https://doi.org/10.1109/NEUREL.2018.8587031
6. Jennings, N.R.: The archon system and its applications (1994). https://eprints.soton.ac.uk/252176/
7. Lee, J., Davari, H., Singh, J., Pandhare, V.: Industrial artificial intelligence for industry 4.0-based manufacturing systems. Manuf. Lett. 18, 20–23 (2018)
8. Lee, Y., Strong, D., Kahn, B., Wang, R.: AIMQ: a methodology for information quality assessment. Inf. Manag. 40, 133–146 (2002). https://doi.org/10.1016/S0378-7206(02)00043-5
9. Li, Q., Wen, Z., Wu, Z., Hu, S., Wang, N., He, B.: A survey on federated learning systems: vision, hype and reality for data privacy and protection (2019)
10. Liu, B., Wang, L., Liu, M., Xu, C.: Lifelong federated reinforcement learning: a learning architecture for navigation in cloud robotic systems. CoRR abs/1901.06455 (2019). http://arxiv.org/abs/1901.06455
11. McMahan, H.B., Moore, E., Ramage, D., Hampson, S., Arcas, B.A.: Communication-efficient learning of deep networks from decentralized data (2016). https://arxiv.org/abs/1602.05629
12. Nishio, T., Yonetani, R.: Client selection for federated learning with heterogeneous resources in mobile edge. In: 2019 IEEE International Conference on Communications (ICC), pp. 1–7 (2019). https://doi.org/10.1109/ICC.2019.8761315
13. Shokri, R., Shmatikov, V.: Privacy-preserving deep learning. In: Proceedings of the 22nd ACM SIGSAC Conference on Computer and Communications Security, CCS 2015, pp. 1310–1321. Association for Computing Machinery, New York (2015). https://doi.org/10.1145/2810103.2813687
14. Torrey, L., Shavlik, J.: Transfer learning. In: Handbook of Research on Machine Learning Applications and Trends: Algorithms, Methods, and Techniques, pp. 242–264. IGI Global (2010)
15. Van Dyke Parunak, H.: Applications of distributed artificial intelligence in industry. Found. Distrib. Artif. Intell. 139–164 (1996)

Evaluating Interpretability in Machine Teaching

Lars Holmberg[1]([⊠]) [iD], Paul Davidsson[1][iD], and Per Linde[2][iD]

[1] Department of Computer Science and Media Technology,
Malmö University, 205 06 Malmö, Sweden
{lars.holmberg,paul.davidsson}@mau.se
[2] Arts and Communication, Malmö University,
205 06 Malmö, Sweden
per.linde@mau.se

Abstract. Building interpretable machine learning agents is a challenge that needs to be addressed to make the agents trustworthy and align the usage of the technology with human values. In this work, we focus on how to evaluate interpretability in a machine teaching setting, a setting that involves a human domain expert as a teacher in relation to a machine learning agent. By using a prototype in a study, we discuss the interpretability definition and show how interpretability can be evaluated on a functional-, human- and application level. We end the paper by discussing open questions and suggestions on how our results can be transferable to other domains.

Keywords: Machine learning · Machine Teaching · Trustworthiness · Interpretability

1 Introduction

A missing keystone in the quest of building trustworthy AI agents is the ability for the agent to present results that are explainable and interpretable. Interpretability put demands on a human to be able to understand the result, explainability put demands on that the result is presented so it can be understood and traced by a human being [9].

Whilst interpretability of machine learning, from a computer science perspective, is an emerging field [3,6,11]. There is a growing interest in addressing interpretability through a model-agnostic approach [8,12,17,20,22] but there are to our knowledge a lack of real world case studies.

In this work, we explore how interpretability can be evaluated in a machine learning process that uses the paradigm of Machine Teaching (MT) [21]. A setting where a human teacher is in control of the machine learning process.

We will consequently focus on the following research question.

This work was partially financed by the Knowledge Foundation through the Internet of Things and People research profile.

F. De La Prieta et al. (Eds.): PAAMS 2020 Workshops, CCIS 1233, pp. 54–65, 2020.
https://doi.org/10.1007/978-3-030-51999-5_5

– How can interpretability be evaluated for an MT agent?

To shed light on this question, we created an MT prototype targeting the personal knowledge domain commuting. As a domain, commuting is well-known even if commute patterns are individual and a commuter is the only expert in their patterns. A commuter, using our prototype, can teach the agent selected commutes. Results in this area can give indication and inspiration regarding future studies in shared domains, for example, radiology [14] or personal domains, for example, personalisation of intelligent personal assistants and assistive technology.

We aimed at evaluating interpretability inspired by the considerations that Doshi-Velez and Kim [4] outline. Our results are in line with that work, but our work adds practical knowledge on how the considerations can be applied and used in a real setting. We also unpack local and global interpretability in relation to evaluation. Our focus also add awareness around how explanations and interpretability relates to the end user of the agent. We do this by drawing attention to the term explicability, in this work defined as a term between interpretability and explanations that implies that a domain expert, on their own, can formulate an explanation for an explicable agent.

We proceed as follows, first, we give an overview of related work and introduce our approach. We then outline the study setup that we evaluate in a result and analysis section. Before concluding the results are elaborated in a discussion section.

2   Related Work

The report Ethics guidelines for Trustworthy AI [9] highlights three components of AI agents: ethical, robust and lawful. Important for the ethical component is that the agent is explicable, implying a transparency that makes the agent explainable and contestable to those affected [9]. In the report, the terms explicability and explicable are used, according to Merriam-Webster explicable means *capable of being explained*[1]. The report also highlights that demands concerning explicability is highly dependent on the context and severity of the consequences. In this work, we will have a focus on interpretability, explicability, and explainability as an important part of the ethical component and less focus on the components robustness and lawful.

One view on interpretability is the coupling to transparent algorithms, like linear models or decision trees, algorithms that can make the entire model transparent and simultaneity is possible for a human. This coupling is contested [15,16] in that interpretability challenges has less to do with the choice of model and are more connected to the complexity of the agent and thus, that, for example, linear models are not automatically interpretable and neural networks not automatically black-boxes from an explainability perspective. If the features and labels used in a neural network are understandable, a human can

---

[1] Merriam-Webster dictionary, accessed 2020-01-24.

in some cases explain the predictions using the relation between feature values and labels, even if the network as such is a black box.

In an overview of explanations and justification in machine learning Biran and Cotton [1] provides this definition of explainability and interpretability:

> Explanation is closely related to the concept of *interpretability*: systems are interpretable if their operations can be understood by a human, either through introspection or through a produced explanation.

In this work, we define an end user as anyone that uses the system, a usage that does not demand any ML or domain expertise. Among these end users, there are domain experts/teachers with a teaching goal, this goal is manifested as a knowledge transfer from the teacher to the ML agent. This transfer is performed without any need for ML expertise. We use the terms domain expert and teacher interchangeable.

There exists, in related literature, a limited discussion on requirements on the end user's capability to understand the explanation, although the complexity in providing good explanations are acknowledged [4, 18]. In this work, we will focus on the end user and therefore we distinguish between interpretability, explicability, and explainability in relation to the end user. We define interpretability as a property of the agent in line with the Biran and Cotton [1] definition, which can imply a need for Machine Learning (ML) expertise and/or domain expertise to produce an, for an end user, understandable explanation. For an explicable ML agent, we define that, a domain expert is needed to adapt or rephrase the explanation in understandable terms to the end user. Explainability is then, as we define it, a quality of an ML agent that does not need any human intermediary to adapt or rephrase an explanation to be understood by an end user. An ML agent can then provide, depending on the situation, predictions that are interpretable, explicable or formulate an explanation concerning the prediction. Implementing agents that are capable of providing explanations implies understanding what constitutes a good explanation [18]. The focus in this work is, instead of the problem of formulating good explanations, on interpretability and explicability and ML systems that involves a human domain expert capable of formulating explanations.

Doshi-Velez and Kim [4] emphasize that a need for interpretability builds on downstream goals as fairness, privacy, reliability, robustness, causality, usability and trust. The authors also urge researchers to both define these goals as well as question if interpretability is the right tool to achieve these goals. Interpretability is seen as a quality needed when the problem formulation is incomplete. The authors also state three modes of interpretability evaluation with increasing specificity and cost: Functionally-grounded evaluation with no real humans and proxy tasks, Human-grounded evaluation with real humans and simple tasks and finally Application-grounded evaluation with real humans and real tasks.

2.1   Machine Teaching

Simard et al. [21] primarily sees MT as a paradigm shift decoupling the domain experts from the ML experts in order to build systems that can be trained-deployed and used without the involvement of ML experts. In that work, the importance of a domain-specific language is highlighted, a language that builds on the taxonomy for the specific domain. MT is then, as we define it, an approach that gives a domain expert control over subjectively selected knowledge to be transferred to a model in a machine learning agent using a domain-specific language. An important part of this language is the user interface that facilitates human-agent interaction.

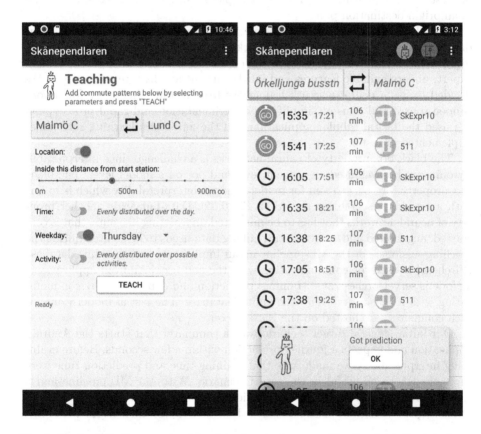

Fig. 1. To the left, the apps teaching interface is shown and to the right, the interface for the predictions is shown.

3   Research Setting

The domain commuting has some qualities that makes it interesting as a research domain in the area of interpretable MT, the domain is well-known, accessible but still commute patterns are individual. This implies that a commuter is domain expert in their commute patterns. We built a functioning prototype for the commuting domain that consist of a MT interface and a prediction interface. The final design can be seen in Fig. 1.

An important part of any machine learning implementation is the selection of features to use. This is also central in an MT implementation since an available orthogonal feature adds an extra dimension to the feature space and thus gives the teacher further possibilities to separate classes. For commuting the end user's location, day and time seemed to be a natural selection, we also added the end user's activity (still, walking running, in vehicle) as a feature. Since we are interested in commuting we chose the complete journey as our label, consisting of an origin-destination pair.

Neural networks can handle multiple levels of representation and raw input data [10,13]. By selecting neural networks as our ML method we can simplify interpretation since the learner and the commuter uses the same, for a domain expert, understandable features and labels without any feature engineering. We decided to use a neural network framework from fast.ai[2] since that framework is open source and aims at simplifying experimentation and rapid prototyping. We used the fast.ai tabular application and the automatic learning rate finder implemented in fast.ai.

The black box property of neural networks is a challenge since interpretability only can be evaluated on a agent level and not on a model level. The black box property forces us to aim for model agnostic interpretability which is in line with a growing research interest [8,12,17,20,22]. Data-hunger is another property of neural networks that has to be mitigated. In a setting like ours, that is cold started, augmented and/or synthetic training data needs to be created during the teaching sessions. For the ML-pipeline in our implementation an online database (Firebase) is used for communicating with the end users Android applications, a Node.js server orchestrates training, prediction and deployment by communicating with a Flask server and the online database. The fast.ai models, one for each commuter, are hosted on the Flask server.

Our initial general target scenario was: a commuter that starts the Android application and expects a journey prediction within a few seconds. Before evaluating interpretability we made sure that training time and prediction time were short enough to be useful in the target scenario. With our ML pipeline and a small neural network we reached prediction times in the area of a few seconds a retraining time around 15 s, we assessed these metrics as sufficient for the study.

4   Methodology

To evaluate interpretability from a functional and human perspective we created three personas [19][3] based on personas created for a local transport provider.

---

[2] fast.ai.

[3] https://github.com/k3larra/commuter#personas.

For interpretability evaluation on an application level, we conducted an eight-week study. As study participants, we selected eight participants, four males, and four females, with experience from computer science and interaction design. Two were from the industry and six from the University. The participants used the app daily and we conducted six meetings and workshops. At the meetings, we discussed and compared experiences from last week and discussed the tasks for next week. We analyzed recorded interviews using content analysis [7] focusing on comments on interpretability. The participants were reimbursed by free journeys during the study.

5   Result and Analysis

In this section, we describe the process of evaluating interpretability for the prototype. The steps in this process are presented in a chronological order and for each step we move closer to application level evaluation. The focus is on producing predictions that full-fills the downstream goals of being causal, trustworthy and usable. Causal so that predictions map the commuters intentions, trustworthy and usable so the predictions reflect the context cue of the commuter. Our problem formulation is incomplete and can thus benefit from being interpretable since individual commute patterns cannot be defined in advance and are subject to change [4].

For the prototype, we aimed for an explicable agent, for which, a domain expert/commuter can formulate explanations for performed predictions. For example, based on a given journey prediction, a commuter could formulate the following explanation "Since it is Tuesday evening I am going to town to meet Johan and play boule". When predictions do not match the commuter's expectations there could be three types of reasons. Either, since it is an MT setting, the commute pattern has not been taught to the agent, the commute patterns shifted or the agent is not robust and cannot provide an explicable prediction. The information that is intended to be explicable consists of the predicted journey and the context cue (location, time, day and activity).

5.1   Functionally-Grounded Evaluation: No Humans, Proxy Tasks

In this more general and global evaluation, we aimed to make predictions interpretable in relation to the different features. In this MT setting no data exists initially to train from, and the data is created in a teaching session by selecting sub-spaces in the feature space using the interface in Fig. 1.

We experimented and found that using two hidden layers (200|100 neurons), and creating under 100 examples inside the sub-space made it possible for the training to converge in less than 20 epochs[4]. With this setting, retraining time is still under 30 s for training data consisting of up to a few thousand rows on a non GPU cloud server.

---

[4] https://github.com/k3larra/commuter/blob/master/machine_teaching/mt.ipynb.

We then evaluated the interpretability by keeping all features constant except one so we could investigate how the generalization maps to interpretability. A visualization of one experiment can be seen in Fig. 2 where all features except location is kept constant and four different journeys are predicted, represented by the different colors. The images shows a situation where the generalization is designed so a journey should be predicted from the closest station.

In the scenarios we created for our personas we defined that a commuter only wants to make predictions centred around an origin station. An alternative edge scenario could be a commuter that wants to teach the prototype to make predictions for someone else, for example, a child, based on a location different from the origin station's location. The result would be, if for example more red teaching data (Fig. 2) was placed at a location to the left, that classification boundaries would be more complex. To avoid this, since we judged that this would result in predictions that would not be explicable, we only allowed one location, with user-defined size, surrounding the origin station for a journey.

We made similar tests and reasoning using scenarios concerning the other features, but made no restrictions. As an example, if a journey is taught on Monday mornings we deemed that a logical generalization would be to predict the same journey on all weekdays when no other conflicting journeys exists.

The functional test ended with daily usage by the development team to verify the robustness of the implementation.

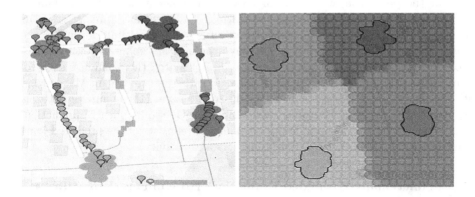

Fig. 2. Location feature space, markers represent predictions, blobs represent teaching data and areas are classification boundaries.

5.2   Human-Grounded Evaluation: Proxy Humans, Simplified Tasks

Compared to the interpretability evaluation that Doshi-Velez and Kim [4] names as human grounded using real humans and simplified task we saw a need for a more controllable and reproducible evaluation than using real humans could give. Using the design team for this was time-consuming and prone to errors, for example, inaccuracy in GPS position and delays in transport made it difficult to reproduce tests. Here our personas were used as a trade-off. For each of our personas, we initially created three scenarios and trained our agent using the teaching interface to make predictions matching the scenarios. A scenario formulated for the persona Andrea (See footnote 3) can be read below:

It is Monday morning 7:23 and Andrea is as usual late for the bus and runs towards the bus stop "Veberöd försköningen". She checks the app while running to see if there are any delays.

To get more realistic data we generated three datasets that mimics one-year journeys for the personas. These datasets were used as our test sets to evaluate the models performance. We used our teaching interface to teach the agent and evaluated the result using visual representations as those that can be seen in Fig. 3. Metrics around how many epochs/time the training needs was balanced towards the amount of teaching data we created (the bar graph). A confusion matrix was used to visualize journeys that are not explicable. Based on these tests the final configurations for the ML pipeline and back-end were decided. (Two hidden layers with (200|100 neurons), 40 synthetic examples created evenly distributed inside the teaching sub-space and training over 7 epochs (See footnote 4).)

Decisions at this level has consequences for the interpretability in-between global and local since we focus on results based on data for our personas. The diversity and complexity of the commute patterns for the personas has a normative influence for the behavior of the agent.

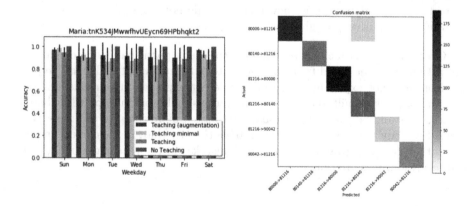

Fig. 3. Tools used during human grounded interpretability evaluation. The test uses synthetic data generated for an envisioned one-year usage for the personas. The data was created using the teaching interface (Fig. 1). To the left accuracy and variance is aggregated over the week using different amount of generated teaching data (No teaching indicates a baseline), to the right precision is mapped in the form of a confusion matrix.

5.3   Application-Grounded Evaluation: Real Humans, Real Tasks

This part of the interpretability evaluation involves real humans and real tasks. A consequence of our MT setting is that it contains a temporal aspect in the form of teaching strategies. The participants explored different strategies, for example, teaching once out of context in the beginning of the week, teaching only when in context, if the predictions were wrong and a combination of these strategies. The focus for this phase was on local explicability, the situation when the end user compares the predicted journey with the intended journey and current context cue.

The participants, in general, found the predictions interpretable in relation to the commute patterns they already taught, or as expressed by one of the participants:

But it did correct .. around half of the times it was wrong. So it is still logic. Even if i doesn't favor me so to say.

The predictions generalized as intended in the sense that if a journey was taught on one day at a specific location and time it was predicted for all other days at that time. We discussed this inherent quality in machine learning compared to applications based on traditional algorithmic programming. We especially discussed the situation when predictions are made with low class probability and how this should be handled. One participant expressed that predictions should only be given "close" to the teaching data:

But I would like to say that if you are under some percentage .. and the app has really no idea of where you want to go.. that a dialog comes up.. or that a question-mark is shown to say "I do not know please teach me where you want to go right now"

Over time and with extensive teaching the study participants found that the predictions given deviated from the commute patterns taught and thus the predictions were not explicable. There are different explanations for this. Firstly, our prototype was built and tested using quite simple commute patterns based on scenarios and personas and those do not match more complex commute patterns. Secondly, the deviation can stem from the fact that, in the current implementation, teaching cannot be undone if mistakes in the teaching is made and erroneous journeys are taught.

6   Discussion

In this work we focus on post-hoc agent-level explicability a situation were a human domain expert can explain the predictions given contextual features like time, day and location and previous teaching. In our setting, we have a one to one relationship between a human domain expert and a machine learning agent. The agent is initially untrained and designed to target the commuting domain.

With our work we add to the interpretability terminology by Lipton [15] and Doshi-Velez and Kim [4]. We use the term explicability to indicate a quality of the agent and distinguish between predictions that are interpretable and those that are explicable. Interpretable predictions does, with this distinction, need both ML expertise and domain expertise to be explained whilst explicable predictions can be explained using domain expertise.

When our prototype is used the end user can, for an explicable prediction, formulate an explanation that matches the intended journey. If the prototype is robust, and the wrong journey is predicted, this can be because it has not yet been taught the commute pattern or that the user for one or another reason chose not to teach the pattern. For our prototype, this local in context explicability, works well for simple commute patterns. A possibility to assess the model's knowledge from a global perspective and not only locally and in context would be an important addition from an explicability perspective.

We designed our prototype with the intention of maximizing the part of the predictions that are explicable. By evaluating interpretability during the design phase from a functional-, human- and application level, we found, in line with Doshi-Velez and Kim [4] that the cost and specificity increases with those levels. From a functional level, it was clear that design consideration had a global impact on the final design. By using personas [19] instead of real humans in the human level evaluation we could strike a balance between a human perspective and still get reproducible results. The impact from this evaluation, which sits between a global and local perspective, to a large extent defines the portions of predictions that in the final application are explicable. A larger and more diverse collection of personas with more complex commute patterns would in our case produce a prototype that is explicable for a more diverse user group. The application-level evaluation gave us insights into the temporal aspect of the models taught knowledge and explicability on a local level.

Over time and in more complex teaching environments it will be crucial to assess the learner, in our case a short description, perhaps in the form of a global explanation, using interpretable decision set [11] could be enough like "If weekday = Yes and Location = A and Time > 18:00 and Time < 22:00 then travel from A to B" to make the predictions explicable. If the areas in the feature space could be named during the teaching using concepts and sub-concepts [21] the interpretable decision set could be used in a more easily interpretable fashion for example: "Exercise = Yes, Rugby = Yes then travel from A to B" or rephrased in natural language. Presenting predictions on a global level by selecting features of interest, from a calendar or map perspective, has parallels with work by Lakkaraju et al. [12] in MUSE framework where features of interest can be selected to investigate predictions in sub-spaces of interest.

The TED [8] and MUSE [12] framework could be an interesting addition, implementing TED in our prototype would be beneficial in that meta-information in the form of concepts and sub-concepts can be added to labels corresponding to specific journeys. This would imply that interpretable information can, for example, be added for the concept "Exercise" that includes all journeys the commuter performs as sub-concepts to "Exercise". The concepts can then be used to inspect sub-spaces of interest in a form similar to MUSE. Our approach has similar goals concerning trust as Teso and Kersting [22] but differs in that the agency in our case is closer to the human teacher that decides the extent of the knowledge that should be transferred.

Our work then suggests that through designing an explicable MT agent for a domain, over time the agent can be trusted. To reach this the agent has to be either, as in our case, matching a significant amount of predictions to the context in an explicable manner and/or support exploration regarding the model so the knowledge transferred can be assessed and understood.

7 Conclusion

This paper set out to explore how interpretability can be evaluated in an MT setting. Addressing evaluation of interpretability is an emerging research field [2,3], to this, our work adds a case study and evaluates interpretability as a design objective. One contribution is an increased focus on explicability as a relational quality of the ML agent. Explicability indicates that a domain expert can explain a prediction so it can be widely understood. How local and global explicability relates to the evaluation of interpretability are other contributions that can be important in many domains. Our work also shows how initial design goals concerning interpretability and explicability for an ML agent deeply influence the final result.

For future work, we suggest an increased focus on tools that support assessing a model's knowledge from an end user's, domain expert's and ML expert's perspective. Further research in this area can strike a balance between explicable and interpretable predictions and thus MT agents that evolve in incremental short cycles [5] in order to adapt to changes and support personalisation.

References

1. Biran, O., Cotton, C.: Explanation and justification in machine learning: a survey. IJCAI Workshop on Explain. AI (XAI) **8**(August), 8–14 (2017)
2. Boukhelifa, N., Bezerianos, A., Lutton, E.: Evaluation of interactive machine learning systems, pp. 1–20 (2018)
3. Doshi-Velez, F., Kim, B.: Towards a rigorous science of interpretable machine learning. arXiv preprint arXiv:1702.08608 (2017)
4. Doshi-Velez, F., Kim, B.: Considerations for evaluation and generalization in interpretable machine learning. In: Escalante, H.J., et al. (eds.) Explainable and Interpretable Models in Computer Vision and Machine Learning. TSSCML, pp. 3–17. Springer, Cham (2018). https://doi.org/10.1007/978-3-319-98131-4_1
5. Dudley, J.J., Kristensson, P.O.: A review of user interface design for interactive machine learning (2018). https://doi.org/10.1145/3185517
6. Gilpin, L.H., Bau, D., Yuan, B.Z., Bajwa, A., Specter, M., Kagal, L.: Explaining explanations: an overview of interpretability of machine learning. In: Proceedings - 2018 IEEE 5th International Conference on Data Science and Advanced Analytics, DSAA 2018 (2019). https://doi.org/10.1109/DSAA.2018.00018

7. Graneheim, U., Lundman, B.: Qualitative content analysis in nursing research: concepts, procedures and measures to achieve trustworthiness. Nurse Educ. Today **24**(2), 105–112 (2004). https://doi.org/10.1016/J.NEDT.2003.10.001

8. Hind, M., et al.: TED: teaching AI to explain its decisions. In: Proceedings of the 2019 AAAI/ACM Conference on AI, Ethics, and Society, pp. 123–129 (2018). https://doi.org/10.1145/3306618.3314273

9. HLEG: Ethics Guidelines for Trustworthy AI (European Commission, 2019). Technical report, High-Level Expert Group on Artificial Intelligence (2019). https://ec.europa.eu/digital-single-market/en/news/ethics-guidelines-trustworthy-ai

10. Hornik, K., Stinchcombe, M., White, H.: Multilayer feedforward networks are universal approximators. Neural Netw. **2**(5), 359–366 (1989). https://doi.org/10.1016/0893-6080(89)90020-8

11. Lakkaraju, H., Bach, S.H., Leskovec, J.: Interpretable decision sets: a joint framework for description and prediction. In: Proceedings of the ACM SIGKDD International Conference on Knowledge Discovery and Data Mining, vol. 13–17-August, pp. 1675–1684 (2016). https://doi.org/10.1145/2939672.2939874

12. Lakkaraju, H., Kamar, E., Caruana, R., Leskovec, J.: Faithful and customizable explanations of black box models. In: Proceedings of the 2019 AAAI/ACM Conference on AI, Ethics, and Society, pp. 131–138. ACM (2019). www.aaai.org

13. Lecun, Y., Bengio, Y., Hinton, G.: Deep learning. Nature **521**(7553), 436–444 (2015). https://doi.org/10.1038/nature14539

14. Lindvall, M., Molin, J., Löwgren, J.: From machine learning to machine teaching. Interactions **25**(6), 52–57 (2018). https://doi.org/10.1145/3282860

15. Lipton, Z.C.: The mythos of model interpretability. In: ICML Workshop on Human Interpretability in Machine Learning, WHI (2016)

16. Lou, Y., Caruana, R., Gehrke, J.: Intelligible models for classification and regression. In: Proceedings of the ACM SIGKDD International Conference on Knowledge Discovery and Data Mining, pp. 150–158 (2012). https://doi.org/10.1145/2339530.2339556

17. Lundberg, S., Lee, S.I.: An unexpected unity among methods for interpreting model predictions. arXiv preprint arXiv:1611.07478 (2016)

18. Miller, T.: Explanation in artificial intelligence: insights from the social sciences (2019). https://doi.org/10.1016/j.artint.2018.07.007

19. Nielsen, L.: Personas - User Focused Design. Springer, London (2013). https://doi.org/10.1007/978-1-4471-4084-9

20. Ribeiro, M.T., Singh, S., Guestrin, C.: Why should I trust you? In: Proceedings of the 22nd ACM SIGKDD International Conference on Knowledge Discovery and Data Mining, KDD 2016, pp. 1135–1144. ACM Press, New York (2016). https://doi.org/10.1145/2939672.2939778

21. Simard, P.Y., et al.: Machine teaching: a new paradigm for building machine learning systems. Technical report, Microsoft Research (2017). http://arxiv.org/abs/1707.06742

22. Teso, S., Kersting, K.: Explanatory interactive machine learning. In: Proceedings of the 2019 AAAI/ACM Conference on AI, Ethics, and Society, pp. 239–245. ACM (2019). https://doi.org/10.1145/3306618.3314293

Workshop on Character Computing (C2)

Workshop on Character Computing (C2)

The third consecutive workshop on Character Computing presents the emerging field and the opportunities and challenges it poses. Following the visibility of the first version of the workshop and the appeal of the concept of Character Computing, the first book about the topic is finalized and will be published as part of the Human-Computer Interaction series by Springer Nature (https://www.springer.com/gp/book/9783030159535) in 2020.

Individual people and institutional organizations from all over the globe are about to move their private life and notably their labor and education activities to the Internet. This calls for these systems to adapt to their current user to ensure the most efficient and seamless interaction. To enable systems to truly adapt to their users, there is a need for the systems to know their users. This does not restrict to only the user's current states but also to the user's traits.

In recent years there has been a lot of research within the field of Affective Computing on how to understand, adapt to, and simulate people's states i.e. affect. This resulted in various diverse applications. Another field of research, namely Personality Computing aims at providing technologies for dealing with the personality traits of humans from three main perspectives; Automatic Personality Recognition, Automatic Personality Perception, and Automatic Personality Synthesis.

However, personality or affect alone do not entail how a person would behave in a specific situation, and thus Affective and Personality Computing need to be extended. Considering the human as a whole i.e. the character is required. The character is the individual person with all his/her defining or describing features. This includes stable personality traits, variable affective, cognitive and motivational states, as well as history, morals, beliefs, skills, appearance, and socio-cultural embeddings, to name a few.

As the next step towards further putting humans at the center of technology, novel interdisciplinary approaches such as Character Computing are developing. The extension and fusion between the different computing approaches, e.g. Affective and Personality Computing, within Character Computing is based on well-controlled empirical and theoretical knowledge from Psychology.

This is done by including the whole human character as a central part of any artificial interaction. Character Computing is any computing that incorporates the human character within its context. In practical terms, depending on the application context, it is computing that senses, predicts, adapts to, affects, or simulates 1) character based on behavior and situation, 2) behavior based on character and situation, or 3) situation based on character and behavior.

Character Computing has three main modules that can be investigated and leveraged separately or together:

- Character sensing and profiling
- Character-aware adaptive systems
- Artificial characters

As in previous years, the present workshop is organized by a team of researchers from the German University of Cairo (GUC) and from Ulm University (UUlm) from the fields of Computer Science and Psychology who combine computational and psychological scientific knowledge in an attempt to integrate the expertise of the field of Psychology and Computer Science into Character Computing.

In this workshop we will discuss the possible applications of Character Computing in a diverse number of research fields at the interface of Psychology and Computer Science. We also aim at discussing a more foundational background for Character Computing by integrating the expertise of the field of Psychology. In particular, we aim to show that Character Computing provides a novel perspective on Affective and Personality Computing, that can enable the presence of ubiquitous and non-obtrusive character-aware adaptive systems if Psychology and its fields of research are integrated into the Character Computing approach.

Organization

Organizing Committee

Alia El Bolock	University of Cairo, Egypt, and Ulm University, Germany
Slim Abdennadher	German University in Cairo, Egypt
Cornelia Herbert	Ulm University, Germany

Program Committee

Yomna Abdelrahman	Bundeswehr University, Germany
Florian Alt	Bundeswehr University, Germany
Patrick Weis	George Mason University, USA, and Ulm University, Germany
Jailan Salah	German University in Cairo, Egypt
Dirk Reichardt	DHBW Stuttgart, Germany

VRacter: Investigating Character-Based Avatar Preference in Education

Basma Mohamed Afifi[1]($\boxtimes$), Alia El Bolock[1,2], Mostafa Alaa[1],
Cornelia Herbert[2], and Slim Abdennadher[1]

[1] German University in Cairo, Cairo, Egypt
basma.afifi@student.guc.edu.eg, aliaelbolock@gmail.com,
mostafa.talaat@guc.edu.eg
[2] Ulm University, Ulm, Germany

Abstract. Finding the best match for students and teachers is seen as a very promising way to maximise the learning gain and enhance the learning experience in any prestigious educational institute. Character, i.e. traits that distinguish between individuals, such as personality, are a key aspect in any human interaction, including student-teacher ones. Character defines how a person behaves given a specific situation. In the current paper, we focus on students in a virtual learning environment with a teacher avatar embodying a specific teaching style and the resulting learning gain. The main research question is how certain character components of the student affect his/her learning gain given the different situations (teachers with different styles). Using a controlled yet customizable environment such as virtual reality is well suited for investigating this fit between different teacher and student styles. This paper investigates the relation between different embodiments of pedagogical agent characters and the students' personalities in reference to their gain of knowledge. The different agent characters are embodied through body language and speech style, modeled through different movement animations and the pace and tone of speech. The learning gain of each student resulting from attending two short VR lectures for two virtual teachers with different teaching styles is calculated and related to the student's personality.

Keywords: Pedagogical agents · Virtual reality · Personality · Education · Character Computing

1 Introduction

Virtual reality (VR) as a platform for research studies has shown now for years how dependable and controllable it can be for researchers. Also, safety is a great privilege provided by the VR environments. At the same time, the most desired aspects of research experiments in the educational field are safety and control while still offering flexibility. Therefore, the use of VR teachers or pedagogical agents is on the rise in education related studies these years. As we focus on the

© Springer Nature Switzerland AG 2020
F. De La Prieta et al. (Eds.): PAAMS 2020 Workshops, CCIS 1233, pp. 71–82, 2020.
https://doi.org/10.1007/978-3-030-51999-5_6

educational field studies, personalities and characters of teachers and students seems to be a very interesting side of the student-teacher relation to investigate. Is there a combination of characteristics that form a teacher's character that might increase the learn gain for certain student's personalities? And how can we extract the effect of the traits alone while excluding the effect of other aspects such as the appearance, gender, age, race and many other aspects? Those were the main questions motivating the presented work.

Character, i.e. the traits that distinguish between individuals, such as personality, are a key aspect in any human interaction [13], including student-teacher ones. Character defines how an individual behaves given a specific situation (see Fig. 1) [14,20]. In this paper, we investigate how certain attributes of the character of a student affect the learning experience and performance based on the teacher's teaching style and embodiment of character. Accordingly, we design a virtual learning environment with two pedagogical agents of contrasting teaching styles, calm and lively. The teaching styles are represented through different body movements and tones of speech while keeping the model of the teaching agent itself constant. The environment was tested on 38 participants i.e. students while collecting information about their character attributes of interest to align with their performance with each agent. The results were analyzed using statistical methods as well as machine learning.

The rest of the paper is organized as follows. In Sect. 2, we present the background of character and personality as well as the related work. In Sect. 3, we outline the followed approach for designing and realizing the VR environment. We give an overview of the experiment design and a discussion of its results in Sects. 4 and 5, respectively. Finally, we conclude the paper and discuss the future work in Sect. 6.

2   Background and Related Work

2.1   Character

According to Oxford Dictionary, a character is all the qualities and features that make a person, groups of people, and places different from others. When developing a character, we can distinguish between explicit and implicit characteristics. Explicit or visible characteristics are represented in body shape, facial-expressions, gestures, voice, age, gender, race, and clothing. A summary of some studies that investigated those features can be found in Table 1. Explicit characteristics can be seen as the reflection of the implicit ones. The implicit characteristics include personality, affect, morals, beliefs, culture, and health. The explicit and implicit characteristics together form an individual's character [13]. This was first defined as such by the merging inter-disciplinary field of Character Computing [12,14–16]. Character Computing is any computing that is based on, detects and adapts to human character traits. Unlike Affective Computing [27] which focuses on affect or Personality Computing [30] which focuses on personality traits, Character Computing targets an individual's character as a whole. It may be considered a combination and extension of Affective Computing and Personality Computing. According to [13] character cannot be explained or considered alone but rather as part of an interaction of three edges of a triad consisting of character, behavior and situation, denoted the Character-Behavior-Situation (CBS) triad (depicted in Fig. 1). Any of the three edges of the triad can be explained or analysed using the other two.

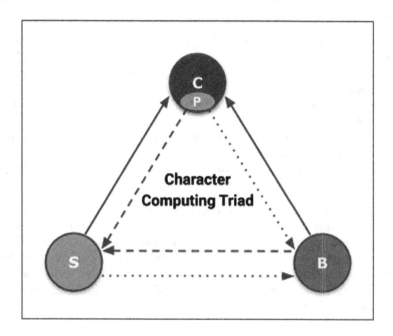

Fig. 1. The Character-Behavior-Situation (CBS) triad illustrated in [13]

2.2 Personality

For decades, scientists and researchers considered understanding what personality means and how it affects human interactions, as a crucial and challenging field of science. They also believed that it is the gateway to many novel interaction systems and inventions in all kinds of research fields. "Personality is the collection of individual differences, dispositions, and temperaments that are observed to have some consistency across situations and time" [10]. The trait theory as referred to by (Chamorro-Premuzic, 2014; Derlega, Winstead and Jones, 2005; Feist, Feist and Roberts, 2013) [25] is the approach of deciding the personality composition of a person. The journey to identifying a clear and precise list of personality traits started as early as [2] who provided an extremely detailed and comprehensive dictionary of personality traits that was considered the strongest at its time. Later on, they reduced that to 4500 adjectives. A further reduction using synonyms and antonyms was done by Cattell (1957, 1970) [9] to bring it to 171 trait. Factor analysis identified 16 personality factors, which then was reduced by Eysenck (1975) [3] to three. However the last and most significant update was done by Costa and McCrae [6] who re-increased the number to five traits, famously known as the Five Factor Model of Personality or Big Five. The Big Five is widely used in Computer Science as well as Psychology research and is thus the model followed in this paper. The big five traits are explained in the following.

- Openness (to Experience): defines how much a person is willing to share and interact with others.
- Conscientiousness: defines how conscious a person is of right and wrong and how he/she reacts toward them.
- Extraversion: defines how outgoing is that person. Also referred to as friendliness and dominance.
- Agreeableness: defines the percentage of cooperation and social cohesion (Graziano and Tobin, 2002) [17].
- Neuroticism: is the percentage of anxiety, moodiness and jealousy (Thompson, 2008) [21]. Also referred to as Stability.

Regarding the effect of personality traits of a teacher on the teacher-student relationship, a study by Kok, Mando and Meyer (2018) [25] states that teachers with high percentage on Extroversion and Agreeableness had the greatest impact on students learning capabilities. Another study by De Jong, Romi and Mainhard (2014), [8] investigated pre-service teachers' personality traits and added other perspectives when investigating a personality which included self-efficacy, discipline and teaching strategy.

2.3   Related Work

Pedagogical agents, or virtual teachers, started from being 2D models, and 3D computer models, to 3D VR models. The interaction of students with pedagogical agents has been widely investigated by researchers focusing on many aspects. Table 1 gives an overview of the features used to differentiate between pedagogical agents, that are investigated in the literature. A study by Wang, Ning and Johnson [31] investigated the effect of politeness as a personality trait mapped on 2D pedagogical agents. The model was viewed and interacted with through a primitive computer monitor by college students with varying computer skills. The agents were scripted by different levels of politeness dialogues to guide the students through an engineering related tutorial. The results of this study showed that the polite agent had the most positive effect on students who scored high on extroversion or need of cognition. 3D models were used in many studies, each of which, were targeting diverse perspectives in conveying characters. Shiban, Youssef and Schelhorn [29] discussed how the performance and motivation of college students would be affected by adding the appearance stereotypes that shows, for example, an old man who is dressed formally would be considered as someone professional, on the other hand a young, smartly dressed woman, would be conveyed as fun and easy going. The results showed that the old man helped enhance the performance of the students, however he had no great impact on their motivation levels. On the other hand the young lady had a positive impact on the students' level of motivation to learn the explained topic, but had no great effect on their performance. However none of these studies related to the student's personality and how that affects the situation and experience with a pedagogical agent.

Table 1. Pedagogical agent features in previous papers.

Feature	Paper
Facial expressions	[4, 11]
Gestures	[4, 31]
Clothing	[11, 24]
Gender	[8, 23, 24]
Rendering	[18]
Voice	[7]
Body shape, style, realism, body language, contact with ground, hair and graphical representation	[11]
Age, speech pace and race	[24]
Self-efficacy, culture, and discipline strategies	[8]

3 Approach

Based on the previous work and the feedback from the Psychology expert involved in this paper, we designed two contrasting pedagogical agents. The two embodies teaching styles were, the so called, calm and lively teachers. As we mentioned in the Sect. 2, the triad model of Character, Behavior and Situation can be used as a basis for investigating any one of the three edges based on the other two. In this paper, the main interest is the performance and teacher liking of a student (situation) based on a specific situation (pedagogical agent's teaching style) and the student's personality and background information (character attributes). How the three edges of the triad were realized will be explained in more detail:

1. Situation: we designed two identical situations with the exception of the agent's teaching style. The student's were immersed in a virtual classroom with minimal objects to avoid any distractions. In order to exclude the effect of the appearance as well as any materialized factor that can manipulate

the student's perception of the pedagogical agent, we fixed the 3D model for both teachers and only manipulated their style of teaching. Accordingly, for each teacher we used a different speaking tone, pace, and style. Moreover, we changed the style of movement, face expressions, gestures and declamation.

(a) The first pedagogical agent is calm, speaks in a relatively slow pace, does not use extensive motion or gestures, and has minimal face expressions.

(b) The second pedagogical agent is lively, highly expressive in terms of hand gestures and facial expressions - frequently moving around the room - and speaks in a relatively fast paced manner.

Both agents were designed using the same 3D model of a male character, to exclude the effect of any external appearance or gender biases. The 3D model was ready downloaded from a 3D models website called Sketchfab. The model was refined on Blender application to have the needed face animation bases called blendshapes. Blendshapes are face mesh formations that represent a face expression. To sync the lip movement with the speech given by the pedagogical agents, Crazy Minnow Studio's SALSA lip syncing package for unity 3D was used. As for the animation different strategies were used to either characters. For the lively character Mixamo animation clips were downloaded, modified and combined to create a smooth animation sequence. On the other hand the animation for the calm character was recorded using a Kinect sensor and modified to match the speech given by the character, that is because the behaviour of the calm character required very specific few movements that is not provided by Mixamo. Finally the different speech files were extracted from YouTube to match the desired explanation style.

2. Behavior: The student's learning gain from both teachers was the main behavior measure. We also measured their virtual reality experience and how they felt during the whole interaction.

3. Character: The main considered character attributes are personality, affect, culture and history. The personality is measured in terms of the Big Five model and affect based on the valence, arousal, pleasure model [26]. The background information, gender, VR experience (current and previous) are also important attributes, defining the current student. For example, we need to distinguish between the history of students with respect to whether they are beginner or experienced VR users, due to the novelty effect experienced by novel VR users [22].

4 Experiment

We designed an experiment to collect data the represents each participant's personality traits, performance during the virtual teacher's presence, and how she/he perceived the teacher's character.

4.1 Participants

38 participants (17 female) took part in this experiment. The participants were mostly undergraduate and masters students at the German University in Cairo

from majors ranging between Engineering, Management, Pharmacy and Applied Arts with an age group of 19–24 years old.

4.2 Procedure and Setup

Upon arrival, each participant was provided with a consent form, a clear explanation of the collected data and an overview of the experiment. The clear research question and the difference between the pedagogical agents was only explained after the experiment to void any biases. Then, they were each given a brief tutorial on how to use the VR headset and controllers, before being immersed in the VR environment. In order to insure full immersion in the virtual environment some steps was taken. Firstly, the chair on which the participant sits was a replica of the real life chair he was actually sitting on and by looking downwards the participant sees the chair. Secondly, during the experiment participants wore noise cancelling headphones that ensured no sound from the real world would interfere with the virtual experience. Each participant had to listen to two brief lessons within the VR classroom given by the two different pedagogical agents. The agents gave the students a brief overview of black-holes without going into any technical details, making the lessons accessible to students with various backgrounds and interests. The sequence in which the virtual teachers were presented was randomized, excluding any biases. After each lesson, the participant's knowledge gain was assessed through a few related multiple choice questions presented within the VR environment to avoid breaking out of immersion. The whole VR interaction lasts approximately 4:50 min, with each lesson going on for about 2 min.

4.3 Test and Questionnaires

To collect subjective information and feedback from the participants we used multiple online forms. There were four forms each targeting a different aspect. The first form included the Big Five Inventory (BFI) [28], consisting of 44 question with subcategories each targeting one of the Big Five traits (OCEAN) Sect. 2.2. Followed by the Self Assessment Manikin (SAM) to determine the participant's arousal, valence, and dominance [5]. The SAM is a pictorial scale that the participant should relate to his/her state of happiness, excitement, and control while going through the experience as a whole. The third questionnaire was the Igroup Presence Questionnaire (IPQ) [1]. It was included as a subjective scale to measure the sense of realism and presence experienced by the participants in the virtual environment. The last questionnaire collected the participant's demographics alongside questions to determine whether 1) the participants had prior knowledge about the topics discussed by the virtual agents, 2) this was their first time experiencing virtual reality, 3) they were distracted by the virtual environment itself rather than the agents and their lessons, 4) whether they enjoyed the experience overall and liked the different pedagogical agents. All collected data aims to determine which factors has the most impact on the participants' performance.

5 Results and Discussion

To analyze our implicitly and explicitly collected data, we used two approaches: statistical analysis using SPSS and Machine Learning analysis using Weka. The main goal was to discover relationships between the collected attributes and each other.However, our focus was mainly on the relationship between the preference of the students to either of the pedagogical agents and their personality traits and how does this relationship gets effected by other collected attributes.

The values of the personality traits of the participants, that was collected using the BFI questionnaire mentioned in Sect. 4.3, follows a mainly normal distribution. Table 2 shows the mean values of all measured attributes:

Table 2. The mean values for the measured attributes

Attribute	Mean
Big Five Inventory	
Openness	41.1
Conciseness	31.4
Extraversion	25.4
Agreeableness	34.3
Neuroticism	24.5
Igroup Presence Questionnaire	
General presence	4.7
Spatial presence	3.2
Involvement	3.0
Experienced realism	3.4
Self Assessment Manikin	
Valence	1.83
Arousal	2.58
Dominance	3.11

5.1 SPSS Analysis

To discover various correlations, We applied linear regression analysis on the data-set with the dependent variable varying between all the measured attributes.

We found that when having the score the participant got with the calm character pedagogical agent as the dependent variable, the score was highest correlated with the Experienced Realism attribute with a significance value of 0.153.

As for the personality traits, the highest trait correlated with the calm teacher was the Neuroticism trait with a significance value of 0.520. On the other hand, when the score with the lively teacher was put as the dependent variable, the highest correlation value appeared with Involvement attribute with a significance value of 0.065, and the most correlated personality trait was the Conciseness trait with a significance value of 0.155. Further analysis was done with the dependent variable set to the numerically coded variable "Prefers", which represents the preference of the participant to either of the pedagogical agents. The Table 3 shows a summary of the most significant results running different analysis algorithms with the "Prefers" variable set as the dependent variable and all other variables set as the independent variables.

Table 3. Summary of the most significant results with Prefers as the dependent variable

Analysis	Highest sig.	Attribute
Univariate analysis of variance	0.002	**Neuroticism**
Correlations	0.042	Dominance
Non parametric correlations	0.041	**Neuroticism**
T-test (equal variances assumed)	0.058	1st time in VR
T-test (equal variances not assumed)	0.019	Involvement

5.2 Machine Learning Models

We used Weka [19] to analyse the result using different machine learning algorithms. As shown in Table 4, we used multiple models to compare and predict output from our data set. A summary of the models used and their results is shown in the table. The class that those models were trained to predict was the "Prefers" attribute which is a number coded attribute symbolizing the preferred agent of each participant between the two pedagogical agents. The attribute is decided upon the participant's score with each pedagogical agent as well as their verbal feedback collected in one of the post experiment questionnaires that was carried out. Figure 2 shows the visualization of all the attributes used by the machine learning models against the attribute Prefers.

The highest prediction accuracy was achieved with the Decision table model with a coefficient of 0.9, a Root Mean Squared Error (RMSE) of as low as 0.3, a Relative Absolute Error of 16.72%, and finally a Root relative Squared Error of 43.52%.

Table 4. Results summary for the ulsvarious Machine Learning models on Weka

Model	Correlation coefficient	RMSE	Relative ABS.ERR	RRSE
Gaussian processes	0.4236	0.6261	99.32%	88.86%
Linear regression	0.622	0.5692	92.36%	80.78%
SMOreg (SVM)	0.55	0.6089	88.88%	86.42%
Additive regression	0.4897	0.6133	91.26%	87.03%
Bagging	0.0677	0.7003	105.67%	99.38%
Random committee	0.3919	0.6413	92.52%	91.02%
Randomizable filtered classifier	0.4066	0.7255	62.02%	102.96%
Random subspace	0.0574	0.6881	99.98%	97.66%
Regression by discretization	0.3737	0.7068	76.73%	100.30%
Decision table	**0.9056**	**0.3033**	**16.72%**	**43.05%**
Decision stump	0.4808	0.6026	87.28%	85.52%

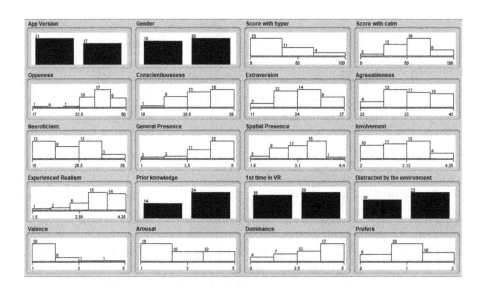

Fig. 2. Visualisation for the attributes included to predict preference.

6   Conclusion and Future Work

In this paper, we investigated the effect of different teaching styles (calm and lively) embodied through virtual agents in a VR classroom on the performance of students with different characters. The character was measured through personality, affect, background and history. The results achieved by this study are promising and motivate future investigations. To the best of our knowledge, that does not separately focus on the student or teacher personality but rather the interaction of the two and how they affect each other. It also takes it one step further by considering other student character attributes alongside personality.

In the future, we suggest investigating more different teacher styles, alongside the two chosen extremes of calm and lively. We also need to investigate different ways to embody the character of the agents e.g., by manipulating appearance, clothes, 3D models, or different animations than the already used ones. The interaction of different models and styles should also be investigated by for example mismatching the animation and the body image of the agent or the voice and appearance. We also suggest relying on other means to measure the student's learning gain or experience. This can be done by using different sensors such as eye trackers to give a more precise measure for the participant's attention on the lessons of the different pedagogical agents. Also, having longer and more diverse lessons presented by the agents would give us more detailed data which could lead to better insights.

References

1. Igroup presence questionnaire. http://www.igroup.org/pq/ipq/index.php
2. Allport, G.W., Odbert, H.S.: Trait-names: a psycho-lexical study. Psychol. Monographs **47**(1), i (1936)
3. Allsopp, J., Eysenck, H.: Extraversion, neuroticism, and verbal reasoning ability as determinants of paired-associates learning. Br. J. Psychol. **66**(1), 15–24 (1975)
4. Baylor, A.L., Kim, S.: Designing nonverbal communication for pedagogical agents: when less is more. Comput. Hum. Behav. **25**(2), 450–457 (2009)
5. Bradley, M.M., Lang, P.J.: Measuring emotion: the self-assessment Manikin and the semantic differential. J. Behav. Ther. Exp. Psychiatry **25**(1), 49–59 (1994)
6. Costa Jr., P.T., McCrae, R.R.: The Revised NEO Personality Inventory (NEO-PI-R). Sage Publications, Inc. (2008)
7. Craig, S.D., Schroeder, N.L.: Reconsidering the voice effect when learning from a virtual human. Comput. Educ. **114**, 193–205 (2017)
8. De Jong, R., Mainhard, T., Van Tartwijk, J., Veldman, I., Verloop, N., Wubbels, T.: How pre-service teachers' personality traits, self-efficacy, and discipline strategies contribute to the teacher-student relationship. Br. J. Educ. Psychol. **84**(2), 294–310 (2014)
9. Digman, J.M.: Personality structure: emergence of the five-factor model. Annu. Rev. Psychol. **41**(1), 417–440 (1990)
10. Dryer, D.C.: Getting personal with computers: how to design personalities for agents. Appl. Artif. Intell. **13**(3), 273–295 (1999)
11. Ekström, H.: How can a character's personality be conveyed visually, through shape (2013)
12. El Bolock, A.: Defining character computing from the perspective of computer science and psychology. In: Proceedings of the 17th International Conference on Mobile and Ubiquitous Multimedia, pp. 567–572. ACM (2018)
13. El Bolock, A.: What is character computing? In: El Bolock, A., Abdelrahman, Y., Abdennadher, S. (eds.) Character Computing. HIS, pp. 1–16. Springer, Cham (2020). https://doi.org/10.1007/978-3-030-15954-2_1
14. El Bolock, A., Abdelrahman, Y., Abdennadher, S. (eds.): Character Computing. HIS. Springer, Cham (2020). https://doi.org/10.1007/978-3-030-15954-2
15. El Bolock, A., Salah, J., Abdelrahman, Y., Herbert, C., Abdennadher, S.: Character computing: computer science meets psychology. In: 17th International Conference on Mobile and Ubiquitous Multimedia, pp. 557–562. ACM (2018)

16. El Bolock, A., Salah, J., Abdennadher, S., Abdelrahman, Y.: Character computing: challenges and opportunities. In: Proceedings of the 16th International Conference on Mobile and Ubiquitous Multimedia, pp. 555–559. ACM (2017)

17. Graziano, W.G., Tobin, R.M.: Agreeableness: dimension of personality or social desirability artifact? J. Pers. **70**(5), 695–728 (2002)

18. Haake, M., Gulz, A.: A look at the roles of look & roles in embodied pedagogical agents-a user preference perspective. Int. J. Artif. Intell. Educ. **19**(1), 39–71 (2009)

19. Hall, M., Frank, E., Holmes, G., Pfahringer, B., Reutemann, P., Witten, I.H.: The weka data mining software: an update. ACM SIGKDD Explor. Newslett. **11**(1), 10–18 (2009)

20. Herbert, C., El Bolock, A., Abdennadher, S.: A psychologically driven, user-centered approach to character modeling. In: El Bolock, A., Abdelrahman, Y., Abdennadher, S. (eds.) Character Computing. HIS, pp. 39–51. Springer, Cham (2020). https://doi.org/10.1007/978-3-030-15954-2_3

21. Hirsh, J.B., Inzlicht, M.: The devil you know: neuroticism predicts neural response to uncertainty. Psychol. Sci. **19**(10), 962–967 (2008)

22. Huang, H.M., Rauch, U., Liaw, S.S.: Investigating learners' attitudes toward virtual reality learning environments: based on a constructivist approach. Comput. Educ. **55**(3), 1171–1182 (2010)

23. Jin, S.A.A., Sung, Y.: The roles of spokes-avatars' personalities in brand communication in 3D virtual environments. J. Brand Manag. **17**(5), 317–327 (2010)

24. Johnson, A.M., DiDonato, M.D., Reisslein, M.: Animated agents in K-12 engineering outreach: preferred agent characteristics across age levels. Comput. Hum. Behav. **29**(4), 1807–1815 (2013)

25. Kok, R., Meyer, L.: Towards an optimal person-environment fit: a baseline study of student teachers' personality traits. South Afr. J. Educ. **38**(3), 2–3 (2018)

26. Mehrabian, A., Russell, J.A.: An Approach to Environmental Psychology. The MIT Press (1974)

27. Picard, R.W.: Affective computing: challenges. Int. J. Hum.-Comput. Stud. **59**(1–2), 55–64 (2003)

28. Rammstedt, B., John, O.P.: Measuring personality in one minute or less: a 10-item short version of the big five inventory in English and German. J. Res. Pers. **41**(1), 203–212 (2007)

29. Shiban, Y., et al.: The appearance effect: influences of virtual agent features on performance and motivation. Comput. Hum. Behav. **49**, 5–11 (2015)

30. Vinciarelli, A., Mohammadi, G.: A survey of personality computing. IEEE Trans. Affect. Comput. **5**(3), 273–291 (2014)

31. Wang, N., Johnson, W.L., Mayer, R.E., Rizzo, P., Shaw, E., Collins, H.: The politeness effect: pedagogical agents and learning outcomes. Int. J. Hum.-Comput. Stud. **66**(2), 98–112 (2008)

Who, When and Why: The 3 Ws
of Code-Switching

Alia El Bolock[1,2(✉)], Injy Khairy[3], Yomna Abdelrahman[4],
Ngoc Thang Vu[3], Cornelia Herbert[1], and Slim Abdennadher[1]

[1] German University in Cairo, Cairo, Egypt
{alia.elbolock,slim.adbennadher}@guc.edu.eg
[2] Ulm Univeristy, Ulm, Germany
cornelia.herbert@uni-ulm.de
[3] Stuttgart University, Stuttgart, Germany
{injy.hamed,ngoc-thang.vu}@ims.uni-stuttgart.de
[4] Bundeswehr University, Munich, Germany
yomna.abdelrahman@unibw.de

Abstract. With the rise of globalization, the use of mixed languages in
daily conversations, referred to as "code-switching" (CS) has become
a common linguistic phenomenon among bilingual/multilingual communities. It has become common for people to alternate between distinct languages or "codes" in daily conversations. This has placed a
high demand on Natural Language Processing (NLP) applications to
be able to deal with such mixed-language input. Researchers have lately
achieved advancements in multilingual NLP applications, however, few
work has been done to adapt these applications to users' CS behaviour.
In this work, we take the first steps towards this goal by investigating
the CS behavior and its correlation with the users' profiles in our case
study on Egyptian Arabic-English code-switching. Although these factors have been investigated by linguists, the findings have been mostly
made through theoretical studies. We provide empirical evidence based
on a user study with 50 participants showing initial correlations between
user traits and the CS frequency, which can be used to predict users'
CS. Our findings imply that in the scope of our study, people (who)
code-switch in specific discourse domains more than others (when) and
depending on their background and social factors (why). The study also
shows that to be able to properly investigate who code-switches more
data needs to be collected and further analysis is required.

Keywords: Character computing · Code-switching · Code-mixing ·
Personality · Arabic-English

1 Introduction

Verbal communication is a basic and main means of communication between
individuals. The most known obstacle is the language barrier. Over the past

F. De La Prieta et al. (Eds.): PAAMS 2020 Workshops, CCIS 1233, pp. 83–94, 2020.
https://doi.org/10.1007/978-3-030-51999-5_7

years a phenomenon called *Code-switching* (CS) became common with the rise of mixed languages [24]. CS occurs when a bilingual/multilingual person alternates between two or more languages, intentionally or unintentionally, in the context of one conversation. It became an increasingly topical and important field of research in several fields such as, Natural Language Processing (NLP), Cognitive Science, and Socio-Linguistics. CS is an obstacle that could hinder communication between two speakers with the same mother-tongue. This is especially the case when interacting with technology, that attempts to automatically detect speech.

In this work, we aim to investigate whether it could be possible to predict user's CS behavior based on user knowledge. This information can then be used for user-profiling to build user-adaptive NLP applications that can process information more accurately. By knowing the factors that affect the user's CS behavior, we can predict the user's CS frequency based on given user information. This can then be integrated into a system to build a user-adaptive model that would perform better.

A lot of research investigates CS and its reasons. It has been often attributed to various psychological, social, and external factors [3,7,14,17,18,25,26,28,29]. In this paper, we aim to advance the state of the art by investigating who is more prone to code-switching, as well as why and when people code-switch. Like any other behavior, the CS behavior of the same person could vary in different situations and depending on their different traits and states (i.e., their character) [9,11,13]. This paper tackles the 3 "W"s of CS: who, why and when, by investigating the correlation between 1) the personality of an individual, 2) the domain and topic of discourse, 3) the individual's background and history, and the CS behavior, respectively. We conducted a user study where we collected speech data as well as background and personality information from 50 participants to generate the needed dataset. We labeled the dataset to get insights into the correlations between the frequency of CS and the aforementioned attributes; who, when and why. This paper contributes the investigation of factors that affect individuals' CS behavior and the collected dataset of Arabic-English CS speech.

The remainder of the paper is structured as follows. We first present a summary of existing related work, and define the needed concepts in Sect. 2. Next, in Sect. 3, we describe our study design and the dataset generation. We then discuss the analysis and results in Sect. 4. Finally, we make conclusions and discuss the future work in Sect. 5.

2   Related Work

Many scientific fields have been interested in understanding the processes behind code switching, from its measurement to its modeling. Given that CS is a user-dependent behaviour, where each user code-switches differently, it would be useful to incorporate the different code switching frequencies in the NLP applications to make them user-adaptive. A pre-condition for this is the ability to understand the code switching behavior of users. In this section, we discuss the types of code switching and as well as the work done by socio- and psycholinguistics to determine the factors that affect the individual's CS behavior.

2.1   Code-Switching (CS)

Code-switching (CS) is the act of using more than one language in a conversation. This phenomenon has become popular, especially among urban youth. It evolved as a result of several factors, including globalization, immigration, colonization, the rise of education levels, and international business and communication. CS can be seen in several bilingual/multilingual societies, such as: Cantonese-English in Hong Kong [19], Mandarin-Taiwanese in Taiwan [6], Mandarin-English in Singapore and Malaysia [20], Spanish-English in Hispanic communities in the United States [1], Turkish-German in Germany [5], Italian-French and German-Italian in Switzerland [2], Arabic-English in Egypt [16] and Arabic-French in Tunisia [27], Algeria [8] and Morocco [4].

In [23], the author categorized CS into the following three types:

- Inter-sentential switching: happens at clausal or sentential level where each clause or sentence is in one language or another. For example, "Du musst immer optimistisch bleiben. Every cloud has a silver lining." (You must stay optimistic. Every cloud has a silver lining).
- Intra-sentential switching: the most complex type among the three, can take place at clausal, sentential or even word level. For example, "Als Alice gesagt hat "that's great", waren sie alle zufrieden" (When Alice said "that's great", everyone was happy).
- Tag-switching: involves inserting a borrowed word in one language into an utterance that is otherwise entirely in another language. For example, "Das ist mein Lifestyle!" (This is my lifestyle!).

2.2   Reasons of Code-Switching

Researchers have investigated the factors that motivate code-switching. Bilinguals are driven towards code-switching whenever the second language is linguistically easier, for example, whenever a word is not accessible in the first language [7,17,28], and whenever some words are easier, more distinguishable and easier to use or the concepts involved are easier to express in that languages [7]. Ritchie and Bhatia [26] also reported that code-switching is affected by the Participant Roles and Relationship; whether bilinguals code-mix or not depends on whom they talk to. The authors also stated that the topic of the conversation affects the code-switching behavior [29]. This finding was also confirmed by Velásquez [29], where it was found that code-switching stood out in certain topics, including family, school, ethnicity, and friends. Code-switching is also affected by social factors, such as age, gender, religion, level of education and social class [3,25,26]. It was also found that code-switching can be done intentionally for the speaker's own benefit. Janet Holmes [18] has mentioned that code-switching can be used on purpose in order to attract attention and to persuade an audience. Nerghes [22] also reports on the impart of code-switching to reflect a certain socioeconomic identity which can give the speaker more credibility and reliability. Cheng [7] also reported that code-switching can be used to capture attention, appeal to the literate/illiterate, or exclude another person from the dialog. It has also been agreed by several researchers that a speaker may code-switch intentionally to express group solidarity [7,14,25,28] or reflect social status [14]. As stated by Peter Auer [2], "Code-switching carries a hidden prestige which is made explicit by attitudes". In this paper we aim at further investigating some of the aforementioned factors as well as filling the gap by investigating the speaker's personality factors that affect code-switching, as well as the speaker's background and past experiences.

2.3   Temperament and Character Inventory

The Temperament and Character Inventory (TCI) [15] is a self-report questionnaire specifically designed to identify the intensity of its seven basic personality dimensions and the relationship between them. The seven dimensions interact together to make up the individual's personality. The TCI consists of four temperament dimensions: Novelty Seeking (NS), Harm Avoidance (HA), Reward Dependence (RD) and Persistence (PS) and three character dimensions: Self-Directedness (SD), Cooperativeness (CO), Self-Transcendence (ST). Each of these dimensions in turn has its own sub-dimensions. The TCI was chosen instead of the more commonly used Five Factor Model [21] as it offers more detailed sub-dimensions that are of interest for the designed virtual environments. Both models can be mapped to each other.

3   Study

To answer our research questions and get more insights about the correlations of code-switching behavior with personality, character and background, we conducted a user study in which we recorded the following:

1. Temperament and Character Inventory profile
2. Interview speech annotated with Arabic, English, idle utterances and domain of discourse per utterance
3. Background information from a questionnaire
4. Self-awareness and general code-switching questionnaire
5. Electroencephalography (EEG) recordings throughout the interview
6. Heart rate variability (HRV), heart rate (HR) and galvanic skin response (GSR) throughout the interview

Although the data from the bio-sensors were not used in the scope of this work, it can be used in future work to investigate the relation between CS and cognitive load, and to correlate it with user profile and imply whether CS is done intentionally or intuitively.

3.1   Study Timeline

In Fig. 1, we present the overall plan of our work. Our study consisted of three phases: personality profiling (TCI), interview and post-questionnaire. In future work, we plan to use our collected data and findings, to build a predictive model using machine learning, that would learn to predict user CS frequency based on given information, including the user profile, background and conversation domain.

Prior to the interview, the participants signed a consent form and filled the TCI profile questionnaire. Then, in the interview, we collected spontaneous code-switched speech. The interview was semi-structured and consisted of a series of open-ended questions. The duration of the interview ranged from 25 to 35 min. To not affect users' behavior, we designed the questions to cover a wide range of topics e.g., family, university life, hobbies, quotes, songs, movies, books, and traveling. After finishing the interview questions, the participants were asked to describe seven different pictures. The idea behind this part of the interview is to control the answers and thus have a fair comparison between the different CS frequencies across users. In order to examine the effect of the language used by the interviewer, the questions in the first part of the interview were asked in monolingual Arabic and then in mixed code-switched Arabic-English. After the interview, the participants filled a questionnaire to provide background information (gender, age, educational level, history and travel experience), as well as feedback about their self-awareness of their code-switching behavior.

3.2   Participants and Procedure

We recruited 50 participants (25 males, 25 females) with an average age of 22.1 years ($SD = 3.32$) using university mailing lists. Participants were teaching assistants and students from different majors ranging from computer science to management and applied arts (17 graduates, 33 undergraduates). All participants are native Arabic speakers who have at least English as a second language. The participants were assigned to the TCI test before coming to the study. Upon arrival, participants were asked to sign a consent form, and we explained the procedure of the study. The aim of the study was explained after the study to avoid any biases. There were three speakers in each setup, two interviewers, a male and a female and the interviewee. The interviewees' speech was recorded using a noise cancellation microphone. Afterwards, the participants were asked to fill the questionnaire.

3.3   Data Analysis

To be able to answer our research question using the collected dataset, we first annotated the data as well as the dependent variables for analysis. Our independent variables included the TCI profile and the interview and questionnaire questions while the dependent variables included the bio-sensor data and the CS behavior of the participants. Two researchers annotated the recorded

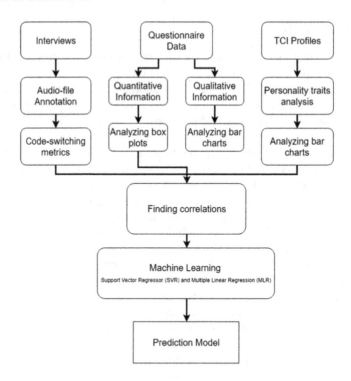

Fig. 1. Flow chart of the data analysis phase

speech using the TranscriberAG annotation tool, to distinguish between English, Arabic and Idle/Interviewer segments. After identifying the boundaries of each language-switching point. The CS percentage was calculated using Eq. 1

$$\frac{\sum (English Seconds PerUtterance \div Seconds PerUtterance)}{\#utterances} * 100 \qquad (1)$$

We also divided the interview audio file into five separate domains of discourse based on the interview questions: Background, Travel, Interests and Hobbies, Personality and Character, and Pictures. We then calculated the CS percentage separately for each domain.

4   Results

We analyzed the data to investigate who, why and when participants code switch.

4.1   Who: Personality vs. Code-Switching %

For the purpose of our study, we only analyzed the dimensions and sub-dimensions that may affect that may influence the speech behavior. These sub-dimensions include: impulsiveness, fear of uncertainty, shyness with strangers, sentimentality, openness to warm communication, eagerness of effort, perfectionism, self-acceptance, self-actualization, social acceptance, helpfulness and pure-hearted conscience. The character and personality of the participants are logistically distributed. Table 1 shows the Pearson's correlations between the CS percentage and the different relevant character and temperament sub-dimensions pinpointed by a TCI expert. It also shows the mean and average values for each of the sub-dimensions (values ranging from 1 to 5). All of the sub-dimensions show a weak correlation with the CS percentage or no correlation at all. This means that no single sub-dimension contributes to the code-switching on its own. The strongest correlations were found for sentimentality and self-acceptance. This could be due to the confidence acquired from self-acceptance [22]. The negative correlation with sentimentality is in-line with previous research, showing that individuals may code-switch to express certain feelings and attitudes [14] or to distant themselves from emotional events [17]. The weak correlations found in case of the personality traits can be explained by the fact that the situation was kept as a constant for all the collected data which means that the trigger points to affect CS based on personality were not present. This is because depending on the personality type and the situation the CS behavior would vary [10]. The older age group showed higher CS than the younger one. This observed changed behavior is found to relate to the occupation rather than the age. As the older target group were teaching assistants with the teaching language as English, hence, their natural language is code-switched more than students i.e., the younger age group.

Table 1. Results of correlation and statistics of the CS percentage and the TCI sub-dimensions

	Pearson's r	Mean	SD
CS %		22.92	13.08
Impulsiveness	−0.01	2.48	0.70
Fear of uncertainty	−0.01	3.41	0.67
Shyness with Strangers	−0.10	3.04	0.85
Sentimentality	−0.25	3.77	0.53
Openness to warm comm.	−0.22	3.59	0.59
Eagerness of effort	0.051	3.48	0.61
Perfectionist	0.11	3.54	0.52
Self-acceptance	0.25	2.66	0.73
Self-actualization	−0.15	3.35	0.49
Social acceptance	−0.16	3.91	0.59
Helpfulness	−0.05	3.65	0.36

4.2   When: Domain of Discourse vs. Code-Switching %

We compared the percentage of CS throughout the whole interview with the percentages of CS per domain of discourse. Table 2 shows the means and standard deviation of code-switching per domain. It also shows the r Pearson correlation coefficient between the general CS and CS within a specific domain, proving that CS varying according to the domain, (supported by 92% of the questionnaire responses to belonging questions and [26,29]). The fact that describing interests and pictures has a high percentage of CS, could be explained by the fact that keywords describing the words often come to mind in the CS language (supported by 80% of the questionnaire responses to belonging questions and [7,17,28]).

Table 2. Results of correlation and statistics of the CS percentage per domain

	Background	Traveling	Interests	Personality	Pictures
Mean	23.8565418	17.41	28.15	24.15	26.47
SD	14.36	14.41	18.43	15.24	16.56
r	0.80	0.67	0.77	0.82	0.77

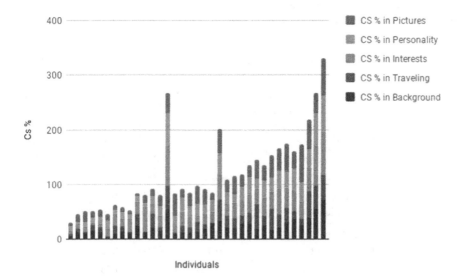

Fig. 2. Stacked step area chart of the CS percentages per domain of discourse.

Figure 2 shows the comparison between the CS percentages per domain. It shows that while talking about the interests and describing pictures the CS is highest while it is lowest when talking about traveling. The pair-wise p value is <0.00001 between the CS percentages of any two domains.

4.3   Why: Background Information vs. Code-Switching %

We analyzed the background information and demographics of the participants
with respect to their code-switching behavior during the interview. The data
for this consideration is extracted from responses to the questionnaire questions dealing with the background and history of the participants. Males exhib-
ited lower percentage of CS (mean = 20.79, SD = 13.65) as opposed to females
(mean = 24.73, SD = 12.63). The older age group tends to code-switch more often
(mean = 28.19, SD = 15.03) than the younger one (mean = 19.71, SD = 15.03).
Unexpectedly, the longest stay in a foreign country of the subjects didn't show
any correlation with the code-mixing percentage. Our analysis also showed a
negative correlation between whether family spoke various languages and the
CS percentage, where individuals from uni-lingual families tend to code-switch
more. The participants' school type (national or international), showed a correlation with the CS percentage, with some out-liners. In Fig. 3, we present some
of the factors perceived by participants as gained benefits from code-switching.

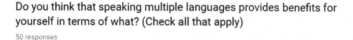

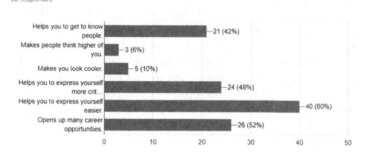

Fig. 3. Perceived benefits provided to the participants from CS.

4.4   Self-awareness

We investigated if participants could rate their own rate of code-switching behavior through self-awareness questions. The participants' answers showed their
awareness of their CS behavior, as there is a high correlation (p < 0.01) between
their reported level of code-switching and the calculated code-mixing percentage. The language considered as the mother tongue by the participants did not
show a correlation as the participants who chose pure Arabic as their mother-
tongue have very similar CS percentage (MEAN = 22.46) to those who viewed
their mother-tongue as code-switched (MEAN = 24.81). On the other hand, the
minimum and maximum values are higher in the participants who consider their
mother tongue to be code-switched (Arabic-English). According to the subjects'

answers on how often they code-switch the results showed a positive correlation between their own prediction of their CS frequency and the calculated code-mixing percentage. The participants' replies showed a correlation between how often do their friends' code-switch and the calculated CS percentage which proves that people adjust their language and thus CS behavior depending on the people they are surrounded with. Only 8% believed that their CS behavior did not vary depending on the environment, which were all participants with low CS percentages.

4.5   Potential Use-Cases

Finding correlations between an individual's code-switching level and his/her character and background has numerous use cases. This correlation can be used to predict the code-switching percentage of an individual which in turn can be used to adapt the NLP applications to suit the individual's CS behavior and thus achieve higher accuracies. This is particularly useful for smart assistants as it would improve the processing of user's input. It can also be later used to have the smart assistant talk to the user in the same manner as the user making it more familiar and human like. This would be done by programming the smart assistant to mimic the user's talking style by enforcing the same percentage of code switching. Another possible use case is for Facebook Translate. During translation and dictation having a prediction of the a user's code-switching frequency can help improve the system accuracy. In general, User-profiling in terms of CS behavior can be used to generate user-adaptive models, which can help improve the performance of the NLP application involved. Our research can also be used to ease communication by using the profile of the people we are talking to, in order to predict their code-switching behavior. These profiles can be extracted from different daily cues to provide the needed features of a specific individual as proposed in [12].

5   Conclusion and Future Work

In this work, we proposed our investigation on the correlation between users' profiles and code switching behavior in the scope of Egyptian Arabic-English language. Through our review of related work, we concluded that no prior work explored the correlation between code-switching behavior and users' personality and background, as well as the lack of experimental studies supporting theoretical theories on the reasons of code-switching. We investigated the effects of personality (TCI profile), background (stay in foreign country, school type, language requirements, having multilingual family and friends), domain of discourse on the code-switching behavior. Our findings gave initial insights on the correlation between code-switching and the investigated factors. Our findings also highlight that users showed high level of awareness concerning their code switching behavior. This would pave the road to enhanced NLP applications, since users can feed to the system their percentage of code switching, and the system can adapt accordingly. In summary, our results reveal the feasibility of having a system that predicts the code-switching behavior based on their background, personality and context. Hence, we envision that our work can serve as an initial building block to understanding the code-switch behavior.

To further extend the results of this research, we need to collect a larger sample of interview speech with a wider range of participants. We need to conduct the study with participants of more diverse age groups, occupations, educational background and social classes, as our preliminary findings showed that these might have an effect on CS behavior. We also intend to include the personality traits from the Five Factor Model of Personality, as well as other factors affecting behavior, i.e. different character attributes [10]. A bigger dataset would enable us to use different machine learning techniques to predict the code-switching behavior from the features of the three measured cues of personality traits, background information and domain of discourse. Moreover, we can combine the collected data with bio-sensor information (EEG, HRV, eye trackers) to help measure the physiological state and cognitive load in various instances of CS. It would be interesting to investigate whether the cognitive load at CS points can be used to distinguish between intentional and intuitive CS. Also, although our findings are in-line with previous socio- and psycho-linguistic studies, we cannot generalize them to other language pairs, as CS is language-dependent, where the behaviour of users varies across language pairs. Therefore, it would be interesting to conduct the same study on different language pairs, and explore the similarities and differences of users' CS behaviour across languages and cultures. Finally, this work is to be extended to adapt NLP applications based on users' profiles.

References

1. Ardila, A.: Spanglish: an anglicized Spanish dialect. Hispanic J. Behav. Sci. **27**(1), 60–81 (2005)
2. Auer, P.: Code-Switching in Conversation: Language, Interaction and Identity. Routledge (2013)
3. Benguedda-Kesraoui, A.: Sociolinguistic dimensions of code switching: the role of social factors in its occurrence in an Algerian context, Tlemcen speech community. Ph.D. thesis (2017)
4. Bentahila, A.: Language Attitudes Among Arabic-French Bilinguals in Morocco. Multilingual Matters Clevedon (1983)
5. Çetinoglu, Ö.: A Turkish-German code-switching corpus. In: LREC (2016)
6. Chen, C.M.: Two types of code-switching in Taiwan. In: 15th Sociolinguistics Symposium (2004)
7. Cheng, K.K.Y.: Code-switching for a purpose: focus on pre-school Malaysian children. Multilingua **22**(1), 59–78 (2003)
8. Cotterell, R., Renduchintala, A., Saphra, N., Callison-Burch, C.: An Algerian Arabic-French code-switched corpus. In: Workshop on Free/Open-Source Arabic Corpora and Corpora Processing Tools Workshop Programme, p. 34 (2014)
9. El Bolock, A.: Defining character computing from the perspective of computer science and psychology. In: Proceedings of the 17th International Conference on Mobile and Ubiquitous Multimedia, pp. 567–572. ACM (2018)

10. El Bolock, A.: What is character computing? In: El Bolock, A., Abdelrahman, Y., Abdennadher, S. (eds.) Character Computing. HIS, pp. 1–16. Springer, Cham (2020). https://doi.org/10.1007/978-3-030-15954-2_1

11. El Bolock, A., Abdelrahman, Y., Abdennadher, S. (eds.): Character Computing. HIS. Springer, Cham (2020). https://doi.org/10.1007/978-3-030-15954-2

12. El Bolock, A., Abdennadher, S., Herbert, C.: Applications of character computing from psychology to computer science. In: El Bolock, A., Abdelrahman, Y., Abdennadher, S. (eds.) Character Computing. HIS, pp. 53–71. Springer, Cham (2020). https://doi.org/10.1007/978-3-030-15954-2_4

13. El Bolock, A., Salah, J., Abdelrahman, Y., Herbert, C., Abdennadher, S.: Character computing: computer science meets psychology. In: 17th International Conference on Mobile and Ubiquitous Multimedia, pp. 557–562. ACM (2018)

14. Eldin, A.A.T.S.: Socio linguistic study of code switching of the arabic language speakers on social networking. Int. J. Eng. Linguist. **4**(6), 78 (2014)

15. Gutierrez-Zotes, J., et al.: Temperament and character inventory-revised (TCI-R). Standardization and normative data in a general population sample. Actas españolas de psiquiatría **32**(1), 8–15 (2004)

16. Hamed, I., Elmahdy, M., Abdennadher, S.: Collection and analysis of code-switch Egyptian Arabic-English speech corpus. In: LREC (2018)

17. Heredia, R.R., Altarriba, J.: Bilingual language mixing: why do bilinguals code-switch? Curr. Dir. Psychol. Sci. **10**(5), 164–168 (2001)

18. Holmes, J., Wilson, N.: An Introduction to Sociolinguistics. Routledge (2017)

19. Li, D.C.: Cantonese-English code-switching research in Hong Kong: a Y2K review. World Engl. **19**(3), 305–322 (2000)

20. Lyu, D.C., Tan, T.P., Chng, E.S., Li, H.: An analysis of a Mandarin-English code-switching speech corpus: Seame. Age **21**, 25–8 (2010)

21. McCrae, R.R., John, O.P.: An introduction to the five-factor model and its applications. J. Pers. **60**(2), 175–215 (1992)

22. Nerghes, A.: The impact of code-switching on persuasion: an elaboration likelihood perspective. Wageningen University (2011)

23. Poplack, S.: Sometimes I'll start a sentence in Spanish y termino en Espanol: toward a typology of code-switching. Linguistics **18**(7–8), 581–618 (1980)

24. Poplack, S.: Code-switching (linguistic). In: Smelser, N.J., Baltes, B. (eds.) International Encyclopedia of the Social and Behavioral Sciences, pp. 2062–2065 (2001)

25. Rihane, W.M.: Why do people code-switch: a sociolinguistic approach (2007)

26. Ritchie, W.C., Bhatia, T.: 15 social and psychological factors in language mixing. In: The Handbook of Bilingualism and Multilingualism, p. 375 (2013)

27. Sayahi, L.: Code-switching and language change in Tunisia. Int. J. Sociol. Lang. **2011**(211), 113–133 (2011)

28. Tariq, A., Bilal, H., Abbas, N., Mahmood, A.: Functions of code-switching in bilingual classrooms. Res. Hum. Soc. Sci. **3**(14), 29–34 (2013)

29. Velásquez, M.C.: Language and identity: bilingual code-switching in Spanish-English interviews. Ph.D. thesis (2010)

Towards a Generic Framework
for Character-Based Chatbots

Walid El Hefny[1]([⊠]), Alia El Bolock[1,2], Cornelia Herbert[2],
and Slim Abdennadher[1]

[1] German University in Cairo, Cairo, Egypt
{walid.elhifny,alia.elbolock,slim.abdennadher}@guc.edu.eg
[2] Ulm University, Ulm, Germany
cornelia.herbert@uni-ulm.de

Abstract. A sudden interest in chatbots occurred in 2016 due to the advancements in machine learning and artificial intelligence technologies. The increase of mobile messaging applications and the introduction of chatbot development frameworks allowed researchers to explore different paradigms for building chatbots. A major issue related to the user experience with chatbots was detected. Users with different personalities, preferences, and needs receive the same responses when they interact with a particular chatbot. This can create unpleasant experiences towards certain user groups. There were multiple efforts to create personalized chatbots in order to overcome such experiences. In this paper, a systematic review for personalized chatbots is conducted to investigate the attempts of building psychologically-driven personalized chatbots. Accordingly, we propose a generic framework for building character-based chatbots using the principles of Character Computing based on psychological theorizing. Our goal is to allow users to create their individual chatbot characters by selecting their preferred character traits. To this end, we introduce a retrieval-based approach for implementing our proposed framework.

Keywords: Conversational agents · Chatbots · Character Computing

1 Introduction

Conversational agents were introduced in the 1960s to deceive users into believing that they are humans [19]. Researchers are trying to answer Alan Turing's significant question "Can machines think?" through the visualization of an intelligent machine behaviour using conversational agents [12]. The term chatbot was introduced in 1994 to describe conversational agents, and was defined as a software system with the role of simulating a conversation with the user in an intelligent way [24]. Nowadays, chatbots are used in multiple fields such as business, entertainment, education, health, and information retrieval [25].

A sudden interest in chatbots began in 2016 due to the enormous advancements in artificial intelligence, machine learning, and natural language processing [20]. Mobile messaging applications such as Facebook Messenger, Skype,

© Springer Nature Switzerland AG 2020
F. De La Prieta et al. (Eds.): PAAMS 2020 Workshops, CCIS 1233, pp. 95–107, 2020.
https://doi.org/10.1007/978-3-030-51999-5_8

and Viber were major factors in the rise of chatbots. More than 3 billion people used messaging applications in 2016, paving the way for chatbots to reach more people through their deployment on such applications. More than 1 million chatbots were deployed on such platforms with Facebook Messenger having around 300,000 chatbots [2].

The authors in [3] believe that developers and designers must understand the user needs and their attitudes experience and experiences with and towards chatbots, as it will affect the way they engage with the chatbot data and conversational services online. Crucially, from a psychological point of view, the quality and quantity of a conversation is considered to be influenced by a number of factors, most notably the human user's characters i.e. his/her affect, motivation, intention and the user's metacognitive beliefs about other people's actions and beliefs. It is considered one of the important success factors for chatbots to support the user needs efficiently and seamlessly throughout the conversation [20]. Oracle stated that by 2020 80% of consumer brands will use chatbots to engage with customers [17].

In this paper, we review the current implementations of personality-based chatbots. Accordingly, we propose a framework for building character-based chatbots to generalize the personalization process and enhance the user experience. This approach will be guided by psychological theorizing and allowing users to build their favorite chatbot characters. Moreover, a retrieval-based implementation of our framework is introduced. The structure of this paper is as follows: Sect. 2 presents the literature review. Section 3 describes our framework for building character-based chatbots. Section 4 discusses an approach for implementing our proposed framework. Finally, Sect. 5 concludes the paper and presents future work.

2 Literature Review

2.1 Classification of Chatbots

Chatbots can be classified according to various parameters such as knowledge domain, service provided, goal, and response generation method. The categories can exist in varying proportions as chatbots can belong to multiple categories at the same time [15].

Knowledge Domain - Chatbots are classified based on the amount of data they can access or are trained upon. Open domain agents can tackle general topics and respond accordingly such as Amazon Alexa, Apple Siri, and Google Assistant, while closed domain agents can only respond to a specific knowledge domain such as restaurant booking chatbots [15].

Service Provided - Chatbots are classified according to the sentimental proximity of the chatbot to the user. It is related to the proxemics field which is the study of man's perception and use of space [10]. Interpersonal agents fall under the social or personal distance range. Their role is to retrieve information for the user while being friendly. However, they are not supposed to be companions to the user. The second type are intrapersonal agents, which perform tasks that lie in the personal domain of the user, similar to chat applications. Unlike interpersonal agents, they are companions to the user, and understand the user's needs like humans. Finally, inter-agents are chatbots that can communicate with each other to perform a certain task. This type is more dominant in Internet of Things (IoT) applications [15].

Goals - Chatbots are classified based on the primary goal they aim to fulfill. Informative agents are information retrieval chatbots that provide the user with the required information through fetching the result of the user query from a database, or by performing string matching. Secondly, chat-based agents are chatbots built with the aim of chatting with the user and maintaining the conversation. They use techniques such as cross questioning, evasion, and deference. The last type in the goals classification is task-based agents. They perform specific tasks requested by the user. The actions and flow of events are predetermined [13,15].

Response Generation - Chatbots are classified according to the response generation techniques. Intelligent agents use generation-based methods to generate the response. It is used when having a limited domain and sample data for training. An encoder-decoder framework is used based on recurrent neural networks (RNN) [22,23]. It generates the reply sentence word by word [26]. On the other hand, rule-based agents use retrieval-based methods such as pattern and string matching. It is used when a fixed number of outcomes is known. The user issues an utterance, in which the best response from a set of predefined responses is chosen [22]. Finally, hybrid agents are a mix of intelligent and rule-based agents, where a flow chart is used for managing the conversation direction, but the response is generated through machine learning techniques [15].

2.2   Challenges of Chatbots

Due to the difficulty of developing open domain chatbots, neglecting the user needs, and rushing to deploy chatbots for businesses, current chatbots often fail. In 2016 Microsoft deployed its intelligent chatbot Tay on Twitter to imitate the personality of an 19 year old girl through learning from the tweets of other users. Some Twitter users were interacting with Tay through writing hateful comments. An unexpected behavior was expressed by Tay resulting in hateful and racist tweets. Microsoft decided to discontinue Tay and removed it from Twitter [3,18].

The authors in [3] stated that chatbot dialogues must focus on the engagement and user experience. They decided to put some questions for developers and designers to take into consideration while building chatbots. The questions included: "How friendly should they make the chatbot?", "How humanlike or personal the chatbot should be?", and "Should the chatbot have a gender?".

Multiple variables exist that shape the users expectations towards chatbots. It was found that age and behavior trends had an impact on the type of responses and engagements between users and chatbots. In order to achieve success with the public audience, it is required to design and evaluate chatbots for users with diverse perspectives [27]. The authors in [17] urged researchers to focus on user-centered research since the majority of users have different expectations and perspectives. They defined some future research directions which include elements such as the interaction style, appropriate tasks, and trustworthiness.

Chatbots interact with users having different characteristics and personalities. The authors in [8] stated that current chatbots are built using the one-size-fits-all approach. Chatbots respond to users with different preferences, needs, and degrees of digital literacy in the same way and language. Such default responses may create unpleasant biases towards certain user groups or not. Therefore, it was proposed to create chatbots that adapt to different user groups.

2.3 Character Computing

When it comes to Human Computer Interaction (HCI), we find that subfields such as Affective Computing and Personality Computing focus on putting the human factors at the center of technology. Affective Computing attempts to add the human emotions into the computational considerations to create personalized user experiences. It mainly focuses on detecting the emotional states and trying to adapt to them [16]. On the other hand, Personality Computing deals with the human personality instead of emotions. It constantly attempts to detect, perceive, and synthesize the human personality which is represented using the Five Factor Model (FFM) [9].

It was proposed to take the character as a whole instead of focusing on the emotions or personality individually, since the same person may express different emotions at the same situation. Moreover, given the same situation, two persons with different personality traits may express different emotions. It was concluded that personality traits may reflect the differences between humans, while emotions may reflect the differences within the same human. When it comes to the character as a whole, psychologically speaking, it can be seen as the individual person with all of their features such as personality traits, affective, cognitive, and motivational states, beliefs, sociocultural embeddings, and morals [5]. This resulted in a new field named Character Computing which puts the whole human character at the center of any artificial interaction [6,7].

Character Computing tackles any type of computation that includes the human character within its context. It consists of three modules "character sensing and profiling, character-aware adaptive systems, and artificial characters" which supplement each other. The adaptation to human character was always questioned from the perspective of computer science or psychology alone. However in Character Computing, these questions are tackled from a joint perspective of both research fields in parallel [11]. It extended the Personality-

Behaviour-Situation triad tackled in Personality Psychology to the Character-Behaviour-Situation triad, highlighting the importance of the whole human character instead of the personality alone [5,11].

2.4 Character-Based Chatbots

One of the early attempts to create personalized chatbots was in [14] when the authors developed chatbots based on characters from famous TV shows. This allowed users to interact and chat with their favorite fictional characters. Each chatbot was imitating the personality of the character it represents, and was trained on data extracted from dialogues. The authors proved that more than 50% of the users will believe the result came from the actual character. Although the participants did not have the option to customize the chatbot personality, they chose a chatbot from a list of chatbots, each having a different personality than the others.

A framework was proposed by [21] for building user-centered chatbots through a design process with personality as its main factor. The framework focused on choosing the tone of voice and identifying the intended chatbot personality using the Five Factor Model. Characteristics, qualities, and personality traits were also defined as part of the framework. The authors tested the framework by developing a chatbot named Bella for the healthy food domain, and compared it to a non personalized task-oriented chatbot. It was found that the personalized chatbot had a positive effect on the user experience compared to the non personalized chatbot.

Recently the authors in [4] applied the principles of Character Computing on an in-car voice assistant. Famous characters from TV shows were analyzed using the model of attitudes to create 8 different assistant personalities. The participants were asked to fill a questionnaire about the likability and trust, usefulness and satisfaction, emotional satisfaction, and character assessment of the tested assistants. It was found after conducting personal interviews that there are 7 main reasons for preferring some assistants over the others. The categories were recognition, humor, intelligence, number of words, relational level, balance of power, and professionalism. Friendly and open assistants were preferred by most of the participants, while unfriendly and excessive talking assistants were disliked by them. Other categories such as the balance of power and professionalism had mixed preferences. As a result, the authors proposed a model containing fixed personality traits universally accepted by most users, while having a 2-dimensional trait that can be manually adjusted.

The authors in [1] proved that users comply more with robots that matched their personality, and the users gave these robots high ratings in terms of performance. Therefore, we need to allow users to choose their preferred chatbot personality. Currently, there exists no formal process for developing chatbots with multiple personalities. All personality-based chatbots existing in the literature do not support the change of their personality in the middle of the conversation. When it comes to testing multiple personalities, researchers build a chatbot for each personality.

3   Framework for Character-Based Chatbots

We propose a generic framework for building character-based chatbots. The framework consists of multiple modules that can be customized according to the purpose of the chatbot. Our goal is to build chatbots with variable n-dimensional character traits. This is an attempt to remove any digital divides and biases towards certain user groups, as chatbots will no longer respond to all users with the same response rather, the responses will be customized according to the user selected character. A user can freely change the n-dimensional character traits during the conversation, which will change the behavior of the chatbot. A chatbot may have multiple responses for a user query, but the most suitable response will be retrieved according to the chosen character. The framework is based on existing chatbot development components. The components are broken down into modules that can be adjusted easily to provide a direct and systematic way for building character-based chatbots.

3.1   N-Dimensional Traits

Our goal is to apply the principles of Character Computing to build chatbot characters according to the user preferences. We want to include the human character components in the chatbot development process to create artificial personalities. Each component can have n-dimensional traits were the user can choose between.

One of the main character components is the personality traits. There exist multiple models for representing personality traits such as the Five Factor Model (FFM). One of the Five Factor Model personality traits is extraversion. If we apply our n-dimensional approach to the extraversion trait, we can have a 2-dimensional trait where the user can choose between introversion or extroversion. However, extraversion can be deconstructed into multiple n-dimensional traits. We can have other 2-dimensional options representing the extraversion trait such as sociable-intimate, humorous-serious, and adventurous-inactive.

Our approach can be applied to any character component trait consisting of 2 or more dimensions. The challenge is to have responses representing all the different character combinations. For example, if the user can only choose between humorous or serious, and emotional or emotionless, we will have a total of 4 characters representing the 4 different combinations (humorous-emotional, humorous-emotionless, serious-emotional, and serious-emotionless).

3.2   Modules

Our framework consists of five modules that interact together. The modules are the conversational user interface, entities, intents, webhook, and database as shown in Fig. 1. Each module can be easily customized without affecting the rest of the system.

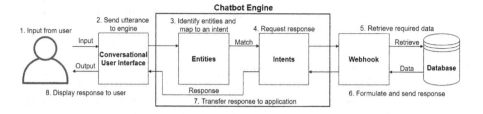

Fig. 1. The proposed generic framework for building character-based chatbots.

Conversational User Interface - In our framework, the conversational user interface (CUI) represents the front-end of the chatbot. It is responsible for taking an input from the user and displaying an output to the user. Users can interact with chatbots through text or speech depending on the platform they are deployed on. Conversational user interfaces are based on the principles of human-human interaction. Instead of having graphical elements such as buttons and links, it focuses on natural language and emotions. Mobile applications, web applications, and smart speakers are examples of platforms that support conversational user interfaces.

Intents - The intention of a user for one conversation turn is called an intent. A chatbot should have a list of intents that handles a complete conversation. Each intent is provided with training phrases and a list of responses during its creation. When a user message (user utterance) is matched to an intent, one of the intent responses will be retrieved randomly. The intent handles the keywords extraction in a user utterance. Keywords can be used as parameters for the chatbot to perform some logic or generate responses. The list of intents differs from one chatbot to another according to the purpose of the chatbot. In our approach, the list of intents is considered as a module that can be replaced or customized freely. For example, we can have a welcome intent. If the user says "hello" or "hi", which are phrases that exist in the training phrases of the welcome intent, it will match to it. A suitable response will be given to the user from the intent's list of responses such as "Hey there".

Entities - An entity is used to identify keywords in a user utterance. Developers can create custom entities to match custom data which is used in the training phrases of an intent. The intent will add the entity related to the custom data to its input parameters, which enhances the intent matching process to a user utterance. An example of an entity is a city. If the user types "Berlin", the chatbot engine realizes that Berlin is a city, and matches it to an intent that requires a city as an input parameter. The developer must define the city entity beforehand, including all possible cities. The intent and entities modules form the chatbot engine. In our approach, character traits are defined as entities. For example, if we create an entity named "extraversion", we can have values such as "sociable" and "intimate" included in the entity. If the user types "I want the chatbot to be sociable", it will alert the engine that the user chose the extraversion trait to be sociable.

Webhook - A webhook is a user-defined HTTP callback which can store and retrieve data from an event. It is used to pass and retrieve data from web services. Webhooks are used for actions that require dynamic data or communication with external systems. In our approach, when an intent is matched, the chatbot engine requests a customized response from the webhook. Since our aim is to allow users to build their chatbot character, we need to keep track of the selected character. The webhook is responsible for retrieving the selected character and requesting a customized response matching the selected character. It acts as a link between the chatbot engine and the database. It does not require constant polling as it is only triggered when an intent is matched and a response is needed. A webhook can be seen as a server that receives requests and sends back responses.

Database - A database is needed to store user data and customized responses. The user data contains information gathered from the conversation such as the user's name, age, and gender. The selected chatbot character is also stored allowing the webhook to figure which customized response is needed to be retrieved. Each chatbot character has a list of customized responses stored in the database. The webhook interacts multiple times with the database until it retrieves all the required data to formulate the customized response and sends it back to the chatbot engine. Current chatbots with one personality have the list of responses embedded inside the intent itself. In order to support multiple characters, a database is needed to store the list of responses of each character per intent. For example, if we have empathetic and tough characters, the responses representing these characters for each intent are stored in the database and retrieved according to the selected character.

3.3 Approach Variations

We could have multiple variations regarding the chatbot characters. We described the general case of having variable n-dimensional traits, but our approach can support having static characters were the user can choose directly from. For example, a chatbot can have a friendly, formal, and tough characters were the user can select. This can be performed by creating a universal entity named "Character" containing all the predefined characters. When the user types "I want the friendly character", the friendly character responses for the upcoming user utterances will be retrieved from the database. Other variations include having fixed traits with one or more n-dimensional traits. For example, we can have a friendly character but the user can control its level of humour. In this case, we can have an entity representing the level of humour the user wants.

4   Retrieval-Based Implementation

We propose a retrieval-based approach for implementing character-based chat-bots using our proposed framework. The implementation consists of four main components which are the messaging application, agent, web server, and database as shown in Fig. 2. Each component corresponds to one or more modules in our proposed framework. Since the chatbot responses are retrieved from a database and are not generated using machine learning algorithms, our approach falls under the retrieval-based category.

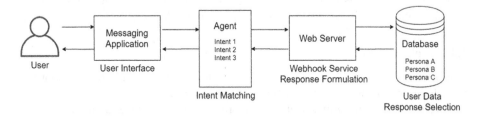

Fig. 2. Retrieval-based implementation of our proposed framework.

4.1   Messaging Application

Messaging applications are a major factor in the rapid increase of chatbots. Most of the well-known messaging applications support the integration and deployment of chatbots onto their platforms such as Facebook Messenger, WhatsApp, and Skype. Chatbots can also be deployed on Intelligent Personal Assistants such as Google Assistant (Actions on Google) and Alexa (Alexa Skills). Developers will no longer worry about developing user interfaces for their chatbots as it will be maintained by messaging applications. No user authentication is needed as it is handled internally through the messaging platforms. Messaging applications were restricted to mobile devices, but nowadays they can be found on personal computers and on the web.

   In our approach, users interact with a chatbot through a messaging application. Therefore, the messaging application acts as the conversational user interface present in our framework. The user utterance will be transferred from the messaging application to the chatbot engine in order to retrieve a response and output it to the user. Messaging applications support taking an input from a user and displaying a response from a chatbot in text and audio formats.

4.2   Agent

The agent acts as the chatbot engine containing the list of intents and defined entities. After receiving the user utterance, it is matched to one of the intents.

The agent will request a customized response from the web server, and the response will be retrieved according to the chosen character traits by the user.

There are multiple frameworks for developing chatbots such as Google's Dialogflow, Microsoft Bot Framework, Amazon Lex, and IBM Watson. The frameworks are easy to use and do not require any advanced machine learning or natural language knowledge. They provide a friendly web interface for developers to build chatbots.

The entities recognition and intent matching processes are handled internally without the developer's interference. Moreover, the frameworks support the integration of chatbots to most of the mobile messaging applications seamlessly. Other features such as speech-to-text, text-to-speech, and sentiment analysis on user utterances are included in most of the frameworks.

4.3   Web Server

The previously mentioned frameworks allow developers to add static responses to each intent. In case a user utterance was matched to an intent, one of the static responses will be randomly selected as the response. However dynamic responses are not supported internally. The engine will request the response from the web server. The request contains information about the matched intent.

A web server is needed to host the webhook code from our framework and initialize the database connections. There are multiple hosting platforms, such as Google Firebase Hosting, Amazon Web Services (AWS), and Heroku that use the latest cloud technologies. The webhook interacts with the database multiple times per user utterance to retrieve data such as the user information, chatbot character selected by the user, and the customized response. Any calculations or Application Programming Interfaces (APIs) requests are done through the webhook.

4.4   Database

There are various relational and non-relational online databases such as Amazon Relational Database Service (RDS), Heroku Postgres, Google Firebase, and Google Cloud Firestore. The responses are stored in a key-value pair under the correct character. For example, if we have 3 characters, we will have 3 documents in the database. Each document represents a character and contains all responses that represent it in a key-value pair. Each intent has a list of keys for each chatbot character where the webhook randomly selects a key and retrieves its value from the database. After the customized response is retrieved, the webhook sends it to the agent which sends it back to the messaging application to be displayed. Database responses can be collected from personality-tagged datasets.

5   Conclusion and Future Work

Current chatbots respond to users having different personalities with the same responses. A major question was raised whether such default responses create unpleasant biases towards certain user groups or not. After reviewing the current personality-based chatbots in the literature, we present an approach for building character-based chatbots based on the principles of Character Computing. Our framework consists of five components which are the conversational user interface, entities, intents, webhook, and database. Our goal is to have multiple n-dimensional traits based on the human character components where the user can choose between to create their preferred character. A retrieval-based implementation for our framework was introduced, based on four main components which are the messaging application, agent, web server, and database.

Further research is needed to evaluate our framework by building chatbots for different domains such as business, education, health, and entertainment using our proposed implementation. Chatbots built based on our framework can be easily adapted to other domains since it is module-based. Each module can be amended without affecting the rest of the system. We can expand the current framework by adding new modules or deconstructing existing ones. Other variations of our implementation include the introduction of generation-based responses instead of the retrieval-based approach. We can replace the messaging application with an intelligent personal assistant to make the interaction fully based on speech. Our framework supports the existence of n-dimensional traits from different character components together. We can investigate the simulation of multiple character components such as personality traits, affective states, and cultural aspects individually and collectively, and observe the differences. We can ask the participants about their experience toward the multiple chatbot characters. This will help us create adaptive chatbots in which the chatbot character can be selected based on the user character.

References

1. Andrist, S., Mutlu, B., Tapus, A.: Look like me: matching robot personality via gaze to increase motivation. In: Proceedings of the 33rd Annual ACM Conference on Human Factors in Computing Systems, pp. 3603–3612 (2015)
2. Brandtzaeg, P.B., Følstad, A.: Why people use chatbots. In: Kompatsiaris, I., et al. (eds.) INSCI 2017. LNCS, vol. 10673, pp. 377–392. Springer, Cham (2017). https:// doi.org/10.1007/978-3-319-70284-1_30
3. Brandtzaeg, P.B., Følstad, A.: Chatbots: changing user needs and motivations. Interactions 25(5), 38–43 (2018)
4. Braun, M., Alt, F.: Identifying personality dimensions for characters of digital agents. In: El Bolock, A., Abdelrahman, Y., Abdennadher, S. (eds.) Character Computing. HIS, pp. 123–137. Springer, Cham (2020). https://doi.org/10.1007/ 978-3-030-15954-2_8
5. El Bolock, A.: What is character computing? In: El Bolock, A., Abdelrahman, Y., Abdennadher, S. (eds.) Character Computing. HIS, pp. 1–16. Springer, Cham (2020). https://doi.org/10.1007/978-3-030-15954-2_1
6. El Bolock, A., Salah, J., Abdelrahman, Y., Herbert, C., Abdennadher, S.: Character computing: computer science meets psychology. In: Proceedings of the 17th International Conference on Mobile and Ubiquitous Multimedia, pp. 557–562 (2018)

7. ElBolock, A.: Defining character computing from the perspective of computer science and psychology. In: Proceedings of the 17th International Conference on Mobile and Ubiquitous Multimedia, pp. 567–572 (2018)

8. Følstad, A., Brandtzæg, P.B.: Chatbots and the new world of HCI. Interactions **24**(4), 38–42 (2017)

9. Goldberg, L.R.: The development of markers for the big-five factor structure. Psychol. Assess. **4**(1), 26 (1992)

10. Hall, E.T., et al.: Proxemics (and comments and replies). Curr. Anthropol. **9**(2/3), 83–108 (1968)

11. Herbert, C.: An experimental-psychological approach for the development of character computing. In: El Bolock, A., Abdelrahman, Y., Abdennadher, S. (eds.) Character Computing. HIS, pp. 17–38. Springer, Cham (2020). https://doi.org/10.1007/978-3-030-15954-2_2

12. Lokman, A.S., Zain, J.M.: Extension and prerequisite: an algorithm to enable relations between responses in chatbot technology. J. Comput. Sci. **6**(10), 1212 (2010)

13. Neff, G., Nagy, P.: Automation, algorithms, and politics—talking to bots: symbiotic agency and the case of tay. Int. J. Commun. **10**, 17 (2016)

14. Nguyen, H., Morales, D., Chin, T.: A neural chatbot with personality (2017)

15. Nimavat, K., Champaneria, T.: Chatbots: an overview. Types, architecture, tools and future possibilities, October 2017

16. Picard, R.W., Picard, R.: Affective Computing, vol. 252. MIT Press, Cambridge. EEG-detected olfactory imagery to reveal covert consciousness in minimally conscious state. Brain Injury **29**(13–14), 1729–1735 (1997)

17. Piccolo, L., Mensio, M., Alani, H.: Chasing the chatbots: directions for interaction and design research (2019)

18. Price, R.: Microsoft is deleting its AI chatbot's incredibly racist tweets. Business Insider (2016)

19. Shawar, B.A., Atwell, E.: Chatbots: are they really useful? Ldv Forum. **22**, 29–49 (2007)

20. Shevat, A.: Designing bots: creating conversational experiences. O'Reilly Media, Inc. (2017)

21. Smestad, T.L.: Personality matters! Improving the user experience of chatbot interfaces-personality provides a stable pattern to guide the design and behaviour of conversational agents. Master's thesis, NTNU (2018)

22. Song, Y., Yan, R., Li, C.T., Nie, J.Y., Zhang, M., Zhao, D.: An ensemble of retrieval-based and generation-based human-computer conversation systems (2018)

23. Song, Y., Yan, R., Li, X., Zhao, D., Zhang, M.: Two are better than one: an ensemble of retrieval-and generation-based dialog systems. arXiv preprint arXiv:1610.07149 (2016)

24. Valtolina, S., Barricelli, B., Gaetano, S., Diliberto, P.: Chatbots and conversational interfaces: three domains of use. In: International Workshop on Cultures of Participation in the Digital Age: Design Trade-offs for an Inclusive Society Co-located with the International Conference on Advanced Visual Interfaces, vol. 2101, pp. 62–70. CEUR-WS (2018)

25. Wu, Y., Wu, W., Xing, C., Zhou, M., Li, Z.: Sequential matching network: a new architecture for multi-turn response selection in retrieval-based chatbots. arXiv preprint arXiv:1612.01627 (2016)

26. Yan, Z., et al.: DocChat: an information retrieval approach for chatbot engines using unstructured documents. In: Proceedings of the 54th Annual Meeting of the Association for Computational Linguistics (Volume 1: Long Papers), vol. 1, pp. 516–525 (2016)

27. Zamora, J.: I'm sorry, Dave, I'm afraid I can't do that: chatbot perception and expectations. In: Proceedings of the 5th International Conference on Human Agent Interaction, pp. 253–260. ACM (2017)

The Effects of Personality Traits on the Lifetime of a Rumor

Merna Mikhaeil$^{(\boxtimes)}$ and Amr El Mougy$^{(\boxtimes)}$

Department of Computer Science and Engineering,
German University in Cairo, Cairo, Egypt
{merna.mikhaeil,amr.elmougy}@guc.edu.eg

Abstract. Social media platforms have limited mechanisms for authenticating the veracity of the shared information. This leads to widespread rumors and misinformation. Quite often, these rumors can lead to drastic consequences such as shocking the stock market or violent actions against target groups. Understanding the factors that lead to rumor propagation is key to its detection and eventual mitigation. Accordingly, this paper studies the possible factors that may influence how a rumor spreads. We discuss the types of personality traits that are more likely to participate in the propagation of a rumor, and present a survey of pertinent research efforts that support this claim. In addition, we offer an analysis of the lifetime of a rumor using a large dataset collected from Twitter, which shows that people with a higher number of followers are generally regarded to be more trustworthy and thus can influence the rate of propagation of a rumor. Our study leads us to confirm that personality traits affect the rate of spreading of a rumor.

Keywords: Social media · Personality · Rumors propagation

1 Introduction

Social media platforms now allow billions of people to share information on a scale that would have been inconceivable only a decade ago. On these platforms, people can share their opinions, thoughts, news and product reviews [1]. However, just as they can be used to share knowledge and positive experiences, they can also be used to share rumors and misinformation [2]. Social media users spread information rapidly and widely without content authentication, as they may lack the capacity to determine the veracity of the information they receive [3]. This situation is getting worse with time and often leads to drastic consequences.

Social psychology literature [4–6] defines Rumors as a piece of information that has not been confirmed as a fact before spreading. In addition, many dictionaries define rumor as "information that is passed from one person to another but has not been proven to be true" [10]. Accordingly, a rumor can be resolved as true (factual), false (non-factual) or unresolved after being propagated. The

© Springer Nature Switzerland AG 2020
F. De La Prieta et al. (Eds.): PAAMS 2020 Workshops, CCIS 1233, pp. 108–117, 2020.
https://doi.org/10.1007/978-3-030-51999-5_9

main characteristic of a piece of information, to be classified as a rumor, is that it is not verified at the time of posting [6]. In order to develop ways detecting rumors and mitigating their propagation, it is important to study the factors that lead to their spreading.

Different researchers [6–8] explored various factors and characteristics that affect the rumor behavior and rate of spreading. The work in [7] focused on understanding rumor behaviour by measuring the speed of re-transmission of a rumor during crisis event in co-relation with the information content(e.g. URLs, Topics) [7]. Another study [6] focused on the topic of a rumor. It tackled the problem of identifying breaking news rumors of emerging topics. The frequency of the rumors is directly proportional to the individuals' interest in the topic. The rumors' circulation is effectively higher when the topic become more sensitive or spreading breaking news (e.g. Earthquakes) [6].

However, recently there has been increasing interest in studying the personality traits that lead to rumor spreading. For example, the work in [8] showed a co-relation between individual's personality and motivation as well as the information content with spread of rumor. The results show significant potential to understanding what makes a rumor spread. Nevertheless, this is a direction that requires more attention from the research community [2,6]. In the light of this gap, this article attempts to address different rumor spreading factors that have not been investigated before. We collect data from Twitter about a well known rumor and use this data to investigate whether the diffusion of the rumor is dependent on the rumor initiator. We try to answer the following questions: does the personality affects the dissemination of rumors? Are certain topics more likely to spread by certain personalities?

The remaining sections of this paper are organized as follows. Section 2 explains our experiment and results; Sect. 3 surveys previous research about personality traits and their impact on rumor spreading; while Sect. 4 offers concluding remarks.

2 Studying Various Rumor-Related Features and Characteristics

Studying the rumors behavior and characteristics has been an attractive research area. Different researchers proved that rumor characteristics could have a role in the transmission and propagation of a rumor such as speed, topic and lifetime.

Li Zeng et al. [7] studied the speed of information transmission during crisis events. They found an association between the speed of re-transmission and rumor-related features of the messages. Firstly, they studied the speed of propagation of each rumor, which they defined as the length of the waiting time for a tweet to be re-tweeted i.e re-transmitted by another user. In case an original tweet was re-posted multiple times, i.e it was retweeted by more than one user, and hence multiple associated waiting times, they calculated the average waiting times. Moreover, the study extracted several features as shown in Fig. 1 and associated them with longer/shorter median waiting time. For example, the analysis demonstrates that rumor-affirming content tends to have longer waiting times than rumor-denying content.

Tweet element	The presence of URLs, the presence of hashtags, the presence of user mentions
Rumor	Rumor stance, uncertainty, true or false rumor, sentiment
Interest	Retweet counts, favorite counts
Exposure	Average exposure degree (in-degree), average attention degree (out-degree), popularity of original poster, outgoingness of original poster
Seasonality	Time of day when original tweet was posted

Fig. 1. Tweet features and characteristics.

Another study [18] focused on the content of the rumors. They divided the rumors collected into 4 categories: information-related, emotion-related, deliberation, and call-to-action. The study proved that the four message categories were found to differ in the life of rumors. The life of a rumor means how long it lasts; and it typically varies from 2 days to 12 weeks. Information and emotion-related messages were high in proportions in the initial stages of rumors as information triggers interest and emotion adds fuel to the interest [18]. However, information- and emotion-related messages showed a decrease in proportions with progress in the life of rumors, while the proportion of deliberation messages showed an increasing trend with progress in the life of rumors. Finally, The proportion of call-to action messages showed an increasing trend during the first half of the life of rumors, and a decreasing trend thereafter [18]. These findings lead us to study the personality traits that affect the spreading of specific rumor content (topic). Recently there has been increasing interest in studying the personality traits that affects the rumor transmission and propagation.

3   Personality Traits Affect Rumor Propagation

Scarce studies on rumor propagation have previously considered personality as one of the factors. One rumor can be attractive for one to share, but completely uninteresting to others.

Researchers [16] studied the five personality factors (extraversion, agreeableness, conscientiousness, neuroticism, and openness to experience) and showed that extroversion and neuroticism personalities were more associated with online activities. Introverted people were shown to be not as active Internet users as extroverted people. In particular, three of five personality factors showed high usage of social media: extraversion, neuroticism, and openness [16].

Different researches focused on different aspects of personality that affect rumor spreading. Some studies [17] considered age and level of anxiety as a factor, while other studies [8] considered five personality traits and motivation factor.

3.1 Emotional Factors

A study [17] highlighted that a person's emotions is a trigger to rumor sharing. The study claimed that rumor sharing helps reducing anxiety and manage uncertainties. Anxiety is stated as the fear of threats or danger demonstrated in the rumor event/topic. Rumors usually associated with ambiguity and uncertainties which often lead to high level of anxiety. Therefore the rate of sharing the rumor is defined by the level of anxiety of the spreaders. Whenever the level of anxiety increases the probability for person to spread this rumor increases [17]. Furthermore, the research [17] co-relates the age of the person with his state of anxiety. They found that young adults tend to spread rumor as a way to control their emotions.

3.2 Personality Traits and Motivation Factors

While Chen's [8] contribution focuses on the spread of misinformation generally as opposed to rumors specifically, the results apply equally to rumors.To the best of our knowledge, Chen's [8] work is considered the leading work with respect to the effect of the user's personality on the patterns of rumor propagation.

In their study, Chen uses the five-factor model (FFM) [13,14]. The results show that two traits had a significant impact on the user's decision to further spread misinformation. Neuroticism was negatively associated with the sharing of misinformation. Ross et al. [15] explain that neurotic people are more likely to limit and control the information they participated online, hence their reluctance to further share doubtful misinformation. Conversely, openness to experience demonstrated a more encouraging effect on the decision to propagate doubtful information as Chen stated "As open people have wider interests and are more willing to use unusual means, it is possible that they would share more misinformation to explore its novel ideas".

4 Identifying the Influential Rumor Spreader and Likelihood of a User to Spread a Rumor

4.1 Twitter and Rumor Propagation

We have chosen Twitter as the social media platform to study because it is an effective medium to deliver and receive information. Over 300 million people around the world use Twitter. Billions of tweets have been shared between Twitter users [9].

The research in [11] found that Twitter's follow graph exhibits structural characteristics of both an information network and a social network. However, Zubiaga et al. [10] found that users tend to support rather than deny a rumor on Twitter before it is verified. Given the nature of social media, it is adequate for the users to share any information without verifying.

Twitter has proved to be a fertile ground for rumors. For example in 2013, a single tweet reported an explosion at the white house. In six minutes, it had been widely spread and resulted in a dramatic plunge in the stock market, although it was debunked rapidly [6]. Furthermore, In 2018, An Egyptian girl reported a tweet "GIANT BBQ PARTY!!!" that claimed to put a giant grill with a large amount of chicken and meat under NASA rocket before it launches. Surprisingly, this tweet was widely spread all over the world and became a trending topic. Afterwards, The Tweet was classified as a rumor, as the girl claimed that all of these were fake[1].

Our main aim is to identify the influential rumor spreader and what characteristics made them influential. A research by Jiang et al. [12] proved that identifying rumor sources plays a crucial role in reducing the damage caused by them. Our approach was to find the number of re-tweets for every tweet/re-tweet. The highest number of re-tweets indicates the highest spread and accordingly the highest influence. Also, we tried to figure if the number of followers affects the rate of spreading. Thus, the tweeter who lead to the highest number of retweets generated directly/indirectly from their node was considered the most influential one. Furthermore, we extended our study to find the likelihood of a person to spread a rumor based on his interests.

4.2 Data Collection

We collected about 1500 Tweets posted about different rumors: NASABBQ, Hillary Clinton winning the election, white house explosion, John smith committing a suicide using Twitter streaming API and tweepy[2]. The rumors were handpicked based on the fact checking website "Snopes"[3]. The collected tweets include original tweets (created by the account owner) and re-tweets (shared from another one). To be able to study the behavior of the influencers, we started by separating the original tweets from re-tweets. Furthermore, We considered each one of the original tweeters to be a rumor spreader to compare their behavior. After then, using streaming API, we extracted his followers for each rumor spreader. Also, by using the API we were able to collect 100 retweets for every original tweet. Moreover, we collected around 200,000 tweets for 250 users that have participated in any of the previous rumors.

4.3 Experiment

Identifying the Influential Rumor Seed. We tried to find matches between the followers of the tweeter/re-tweeter and the re-tweets of their respective tweet in a chaining algorithm in order to build a propagation graph (i.e. who re-tweeted from whom). However, our main challenge was to investigate the direct source of each retweet even if the source was another re-tweet and not an original tweet, as this information is not provided directly by the Twitter API. In order

---

[1] https://egyptindependent.com/egyptian-tells-nasa-to-use-a-giant-bbq-as-rocket-launch-pad-they-accept/.

[2] An easy-to-use Python library for accessing the Twitter API.

[3] www.snopes.com/.

to tackle this problem, we based our experiment on the characteristics of an information network. The work done by Myers, Seth A. et al. [11] proved that the "Follow" graph in twitter exhibits the information network characteristics. In Twitter unlike other networks, users tend to follow another account to receive new information not because of any meaningful social relationship [11].

Moreover, we extracted the number of followers for each rumor spreader. As the number of followers increases, the probability of spreading increases. Table 1 shows a sample of the follower's count.

Table 1. The number of followers for some of influencers in the collected dataset.

Influencer	Number of followers
Influencer 1	102364
Influencer 2	60662
Influencer 3	62753

The next step was to build the propagation graph i.e. twitter re-tweets graph; connecting each retweet with its direct source, whether the direct source was an original tweet or a re-tweet. Figures 2, 3, 4 illustrate sample of the propagation graphs of influencers 1,2,3 respectively. As illustrated, the node with the most edges is the original rumor tweeter, while the other nodes show the source from which each retweet was taken.

Identifying User Interests. Furthermore, we extended our experiment to study which users are more likely to share in spreading a rumor based on their interests/topics they usually talk about in the social media. In order to extract the interests of each user, we started by classifying his recent tweets to detect topics he usually post about. To achieve this goal, we have used an online classifier *"uClassify"*[4]. uClassify uses multinomial Naive Bayesian classifier with a couple of steps that improves the classification further (hybrid complementary NB, class normalization and special smoothing). The result of classifications are probabilities [0–1] of a document belonging to each class. In our case, we defined 4 classes: social, celebrity, political, medical depending on the type of rumors we collected. Moreover, the collected rumors were classified the same way as the tweets to calculate the score of each category. Consequently, each user and rumor was associated with score for each category.

4.4 Results and Analysis

Figure 2 shows that influencer 1 has the highest spread rate, in terms of number of nodes. Table 1 indicates that influencer 1 has the highest number of followers. Table 2 shows the number of total retweets from every rumor spreader.

---

[4] www.uclassify.com/.

The propagation graph of influencer 2, Fig. 3, has nearly half the nodes of influencer 3, Fig. 4. Although, they almost have the same number of followers. This leads us to another questions, *do personality traits affect rumor propagation?, are certain topic more likely to spread by certain types of personality?*.

Table 2. Illustrates the number of retweets from original tweets.

Influencer	Number of retweets
Influencer 1	58
Influencer 2	21
Influencer 3	43

Fig. 2. Influencer 1 propagation graph.

In order to fill this gap, a weighted formula was used to calculate the probability of a user to believe/spread this type of rumor. The proposed formula, as shown in Fig. 5, was used to indicate whether a user would believe a rumour of a certain topic. The formula is utilizing weighted products and works as follows topic score of a statement is obtained from uClassify using the same method used to obtain the interests of the user, the product of the most prominent topic score of a statement and the topic score of the user is divided by the sum of the product of the topic score of a statement and the topic score of the user for all the topics. This formula checks if a rumor (statement) was spread the probability of a user to share the rumor or talk about this statement. This formula was tested against 250 users and for each user we tested an average of 5 rumors that they tweeted about The formula stood correct for 87.55% of the tweets.

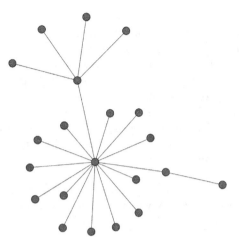

Fig. 3. Influencer 2 propagation graph.

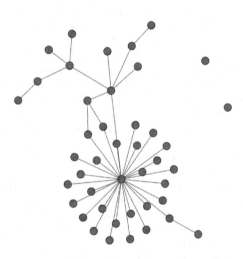

Fig. 4. Influencer 3 propagation graph.

$$\frac{Max\left(Topic\ score\ of\ statement\right)\cdot Topic\ score\ of\ user}{\sum_{n=0}^{Number\ of\ topics}\ Topic\ score\ of\ statement\cdot Topic\ score\ of\ user}$$

Fig. 5. Weighted formula to calculate the probability to spread a rumor.

5   Conclusion

In this survey, we implemented a small experiment to study the effect of different seed nodes in rumor propagation and whether the number of followers affect the rumor spread rate. The experiment showed that the node with higher number of followers leads to a higher rumor propagation than other. However, the result leads to another research question, do the personality affects the rumor spreading. In the light of the research gap, we can investigate how different user personalities affect the rumor propagation. Also, we can further investigate whether some personalities are more vulnerable to share rumors of specific topic more than other personalities.

Acknowledgment. This work has been supported by **Ali Souidan**, a bachelor student in German University in Cairo, who was responsible for the data collection and classifying user interests parts.

References

1. Romero, D.M., Galuba, W., Asur, S., Huberman, B.A.: Influence and passivity in social media. In: Gunopulos, D., Hofmann, T., Malerba, D., Vazirgiannis, M. (eds.) ECML PKDD 2011. LNCS (LNAI), vol. 6913, pp. 18–33. Springer, Heidelberg (2011). https://doi.org/10.1007/978-3-642-23808-6_2
2. Lai, K., et al.: Who falls for rumor? Influence of personality traits on false rumor belief. Personality Individual Differ. **152**, 109520 (2020)
3. Kwon, S., Cha, M., Jung, K.: Rumor detection over varying time windows. PloS One **12**(1), e0168344 (2017)
4. Vosoughi, S., Mohsenvand, M.N., Roy, D.: Rumor gauge: predicting the veracity of rumors on Twitter. ACM Trans. Knowl. Discovery Data (TKDD) **11**(4), 1–36 (2017)
5. Alkhodair, S.A., et al.: Detecting breaking news rumors of emerging topics in social media. Inf. Process. Manag. **57**(2), 102018 (2020)
6. Li, Q., et al.: Rumor detection on social media: datasets, methods and opportunities. arXiv preprint arXiv:1911.07199 (2019)
7. Zeng, L., Starbird, K., Spiro, E.S.: Rumors at the speed of light? Modeling the rate of rumor transmission during crisis. In: 2016 49th Hawaii International Conference on System Sciences (HICSS). IEEE (2016)
8. Chen, X.: The influences of personality and motivation on the sharing of misinformation on social media. In: IConference 2016 Proceedings (2016)
9. Sinnenberg, L., et al.: Twitter as a potential data source for cardiovascular disease research. JAMA Cardiol. **1**(9), 1032–1036 (2016)
10. Zubiaga, A., Liakata, M., Procter, R.: Learning reporting dynamics during breaking news for rumour detection in social media. arXiv preprint arXiv:1610.07363 (2016)
11. Myers, S.A., et al. Information network or social network? The structure of the Twitter follow graph. In: Proceedings of the 23rd International Conference on World Wide Web (2014)
12. Jiang, J., et al.: Rumor source identification in social networks with time-varying topology. IEEE Trans. Dependable Secure Comput. **15**(1), 166–179 (2016)

13. McCrae, R.R., John, O.P.: An introduction to the five-factor model and its applications. J. Personality **60**(2), 175–215 (1992)
14. McElroy, J.C., Hendrickson, A.R., Townsend, A.M., DeMarie, S.M.: Dispositional factors in Internet use: personality versus conitive style. MIS Q. **31**(4), 809–820 (2007)
15. Ross, C., Orr, E.S., Sisic, M., Arseneault, J.M., Simmering, M.G., Orr, R.R.: Personality and motivations associated with Facebook use. Comput. Hum. Behav. **25**(2), 578–586 (2009)
16. Correa, T., Hinsley, A.W., De Zuniga, H.G.: Who interacts on the Web?: the intersection of users' personality and social media use. Comput. Hum. Behav. **26**(2), 247–253 (2010)
17. Sudhir, S., Unnithan, A.B.: Marketplace rumor sharing among young consumers: the role of anxiety and arousal. In: Young Consumers (2019)
18. Chua, A.Y.K., Aricat, R., Goh, D.: Message content in the life of rumors: comparing three rumor types. In: 2017 Twelfth International Conference on Digital Information Management (ICDIM). IEEE (2017)

The Effect of Student-Lecturer Cultural Differences on Engagement in Learning Environments - A Pilot Study

Sherine Safwat[1(✉)], Alia El Bolock[1,2(✉)], Mostafa Alaa[1(✉)],
Sarah Faltaous[3(✉)], Stefan Schneegass[3(✉)], and Slim Abdennadher[1(✉)]

[1] German University in Cairo, Cairo, Egypt
sherine.ashraf.safwat@gmail.com,
{alia.elbolock,mostafa.talaat,slim.abdennadher}@guc.edu.eg
[2] Ulm University, Ulm, Germany
[3] University of Duisburg-Essen, Essen, Germany
{sarah.faltaous,stefan.schneegass}@uni-due.de

Abstract. Recently, virtual reality has taken part in various fields such as education, where virtual reality is used for creating virtual interactive learning environments such as virtual lectures. Culture difference is an effective factor in the learning environment. It affects the students' learning outcome, thus, it is needed to be taken into consideration when designing a virtual learning environment. In this work, we aim to take the initial step in investigating the effect of cultural differences between lecturers and students. We conducted a study where Egyptian students who attended lectures with both Egyptian and German lecturers took different questionnaires. Students answered the Big Five-Inventory 10 (BFI-10) questionnaire, Self-Assessment Manikin (SAM), and designed questions about the impact of student-lecturer cultural differences on students' engagement experience in lectures. Our results showed a significant difference in the valence emotions of students ($p = .023$) in the SAM questionnaire which indicated that Egyptian students thought they were happier in Egyptian lectures over the German ones. We found low correlations with the Big Five Personality traits which were a good indicator of the independence of these personality traits. Finally, more than 50% of participants would be interested in customizing their lecturer's culture as their own culture in an online educational platform. This experiment can pave the road for developers and researchers to have more understanding of new factors that can be included when designing a virtual learning environment.

Keywords: Virtual Reality · Character computing · Culture · Education

1 Introduction

Virtual Reality (VR) provides a new platform for creating highly immersive and interactive media. It utilizes head-mounted displays (HMD) along with motion

© Springer Nature Switzerland AG 2020
F. De La Prieta et al. (Eds.): PAAMS 2020 Workshops, CCIS 1233, pp. 118–128, 2020.
https://doi.org/10.1007/978-3-030-51999-5_10

tracking algorithms to immerse its users in a virtual environment that they can explore and interact with. A virtual environment is a 3D virtual representation of any environment (real or imaginary), where the user can interact virtually with this environment and with other users in said environment [2].

In the past few years, VR has been used in novel and innovative ways across various fields such as; military, gaming, healthcare, tourism, and education [4,13]. With its ability to create immersive virtual environments it is believed that VR can have a pivotal role in the transformation of learning in higher education. For example, virtual lectures that resemble a real lecture could offer a customizable environment suitable for immersive remote learning. Virtual lectures is a novel research field. However, initial studies showed that improvement in social interactions and productivity tools in VR can lead to a greater impact in higher education when compared to conventional learning models [9]. Thus, designing VR educational systems remains an open challenge.

When designing a VR educational system multiple factors should be considered to increase the effectiveness of virtual lectures and motivate students in the class [13]. The lecturer-students relation is very important in the learning process since the learning environment depends on social interaction among lecturers and students. With the tremendously increasing number of international students in universities, a cultural difference can play an important role in affecting student's learning experience. Such differences can lay in the lecturer's verbal communication, reach-ability, equality, students' perception of lecturers' roles, learning traditions, etc. [3,9,12].

Consequently, VR educational systems should take into consideration the cultural differences as a system attribute. This can help VR developers in widening the region of features in their VR learning environment to provide a realistic fruitful learning experience for students.

In this research, we aim to investigate the effect (if any) of the cultural difference between lecturers and students on students' engagement in the lectures. We are concerned with the initial step of understanding if cultural difference between students and lecturers affects the students' engagement in lectures from students' perspective. Hence, our research question arises.

We Formalize Our Research Question as Follows:

– Can culture difference between lecturer and students affect their engagement in lectures in terms of asking/answering questions?

2   Background

Studies were conducted to examine the type of obstacles arose from having multicultural students in lectures from the students' and lecturers' perspectives.

Huerta and poudling wanted to research the challenges faced by overseas students from partner universities in China and India taking the masters degree in software engineering program at BTH University in Sweden. They hypothesized that academic culture diversity between the students' home universities and BTH could be one obstacle for overseas students. The data was collected by interviewing students enrolled in the software engineering program at BTH in focus groups. One of the main themes found in the focus groups was the language difference and using English as the fundamental instruction language. Additionally, the differences in the lecturers teaching methods, wherein the Chinese culture the teachers spoon-feed all knowledge to the students. However; in the Swedish culture lecturers provide only guidance. Besides, Chinese students were unsure about the correct method to contact the lecturers for questions [3].

Another study that discussed the culture difference between students and lecturers from the students' perspective, was conducted by Littlemore. The study investigated the ways the Bangladeshi students interpreted the metaphors used by their academic British lecturers at a British university. Students were asked to interpret and judge the value of some metaphors presented in context. The results suggested that students were most likely to interpret the metaphors and their evaluative function in their value systems and schemata rather than that of their lecturers. Thus, the misinterpretation mainly occurred when the clues in the context were unclear and contained conflicting value systems. This problem could lead students to a misleading interpretation of lecturers' attitudes and conveyed information [5].

On the other hand, Tange examined the problems of the internationalization of Danish higher education from the perspective of the lecturers. Thus, interviews were conducted with administrative and lecturing staff. The findings confirmed an emerging problem for academic staff from the linguistic change from Danish to English during a teaching in international programs. Academic staff reported that this change caused less communication engagement in the lectures. Also, some lecturers who were not used to cultural diversity in the classroom, reported that they couldn't successfully manage the behaviors of some international students that deviated from the practices and norms grounded in the Danish university [12].

Strauss and U conducted semi-structured interviews with lecturers at Auckland University of Technology in New Zealand to investigate the difficulties they faced in group assessments in their multicultural courses. Interviewees highlighted the group selection for projects, reliability, and fairness of the assessment as their main challenges. However, it was noticed that lecturers strongly support multi-culture group projects if assessed correctly as this would enhance the students' social skills and allow sharing knowledge and different views among them [11].

Finally, the previous studies discussed the challenges faced in a multi-cultural classroom from both students' and lecturers' perspective. However, we still miss the engagement side in terms of asking and answering questions in particular from the students' viewpoint. As this engagement part is one of the communication methods in a VR learning environment. Subsequently, this engagement side should be carefully studied so that a better VR learning experience can be offered.

3   Study Design

The principle objective of this research is to investigate if the cultural difference between lecturers and students can affect students' engagement in lectures. Thus, such variables will be taken into consideration when designing a VR educational environment. As an initial step Egyptian students who were given lectures by German and Egyptian lecturers took an online structured questionnaire to collect data and investigate the responses. The questionnaire comprises of 5 sections; respondent's demographics, Big Five-Inventory 10 (BFI-10) questionnaire to describe their personalities and correlate it with their engagement in lectures, Self-Assessment Manikin (SAM) for lectures given by Egyptian lecturer, Self-Assessment Manikin for lectures given by German lecturer to measure the students' emotional responses within the lectures, and finally; students-lecturers culture difference questions rating students' engagement experience in lectures.

3.1   Big Five-Inventory 10 (BFI-10)

The Big Five-Inventory was originally designed by John, Donahue, & Kentle in 1991 as a predominant model for describing personality based on a 44-items scale [7]. The BFI-10 was then developed by Rammstedt et al. for participants with severely limited time [8]. The BFI-10 is an ultra-short version with 10-items scale assessing the Big Five personality traits; extraversion, agreeableness, conscientiousness, emotional stability, and openness [7]. The BFI-10 used in this experiment is shown in Table 1.

Table 1. The Big Five-Inventory-10 (BFI-10) used in the questionnaire

I see myself as someone who..	Disagree strongly	Disagree a little	Neither agree nor disagree	Agree a little	Agree strongly
1. ...is reserved	(1)	(2)	(3)	(4)	(5)
2. ...is generally trusting	(1)	(2)	(3)	(4)	(5)
3. ...tends to be lazy	(1)	(2)	(3)	(4)	(5)
4. ...is relaxed, handles stress well	(1)	(2)	(3)	(4)	(5)
5. ...has few artistic interests	(1)	(2)	(3)	(4)	(5)
6. ...is outgoing, sociable	(1)	(2)	(3)	(4)	(5)
7. ...tends to find fault with others	(1)	(2)	(3)	(4)	(5)
8. ...does a thorough job	(1)	(2)	(3)	(4)	(5)
9. ...gets nervous easily	(1)	(2)	(3)	(4)	(5)
10. ...has an active imagination	(1)	(2)	(3)	(4)	(5)

3.2   Self-Assessment Manikin (SAM)

The Self-Assessment Manikin (SAM) is a picture-oriented questionnaire developed by Lang (1980) to measure emotional responses [6]. The questionnaire is designed to measure three features of emotional response; valence, arousal, and dominance to a given stimuli [1]:

- **Valence:** It measures positive or negative emotion, ranging from unhappy to happy feelings.
- **Arousal:** It measures excited or apathetic emotion, ranging from sleepiness or boredom to excitement.
- **Dominance:** It measures the extent to which the emotion makes the subjects feel in control of the situation, ranging from fully in control to not in control at all [10].

Specifically, there are single-item scales for each factor. Each scale consists of five pictorial representations. The version of the SAM used in this experiment is shown in Fig. 1.

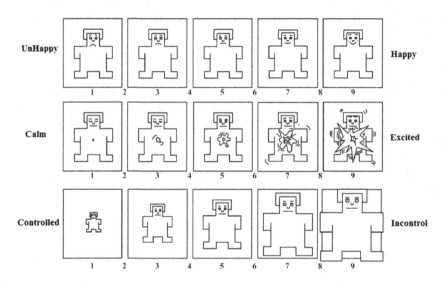

Fig. 1. The Self-Assessment Manikin (SAM) used in the questionnaire

In this version of SAM, the subject can choose any number from 1–9 over each scale.

3.3   Students-Lecturers Culture Difference Questions

A list of 12 questions is prepared to investigate whether the cultural difference between the students and lecturers will affect the engagement of the students with the lecturer in the lectures.

Questions can be divided into two categories; one related to real-life lectures while the other covers online educational platforms. Questions range from multiple choice and yes-no questions the tackling the engagement of students in lectures given by Egyptian, German or both lecturers, communication problems faced in both lectures if exists, and preferences of customization of the lecturer's culture in an online learning environment as presented in Fig. 2.

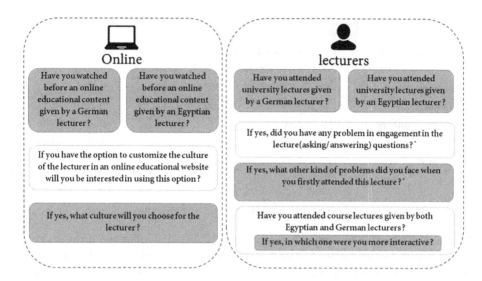

Fig. 2. The engagement in lectures questions used in the questionnaire
* Questions that were asked once for Egyptian lecturers and once for German lecturers

3.4 Participants and Procedures

The sample consisted of 20 Egyptian students (15 male) with ages ranging from 20 to 22 years (M = 20.1, SD = 0.7) studying at the GIU in Berlin for a semester abroad. Students were enrolled in study programs at different faculties including Media Engineering and technology (30%), Information Engineering and Technology (20%), Engineering and Material Science (45%), and Law (5%). Participants answered the online questionnaire once related to the lectures during that semester. Lectures on that semester were given by either German lecturers living in Germany or Egyptian lecturers living in Egypt and coming bi-monthly to give lectures.

4 Results

4.1 Big Five-Inventory 10 (BFI-10)

BFI-10 data were entered into an SPSS for Windows for Pearson's correlation analysis. From the participants' ratings on the BFI-10 items, the average score was calculated for each of the big five personality dimensions. The results are shown in Table 2.

Conscientiousness showed the highest values, while on the other hand neuroticism showed the lowest value. Whilst, agreeableness, extraversion, and openness showed similar values. It was detected the existence of low correlations for the big five traits of personality which is a good indicator of the independence of these personality traits.

Table 2. Average, standard deviation, and correlations for the BFI-10 dimensions

Personality trait score	Matrix of correlations						
	Mean	SD.	Extrav.	Agreeb.	Conscient.	Neurot.	Open.
Extraversion	6.85	2.18	1.00	0.12	0.36	0.17	0.34
Agreeableness	6.8	1.77		1.00	0.11	0.22	−0.14
Conscientiousness	6.9	1.80			1.00	−0.31	0.05
Neuroticism	4.95	1.70				1.00	−0.03
Openness	6.65	1.35					1.00

4.2   Self-Assessment Manikin (SAM)

We analyzed the SAM scales of valence, arousal, and dominance using paired sample t-test, to determine if there was any significant difference in the emotions of the Egyptian students between attending the lectures given by Egyptian and German lecturers. The results showed a significant difference only in the valence emotions of students ($p = .023$). There was an increase in the mean valence scores for Egyptian lecturers over the German lecturers as represented in Fig. 3.

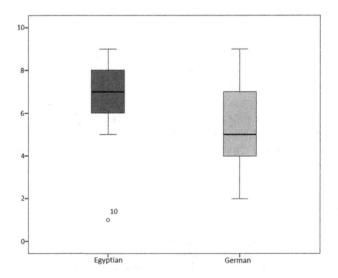

Fig. 3. The SAM valence scores for the Egyptian and German lecturers

4.3   Students-Lecturers Culture Difference Questions

The results of the questionnaire showed that 50% of the students didn't encounter difficulties in the engagement in the lectures given by their German lecturer, whereas only 20% found problems in engagement in the lectures given by Egyptian lecturer as presented in Fig. 4.

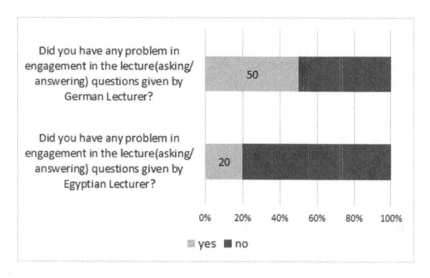

Fig. 4. The percentage of students facing difficulties in lectures

Students who faced difficulties in the prior lectures; reported that these difficulties were related to problems in asking and answering questions due to culture difference, language difference, and different teaching techniques which were aligned with [3]. Students chose the kind of problems they face from our provided choices as elaborated in Fig. 5 and some other mentioned problems as shown in Table 3.

Finally, about 52% of the students would be interested in customizing their lecturers' culture as their own culture in an online educational platform.

Table 3. More problems mentioned by the students during the lectures

Egyptian	German
Different exams style 5%	Different teaching techniques 5%
–	Problem in communicating questions and answers 10%
–	Less interaction 5%

5   Discussion

The purpose of the present study was to investigate whether the cultural difference between students and lecturers can play a role in students' engagement in

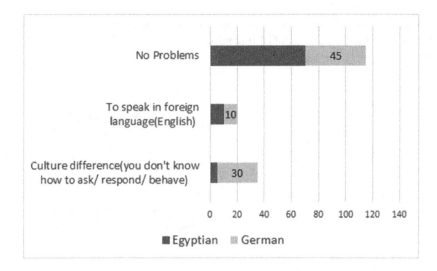

Fig. 5. The percentage of students facing specific problems in lectures

the lecture, and by the engagement we meant specifically asking and answering questions within the lectures. The findings of this initial study can help developers who are interested in designing online educational systems and virtual teachers in widening their metrics of customization in their platforms. These online educational platforms will be taken more into consideration; since they can be sensible choice for students who won't be able to join schools or universities due to various reasons (e.g. abrupt pandemics).

Our analysis showed that students felt happier when attending lecturers having the same culture rather than a different culture. However, the engagement in the lecture didn't depend on the culture of the lecturer. We hypothesis that there could be more factors affecting; such as the personality of the student and the lecturer, using a foreign language in lectures, and the teaching method. More studies are needed to examine these factors and others.

6   Limitations

Limitations of the present study include the fact that only one cohort of students with convergent age from one university, and culture was included in the study. The sample size needs to be increased with much diversity in age, culture, and studies. However, our sample can be considered good for a pilot study where more investigation is required. Additionally, our study didn't take into account other metrics as gender and more variant personality traits. Future studies can be done to consider these factors in their measurements.

7   Conclusion

In conclusion, this study has met its aim of understanding the effect of cultural differences between lecturers and students on the students' engagement in the lectures. Students who attended lectures with Egyptian and German lecturers answered questionnaires; BFI-10, SAM, and questions related to the effect of culture-difference on their engagement in the lectures. The results showed that students can be much happier in lectures given by Egyptians; however, their engagement in the lectures depends on multiple factors, not just the cultural difference.

We hope our work can serve as an initial building block to understanding what increases the engagement of the students in the lectures. We also hope that after understanding how to maximize the engagement of students in lectures, developers can build enhanced VR educational systems taking into account the cultural factor. These systems can be help students in having a better fruitful educational experience.

References

1. Bradley, M.M., Lang, P.J.: Measuring emotion: the self-assessment manikin and the semantic differential. J. Behav. Ther. Exp. Psychiatry **25**(1), 49–59 (1994)
2. Fabri, M., Moore, D.J., Hobbs, D.J.: Face value: towards emotionally expressive avatars. AISB02, Imperial College, London, UK (2002)
3. González-Huerta, J., Poulding, S.: Analysing the impact of differences in academic cultures on the learning experiences of overseas students (2017)
4. Hsieh, M., Lee, J.: Preliminary study of VR and AR applications in medical and healthcare education. J. Nurs. Health Stud. **3**(1), 1 (2018)
5. Littlemore, J.: The effect of cultural background on metaphor interpretation. Metaphor Symbol **18**(4), 273–288 (2003)
6. Morris, J.D.: Observations: SAM: the self-assessment manikin; an efficient cross-cultural measurement of emotional response. J. Advertising Res. **35**(6), 63–68 (1995)
7. Rammstedt, B., John, O.P.: Measuring personality in one minute or less: a 10-item short version of the big five inventory in English and German. J. Res. Pers. **41**(1), 203–212 (2007)
8. Rammstedt, B., Kemper, C.J., Klein, M.C., Beierlein, C., Kovaleva, A.: A short scale for assessing the big five dimensions of personality: 10 item big five inventory (BFI-10). Methods Data Analyses **7**(2), 17 (2017)
9. Slavova, Y., Mu, M.: A comparative study of the learning outcomes and experience of VR in education. In: 2018 IEEE Conference on Virtual Reality and 3D User Interfaces (VR), pp. 685–686, March 2018. https://doi.org/10.1109/VR.2018. 8446486
10. Stevens, F., Murphy, D., Smith, S.L.: The self-assessment manikin and heart rate: responses to auralised soundscapes. In: Interactive Audio System Symposium, New York (2016)
11. Strauss, P., Alice, U.: Group assessments: dilemmas facing lecturers in multicultural tertiary classrooms. High Educ. Res. Dev. **26**(2), 147–161 (2007)

12. Tange, H.: Caught in the tower of babel: university lecturers' experiences with internationalisation. Lang. Intercultural Commun. **10**(2), 137–149 (2010)
13. Theonas, G., Hobbs, D., Rigas, D.: Employing virtual lecturers' facial expressions in virtual educational environments. IJVR **7**(1), 31–44 (2008)

Workshop on MAS for Complex Networks and Social Computation (CNSC)

Workshop on MAS for Complex Networks and Social Computation (CNSC)

Many of the systems that can be found in our environment can be modelled as complex adaptive systems that consist of a dynamic network of agents (which may represent individuals, businesses, services, resources) that perform a set of activities in parallel and react to what other agents are doing. Multi-agent systems are considered a suitable tool for the study of complex adaptive systems and specially those distributed and dynamic. The MAS for Complex Networks and Social Computation (CNSC) workshop is focused on providing a forum in which researchers from many disciplines and methodological backgrounds can discuss ideas, research questions, recent results, and future challenges in this emerging area of research and public interest.

Organization

Organizing Committee

Vicente Botti   Universitat Politècnica de València, Spain
Elena Del Val   Universitat Politècnica de València, Spain

Program Committee

Jaime Andrés Rincón   Universitat Politècnica de València, Spain
Joaquin Taverner   Universitat Politècnica de València, Spain
Angelo Costa   Universidade do Minho, Portugal
Jaume Jordán   Universitat Politècnica de València, Spain
Carlos Carrascosa   Universitat Politècnica de València, Spain
Alberto Palomares   Universitat Politècnica de València, Spain
Víctor Sanchez   Florida Universitaria, Spain

An Ontology of Changes in Normative Systems from an Agentive Viewpoint

Matteo Cristani[1(✉)], Claudio Tomazzoli[1(✉)], Francesco Olivieri[2(✉)], and Luca Pasetto[1(✉)]

[1] Department of Computer Science, University of Verona, Verona, Italy
{matteo.cristani,claudio.tomazzoli,luca.pasetto}@univr.it
[2] Data61, CSIRO, Brisbane, Australia
francesco.olivieri@data61.csiro.au

Abstract. Defeasible deontic logic has shown to be expressive enough to represent a normative system, and therefore compliance to such a system can be automatically checked by means of classical model checking techniques of logical systems. However, normative systems are not static, as they can be actively changed by the legislator over time, directly, by changing one norm. Moreover norms can change passively, either by effect of the change of another piece of the normative system, or by means of the change of meaning that affects terms employed in the norm.

Although some efforts have been carried out by scholars in the field of legal reasoning about norm change, there is a lack of uniformity in the representation of these changes, and this is an issue when we aim at deploying the law as an automated platform: we need to introduce changes as effects in the semantics of derivation in a logical system, when the unified viewpoint admits a unified representation as well. We adopt the logical paradigm of agency and provide a classification of changes from an agentive viewpoint that allows a unified representation within the logical language for agents LegalRuleML.

Keywords: Norm change · Normative systems · Rule-based systems

1 Introduction

Deontic defeasible logic is one of the most successful frameworks for the representation of normative systems. To determine the exact application of a norm we need to identify the structure of the norm from the viewpoint of its *temporal* and *territorial* extensions and its application field, namely the individuals who are subject to the norm.

The usage of deontic defeasible logic is common for two reasons: since the normative systems are represented in a declarative fashion it is relatively easy to manage tests for compliance [11], the process of revision in defeasible logic is easier than it is in classical logic, especially when considered from a conflict-resolution perspective [7,10,12,20,21].

© Springer Nature Switzerland AG 2020
F. De La Prieta et al. (Eds.): PAAMS 2020 Workshops, CCIS 1233, pp. 131–142, 2020.
https://doi.org/10.1007/978-3-030-51999-5_11

Many efforts are known in the literature of deontic defeasible logic for denoting normative systems, and some efforts have been also put on the problem of managing change in normative systems as captured by the above mentioned scheme [3,13,14]. In this paper we deal with the problem of classifying in a general framework the ways in which a norm can change, either actively, namely by means of the intervention of a legislator, or passively, as a consequence of the change in the meaning of terms.

The rest of the paper is organised as follows: Sect. 2 presents the framework used for the definition of the problem, Sect. 3 is devoted to discuss ways in which such a framework provides room for many different explicit changes, and Sect. 4 shows the implicit changes. Finally Sect. 5 takes some conclusions and sketches further work.

2   Norms in Defeasible Deontic Logic

We assume that norms are represented in defeasible deontic logic by the definition that follows.

Definition 1 (Norm). *A norm n is a finite set of rules in defeasible deontic logic, where each rule takes one of the following forms:*

- *A definition $l_1, ..., l_n \rightarrow l$,*
- *A fact l,*
- *An unconditional rule in the norm body $\langle X, t_i, t_f, \tau \rangle : \sim \mathcal{M} l$, or*
- *A conditional rule in the norm body $\langle X, t_i, t_f, \tau \rangle : l_1, ..., l_n \Rightarrow \sim \mathcal{M} l$,*

where $l, l_1, ..., l_n$, with $n \geq 1$, are propositional literals that represent a state, an action, or an event; $\mathcal{M}$ is a deontic operator indicating an obligation O or a prohibition F; X is a string indicating the application group of the rule; t_i is a positive finite number indicating the start date of the rule; t_f is the expiration date of the rule, that is a positive finite number for a temporary rule or $+\infty$ for a non-temporary rule; and τ is a string indicating the territory the rule is applicable in. The operator $\sim$ represents either the empty string or the logical negation $\neg$.

As common in modal logic, the modals are dualised, in the specific case of deontic logic, $\neg Ol \Leftrightarrow \neg F \neg l$, and corresponding duals for $\neg O \neg l$ or $\neg Fl$. There has been a long debate in the community of deontic logic about the form that the logic should have in terms of modal axioms, for different and complex reasons [6,9,18]. Moreover, an explicit focus has been posed on the problem of *explicit permissions*. Usual representation of permits in deontic logic is based on the structural dualisation of prohibition: you have the permission P to do something when you have no duty to do its opposite $Pl \Leftrightarrow \neg O \neg l$. However, as shown in [8], explicit permissions are a more complex matter, that will be treated, for what regards changes, in further studies.

When a norm n changes, the set of the worlds that satisfy n, the *legal worlds*, and the set of the worlds that do not satisfy n, the *illegal worlds*, vary accordingly

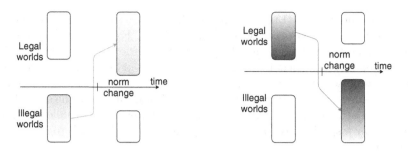

Fig. 1. The effects of changing a norm by extension or by restriction.

[4,5]. In particular, if n is modified by introducing liberalizations or decriminalizations, the set of legal worlds grows and the set of illegal worlds shrinks because some of the illegal worlds become legal, while if n is modified by introducing restrictions, the set of illegal worlds grows and the set of legal worlds shrinks because some of the legal worlds become illegal. The situation is illustrated in Fig. 1.

The legal effects of n can apply also in the past or in the future of its temporal validity. For this reason, whenever a norm n is changed, there may be a transition phase in which its old legal effects still hold. For example, if the norm change includes a restriction, and the action that is being restricted has a prolonged duration, the people involved in the restriction should be allowed some time to change their behaviour. Indeed, since decisions that were taken before the norm change are not contrary to the norm, they have to be protected. This is done by issuing a *transitory norm* that holds during the transition phase. Typically, such a norm consists of one or more *reparation chains* of the form $Ol\ Ol'$, where O is the obligation operator and l, l' are propositional literals indicating states or actions. A reparation chain $Ol\ Ol'$ is read as "Ol' holds whenever Ol is not fulfilled".

3   Explicit Norm Change

We say that norm change is *explicit* when the actual code of a norm n is changed by the legislator [1,2].

Temporal Change and Misalignment of Legal Consequences. We show here six operators that change the temporal validity of a rule in two different combined ways. The intuitive idea is to decrease or increase the start date t_i of the rule or its expiration date t_f. One limitation is that the start date t_i can be anticipated only if it is in the future. If the validity of a norm n has an *expiration date* attached to it, that is, $t_f \neq +\infty$, n is called a *temporary norm* (the problem of modifying temporary norms is addressed by Cristani et al. [3]), whilst in a wider scenario, the problem of abrogations and annulments have been addressed by Governatori et al. [14] from a technical viewpoint and further in details by

Governatori and Rotolo [13]. A change to t_i may be an *anticipation*, when t_i is decreased, or a *postposition*, when t_i is increased. For a temporary norm n, two other kinds of temporal modifications, *anticipation* and *extension* of the expiration date t_f, may occur. Temporal anticipation of t_f consists in decreasing t_f, while temporal extension of t_f consists in increasing t_f. Moreover, for a norm n that is a *non-temporary norm*, i.e., $t_f = +\infty$, modifications to the start date t_i are done by the same operator that works on temporary norms, while changes to t_f are done by a specialized operator, that intuitively corresponds to annulments or abrogations.

These temporal changes for a labelled rule $\langle X,\ t_i,\ t_f,\ \tau \rangle : r$, where r may be conditional or unconditional, are defined through the following norm revision operators, with δ a finite positive number:

- Anticipation of the start date from t_i to $t'_i = t_i - \delta$, with $t_i > t'_i$. For real-world legal systems t'_i is typically in the future with respect to the issuing moment

$$\diagup_{t_i,\delta} (\langle X,\ t_i,\ t_f,\ \tau \rangle : r) = \langle X,\ t_i - \delta,\ t_f,\ \tau \rangle : r$$

- Postposition of the start date from t_i to $t'_i = t_i + \delta$, with $t_i < t'_i$

$$\diagdown_{t_i,\delta} (\langle X,\ t_i,\ t_f,\ \tau \rangle : r) = \langle X,\ t_i + \delta,\ t_f,\ \tau \rangle : r$$

- Anticipation of the expiration date from t_f to $t'_f = t_f - \delta$, with $t_f > t'_f$ and $t_f \neq +\infty$

$$\diagup_{t_f,\delta} (\langle X,\ t_i,\ t_f,\ \tau \rangle : r) = \langle X,\ t_i,\ t_f - \delta,\ \tau \rangle : r$$

- Anticipation of the expiration date from $t_f = +\infty$ to $t'_f = t_i + \delta$, with $t'_f \neq +\infty$

$$\diagup_{+\infty,\delta} (\langle X,\ t_i,\ t_f,\ \tau \rangle : r) = \langle X,\ t_i,\ t_i + \delta,\ \tau \rangle : r$$

- Extension of the expiration date from t_f to $t'_f = t_f + \delta$, with $t_f < t'_f$ and $t'_f \neq +\infty$

$$\diagdown_{t_f,\delta} (\langle X,\ t_i,\ t_f,\ \tau \rangle : r) = \langle X,\ t_i,\ t_f + \delta,\ \tau \rangle : r$$

- Extension of the expiration date from $t_f \neq +\infty$ to $t'_f = +\infty$

$$\diagdown_{t_f,+\infty} (\langle X,\ t_i,\ t_f,\ \tau \rangle : r) = \langle X,\ t_i,\ +\infty,\ \tau \rangle : r$$

The operators are six, and not eight, because we assume that $t_i > 0$ always has to hold in our framework. In the current doctrinal language postposition (and in some cases also anticipation) is named *derogation*. In this paper we employ a more *agentive* term set for the reason that we mean to focus upon the *taxonomies* much more than the legal structures. The main difference among the revision operators is therefore defined on the way in which they modify the norms [15–17,19]. The admissibility in the legal system is treated separately.

Another peculiarity to be aware of is that after a norm n is *issued*, there can be a temporal interval before n is enacted and becomes *valid*, where the temporal validity of n is defined as the interval in which n can be applied. In this paper

Table 1. The nine possible temporal configurations.

Configuration name	Configuration	Configuration class
T_1	$t \leq t' \leq t_i < t_f$	FTR
T_2	$t \leq t_i \leq t' \leq t_f$	FTR
T_3	$t \leq t_i < t_f \leq t'$	FTR
T_4	$t_i \leq t < t' \leq t_f$	PTR
T_5	$t_i \leq t \leq t_f \leq t'$	PTR
T_6	$t_i < t_f \leq t < t'$	PTN
P_1	$t < t' \leq t_i$	FR
P_2	$t \leq t_i \leq t'$	FR
P_3	$t_i \leq t < t'$	PR

we do not analyse effects on the modifiability of the issuing and validity interval, focusing on the modification of temporal validity so far.

We employ t as the issue time instant, t_i as the initial validity time instant and t_f as the final validity time instant. Operators can move either the initial validity time instant forward or backward, and the final validity time instant forward or backward, but cannot move the issue time instant t, as that instant is a fact. There are systems subject to the principle of *natural issue* where it is not possible to provide issue of a norm in the past (lex posterior derogat priori). However, in many systems, at least for certain matters, and in nature of certain operations, it is possible (for instance when a norm is issued in a retroactive form in order to substantiate some principles expressed in other norms, or when some form of discontinuity in the normative system is implemented, in presence, for instance, of the suppression of some sort of previous regime). Therefore, we assume that the original ordering of the three values is free, provided that $t_i < t_f$ is assumed, thereby instituting three ontological classes of norms in terms of temporal issue:

- *Future temporary regulation (FTR)* $t \leq t_i < t_f$;
- *Past temporary repair (PTR)* $t_i < t < t_f$
- *Past temporary norm (PTN)* $t_i < t_f \leq t$.

Legal systems admitting past norms are quite unusual, and generally considered *unfair* as they attribute guilt to behaviours that have not been regulated before. However, there are cases in which past repairs have been introduced, often in the form of regular permanent norms, establishing that something that was *unregulated* in the past is now regulated. The pre-existing norm is issued for foundational principles, as they forbid behaviours that have not been considered in the past. The most commonly known example is the introduction *in judicio* of the notion of *war crime* during the Nuremberg Trials or the Tokyo Trial. Notice that when a norm is *permanent* the types of norms are reduced to two (*Future regulations (FR)* and *Past repairs (PR)*).

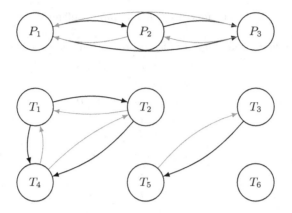

Fig. 2. The transitions on configurations after applying the anticipation of the start date operator $\diagup_{t_i,\delta}$ or the postposition of the start date operator $\diagdown_{t_i,\delta}$.

A summary of the ontological configurations that are possible in this temporal framework is presented in Table 1, where t' is the *reform time*, the time in which the norm is changed. As intuition suggests, we assume that the reform time is after the issue time, that is, $t < t'$. By using one of the four operators defined above we can also substantiate *ontological changes to a norm*, and an overview of the ontological modifications that are provided by the temporal operators is presented by the graphs in Figs. 2, 3, and 4. For instance, Fig. 2 shows the transitions on temporal configurations after the application of the anticipation of the start date operator $\diagup_{t_i,\delta}$ or the postposition of the start date operator $\diagdown_{t_i,\delta}$. Notice how the graph exemplifies that the two operators $\diagup_{t_i,\delta}$ and $\diagdown_{t_i,\delta}$ are symmetric, as the corresponding directed edges are symmetric. In an analogous manner, the graphs in Figs. 3 and 4 show that also the pairs $\diagup_{t_f,\delta}$ and $\diagdown_{t_f,\delta}$ and $\diagup_{+\infty,\delta}$ and $\diagdown_{t_f,+\infty}$ are symmetric.

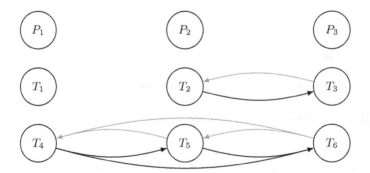

Fig. 3. The transitions on configurations after applying the anticipation of the expiration date operator $\diagup_{t_f,\delta}$ or the extension of the expiration date operator $\diagdown_{t_f,\delta}$.

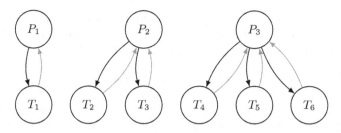

Fig. 4. The transitions on configurations after applying the anticipation of the expiration date operator $\nearrow_{+\infty,\delta}$ or the extension of the expiration date operator $\searrow_{t_f,+\infty}$, that is, the operators that change a finite t_f to $+\infty$, and vice-versa.

Given the three ontological classes and the temporal configurations and having shown how the operators make the configurations transition between each other, we can give the definition of a *pure operator*.

Definition 2 (Pure operator). *A norm revision operator OP is a pure operator if either*

- *for every labelled rule $\langle X,\ t_i,\ t_f,\ \tau \rangle\ :\ r$ of a given ontological class C, when OP is applied to $\langle X,\ t_i,\ t_f,\ \tau \rangle\ :\ r$, the resulting labelled rule $OP(\langle X,\ t_i,\ t_f,\ \tau \rangle : r)$ always has ontological class C', with $C' \neq C$, or*
- *for every labelled rule $\langle X,\ t_i,\ t_f,\ \tau \rangle\ :\ r$ of a given ontological class C, when OP is applied to $\langle X,\ t_i,\ t_f,\ \tau \rangle\ :\ r$, the resulting labelled rule $OP(\langle X,\ t_i,\ t_f,\ \tau \rangle : r)$ always has ontological class C.*

In Examples 1, 2 and 3 we analyze whether the operators presented thus far are pure operators or not.

Example 1. Consider the operators $\nearrow_{t_i,\delta}$ and $\searrow_{t_i,\delta}$. We have that for a rule s in configuration P_1, i.e., with class FR, $\nearrow_{t_f,\delta}(s)$ may be either in configuration P_2, i.e., with class FR, or in configuration P_3, i.e., with class PR. Therefore, the operator $\nearrow_{t_i,\delta}$ is not pure. Indeed, the operator $\searrow_{t_i,\delta}$ is not pure either because it is symmetric to $\nearrow_{t_i,\delta}$.

Example 2. Consider the operators $\nearrow_{t_f,\delta}$ and $\searrow_{t_f,\delta}$. We have that for a rule s in configuration T_4, i.e., with class PTR, $\nearrow_{t_f,\delta}(s)$ may be either in configuration T_5, i.e., with class PTR, or in configuration T_6, i.e., with class PTN. Therefore, the operator $\nearrow_{t_f,\delta}$ is not pure. Indeed, the operator $\searrow_{t_f,\delta}$ is not pure either because it is symmetric to $\nearrow_{t_f,\delta}$.

Example 3. Consider the operators $\nearrow_{+\infty,\delta}$ and $\searrow_{t_f,+\infty}$. These operators always change the ontological class of a norm, as they make a permanent norm temporary, and vice-versa. Therefore, these two operators are pure.

A norm n may be *removed* from a normative system. In general, n may be removed by *annulment* or *abrogation*. Annulment makes a norm n invalid by removing it from the legal system, and usually n is suppressed in a *retroactive* fashion, that is, n is not valid since a time prior to its suppression. Abrogation suppresses only the legal effects of a norm n, and typically it is not retroactive.

Territorial Change. A rule $\langle X, t_i, t_f, \tau \rangle : r$ of a norm n is valid only in the specified territory τ. The territory τ is classified as an element in a hierarchy of territories, where some territories may include τ (the *superterritories* of τ), and other territories may be included in τ (the *subterritories* of τ). For instance, see Fig. 5, which shows a classification of the states that are members of the European Union. The legislator may change the rule $\langle X, t_i, t_f, \tau \rangle : r$ by making it valid in a different territory τ', that may be a superterritory of τ or a subterritory of τ. We give here two operators for this purpose:

- Extension of the territory of validity from τ to one of its superterritories Λ

$$\uparrow_{\tau, \Lambda} (\langle X, t_i, t_f, \tau \rangle : r) = \langle X, t_i, t_f, \Lambda \rangle : r$$

- Shrinkage of the territory of validity from τ to one of its subterritories V

$$\downarrow_{\tau, V} (\langle X, t_i, t_f, \tau \rangle : r) = \langle X, t_i, t_f, V \rangle : r$$

Change in Application Topic. A norm n may regulate a specific action or topic t, for instance $t = fishing$. The legislator may change n by expanding t to t', for instance $t' = fishing\ or\ hunting$; by restricting t to t', for instance $t' = carp\ fishing$; or by changing t to t', for instance $t' = hunting$.

Change in Application Group. A rule $\langle X, t_i, t_f, \tau \rangle : r$ of a norm n is valid only for the specified group X of people. The group X is classified as an element in a hierarchy of groups, where some groups may include X (the *supergroups* of X), and other groups may be included in X (the *subgroups* of X). For instance, see Fig. 6, which shows how different professional groups are classified by the International Labour Organization (ILO) in the International Standard Classification of Occupations (ISCO-08). Notice that a classification based on professional categories is just one among the many ways to classify groups of people, other examples may be classifications by marital status or by native language. The legislator may change the rule $\langle X, t_i, t_f, \tau \rangle : r$ by making it valid for a different group X', that may be a supergroup of X or a subgroup of X. We give here two operators for this purpose:

- Extension of the application group from X to one of its supergroups Δ

$$\Uparrow_{X, \Delta} (\langle X, t_i, t_f, \tau \rangle : r) = \langle \Delta, t_i, t_f, \tau \rangle : r$$

- Restriction of the application group from X to one of its subgroups ∇

$$\Downarrow_{X, \nabla} (\langle X, t_i, t_f, \tau \rangle : r) = \langle \nabla, t_i, t_f, \tau \rangle : r$$

An action that is usually forbidden, but permitted to a group X of people, is called a *privilege* for X. An action that is usually obligatory, but not obligatory for a group X of people, is called an *exemption* for X. An obligation or a prohibition that is applied only to a group X of people is called a *proper obligation* for X or a *proper prohibition* for X, respectively.

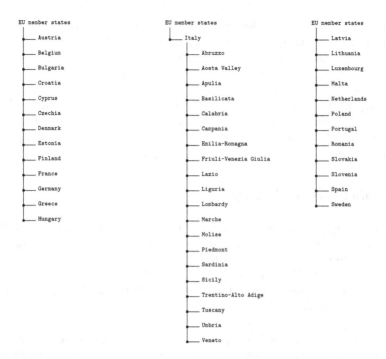

Fig. 5. The classification of the 27 states that are members of the European Union (EU), with a focus on Italy and its 20 regions.

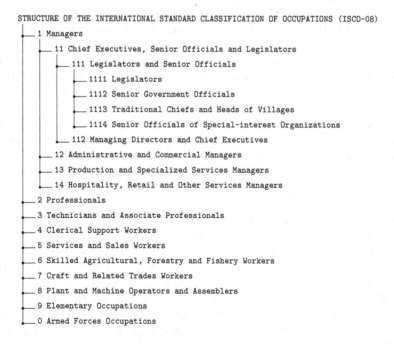

Fig. 6. The ISCO-08 classification of occupational titles, with a focus on the unit group of legislators and senior officials.

Change in Definitions. The legislator may change a norm n by changing the definitions that are adopted by n. Given a definition represented by a strict rule $l_1, ..., l_n \to l$, the definition may be *strengthened*, as in $l_1, ..., l_{n-1} \to l$, *weakened*, as in $l_1, ..., l_n, l_{n+1} \to l$, or *removed* from the normative system.

Change in Applicability Conditions. The legislator may change a conditional rule $\langle X, t_i, t_f, \tau \rangle : l_1, ..., l_n \Rightarrow \sim \mathcal{M} \, l$ by changing the conditions that make it applicable. The rule may be *strengthened*, as in $\langle X, t_i, t_f, \tau \rangle : l_1, ..., l_{n-1} \Rightarrow \sim \mathcal{M} \, l$, or *weakened*, as in $\langle X, t_i, t_f, \tau \rangle : l_1, ..., l_n, l_{n+1} \Rightarrow \sim \mathcal{M} \, l$.

4 Implicit Norm Change

We say that norm change is *implicit* when the actual code of a norm n itself has not changed, but its effects have changed because its context has changed: the region of space or the group of people that n can be applied to have changed independently of it. Norm n may also change because the semantics of legal terminology has changed, for instance because there has been a shift in how some topics are perceived by the public.

Territorial Change. A labelled rule $\langle X, t_i, t_f, \tau \rangle : r$ of a norm n is subjected to an implicit territorial change when the region of space τ that it refers to has changed. Spatial boundaries may be *bona fide* boundaries or *fiat* boundaries. Bona fide boundaries are marked by physical features of the area they constrain, while fiat boundaries are induced through human demarcation.

A rule r that is valid only in a specific region τ of space changes its effects when τ changes. Bona fide boundaries may change because of a change in the physical features of the area, or they may be converted to fiat boundaries. Fiat boundaries of a region τ of space may be changed in order to capture a different region τ' of space, or they may be converted to bona fide boundaries.

Change in Application Group. A labelled rule $\langle X, t_i, t_f, \tau \rangle : r$ of a norm n is applicable only to a specific group X of people and implicitly changes its effects whenever X changes independently of r. This may happen because an external norm that defines group X has changed, or because the perception of what people constitute group X has changed in society.

Change in Semantics of Legal Terminology. Whenever the meaning of legal terminology adopted in norm n changes, the effects of n change accordingly. This implicit change may happen because of a modification in other norms that give the legal terminology, similarly to an explicit change in the definitions of the norm, or because society has changed its perception of the meaning of some words. For example, the Eighth Amendment to the United States Constitution states that a *cruel and unusual* punishment should not be inflicted, but what makes a punishment cruel and unusual is something that gets revised as acceptance in society evolves.

Change in the Norms Hierarchy. Each norm n is part of a norms hierarchy, where norms are ordered by the body of law that issued them and by application topic. The *lex superior* doctrine states that, when in conflict, a law issued by a body of law of greater legitimacy overrides a law issued by an inferior body of law. The *lex specialis* doctrine states that, when in conflict, a law governing a specific topic overrides a law that governs a more general subject. Therefore, the effects of norm n may implicitly change also because a norm that overrides n in the hierarchy has been added, changed or removed from the normative system.

5   Conclusions and Further Work

In this paper we discussed a general framework within which we classify the possible types of changes that a norm can be subject to. The classification is defined in an abstract way and many efforts are still required to solve the problems arising from the application of the peculiarities of the classes to single cases in order to make the model work in an appropriate way in all the specific cases. More in detail we are investigating extensions to the issue and reform models, exploring the non-trivial relationship between application group and application topic of a norm, and studying the ways in which territorial changes can interfere with temporal ones.

References

1. Broersen, J.: Issues in designing logical models for norm change. In: Vouros, G., Artikis, A., Stathis, K., Pitt, J. (eds.) OAMAS 2008. LNCS (LNAI), vol. 5368, pp. 1–17. Springer, Heidelberg (2009). https://doi.org/10.1007/978-3-642-02377-4_1
2. Castelfranchi, C.: A cognitive framing for norm change. In: Dignum, V., Noriega, P., Sensoy, M., Sichman, J.S.S. (eds.) COIN 2015. LNCS (LNAI), vol. 9628, pp. 22–41. Springer, Cham (2016). https://doi.org/10.1007/978-3-319-42691-4_2
3. Cristani, M., Olivieri, F., Rotolo, A.: Changes to temporary norms, pp. 39–48 (2017)
4. Dastani, M., Meyer, J.J., Tinnemeier, N.: Programming norm change. J. Appl. Non-Class. Log. **22**(1–2), 151–180 (2012)
5. De, S., Nau, D., Gelfand, M.: Understanding norm change: an evolutionary game-theoretic approach, vol. 3, pp. 1433–1441 (2017)
6. Governatori, G., Olivieri, F., Calardo, E., Rotolo, A., Cristani, M.: Sequence semantics for normative agents. In: Baldoni, M., Chopra, A.K., Son, T.C., Hirayama, K., Torroni, P. (eds.) PRIMA 2016. LNCS (LNAI), vol. 9862, pp. 230–246. Springer, Cham (2016). https://doi.org/10.1007/978-3-319-44832-9_14
7. Governatori, G., Olivieri, F., Cristani, M., Scannapieco, S.: Revision of defeasible preferences. Int. J. Approx. Reason. **104**, 205–230 (2019)
8. Governatori, G., Olivieri, F., Rotolo, A., Scannapieco, S.: Computing strong and weak permissions in defeasible logic. J. Philos. Log. **42**(6), 799–829 (2013). https://doi.org/10.1007/s10992-013-9295-1
9. Governatori, G., Olivieri, F., Rotolo, A., Scannapieco, S., Cristani, M.: Picking up the best goal an analytical study in defeasible logic. In: Morgenstern, L., Stefaneas, P., Lévy, F., Wyner, A., Paschke, A. (eds.) RuleML 2013. LNCS, vol. 8035, pp. 99–113. Springer, Heidelberg (2013). https://doi.org/10.1007/978-3-642-39617-5_12

10. Governatori, G., Olivieri, F., Scannapieco, S., Cristani, M.: Superiority based revision of defeasible theories. In: Dean, M., Hall, J., Rotolo, A., Tabet, S. (eds.) RuleML 2010. LNCS, vol. 6403, pp. 104–118. Springer, Heidelberg (2010). https://doi.org/10.1007/978-3-642-16289-3_10

11. Governatori, G., Olivieri, F., Scannapieco, S., Cristani, M.: Designing for compliance: norms and goals. In: Olken, F., Palmirani, M., Sottara, D. (eds.) RuleML 2011. LNCS, vol. 7018, pp. 282–297. Springer, Heidelberg (2011). https://doi.org/10.1007/978-3-642-24908-2_29

12. Governatori, G., Olivieri, F., Scannapieco, S., Cristani, M.: The hardness of revising defeasible preferences. In: Bikakis, A., Fodor, P., Roman, D. (eds.) RuleML 2014. LNCS, vol. 8620, pp. 168–177. Springer, Cham (2014). https://doi.org/10.1007/978-3-319-09870-8_12

13. Governatori, G., Rotolo, A.: Changing legal systems: legal abrogations and annulments in defeasible logic. Log. J. IGPL **18**(1), 157–194 (2010)

14. Governatori, G., Rotolo, A., Riveret, R., Palmirani, M., Sartor, G.: Variants of temporal defeasible logics for modelling norm modifications, pp. 155–159 (2007)

15. Gómez-Sebastià, I., Napagao, S., Salceda, J., Felipe, L.: Towards runtime support for norm change from a monitoring perspective, vol. 918, pp. 71–85 (2012). https://www.scopus.com/inward/record.uri?eid=2-s2.0-84891822441&partnerID=40&md5=685e5bf57faaf9f393c12e85e4ee8bae

16. Horty, J.: Norm change in the common law. In: Hansson, S.O. (ed.) David Makinson on Classical Methods for Non-Classical Problems. OCL, vol. 3, pp. 335–355. Springer, Dordrecht (2014). https://doi.org/10.1007/978-94-007-7759-0_15

17. Knobbout, M., Dastani, M., Meyer, J.J.: A dynamic logic of norm change. Front. Artif. Intell. Appl. **285**, 886–894 (2016)

18. Olivieri, F., Cristani, M., Governatori, G.: Compliant business processes with exclusive choices from agent specification. In: Chen, Q., Torroni, P., Villata, S., Hsu, J., Omicini, A. (eds.) PRIMA 2015. LNCS (LNAI), vol. 9387, pp. 603–612. Springer, Cham (2015). https://doi.org/10.1007/978-3-319-25524-8_43

19. Rouleau, M.: NormSim: an agent-based model of norm change (2016). https://www.scopus.com/inward/record.uri?eid=2-s2.0-84978428157&doi=10.1109%2fICoCS.2015.7483251&partnerID=40&md5=825116789dda19ec5a3e6fd152bd61eb

20. Scannapieco, S., Governatori, G., Olivieri, F., Cristani, M.: A methodology for plan revision under norm and outcome compliance. In: Boella, G., Elkind, E., Savarimuthu, B.T.R., Dignum, F., Purvis, M.K. (eds.) PRIMA 2013. LNCS (LNAI), vol. 8291, pp. 324–339. Springer, Heidelberg (2013). https://doi.org/10.1007/978-3-642-44927-7_22

21. Tomazzoli, C., Cristani, M., Karafili, E., Olivieri, F.: Non-monotonic reasoning rules for energy efficiency. J. Ambient Intell. Smart Environ. **9**(3), 345–360 (2017)

Cooperation Through Income Sharing

Franciszek Seredyński and Jakub Gąsior$^{(\boxtimes)}$

Department of Mathematics and Natural Sciences,
Cardinal Stefan Wyszyński University, Warsaw, Poland
{f.seredynski,j.gasior}@uksw.edu.pl

Abstract. We consider an artificial social system modeled by a multi-agent system composed of the second-order Cellular Automata (CA)-based agents, where a spatial Prisoner's Dilemma (PD) game describes interaction between agents. We are interested in studying conditions of emerging in such systems of a collective behavior measured by the average total payoff of agents in the game or by an equivalent measure–the total number of cooperating players. While emerging collective behavior depends on many parameters, we introduce to the game and study the influence of a local income sharing mechanism, giving a possibility to share incomes locally by agents wishing to do it. We present results of an experimental study showing that under some game conditions, the introduced mechanism can increase the level of collective behavior up to around 50%.

Keywords: Collective behavior · Income sharing · Multi-agent systems · Spatial Prisoner's Dilemma game · Second-order Cellular Automata

1 Introduction

Observed in last decade fast development of computer-communication technologies like e.g., fog and edge computing [1] faces researches with new types of massive artificial systems. Centralized control in them is no more possible and must be replaced by distributed, self-organized control systems exhibiting intelligent collective behavior being a result of local interactions of a huge number of simple components [4,11,16]. Indeed, a massive appearance of the Internet-of-Things (IoT) systems generating big data volumes which need to be processed collectively in real-time applications requires new computing paradigms. They should assume an increasing degree of computational intelligence of a huge number of small heterogeneous IoT devices and their ability to perform control, analytic and machine-learning tasks collectively.

In such systems, one can rely on a distributed problem solving by several independent entities that can use only some local information but may face a conflict of local goals. Therefore, we consider a large scale multi-agent system approach, where agents are capable of solving optimization problems by local

© Springer Nature Switzerland AG 2020
F. De La Prieta et al. (Eds.): PAAMS 2020 Workshops, CCIS 1233, pp. 143–153, 2020.
https://doi.org/10.1007/978-3-030-51999-5_12

interaction to achieve, on one side, some compromise between their local goals but at the same time to show a particular ability of global collective behavior. We will study the phenomena of the emergence of global collective behavior of systems composed of CA [21] based agents, where they act in an environment described in terms of non-cooperative game theory [14] with the use of Spatial Prisoner's Dilemma (SPD) game. We will be using the *second-order* CA [10], which in opposite to classical CA have adaptability features.

The phenomenon of emerging cooperation in systems described by SPD game has been a subject of current studies [5,9,15,19] which show that it depends on many factors such as payoff parameters, a type of learning agent, a way of interaction between agents. In this paper, we introduce a new mechanism of interaction between players, based on a possibility of a local income sharing by agents participating in the game, and we show a significant influence of this mechanism on emerging of global cooperation. To our knowledge it is the first attempt to apply this mechanism in the context of CA-based SPD games.

The structure of the paper is the following. The next section presents related work. In Sect. 3 SPD game is presented. Section 4 contains a description of the CA-based multi-agent system acting in the SPD game environment. Section 5 presents a basic mechanism of the game, including income sharing. Section 6 presents some results of the experimental study, and the last section concludes the paper.

2   Related Work

PD game [14] is one of the most accepted game-theoretical models, where both *cooperation* (C) and *defection* (D) of rational players can be observed. Tucker formalized the game as the 2-person game and in the 1980's Axelrod organized the first tournament [2] to recognize competitive strategies in this game. The winner was a strategy Tit-For-Tat (TFT) which assumes cooperation of a player on the first move and subsequent repeating actions of the opponent player used in the previous move. Next, Axelrod proposed [3] to apply Genetic Algorithms to discover strategies enabling cooperation in the 2-person PD game. Genetic Algorithms (GAs) were able to discover the TFT strategy and several interesting strategies specific for humans.

Discovering strategies of cooperation in N-person PD games ($N > 2$) is a more complex problem. Therefore, Yao and Darwen proposed in [22] another approach where GAs are still applied but the payoff function was simplified. The main idea was that a payoff of a given player depends on a number of cooperating players among the remaining $N - 1$ participants. Under these assumptions, GAs were able to find strategies enabling global cooperation for up to 10 players. For more players, such strategies were not discovered by GA. One of the main reasons for that is the form of the payoff function which assumes participation of a player with a "crowd" – a large number of anonymous players.

A concept of spatial games with a neighbor relation between players helps to solve the crowd problem. Among the first concepts related to SPD game was the game on the ring considered by Tsetlin [20] in the context of learning automata games, where a payoff of a given player depends on its action and actions of two immediate neighbors. Later such a game in the context of homogeneous learning automata and GA-based models was studied in [17].

A number of SPD games on 2D grids have been studied recently. Nowak and May proposed [12] an original SPD game on a 2D grid with only two types of players – players who always cooperate (all-C) and players who always defect (all-D). Players occupy cells of 2D space and each of them plays the PD game with all neighbors, and depending on the total score it is replaced by the best performing player in the neighborhood.

Ishibuschi and Namikawa studied in [9] a variant of SPD game with two neighborhoods: one for playing locally defined PD game with randomly selected neighbors, and the second one for matching strategies of the game by a locally defined GA. Howley and O'Riordan considered in [8] a N-person PD game with all-to-all interactions between players and the existence of a tagging mechanism in subgroups of players. Katsumata and Ishida in [10] extended the model of SPD game proposed by [13] by considering 2D space as the 2D CA and introducing an additional strategy called k-D, which tolerates at most k defections in a local neighborhood in the case of cooperation.

3   Iterated Spatial Prisoner's Dilemma Game

We consider a 2D spatial array of size $n \times m$. We assume that a cell (i, j) will be considered as an agent-player participating in the SPD game [10,13]. We assume that a neighborhood of a given player is defined in some way. Players from this neighborhood will be considered as his opponents in the game. At a given discrete moment of time, each cell can be in one of two states: C or D. The state of a given cell will be considered as an action C (cooperate) or D (defect) of the corresponding player against an opponent player from his neighborhood. The payoff function of the game is given in Table 1.

Table 1. Payoff function of a row player participating in SPD game.

Player's action	Opponent's action	
	Cooperate (C)	Defect (D)
Cooperate (C)	$R = 1$	$S = 0$
Defect (D)	$T = b$	$P = a$

Each player playing a game with an opponent in a single round (iteration) receives a payoff equal to R, T, S or P, where $T > R > P > S$. We will assume that $R = 1$, $S = 0$, $T = b$, and $P = a$. The values of a and b can vary depending on the purpose of an experiment.

If a player takes action C and the opponent also takes action C, then the player receives payoff $R = 1$. If a player takes the action D and the opponent player still keeps the action C, the defecting player receives payoff $T = b$. If a player takes the action C while the opponent takes action D, the cooperating player receives payoff $S = 0$. When both players use the action D, then both of them receive payoff $P = a$.

It is worth to notice that choosing by all players the action D corresponds to the Nash equilibrium point [14] and it is considered as a solution of the one-shot game. Indeed, if all players select the action D, each of them receives a payoff equal to a, and there is no reason for any of them to change the action to C while the others keep their actions unchanged, what would result in decreasing his payoff to value 0.

The average total payoff of all players in the Nash equilibrium point is also equal to a. Looking from the point of view of the global collective behavior of players, this average total payoff of all players is low. We would rather expect to choose by all players the action C, which provides the highest value of the average total payoff of all players equal to 1. For this instance of the game, it is the maximal value of a possible average total payoff of all players, and it will be achieved when all players decide to select the action C. We are interested in studying conditions when such behavior of players in iterated games is possible.

4   CA-Based Players

We will be using CA-based agents as players in the game. CA are spatially and temporally discrete computational systems (see, e.g., [21]) originally proposed by Ulam and von Neumann and today are a powerful tool used in computer science and natural science to solve problems and model different phenomena.

When a cell (i, j) is considered as a CA-based player it will be assumed that it is a part of the 2D array and at a given discrete moment of time t, each cell is either in state D or C. The value of the state is used by CA-based player as an action with an opponent player. For each cell, a local neighborhood is defined. Because we employ a 2D finite space, a cyclic boundary condition is applied. We will assume that the Moore neighborhood is used with eight immediate neighbors. It means that each player has eight opponents in the game.

In discrete moments, CA-based players will select new actions according to local rules (also called strategies or transition functions) assigned to them, which will change the states of the corresponding cells. We will be using some number of rules among which one of them will be initially randomly assigned to each CA cell, so we deal with a non-uniform CA.

To each cell one of the following rules: *all-C* (always cooperate), *all-D* (always defect), and *k-D* (k - level of tolerance) will be assigned. The strategy *k-D* tolerates at most k defections in a local neighborhood. It means that an agent with this strategy will choose the action C when the number of defecting neighbors does not exceed the value of k and will choose the action D in the opposite case. It is worth to notice that the *k-D* strategy is a generalized TFT strategy, and when $k = 0$ it is exactly the well known in the literature TFT strategy.

5 Competition and Income Sharing Mechanisms

To study the possibility of the emergence of global collective behavior of CA-based players, we will introduce some local mechanisms of interaction between players.

The first mechanism is a competition that is based on the idea proposed in [13]. Each player associated with a given cell plays in a single round a game with each of his neighbors, and this way collects some total score. If the competition mechanism is turned *on*, after a q number of rounds (iterations), each agent compares its total payoff with the total payoffs of its neighbors. If a more successful player exists in the neighborhood, this player replaces their own rule by the most successful one. This mechanism converts a classical CA into the *second-order* CA, which is able to adopt in time.

The second mechanism called income sharing mechanism (ISM), which we propose provides a possibility of sharing payoffs by players. Some kind of hard local sharing was successfully used [17] in the context of learning automata games. Here we will be using a soft version of sharing, where a player decides to use it or not. It is assumed that each player has a tag indicating whether he wishes (*on*) or not (*off*) to share his payoff with players from the neighborhood who also wish to share. The sharing works in such a way that if two players both wish to share, each of them receives half of the payoff from the sum. Before starting the iterated game, each player turns on its tag with a predefined probability $p_{sharing}$. Due to the competition mechanism, rules with tags containing information about willing to share incomes can be potentially spread or dismissed during the evolution of the system.

6 Experimental Results

Several sets of experiments with the proposed system have been conducted. A 2D array of the size 50×50 was used, with an initial state C or D (player actions) of each cell was set with probability 0.5. Initially, the rule k-D was assigned to CA cells with probability 0.5, and the remaining rules *all-C* and *all-D* were assigned with probability 0.3 and 0.2, respectively. To an agent with the rule k-D, a value k randomly selected from the range $(0..7)$ was assigned. Updating of rules assigned to agents by the competition mechanism was conducted after each iteration $(q = 1)$. Results presented below were averaged on the base of 10 runs. Each run lasted 50 iterations.

Figure 1 shows the results of the first set of experiments that discover the potential influence of ISM on the behavior of players in the game. The experiments were conducted under values of parameters of the payoff table, $b = 1.2$ and $a = 0.3$, and plots show runs of games during the first 30 iterations.

Figure 1 (upper) shows averaged results of games without and with ISM. When ISM was applied, each agent was initially ready to share incomes with probability 0.5. The results are shown via two parameters characterizing the level of collective behavior: the average number of cooperating agents and related to

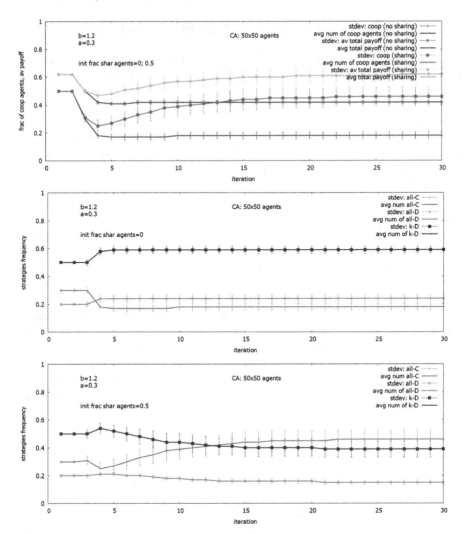

Fig. 1. Runs of games for payoff table parameters $b = 1.2$ and $a = 0.3$: level of cooperation and the average total payoff of players in games without and with ISM (upper), distribution of strategies in games without of ISM (middle), and distribution of strategies in games with ISM (lower) (Color figure online)

it the average total payoff of players in the game. One can see that in the game without ISM the players, according to initial settings, start the game from the level of cooperation equal to around 50% of cooperating players (i.e., frequency of cooperating agents is around 0.5) and this level of cooperation quickly drops to 0,18 (in blue). Corresponding average total payoff of players starts from the value equal to 0.62 and drops to 0.42 (in green). Introducing ISM significantly changes the game. Players achieve the level of cooperation equal to 0.46 (in red), which corresponds to the average total payoff equal to 0.62 (in orange).

Figures 1 (middle) and (lower) give some insight into both types of the game. In the game without ISM (see, Fig. 1 (middle)) strategy k-D is dominating and reaches the value of frequency equal to 0.59 (in green). After few iterations, the strategy all-D becomes the second dominating strategy reaching the frequency equal to 0.24 (in blue) while the frequency of the strategy all-C is decreased to the value equal to 0.17 (in red). Introducing ISM changes dynamics of the game (see, Fig. 1 (lower)). We can see the process of increasing the frequency of the all-C strategy, which becomes dominant, and at the same time, decreasing the frequency of the strategy k-D, and also a slight decrease in the frequency of the strategy all-D. It is also worth to mention that the number of agents ready to share income changes in time. It starts (not shown) from around 50% of agents ready to share income and decreases to achieve a stable value equal to around 30%.

Results of the first set of experiments were enough encouraging to study the influence of ISM deeply and Fig. 2 reports some of them. Figure 2 (upper) shows how the level of cooperation in the multi-agent system depends on values a and b of the payoff function in the game without ISM. Let us see results for already mentioned parameter $b = 1.2$ (in red). One can see that the highest level of cooperation close to 84% is achieved for the value of a from the range 0..0.25. It is a result of a small difference between the values b and $R = 1$ (see, payoff table). The difference not greater than 0.2 is too small to be attractive for a player to change its action from C into D and continue to play D. However, when the value of a increases, players selected D will be more and more attracted by the Nash equilibrium point defined by a value of a, and returning to cooperation will be more difficult. Indeed, the number of cooperating agents decreases with the increase of the value of a. When $a = 0.3$, the number of cooperating players suddenly drops to around 18% and continues decreasing with increasing the value of a. When $a = 0.7$ the cooperation level is close to 0. When the value of b increases, the conditions for cooperation decreases faster, and for $b = 1.6$ (in orange), some level of cooperation close to 0.45 is possible only when a is close to 0. One can conclude that a higher value of b means higher payoff, enabling escaping from cooperation, which results in disrupting cooperation.

Figure 2 (middle) shows what happens when ISM is used in the game, and details of a set of experiments with the value of $b = 1.2$ are presented. The figure shows how the level of cooperation depends on an initial fraction of agents wishing to share their incomes with neighbors. This fraction changes from 0 (sharing is off) to 0.8 and is set by the value of parameter $p_{sharing}$. The bottom curve (in red) represents the results of the game without ISM. One can see that for small values of $a \leq 0.2$, ISM can improve the level of cooperation only slightly, on a few percent. However, the situation significantly changes for values of $a \geq 0.3$. For $a = 0.3$ the level of cooperation is equal to 0.19 when sharing is off. However, when ISM is turned on the cooperation level is increased to 0.34 (in green) when the initial ratio of agents wishing to cooperate is equal to 0.3 and reaches the level of cooperation equal to 0.57 (in orange) or 0.81 (in dark blue) for the initial ratios of agents wishing to cooperate equally to 0.6 and 0.8,

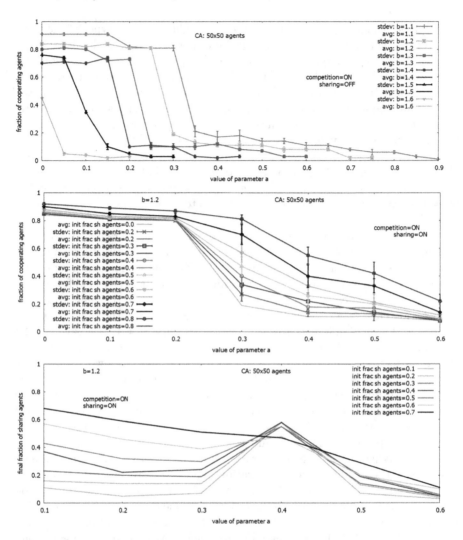

Fig. 2. Comparison of games without and with ISM: level of cooperation and the average total payoff of players in games without ISM as a function of parameters b and a (upper), level of cooperation in games with ISM for $b = 1.2$ (middle), and a final number of agents ready to share income as a function of parameter a (lower). (Color figure online)

respectively. One can see also significant improvement of the level of cooperation for the values $a = 0.4$ and $a = 0.5$.

Figure 2 (lower) gives some inside into the dynamics of the process of the income sharing with ISM. It shows for the game with $b = 1.2$ and ISM the dependence between the final ratio of agents participating in the income sharing and such parameters as an initial ratio of agents wishing to participate in the process of sharing and values of the parameter a. The figure contains a number

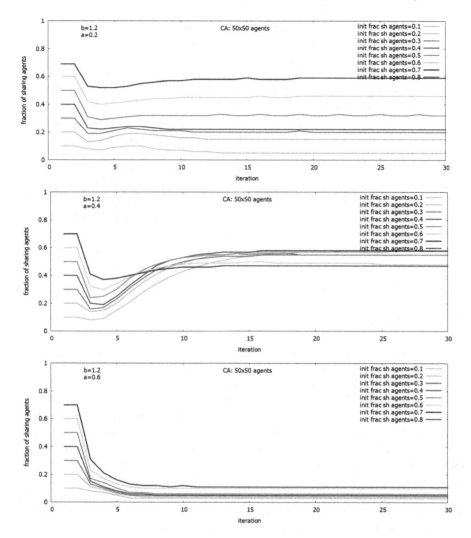

Fig. 3. Change in time of a number of agents ready to share income as a function of parameter a: $a = 0.2$ (upper), $a = 0.4$ (middle), and $a = 0.6$ (lower).

of curves, each dedicated to some initial ratio of agents wishing to participate in the process of sharing and showing the influence of the value of a. We can notice several regions of the behavior of each curve depending on values of a. For values of a in the range $(0.1..0.2)$, the final number of agents wishing to participate in sharing is slightly lower than an initial ratio of agents wishing to participate in sharing. For a in the range $(0.2..0.3)$ and an initial ratio of agents wishing to participate in sharing below 0.5, we can notice some increase of the final ratio of agents participating in the income sharing, and for $a = 0.4$ we notice a strong jump of the final ratio of agents participating in the income sharing to the average value close to 0.6 for all initial ratios of agents wishing to participate in sharing. When the value of a is increasing, we can see again strong lowering the final ratio of agents ready to share incomes.

Figure 3 shows more details for the experiments from Fig. 2 by presenting averaged runs for different initial ratios of agents wishing to participate in sharing and different values of a. One can see that the process of developing the final ratio of agents participating in the income sharing mostly depends on the value of a, and three classes of such a process can be pointed. When a is relatively small, e.g. $a = 0.2$ (see, Fig. 3 (upper)) we can initially observe some drop in the number of agents participating in income sharing, but soon this number increases to reach some final stable ratio close to the initial ratio. This initial drop is proportional to a ratio of agents wishing to share income. When a is close to 0.4 (see, Fig. 3 (medium)), the final ratio of agents wishing to share reaches some value close to 0.5 and generally it does not depend on the initial ratio of agents wishing to share. And finally, when a is larger than 0.5, e.g., equal to 0.6 (see, Fig. 3 (lower)) the final ratio of agents wishing to share stabilizes on the value close to 0.1 and this process does not depend on an initial ratio of agents wishing to share.

7   Conclusions

The phenomenon of cooperation, which can emerge in natural or artificial systems is a subject of multiple studies conducted for many years. Some conditions of emerging cooperation are already known, but some of them yet to be discovered. In this paper, we have studied this phenomenon in a model created by a CA-based multi-agent system with agents interacting according to principles of a spatial PD game. We have proposed for this model a mechanism of income sharing and have shown experimentally that it may lead to a significant enlarging degree of cooperation in such systems. We believe that these results can be useful for solving distributed optimization problems in emerging computer-communication technologies by organizing the collective behavior of large teams. These concepts of collective behavior of automata are currently applied in our studies related to cloud computing [6,18] and IoT [7].

References

1. Östberg, P., Byrne, J., et al.: Reliable capacity provisioning for distributed cloud/edge/fog computing applications. In: 2017 European Conference on Networks and Communications (EuCNC), pp. 1–6 (2017)
2. Axelrod, R.: The Evolution of Cooperation. Basic Books Publishing, New York (1984)
3. Axelrod, R.: The evolution of strategies in the iterated prisoner's dilemma. In: The Dynamics of Norms (1987)
4. Brambilla, M., Ferrante, E., Birattari, M., Dorigo, M.: Swarm robotics: a review from the swarm engineering perspective. Swarm Intell. **7**(1), 1–41 (2013)
5. Fernández Domingos, E., et al.: Emerging cooperation in n-person iterated prisoner's dilemma over dynamic complex networks. Comput. Inform. **36**(3), 493–516 (2017)

6. Gąsior, J., Seredyński, F.: Security-aware distributed job scheduling in cloud computing systems: a game-theoretic cellular automata-based approach. In: Rodrigues, J.M.F., et al. (eds.) ICCS 2019. LNCS, vol. 11537, pp. 449–462. Springer, Cham (2019). https://doi.org/10.1007/978-3-030-22741-8_32

7. Gąsior, J., Seredyński, F., Hoffmann, R.: Towards self-organizing sensor networks: game-theoretic ε-learning automata-based approach. In: Mauri, G., El Yacoubi, S., Dennunzio, A., Nishinari, K., Manzoni, L. (eds.) ACRI 2018. LNCS, vol. 11115, pp. 125–136. Springer, Cham (2018). https://doi.org/10.1007/978-3-319-99813-8_11

8. Howley, E., O'Riordan, C.: The emergence of cooperation among agents using simple fixed bias tagging. In: 2005 IEEE Congress on Evolutionary Computation, vol. 2, pp. 1011–1016 (2005)

9. Ishibuchi, H., Namikawa, N.: Evolution of iterated prisoner's dilemma game strategies in structured demes under random pairing in game playing. IEEE Trans. Evol. Comput. 9(6), 552–561 (2005)

10. Katsumata, Y., Ishida, Y.: On a membrane formation in a spatio-temporally generalized prisoners dilemma. In: Umeo, H., Morishita, S., Nishinari, K., Komatsuzaki, T., Bandini, S. (eds.) ACRI 2008. LNCS, vol. 5191, pp. 60–66. Springer, Heidelberg (2008). https://doi.org/10.1007/978-3-540-79992-4_8

11. Khaluf, Y., et al.: Scale invariance in natural and artificial collective systems: a review. J. R. Soc. Interface 14(136), 20170662 (2017)

12. Nowak, M.A., Bonhoeffer, S., May, R.M.: More spatial games. Int. J. Bifurcati Chaos 04(01), 33–56 (1994)

13. Nowak, M.A., May, R.M.: Evolutionary games and spatial chaos. Nature 359, 826 (1992)

14. Osborne, M.: An Introduction to Game Theory. Oxford University Press, New York (2009)

15. Peleteiro, A., Burguillo, J.C., Bazzan, A.L.: Emerging cooperation in the spatial IPD with reinforcement learning and coalitions. In: Bouvry, P., González-Vélez, H., Kołodziej, J. (eds.) Intelligent Decision Systems in Large-Scale Distributed Environments. Studies in Computational Intelligence, vol. 362, pp. 187–206. Springer, Heidelberg (2011). https://doi.org/10.1007/978-3-642-21271-0_9

16. Rossi, F., et al.: Review of multi-agent algorithms for collective behavior: a structural taxonomy. IFAC-PapersOnLine 51(12), 112–117 (2018)

17. Seredyński, F.: Competitive coevolutionary multi-agent systems: the application to mapping and scheduling problems. J. Parallel Distrib. Comput. 47(1), 39–57 (1997)

18. Seredyński, F., Gąsior, J., Hoffmann, R., Désérable, D.: Experiments with heterogenous automata-based multi-agent systems. In: Wyrzykowski, R., Deelman, E., Dongarra, J., Karczewski, K. (eds.) PPAM 2019. LNCS, vol. 12044, pp. 433–444. Springer, Cham (2020). https://doi.org/10.1007/978-3-030-43222-5_38

19. Seredyński, F., Gąsior, J.: Collective behavior of large teams of multi-agent systems. In: De La Prieta, F., et al. (eds.) PAAMS 2019. CCIS, vol. 1047, pp. 152–163. Springer, Cham (2019). https://doi.org/10.1007/978-3-030-24299-2_13

20. Tsetlin, M.L.: Automaton Theory and Modeling of Biological Systems. Academic Press, Cambridge (1973)

21. Wolfram, S.: A New Kind of Science. Wolfram Media, Champaign (2002)

22. Yao, X., Darwen, P.J.: An experimental study of n-person iterated prisoner's dilemma games. In: Yao, X. (ed.) EvoWorkshops 1993-1994. LNCS, vol. 956, pp. 90–108. Springer, Heidelberg (1995). https://doi.org/10.1007/3-540-60154-6_50

A Second-Order Adaptive Social-Cognitive Agent Model for Prisoner Recidivism

Dorien Melman, Janne B. Ploeger, and Jan Treur$^{(\boxtimes)}$ ⓘ

Social AI Group, Vrije Universiteit Amsterdam, Amsterdam, The Netherlands
dorienmelman@hotmail.com, janneploeger@gmail.com,
j.treur@vu.nl

Abstract. In this study, a second-order adaptive social-cognitive agent model is introduced to examine prisoner recidivism. For comparison between different kinds of prisons and prison policies, recidivism rates from Norway and the USA are used. Two scenarios were used to model the effects of environmental, prison-related, and personal influences on recidivism rates. The presented adaptive social-cognitive agent model is based on a second-order reified network model. The model allows to computationally explore the effects on prisoner recidivism and the learning process for a prisoner's social-cognitive state of mind as a main determinant of recidivism risk.

Keywords: Prisoner recidivism · Hebbian learning · Adaptive agent model

1 Introduction

One of the main goals of imprisonment is to rehabilitate prisoners to a life without crime [1]. However, many studies have shown that a large proportion of prisoners recidivate within a short time [2, 3]. In fact, literature suggests that some prisons have criminogenic effect [4]. In other words, offenders become more, rather than less, criminally oriented due to their experience in prison. Recidivism rates demonstrate - among other things - a prison system's capacity to rehabilitate its offenders [5].

A country that is well-known for its low recidivism rate is Norway [6]. This is remarkable, as Norway is also seen as exceptional in that they have moderate punitive policies. Twenty years ago, Norway exchanged a punitive 'lock-up' approach for prisons that focus on rehabilitation and maintain exceptionally humane conditions [7, 8]. As a consequence, the prison environment is relatively similar to the outside world, except for the restriction of freedom. For example, prisoners are not locked up between bars, kitchens are fully equipped with sharp objects, and prison guards are more concerned with the prisoners. Although it may be against a more revenge-oriented sense of justice to treat criminals well, the recidivism rate has shown an impressive decrease since this change in the prison system and is with 20% now one of the lowest of the world [9]. In contrast to Norway, the recidivism rates are very high for the USA: 60% of the released prisoners is reconvicted within two years [9]. These high recidivism rates suggest that many American offenders are not moved by imprisonment to stay out of trouble [4]. A comparison of the prisons in the USA and the Norwegian prison system reveals large differences. The approach of the USA is much more

© Springer Nature Switzerland AG 2020
F. De La Prieta et al. (Eds.): PAAMS 2020 Workshops, CCIS 1233, pp. 154–167, 2020.
https://doi.org/10.1007/978-3-030-51999-5_13

punitive. Guards have a more hierarchical role and are less concerned with the educational aspect for prisoners and more focused on the punishment against them. More custodial sanctions are being imposed on prisoners, which risk disrupting conventional relationships and pushing offenders into more antisocial contexts [4].

The major differences in prison systems and recidivism rates have created a demand for a better understanding of the relationship between prison environment, societal norms and recidivism. There has been much research into possible influences on prisoner recidivism. For example, one prominent strand of research has focused on how prison experiences influence offending [10–12]. For instance, Mitchel et al. [13] have investigated the impact of personal aspects such as age, race, and gender. Their analysis indicates that imprisonment has a more criminogenic effect among males than females.

Other studies have focused on examining prison policies and practices that improve reentry outcomes [14, 15]. It has been suggested, for example, that visitation reduces recidivism. As [16] has emphasized, the loss of contact with the outside world - especially with regard to family members - might have negative consequences for reintegration back into society. This thought is supported by Mears et al. [17], who found that the extent of visitation has a significant effect in reducing recidivism of all types, which suggests that visitation improves the reintegration of ex-prisoners back into society. Another example of a concept that is related to recidivism is post-release employment. The transition from prison to employment can be very difficult for released prisoners. However, investigation of the relationship between post-release employment and recidivism shows that employment reduces the risk of recidivism. Hence, prisoners benefit from getting a suitable job.

The aim of the study reported here was to model from a Social Cognition perspective the influences on prisoner recidivism using an adaptive agent model based on an adaptive mental network, i.e., a network of mental states that describes the agent's social-cognitive functioning [18, 19, 23, 24]. In Sect. 2 the designed adaptive social-cognitive agent model is introduced. Section 3 illustrates the agent model by example simulations and indicates how parameter tuning was applied. Validation of the model by comparison to empirical data is discussed in Sect. 4. Section 5 provides verification of the model by mathematical analysis.

2   The Adaptive Agent Model

A Network-Oriented Modeling approach was used to design the adaptive agent model with a focus on Social Cognition [18, 19, 23, 24]. This approach can be considered generic and was suitable to create a second-order adaptive agent model for the social-cognitive processes described in Sect. 1. The modeling approach used can be considered as a branch in the causal modeling area which has a long tradition in AI; e.g., see [20–22]. It distinguishes itself by a dynamic perspective on causal relations, according to which causal relations exert causal effects over time, and in addition these causal relations themselves can change over time as well. The basic type of network model used is called *temporal-causal network model*. It provides a useful concept to translate (supported by a dedicated modeling environment [23]) qualitative processes as known from empirical literature into dynamic, numerical computational models that can be used for simulation. It takes states and their causal effects to other states into account as nodes and connections in a causal network.

The causal effects are represented by the connections between the states, that are labeled with weights that determine the causal strength of the effect. These *connection weights* from state X to state Y are denoted by $\omega_{X,Y}$. A state Y's *speed factor* η_Y expresses how fast a state changes upon causal impact. The causal impacts from multiple incoming connections for a state Y are aggregated by a *combination function* $c_Y(..)$. Some of the states have a single incoming connection, of themselves or of one other state. In that case, the simplest combination function, the identity function **id(.)** can be used, which just multiplies the source state value by the connection weight. For multiple incoming connections, more complex functions can be used like the scaled sum **ssum(..)** or advanced logistic function **alogistic(..)**. All three factors together, the connection weights, speed factors and combination functions specify the *network structure characteristics* defining the conceptual representation of the temporal-causal network model.

Adaptiveness of a model is obtained when some of these characteristics, for example, the connection weights $\omega_{X,Y}$, are dynamic, and represented by additional *reification states* $\mathbf{W}_{X,Y}$. Similarly, the speed factor η_Y of state Y can be made adaptive by representing it by a reification state $\mathbf{H}_Y$. Adding such states leads to a two-level network with the original base states at the base level and the added reification states at the (first-order) reification level. This construction can be repeated, leading to a second-order reification level. In that way network characteristics of the first-order reification level can become adaptive as well. For example, to allow an adaptive speed of adaptation for $\omega_{X,Y}$, the speed factor $\eta\mathbf{w}_{X,Y}$ of reification state $\mathbf{W}_{X,Y}$ can be made adaptive in this way and represented by a second-order reification state $\mathbf{Hw}_{X,Y}$. This results in a second-order adaptive network model [18, 23]. A conceptual representation of this type of network structure is shown in Fig. 1.

The numerical representation derived from a conceptual representation is shown in Table 1. This numerical representation is automatically derived from the conceptual representation by the dedicated modeling environment that has been developed and was used for the simulation experiments; see [23] or [18], Ch. 9.

Table 1. Numerical representation derived from a conceptual representation of a temporal-causal network model [21, 22].

Concept	Representation	Explanation
State values over time t	$Y(t)$	At each time point t each state Y in the model has a real number value in [0, 1]
Single causal impact	$\mathbf{impact}_{X,Y}(t) = \omega_{X,Y}X(t)$	At t state X with connection to state Y has an impact on Y, using connection weight $\omega_{X,Y}$
Aggregating multiple impacts	$\mathbf{aggimpact}_Y(t) = c_Y(\mathbf{impact}_{X1,Y}(t), ...,$ $\mathbf{impact}_{Xk,Y}(t)) = c_Y(\omega_{X1,Y}X_1(t), ..., \omega_{Xk,}$ $_YX_k(t))$	The aggregated causal impact of multiple states X_i on Y at t, is determined using combination function $c_Y(...)$
Timing of the causal effect	$Y(t + \Delta t) = Y(t) + \eta_Y[\mathbf{aggimpact}_Y(t) - Y$ $(t)]\Delta t = Y(t) + \eta_Y[c_Y(\omega_{X1,Y}X_1(t), ... , \omega_{Xk,}$ $_YX_k(t)) - Y(t)]\Delta t$	The causal impact on Y is exerted over time gradually, using speed factor η_Y; here the X_i are all states with connections to state Y

Thus, the following difference and differential equations are obtained:

$$Y(t + \Delta t) = Y(t) + \eta_y [c_y (\omega_{X_1,Y} X_1(t), \ldots, \omega_{X_k,Y} X_k(t)) - Y(t)] \Delta t$$
$$\frac{dY(t)}{dt} = \eta_y [c_y (\omega_{X_1,Y} X_1(t), \ldots, \omega_{X_k,Y} X_k(t)) - Y(t)]$$

(1)

In this study, three combination functions were used. For states with single incoming connections, the identity function **id(.)** was used. This function does not have any additional parameters and is shown in Eq. 2:

$$\mathbf{id}(V) = V$$

(2)

However, two other combination functions were used to aggregate multiple incoming connections, namely the scaled sum functions **ssum$_\lambda$(.)** and the advanced logistic sum function **alogistic(..)** defined in Eq. 3 and Eq. 4 respectively:

$$\mathbf{ssum}_\lambda(V_1, \ldots, V_k) = \frac{V_1 + \ldots + V_k}{\lambda}$$

(3)

$$\mathbf{alogistic}_{\sigma,\tau}(V_1, \ldots, V_k) = [\frac{1}{1 + e^{-\sigma(V_1 + \ldots V_k - \tau)}} + \frac{1}{1 + e^{\sigma\tau}}](1 + e^{-\sigma\tau})$$

(4)

The subscripts indicate the dependence of the parameters. Often, when connection weights are non-adaptive, for the scaled sum, as a normalisation the value of parameter λ is the sum of all incoming connection weights $\omega_{X,Y}$. This ensures that the outcome is always between [0, 1]. However, in this study $\lambda = 1$ is used, which makes it a (non-scaled) sum combination function. In case of the **alogistic** function, σ is the steepness factor and τ the threshold.

This far, all combination functions and connections weights are considered for states in the base level of the agent model. The parameter values and connection weights are mostly static, and have a constant value that differs per state. However, since learning in the sense of improving certain social-cognitive skills plays an important role in prison, some of the parameters and connection weights are made adaptive [19]. To this end a (second-order) multilevel reified network model is used for the agent. There are two states in the base level which have adaptive incoming connection weights, which is discussed in more detail later below. These connection weights are modeled at the first reification level as states with their own dedicated combination function: **hebb$_\mu$(..)**. The idea of this function is that connection weights between base level states are learned. If both states show activity simultaneously, the connection between those states gets stronger and its weight value is therefore learned. This learning process includes some forgetting as well, the extent of which is indicated by the persistence factor μ. A high persistence factor means low level of forgetness, while a low value for the persistence factor shows high level of forgetness which makes learning more difficult [25]. Thus, a fourth combination function used for the adaptive connection weights in the first reification level is the following Hebbian learning function **hebb$_\mu$(..)**:

$$\mathbf{hebb}_\mu(V_1, V_2, W) = V_1 V_2(1 - W) + \mu W$$

(5)

The parameter μ in this function is the persistence factor, V_1 and V_2 indicate the activation levels of the two connected states, and W is the connection weight that changes over time.

The use of the Hebbian learning combination function results within the modeling environment [23] in the following difference and differential equation for a connection weight reification state $\mathbf{W}_{X_1,X_2}$ for $\boldsymbol{\omega}_{X_1,X_2}$ (according to Eq. 1 applied to state $\mathbf{W}_{X_1,X_2}$):

$$\mathbf{W}_{X_1,X_2}(t+\Delta t) = \mathbf{W}_{X_1,X_2}(t) + \boldsymbol{\eta}_{\mathbf{W}_{X_1,X_2}}[X_1(t)X_2(t)\left(1 - \mathbf{W}_{X_1,X_2}(t)\right) + \mu\mathbf{W}_{X_1,X_2}(t) - \mathbf{W}_{X_1,X_2}(t)]\Delta t$$
$$\frac{d\mathbf{W}_{X_1,X_2}(t)}{dt} = \boldsymbol{\eta}_{\mathbf{W}_{X_1,X_2}}[X_1(t)X_2(t)\left(1 - \mathbf{W}_{X_1,X_2}(t)\right) + \mu\mathbf{W}_{X_1,X_2}(t) - \mathbf{W}_{X_1,X_2}(t)]$$

$$(6)$$

In this study, the states that make use of adaptive connection weights are prisoners' social-cognitive mental states. The social-cognitive wellbeing of a person changes in prison over time, hence the related connections should be learned. In this way, the adaptation of these mental states happens gradually.

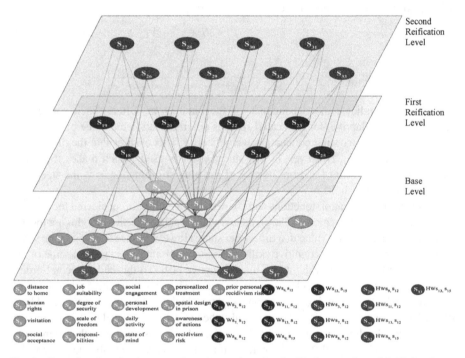

Fig. 1. Second-order adaptive agent based on a three-level reified network model (Color figure online)

The second reification level includes states that enable adaptivity of the speed factor of the adaptive connection weight states for some of the mental states at the base level: the adaptive learning rate. However, a person's ability to learn depends on someone's state of mind in the first place. For example, people that are depressed or stressed seem to show a low learning capacity to get out of that situation. This is due to the high cortisol level and low brain-derived neurotrophic factor (BDNF) level in the body

[26–28]. Together, these levels reduce or block the long-lasting changes in synaptic strength, that are associated with (adaptive) cognitive processes. This block of learning capacity is associated with what has been called negative metaplasticity, which therefore decreases cognitive functioning. Hence, bad cognitive functioning makes it difficult for a person to get out of such a stressed or depressed situation [26–28]. To model this, the speed of the learning process was made adaptive as well: the speed factors of the states in the first reification level are represented by states in the second reification level. The speed factor increases when its input increases. Since the input is learned, the speed factor will be low in the beginning, and raise over time, hand in hand with the learning. Hence, the learning process and the speed of learning are positively correlated in a cyclic manner. The complete model, including both levels of reification states is shown in Fig. 1. The total number of states within the model is 33.

The base level includes 17 states. A distinction is made between states that appear explicitly outside of prison (dark pink) and states that persists both in- and outside prison (light pink). The states outside of prison include S_4 social acceptance to prisoners of society, S_5 job suitability outside of prison, S_{16} recidivism risk, and S_{17} prior recidivism risk of a person.

The last one covers the personal background of an individual. The other states are all states that are maintained in- and outside prison. Two states, S_{12} (state of mind) and S_{15} (awareness of actions) can be seen as the mental states of the prisoner that both are crucial for social-cognitive functioning. Hence, to model the important social-cognitive learning process, these are the states of which most incoming connections are adaptive. A full specification of the adaptive agent model by role matrices [23] can be found at URL https://www.researchgate.net/publication/338547387.

3   Simulation of Example Scenarios

In this section, it is discussed how the influence of prison properties and prisoner states was simulated through the adaptive agent model described in Sect. 2. Two scenarios are taken into account to investigate these influences on a prisoner's social-cognitive mental states and the corresponding recidivism risk. In the first example scenario, both the Norwegian and American imprisonment are simulated for one individual. In the second scenario, the same Norwegian prison is used to simulate different individuals.

3.1   First Scenario: Norway Versus USA

As mentioned above, the first scenario simulates the difference of imprisonment between Norway and the USA for the same individual. This means that for both simulations, the initial values of the personal characteristics' states are equal. These states include S_3 *(family contact)*, S_5 *(job suitability)*, S_9 *(social engagement)*, S_{12} *(state of mind)*, S_{15} *(awareness of actions)*, and S_{17} *(prior personal recidivism risk)*. On the other hand, the prison and country characteristic states are different. These states include S_1 *(proximity to home)*, S_2 *(human rights)*, S_4 *(social acceptance)*, S_6 *(degree of security)*, S_{10} *(personal development)*, S_{11} *(daily activity)*, S_{13} *(personalized treatment)*, and S_{14} *(spatial design)*. The remaining states, which are S_7 *(scale of freedom)*, S_8

(responsibilities), and S_{16} *(recidivism risk)* are equal for both simulations, since they involve general aspects before prison. For example, the individual is not restricted in freedom before prison, independent of personal characteristics or the country.

Figure 2 shows the difference between imprisonment for the same individual between a Norwegian prison (a) and an American prison (b). All 33 states from the conceptual model of Fig. 1 are included. As discussed in Sect. 2, the most important states for the person's social-cognitive functioning and development thereof are the mental states S_{12} *(state of mind)* in bold green and S_{15} *(awareness of actions)* in bold blue, and in relation to them S_{16} *(recidivism risk)* in bold orange. The other lines are the remaining states. In both simulations, eight lines, starting at 0.05 show a linear progression. These lines represent the states in the second reification level, which include the adaptive speed factor of the first reification level states. The linear increase indicates that the speed factor is actually adapted hand in hand with the learning process.

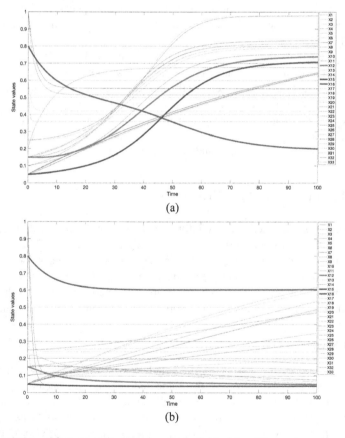

Fig. 2. Simulation of first example scenario: one individual in a Norwegian prison (a) and the same individual in an American prison (b). The y-axis represents the state values, whereas the x-axis represents the time. The time step Δt is set on 0.5. The bold lines represent the most important states: the most relevant mental states in green and blue, and recidivism risk in orange. (Color figure online)

The states in the base level and first reification level show a different course for both Norwegian prison and American prison. First of all, the first-order reification level states that represent the adaptive connection weights, show an seemingly exponential increase until they reach an equilibrium for the Norwegian prison. These states show a different progress for the American imprisonment. Since the imprisonment properties for the USA are in general much lower, the incoming values for the adaptive connection weights are much lower as well. Therefore, these states show a minimal increasing course, after which they decrease to a equilibrium value slightly below the initial state value. Although the speed of learning is slightly learned, the learning itself shows almost no progression.

For the Norwegian imprisonment, the corresponding base level states with adaptive incoming connections (bold green and blue) show an increase that starts more gradually and increase faster when the receiving input gets larger. That is, when the adaptive connection weights have gained a higher value. The slow increase in the beginning of these states and the exponential progress shows that the learning blockade decreases over time. Hence, a Norwegian prisoner learns to be in a better (social-cognitive) state of mind, and during this process, it gets more and more easy to increase this positive state of mind. The final recidivism risk of the Norwegian prisoner shows a value of 0.193.

On the other hand, for the American imprisonment, the corresponding base level states with adaptive incoming connections (bold green and blue) show a slight decrease in the beginning and end up very quick in an equilibrium. The equilibrium value is slightly lower than the initial value, which means that the prisoner even starts feeling worse in prison instead of getting better. The corresponding equilibrium value of the recidivism risk of this prisoner is 0.601.

In order to achieve these outcomes, which almost perfectly match the recidivism rates found by Yukhnenko et al. [9], some model parameters have been tuned automatically. Through Simulated Annealing – a well-known optimization technique that is effective in finding good parameter values for models with a large numbers of parameters [19] – all connection weights to *recidivism risk* (S_{16}) were tuned by using the empirical data in [9]. These weights include $\omega_{S4,S16}$, $\omega_{S5,S16}$, $\omega_{S12,S16}$, $\omega_{S13,S16}$, $\omega_{S15,S16}$, $\omega_{S17,S16}$. The parameter values that resulted in the lowest error after 5000 iterations are included in the final model, of which the results are shown in the subsequent figures.

3.2   Second Scenario: Different Initial Emotional States

The second scenario simulates the difference of imprisonment between two different individuals in a Norwegian prison. This means that for both simulations, the initial values of the prison and country characteristics are equal, whereas the personal characteristics are different. Within this main scenario, two scenarios can be distinguished.

The first scenario is applied to examine the influence of the (social-cognitive) *state of mind* (S_{12}) of the individual on the course of *recidivism risk* (S_{16}). In this scenario, the only difference with the scenario for Norway in Sect. 3.1 is the initial value of the state of mind. The value of 0.2 has been changed into 0.4, which represents a more positive person. The result, depicted in Fig. 3, shows an increase in learning from the

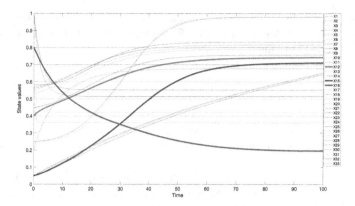

Fig. 3. Simulation of a Norwegian prison for an individual with a relatively positive state of mind.

beginning of the simulation. Due to the more positive initial state of mind, the learning blockade is less which enables an earlier increase in state of mind. This leads to a faster increase of the state of mind and therefore a faster decrease of recidivism risk. The final value of recidivism risk is equal to the value in the simulation of Norway in Sect. 3.1.

The second scenario within the main scenario, focuses on the impact of individual differences in a broader sense. The effects of a Norwegian prison are modelled for two different individuals: one overall more positive person and one person that is in a relatively more tough situation (which we will call 'negative'). The differences between the two individuals can be found in the initial values of states that involve personal characteristics, which include *family contact* (S_3), *job suitability* (S_5), *social engagement* (S_9), *state of mind* (S_{12}), *awareness of actions* (S_{15}), and *prior personal recidivism risk* (S_{17}). The relatively positive person is, in comparison with the negative individual, assigned with higher values for all mentioned personal states (since these characteristics are assumed to lead to less criminal behavior), except for the prior personal recidivism risk. The initial value for this latter state is higher for the more negative individual as a higher value represents a person with a more difficult background. The results are shown in Fig. 4.

It can be observed that the recidivism risk decreases less for the simulation of negative individual (Fig. 4a) when compared to the positive individual (Fig. 4b). This results in a recidivism risk of 0.34 and 0.06 at $t = 100$ for the negative and positive individual respectively. Hence, for both the negative and positive individual the recidivism risk has been decreased from the beginning in the Norwegian prison, but it is more difficult for the negative individual to lower this rate when compared to the positive individual. This difference can be explained by the lower initial values of the 'positive' personal characteristics (i.e., characteristics that are assumed to decrease criminality) and higher value of prior personal risk for the negative individual. Due to these initial values, it takes longer to decrease the learning blockade.

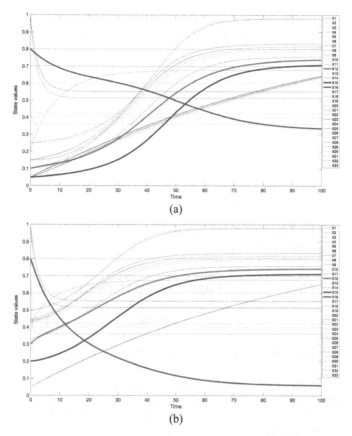

Fig. 4. Simulation of second example scenario: a relatively negative person in a Norwegian prison (a) and a relatively positive person in the same Norwegian prison (b).

4   Validation

The review of criminal recidivism rates worldwide by [9] provided recent recidivism data. Therefore, these recidivism rates were used to validate the results of the proposed adaptive agent model. Since there exist different definitions of recidivism (e.g. reconviction and reimprisonment) and the definition affects the rate, it is important to use rates that result from the same definition for a proper comparison. In this study, the two-year reconviction rates of Norway and USA (federal) are used. According to the review of Yukhnenko et al. [9], 20% of the Norwegian ex-prisoners is reconvicted within two years, while the reconviction rate for this period is 60% for the USA.

A comparison of the simulation results and the empirical data shows that the outcomes of the proposed model are consistent with these data from literature. This is depicted in Fig. 5, where the empirical values are included. The recidivism rates of the individual used in the simulation scenario are 19.3% and 60.1% for Norway and the

USA respectively (represented with orange in Fig. 5). Hence, the Root Mean Square Error (RMSE) is 0.007 for the simulation of Norway and 0.001 for the USA.

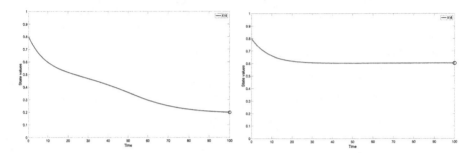

Fig. 5. The simulation results for recidivism of the first example scenario with the empirical data represented in black. (Color figure online)

5   Model Verification by Mathematical Analysis

In order to verify the model, a mathematical analysis of stationary points was performed. This analysis is based on the first scenario for Norway only. The only stationary points verified are the points which reach an equilibrium at the end of the simulation.

A stationary point of state Y at time t is defined as a point where $dY(t)/dt = 0$. The complete model is said to be in an equilibrium at time t when all states, including connections weights, are in a stationary point [18]. As discussed in Sect. 2, the differential Eq. (1) obtained is

$$\frac{dY(t)}{dt} = \eta_y[c_\gamma(\omega_{X_1,Y}X_1(t), \ldots, \omega_{X_k,Y}X_k(t)) - Y(t)]$$

with the X_i all states from which state Y gets incoming connections;
here $c_\gamma(\omega_{X_1,Y}X_1(t), \ldots, \omega_{X_k,Y}X_k(t)) = \textbf{aggimpact}_Y(t)$

Therefore, in a temporal-causal model, there only exist a stationary point if $\eta_Y = 0$ or $\textbf{aggimpact}_Y(t) = Y(t)$. Since all speed factors are non-zero, $\textbf{aggimpact}_Y(t) = Y(t)$ most hold for stationary points at each of the levels. The base level includes 17 states. A distinction is made between states that appear explicitly outside of prison (dark pink) and states that persists both in- and outside prison (light pink). The states outside of prison include S_4 social acceptance to prisoners of society, S_5 job suitability outside of prison, S_{16} recidivism risk, and S_{17} prior recidivism risk of a person. The last one covers the personal background of an individual. The other states are all states that are maintained in- and outside prison. Two states, S_{12} (state of mind) and S_{15} (awareness of actions) can be seen as the most relevant social-cognitive mental states of the prisoner. Hence, these are the states of which most incoming connections are adaptive.

From the simulated model of Scenario 1, the data were extracted for a number of states. A longer time span was used than depicted in Fig. 2(a), to ensure the model has reached an equilibrium if possible. The final values of $Y(t)$ and the corresponding connection weight values of that time t are used the verify if the model reaches an equilibrium; here **aggimpact**$_Y(t)$ is calculated by the corresponding combination function per state. If the derived **aggimpact**$_Y(t)$ is similar to the extracted value of $Y(t)$, the definition of a stationary point is fulfilled. The results are shown in Table 2, which provides insight in the mathematical verification of the model.

Table 2. An overview of the stationary point state values of the non-constant, non-adaptive states, and states with non-adaptive incoming connection weights at time point t = 300 for which the network-model has reached an equilibrium.

States	S_3	S_5	S_7	S_8	S_9	S_{16}
Time point	300	300	300	300	300	300
$S_i(t)$	0.42	0.36	0.552195	0.514057	0.676508	0.193002
aggimpact$_{Si}$(t)	0.42	0.36	0.55219426	0.51405765	0.67650787	0.19300038
Deviation	0	0	−0.0000007	0.0000007	−0.0000002	−0.000002

Hence, all states values in Table 2 fulfill the definition of a stationary point. Additionally, the adaptive connection weights were analyzed as well. Recall the following combination function for the hebbian learning principle: **hebb**$_\mu(V_1, V_2, W) = V_1 V_2(1 - W) + \mu W$. Also this equation can be used to verify the model by substitution of the values at time point t gathered from the simulation. The results are shown in Table 3. Since all deviations are smaller than 0.001, the reification states for the adaptive connection weights in the model show expected behavior as well [18].

Table 3. An overview of the stationary point state values of adaptive connection weight states at time point t = 300 for which the network-model has reached an equilibrium.

States	$W_{S3, S12}$	$W_{S7, S12}$	$W_{S8, S12}$	$W_{S9, S12}$	$W_{S11, S12}$	$W_{S13, S12}$	$W_{S9, S15}$	$W_{S13, S15}$
Time point	300	300	300	300	300	300	300	300
State value	0.756923	0.803692	0.792155	0.833768	0.8164642	0.8164642	0.9799634	0.977096
hebb(..)	0.75692320	0.803691945	0.792154892	0.833768436	0.816462101	0.816462101	0.979635529	0.977098257
Deviation	−0.0000002	0.00000006	0.0000001	−0.0000004	0.000002	0.000002	0.0003	−0.000002

6 Discussion

This paper describes an adaptive social-cognitive agent model for the dynamic and adaptive interplay between prison properties, societal aspects, personal characteristics and mental states relating to social-cognitive functioning, and prisoner recidivism. To enable learning of the connection weights to the relevant social-cognitive mental states of the prisoner and to create an adaptive learning speed, that makes the speed of learning dependent of someone's wellbeing [26], two types of levels were included in the model on top of the base level: one for the adaptive connection weights, and on top of that, one for adaptive learning rates. This resulted in a second-order adaptive social-cognitive agent model. The possible influences on prisoner recidivism were modeled and applied in two scenarios. As far as the authors know, these processes were not modeled computationally before.

The first scenario was used to simulate the effect of different prison systems on one individual. Two countries and their prison systems were taken into account: one concerned Norway, and the second one the USA. A comparison of the two simulations showed that the Norwegian prison system resulted in a lower recidivism risk compared to the USA for the same individual. A validation of the model with empirical data reveals that the results correspond with the criminal recidivism rates in [9].

In the second scenario, different individuals were simulated to examine the effect of a prison on different states of mind. These simulations showed that the recidivism risk of an individual with a more positive state of mind, coming from a better environment and good personal circumstances, decreases faster and to a lower level compared to an individual in a more tough situation.

Validation by parameter tuning and verification by mathematical analysis were performed using a first scenario. The parameter tuning focuses on the values that were available as empirical data: recidivism rates. More detailed data on the exact learning process of a prisoner could be useful to improve the model. However, this kind of data is very hard to quantify. The model verification by mathematical analysis showed that the model behaves as expected.

Although the introduced adaptive agent model is a good attempt in modeling prisoner recidivism by taking into account prison, societal and personal aspects, attention should be given to some limitations of this study. First of all, the generalizability of the model is restricted to one definition of recidivism: recidivism as reconviction after two years has been used in this study. However, more definitions of recidivism exist (e.g., reimprisonment) and these come with different recidivism rates [6]. Besides, the time span of recidivism after prison is important as well, since most measurements are done between one and five years after prison. Secondly, only the learning effect of the connection weights to mental states and the speed of learning were taken into account in the current study; that could be extended to more states. Furthermore, this study focused on Norway and the USA only. In order to make the model more robust, it would be a good improvement to investigate more countries for future work and to validate the model on more recidivism data.

References

1. Skardhamar, T., Telle, K.: Post-release employment and recidivism in Norway. J. Quant. Criminol. **28**(4), 629–649 (2012)
2. Baumer, E.: Levels and predictors of recidivism: the Malta experience. Criminology **35**, 601–628 (1997)
3. Langan, P., Levin, D.: Recidivism of prisoners released in 1994. US Department of Justice, Washington, DC (2002)
4. Cullen, F., Jonson, C., Nagin, D.: Prisons do not reduce recidivism: the high cost of ignoring science. Prison J. **91**(3), 48–65 (2011)

5. US Department of Justice: Why recidivism is a core criminal justice concern (2008)
6. Andersen, S., Skardhamar, T.: Pick a number: mapping recidivism measures and their consequences. Crime Delinquency **5**, 613–635 (2017)
7. Ugelvik, T., Dullum, J.: Nordic Prison Practice and Policy - Exceptional Or Not? Nordic Prison Policy and Practice. Routledge, London (2011)
8. Sterbenz, C.: Why Norway's prison system is so successful. Bus. Insider **11** (2014)
9. Yukhnenko, D., Sridhar, S., Fazel, S.: A systematic review of criminal recidivism rates worldwide: 3-year update. Wellcome Open Res. **4**, 28 (2019)
10. Berg, M., Huebner, B.: Reentry and the ties that bind: an examination of social ties, employment, and recidivism. Justice Q. **28**(2), 382–410 (2010)
11. Nagin, D., Cullen, F., Jonson, C.: Imprisonment and reoffending. Crime Justice **38**, 115–200 (2009)
12. Visher, C., Travis, J.: Transitions from prison to community: understanding individual pathways. Ann. Rev. Sociol. **29**, 89–113 (2003)
13. Mitchell, O., Cochran, J., Mears, D., Bales, W.: Examining prison effects on recidivism: a regression discontinuity approach. Justice Q. **4**, 571–596 (2017)
14. Cullen, F., Gendreau, P.: Assessing Correctional Rehabilitation: Policy, Practice, and Prospects. Policies, Processes, and Decisions of the Criminal Justice System, pp. 109–175 (2000)
15. Gideon, L., Sung, H.-E.: Rethinking Corrections: Rehabilitation, Reentry, and Reintegration. Sage, Thousand Oaks (2010)
16. Adams, K.: Adjusting to prison life. Crime Justice **16**, 275–359 (1992)
17. Mears, D., Cochran, J., Siennick, S., Bales, W.: Prison visitation and recidivism. Justice Q. **29**(6), 888–918 (2012)
18. Treur, J.: Network-Oriented Modeling for Adaptive Networks: Designing Higher-Order Adaptive Biological, Mental and Social Network Models. Studies in Systems, Decision and Control, vol. 251. Springer, Cham (2020). https://doi.org/10.1007/978-3-030-31445-3
19. Treur, J.: Network-Oriented Modeling: Addressing Complexity of Cognitive, Affective and Social Interactions. Springer, Cham (2016). https://doi.org/10.1007/978-3-319-45213-5
20. Kuipers, B., Kassirer, J.: How to discover a knowledge representation for causal reasoning by studying an expert physician. In: Proceedings of IJCAI 1983 (1983)
21. Kuipers, B.: Commonsense reasoning about causality: deriving behavior from structure. Artif. Intell. **24**, 169–203 (1984)
22. Pearl, J.: Causality. Cambridge University Press, Cambridge (2009)
23. Treur, J.: A modeling environment for reified temporal-causal networks: modeling plasticity and metaplasticity in cognitive agent models. In: Baldoni, M., Dastani, M., Liao, B., Sakurai, Y., Zalila Wenkstern, R. (eds.) PRIMA 2019. LNCS (LNAI), vol. 11873, pp. 487–495. Springer, Cham (2019). https://doi.org/10.1007/978-3-030-33792-6_33
24. Treur, J.: Modeling higher-order adaptive evolutionary processes by multilevel adaptive agent models. In: Baldoni, M., Dastani, M., Liao, B., Sakurai, Y., Zalila Wenkstern, R. (eds.) PRIMA 2019. LNCS (LNAI), vol. 11873, pp. 505–513. Springer, Cham (2019). https://doi.org/10.1007/978-3-030-33792-6_35
25. Hebb, D.: The Organisation of Behavior. Wiley, New York (1949)
26. Garcia, R.: Stress, metaplasticity, and antidepressants. Curr. Mol. Med. **2**(7), 629–638 (2002)
27. Kirschbaum, C., Wolf, O., May, M., Wippich, W., Hellhammer, D.: Stress- and treatment-induced elevations of cortisol levels associated with impaired declarative memory in healthy adults. Life Sci. **58**(17), 1475–1483 (1996)
28. Lupien, S., et al.: Stress-induced declarative memory impairment in healthy elderly subjects: relationship to cortisol reactivity. J. Clin. Endocrinol. Metab. **82**(7), 2070–2075 (1997)

Understandable Collaborating Robot Teams

Avinash Kumar Singh, Neha Baranwal, Kai-Florian Richter,
Thomas Hellström, and Suna Bensch$^{(\boxtimes)}$

Department of Computing Science, Umeå University, Umeå, Sweden
{avinash,neha,kaifr,thomash,suna}@cs.umu.se
http://www.cs.umu.se

Abstract. As robots become increasingly complex and competent, they
will also become increasingly more difficult to understand for interacting humans. In this paper, we investigate understandability for teams of
robots collaborating to solve a common task. While such robots do not
need to communicate verbally with each other for successful coordination, human bystanders may benefit from overhearing verbal dialogues
between the robots, describing what they do and plan to do. We present a
novel and flexible solution based on Cooperating Distributed Grammar
Systems and a multi-agent algorithm for coordination of actions. The
solution is implemented and evaluated on three Pepper robots collaborating to solve a task while commenting on their own and other robots'
current and planned actions.

Keywords: Robot teams · Explainable · Understandable · Natural
language generation · Plan derivation · Cooperating Distributed
Grammar System

1 Introduction

As robots become increasingly complex and competent, it will become increasingly more difficult for humans to understand the robots. The area of understandable or explainable robotics specifically addresses this problem [7]. Failure
to take understandability into consideration may affect safety, efficiency, user-
experience, and interaction quality in general [2].

In this paper, we investigate understandability for teams of robots collaborating to solve a common task. While such robots will rarely need to communicate
verbally with each other for successful coordination, human bystanders might
benefit from overhearing verbal dialogues between the robots, describing what
they currently do and plan to do. The scenario becomes more complex if the dialogue between the robots is also reflecting the distribution of work between the
robots. For example, a robot may ask another robot for help, suggest to other
robots to perform actions, or inform the other robots about what it intends to

Supported by the Kempe Foundations.

do. In this paper we present models for collaborative planning and execution of a task, and the generation of actions and utterances. The solution is demonstrated on three Pepper robots solving a pick-and-place task by coordinating the work with each other, and at the same time verbally informing human bystanders.

The paper is organized as follows. In Sect. 2 related work is reviewed. Section 3 describes the overall approach. Details on plan derivation are given in Sect. 4, and the agent model is described in Sect. 5. The technical implementation and conducted experiments are detailed in Sect. 6. The paper ends with a discussion on the results, and ideas for future work in Sect. 7.

2   Related Work

A general theoretical framework for understandable robots is given in [7]. One line of research investigates ways for robots to answer questions related to their recent activity. In [10] and [11] the task is navigation, and the robot answers questions such as "How did you get here?" and "What happened near the elevator?". In [12], the robot verbally explains what and how they conducted domestic tasks.

To the best of our knowledge, architectures supporting verbal understandability for teams of collaborating robots have not been previously addressed. In such teams of collaborating robots, or agents more generally, some form of coordination is required for successful task execution. There are different ways to achieve coordinated behavior. A simple, yet effective approach is a blackboard architecture [4], which provides a common representation of the current state that is accessible to all agents. It has been used in various settings, for example, in distributing tasks in emergency handling [9], but also to coordinate behavior of individual modules of a single robot [8]. Co-operating distributed grammar systems (CDGS) [3] are formal models of blackboard architectures and multi-agent systems, and provide formalizations of notions such as distribution, collaboration, synchronization, and concurrency. These models have been subject to theoretical research but are rarely applied to real world scenarios.

3   Overall Approach

As a basic scenario, a team of independent robot agents operate in a physical environment with human bystanders, see Fig. 1. The robots are given a task, and collaborate to plan and solve the task. The approach is divided into two parts: plan derivation and plan execution. The robots first collaboratively derive a plan by taking into account their individual capabilities to perform actions. The derived plan is then executed, also in collaboration between the robots. During plan execution, the robots describe in natural language what they intend to do or what they request other robots to do.

Plan derivation is modelled using the grammar formalism known as Cooperating Distributed Grammar System (CDGS) [5]. A CDGS is a formal model of blackboard architectures for collaborating multi-agent systems, and is composed of a finite number of so-called *components*, a *shared common string*, and a specified *cooperation protocol*. Each component is a set of rewrite rules that change the shared common string, and the cooperation protocol regulates how long a component can work on the common string. In our CDGS model, we represent the robot agents as components, the blackboard is represented as the shared common string, and the turn taking behaviour among the robots is given by the cooperation protocol.

During plan execution, the robots communicate to decide who should do what when. In most applications, the robots would typically use WiFi to communicate, but here they also generate verbal utterances to explain what is going on to human bystanders. Plan execution and generation of verbal utterances is modelled with an agent-based architecture synchronizing actions and utterances. The following two sections give details on plan derivation and plan execution.

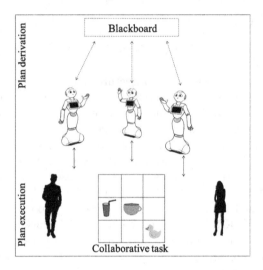

Fig. 1. Illustration of the interaction model in which three robots collaborate to solve a pick-and-place task. See text for details.

4   Plan Derivation

In this section we first give the definition of our grammar systems for plan derivation, followed by an example in Subsect. 4.1. For plan derivation we introduce a CDGS model which is a variant of so-called pure CDGS [1]. A CDGS for plan derivation is an $(n + 2)$-tuple $G = (V, P_1, P_2, \ldots, P_n, \omega)$ where V is a finite set of symbols, ω is a string (the so-called start axiom), and each P_i, $1 \leq i \leq n$ is a finite set of ordered rewrite rules of the following form

$$[\alpha_1 \rightarrow \beta_1, \alpha_2 \rightarrow \beta_2],$$

where $\alpha_1, \alpha_2, \beta_1, \beta_2$ are symbols in V. As indicated by the square brackets the rewrite rules are ordered as a sequence and the first rule must be applied first, followed by the application of the second rule.[1] In particular, an ordered rule describes that a symbol α_1 may be rewritten with a symbol β_1 directly followed by rewriting a symbol α_2 with β_2. In our approach each P_i represents a robot, the string ω represents the initial environment and an ordered rewrite rule represents a robot's specific action capabilities in a given environment.

Let x, y, z be strings consisting of symbols in V and $\rho \subseteq \{P_1, P_2, \ldots, P_n\}$. To indicate that a string x is rewritten into a string y and y is rewritten into a string z by applying a rule, we write

$$x \underset{\rho}{\Longrightarrow} y \underset{\rho}{\Longrightarrow} z.$$

The above holds if and only if for x, y, z one of the following two cases holds

$$x = a_1 a_2 \ldots a_l \alpha_1 a_{l+2} \ldots a_p \alpha_2 a_{p+2} \ldots a_m$$

$$y = a_1 a_2 \ldots a_l \beta_1 a_{l+2} \ldots a_p \alpha_2 a_{p+2} \ldots a_m$$

$$z = a_1 a_2 \ldots a_l \beta_1 a_{l+2} \ldots a_p \beta_2 a_{p+2} \ldots a_m$$

or

$$x = a_1 a_2 \ldots a_f \alpha_2 a_{f+2} \ldots a_l \alpha_1 a_{l+2} \ldots a_m$$

$$y = a_1 a_2 \ldots a_f \alpha_2 a_{f+2} \ldots a_l \beta_1 a_{l+2} \ldots a_m$$

$$z = a_1 a_2 \ldots a_f \beta_2 a_{f+2} \ldots a_l \beta_1 a_{l+2} \ldots a_m$$

and for all P_i in ρ there exists an ordered rewrite rule that is of the form

$$[\alpha_1 \rightarrow \beta_1, \alpha_2 \rightarrow \beta_2].$$

We refer to $x \underset{\rho}{\Longrightarrow} y \underset{\rho}{\Longrightarrow} z$ as two successive *derivation steps*, and x, y, z are called *sentential forms*. We write $v \overset{*}{\Longrightarrow} w$ to indicate that an arbitrary number of derivation steps is applied to derive a string w from a string v. Let z_F be a sentential form that contains a designated symbol $\delta \in V$. In our approach the symbol δ represents a task solution. Let SF be the set of all successively derived sentential forms starting with ω and ending with z_F. The language $L(G)$ generated by a CDGS for plan derivation is the set of all possible SF. The successively generated sentential forms SF represent possible robot moves in a given environment. Generated sentential forms that do not lead to a task solution are not included in the language generated. More formally, we define

$$L(G) = \{\text{SF} \mid \omega \overset{*}{\Longrightarrow} z_F\}.$$

---

[1] A reader familiar with formal grammars might note that regulated rewriting allows for check conditions which we cannot achieve with a context-free approach.

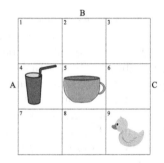

Fig. 2. An example of a table top configuration with a numbered grid, a red glass (R), a green cup (G), and a yellow duck (Y). Three robots A, B and C are placed around the table top, and each robot can reach only some of the cells. (Color figure online)

4.1   Example Plan Derivation

We will use an example with three robots A, B and C, collaborating to solve a pick-and-place task involving a 3×3 grid with three objects. The cells in the grid are numbered 1 to 9 (see Fig. 2). The objects are a red glass (R), a green cup (G), and a yellow duck (Y). The objects are initially placed in different cells of the grid, and the given task is to move R from cell 4 to 9. Each robot can reach only some of the cells, and all capabilities are modelled in the set of rules P_i for each robot.

In our model a string s represents the state of the environment at a time t with the designated string ω representing the initial environment. Thus, in our example in Fig. 2, we represent the initial configuration as the string $123R4G5678Y9$, where 1, 2, 3, $R4$, $G5$, 6, 7, 8, $Y9$ are symbols in V. The symbols 1, 2, 3, 6, 7, 8 represent that the respective cells are empty, whereas the symbols $R4$, $G5$ and $Y9$ represent that the red glass is on cell 4, the green cup is on cell 5 and the yellow duck is on cell 9, respectively.

Starting with the initial string ω, all robots can rewrite strings by taking turns. A robot's capability to change a given environment are represented in the set of rewrite rules P_i. A rewrite rule r can be applied at time t to a string s changing s to a new string s', where s' represents the new environment at time $t + 1$. For example, a typical rule is of the form

$$[R4 \to 4, 1 \to R1],$$

where $R4 \to 4$ describes a robot's capability to grab and lift the red glass up from cell 4 (leaving cell 4 empty) and $1 \to R1$ represents the capability and possibility of placing the red glass on cell 1. In our example illustrated in Fig. 2, we have three sets of rewrite rule for each robot agent, namely P_A, P_B, and P_C, for the robots A, B, and C, respectively. In the following, we list some exemplifying rules that the robots can apply during plan derivation. The entire CDGS for the example is straightforward to generate in the same manner and not fully described here due to space constraints.

$P_A = \{[R4 \rightarrow 4, 1 \rightarrow R1], [R1 \rightarrow 1, 2 \rightarrow R2], \ldots, [G5 \rightarrow 5, 2 \rightarrow G2], \ldots\}$
$P_B = \{[R1 \rightarrow 1, 2 \rightarrow R2], [R2 \rightarrow 2, 3 \rightarrow R3], [R3 \rightarrow 3, 6 \rightarrow R6], \ldots\}$
$P_C = \{[R3 \rightarrow 3, 6 \rightarrow R6], [R6 \rightarrow 6, 9 \rightarrow R9], [G5 \rightarrow 5, 2 \rightarrow G2], [G5 \rightarrow 5, 6 \rightarrow G6], \ldots, [Y9 \rightarrow 9, 6 \rightarrow Y6], [Y6 \rightarrow 6, 5 \rightarrow Y5], \ldots\}$

Consider the initial string $\omega = 123R4G5678Y9$ (depicted in Fig. 2). Given ω we see that robot A could move the red glass from cell 4 to cell 1 (i.e. applying the rule $[R4 \rightarrow 4, 1 \rightarrow R1]$ to ω) as follows

$$123R4G5678Y9 \underset{A}{\Rightarrow} 1234G5678Y9 \underset{A}{\Rightarrow} R1234G5678Y9.$$

The last sentential form represents an environment in which the red glass is on cell 1 and cell 4 is unoccupied. If two robots ρ_1 and ρ_2 are able to apply the same rule r to a alter a string v (because ρ_1 and ρ_2 have the same rule r in P_{ρ_1} and P_{ρ_2}, we write

$$v \underset{\rho_1, \rho_2}{\Longrightarrow} w.$$

In this way we record the set of robots that can reach and move the same object. The successive sentential forms contain information about which object has been moved from a cell to another cell. In our example, given the sentential form $R1234G5678Y9$ robot A as well as robot B could move the red glass on cell 1 to cell 2, which is indicated by the rule $[R1 \rightarrow 1, 2 \rightarrow R2]$ that is in both sets P_A and P_B. In particular, we write

$$R1234G5678Y9 \underset{A,B}{\Longrightarrow} 1234G5678Y9 \underset{A,B}{\Longrightarrow} 1R234G5678Y9.$$

Note that a rule is only applicable if there is an object on a cell that needs to be moved and if the cell that the object should be moved to is unoccupied. Note also that there are many more possibilities to derive alternative sentential forms, since any symbol in a given sentential form can be replaced. In practice this corresponds to a search through the space of all possible derivations, and many alternative search algorithms can be used. Possibilities of derivations that will not yield the desired outcome, that is, sentential forms in which the object R is not on cell 9, are not included in the language generated and thus disregarded. One possibility for plan derivation in our example that is a solution to the given task (i.e. $\delta = R9$ is given as follows (the affected parts are colored in blue):

$$123R4G5678Y9 \underset{A}{\Rightarrow} 1234G5678Y9 \underset{A}{\Rightarrow} R1234G5678Y9 \underset{A,B}{\Rightarrow} 1234G5678Y9 \underset{A,B}{\Longrightarrow}$$

$$1R234G5678Y9 \underset{B}{\Longrightarrow} 1234G5678Y9 \underset{B}{\Longrightarrow} 12R34G5678Y9 \underset{A,C}{\Longrightarrow} 12R345678Y9 \underset{A,C}{\Longrightarrow}$$

$$1G2R345678Y9 \underset{C}{\Longrightarrow} 1G2R3456789 \underset{C}{\Longrightarrow} 1G2R345Y6789 \underset{C}{\Longrightarrow} 1G2R3456789 \underset{C}{\Longrightarrow}$$

$$1G2R34Y56789 \underset{B,C}{\Longrightarrow} 1G234Y56789 \underset{B,C}{\Longrightarrow} 1G234Y5R6789 \underset{C}{\Longrightarrow} 1G234Y56789 \underset{C}{\Longrightarrow}$$

$$1G234Y5678R9.$$

Given an SF containing all successively derived sentential forms from ω to z_F, we extract for each derivation step the set of robots that can reach and move the same object, the object itself, and the cell positions from which the object is moved from and to, in order to construct a so-called *Plan*.

Definition 1. *A* Plan *is a string s of N Action templates a_i seperated by commas: $s = a_1, a_2, \ldots, a_N$.*

Definition 2. *An* Action template *a is a string comprising four substrings: $a = robots\ object\ from\ to$, where robots $\in \{A, B, C, D, AB, AC, AD, BC, BD, CD, ABC, ABD, ACD, BCD, ABCD\}$, object $\in \{R, G, Y\}$, and from, to $\in \{1, 2, 3, 4, 5, 6, 7, 8, 9\}$.*

In our example, the first two derivation steps including the first three sentential forms are used to generate the first Action template $AR41$, representing that robot A may move R from cell 4 to 1. The complete Plan is:

$$AR41, ABR12, BR23, ACG52, CY96, CY65, BCR36, CR69$$

representing possible successive robot actions that lead to a task solution. For example, the substring $BCR36$ is an Action template, denoting that robots B and C are capable of moving object R from cell 3 to cell 6.

Definition 3. *An* Action *is an* Action template *where robots $\in \{A, B, C, D\}$.*

As an example, the Action $CR36$ denotes robot C moving R from cell 3 to cell 6. An Action template differs from an Action in that it may be under-specified in the sense that it does not necessarily specify which robot should perform the action, but rather which robots may perform the action. For example, the Action template $BCR36$ specifies that one of the robots B and C should move R from cell 3 to cell 6. This final decision is made during the plan execution phase.

5   Plan Execution

The plan derived as described in Sect. 4.1 is used as input for plan execution. Our solution comprises a main coordinating component and identical control systems running in parallel on each robot. The coordinating component is given a plan *CurrentPlan*, places it on the blackboard, and starts all robot's control systems. Pseudo-code for these systems is shown in Algorithm 1, and describes how the robots collaborate to generate and execute actions a to be executed, and utterances u to be uttered. Utterance u may be a request for another robot to execute a, or it may declare that the robot itself intends to execute a.

The steps of Algorithm 1 are described below with references to line numbers in parentheses. The robots communicate through the blackboard to execute the plan. In addition to *CurrentPlan*, a string *CurrentAction* (see Definition 3) denoting the action currently scheduled for execution resides on the blackboard.

After each step, *CurrentPlan* is updated by removing the left-most action template in *CurrentPlan*. The main loop (1) runs until *CurrentPlan* is empty. As described above, the first character in an action denotes the robot to execute the action. Since initially, *CurrentAction* is empty, the test in (2) is negative and the else part (11–16) will be executed. After a random delay (11), an empty *CurrentAction* (12) (signalling that no other robot is currently executing an action) causes a new action a and utterance u to be generated (13) from the leftmost action template of *CurrentPlan*. u is uttered by the robot (14), and a is placed on the blackboard as the variable *CurrentAction* (15), such that it can be executed by the assigned robot. If the test in step (2) is positive, *CurrentAction* will be executed by robot r (3). The corresponding action template is then removed (4–5) from *CurrentPlan*, and the team of robots continues with the next action template. The algorithm terminates if and when *CurrentPlan* has been reduced to the empty string (1), which signals that the entire derived plan has been executed, and the goal state has been achieved. The function *DoAction* takes as input an action of the form $roft$ (see Definition 3) and executes it by physically moving object o from f to t. The function *GenUtteranceAndAction* takes a plan (see Definition 1), and generates an action a and an utterance u. It first extracts the leftmost action template $roft$. If r contains more than one letter, the action is planned to be executed by one of the robots referred to by these letters. Based on some strategy (the simplest one being a random choice), robot r_1 is chosen. The function then returns the action r_1oft.

Several approaches are possible to generate the accompanying utterance u. In this experiments, the scheme illustrated in Table 1 was used. The table shows examples of returned action and utterance for different action templates. For example, if the function is executed on robot C, and the action template is "ACR36", the function may return the action "AR36" and the utterance "Robot A, please move the red glass from 3 to 6". Another possibility would be to return the action "CR36" and the utterance "I will move the red glass from 3 to 6". If the action template is "ABG45" the function may return an action "BG45" and an utterance "Robot B please move the green cup from 4 to 5", or an action is set to an empty string "", and an utterance "Robot A and B, either of you have to

Table 1. Actions and utterances generated by robot C for given action templates.

Action template	Action	Utterance
ACR36	AR36	Robot A, please move the red glass from 3 to 6
ACR36	CR36	I will move the red glass from 3 to 6
ABG45	BG45	Robot B please move the green cup from 4 to 5
ABG45		Robot A and B, either of you have to move the green cup

move the green cup". Other interesting behaviors can be easily implemented by modifying the process of generating actions and utterances. These possibilities are further discussed in Sect. 7.

Data: *CurrentPlan* and *CurrentAction* are on the blackboard. *CurrentPlan* is initialized in the plan derivation step. *CurrentAction* is initialized to ""

Result: Step-wise execution of all action templates in *CurrentPlan*.

1 **while** *CurrentPlan* > "" **do**
2   **if** *CurrentAction(1) = r* **then**
3   **if** *DoAction(CurrentAction)* **then**
4   Split up *CurrentAction* into action templates $t_1, t_2, t_3, \ldots$;
5   *CurrentPlan* ← $t_2 t_3 \ldots$ (i.e. remove first action template t_1) ;
6   **else**
7   Report failure, e.g. say "I do not manage";
8   **end**
9   *CurrentAction* ← "" (allow other robots to act);
10   **else**
11   Pause 0-5 seconds at random (to allow for non-determinism);
12   **if** *CurrentAction* = "" **then**
13   *u, a* ← *GenUtteranceAndAction(CurrentPlan)*;
14   Say *u* ;
15   *CurrentAction* ← *a*;
16   **end**
17   **end**
18 **end**

Algorithm 1. Main control loop running on each robot *r*. At each step, an action and an utterance is generated from the leftmost action template in *CurrentPlan*. See text for further details.

---

6   Implementation and Experiments

To demonstrate the developed models and algorithms, Algorithm 1 for plan execution was implemented on three Pepper robots. Although the Pepper robots are not designed to manipulate objects, we managed to grip and move lightweight objects made with a base of polystyrene foam, and a tip of softer rubber foam that allows for safe gripping. Figure 3 shows the experimental setup.

Plan derivation is not yet implemented, and the robots were provided with manually derived plans (see Subsect. 4.1) for given goals. The robots were then activated to collaboratively execute the plan as described in Sect. 5.

The concurrent execution of Algorithm 1 in all three robots results in several randomized operations. The next action is generated by a randomly chosen robot due to the delay in step 11, and due to computational and mechanical delays in all involved robots. The actual generation of the next action and verbal utterance is done by the function *GenUtteranceAndAction*, which also contains several elements of randomization as described in Sect. 5. All together, the behavior for

Fig. 3. Experimental setup showing one of the collaborating robots gripping an object.

a given plan would vary from one execution to another, and several experiments were therefore conducted for evaluation. Some results are presented in a short video[2].

7   Results, Discussion and Future Work

We proposed and evaluated a novel solution for understandable, collaborating robot teams, based on CDGS and a multi-agent algorithm for coordination of actions, and generation of verbal explanations. In our conducted experiments, the robot team successfully collaborated to solve given tasks. The individual robots verbally commented on their own planned actions, and also on actions requested to be performed by other robots. The randomized agent-based approach, together with the under-specified plans, demonstrated considerable variation, both regarding actions and generated utterances.

The approach enables easy implementation of various collaborative strategies. For example, the function *GenUtteranceAndAction* may be modified to allow robots to look beyond the left-most action template in the plan when generating utterances. If the left-most template is "ABR45" and the second left-most template is "CR58", robot C may return the utterance "Robot A or B, please hand me the red glass such that I can move it from 4 to 5".

Another example of the flexibility of our solution concerns automatic handling of malfunctioning robots. Since the capabilities of the robots are stored in the set of rules for each robot, and rules are applied given the current state of the environment, the robot team can easily deal with situations where a robot's capabilities change. For example, a situation where a robot loses its gripping or vision capabilities due to hardware problems can be easily modelled by removing certain rules. In future work, we intend to investigate these possibilities, and also how robots may communicate their failures in natural language, and re-plan in cooperation to compensate for these failures. We also intend to implement the plan derivation as described in Sect. 4, including efficient search algorithms.

---

[2] https://people.cs.umu.se/thomash/UnderstandableCollaboratingRobotTeams.mp4.

As mentioned in the introduction, the underlying motivation for the work presented in this paper is understandability for improved safety, efficiency, and user-experience in HRI. This is relevant for many collaborative human-robot scenarios, including *traded control* [6], where the human's situational awareness would benefit from verbal explanations of the robot's current and planned actions, in particular when the human takes over control from the robot.

References

1. Aydin, S., Bordin, H.: Sequential versus parallel grammar formalisms with respect to measures of descriptional complexity. Fundamenta Informaticae **55**(3–4), 243–254 (2003)
2. Bensch, S., Jevtić, A., Hellström, T.: On interaction quality in human-robot interaction. In: International Conference on Agents and Artificial Intelligence (ICAART), pp. 182–189 (2017)
3. Bordihn, H., Holzer, M.: A note on cooperating distributed grammar systems working in combined modes. Inf. Process. Lett. **108**(1), 10–14 (2008)
4. Botti, V., Barber, F., Crespo, A., Onaindia, E., Garcia-Fornes, A., Ripoll, I., Gallardo, D., Hernández, L.: A temporal blackboard for a multi-agent environment. Data Knowl. Eng. **15**(3), 189–211 (1995). https://doi.org/10.1016/0169-023X(95)00007-F
5. Csuhaj-Varju, E., Kelemen, J., Paun, G., Dassow, J. (eds.): Grammar Systems: A Grammatical Approach to Distribution and Cooperation, 1st edn. Gordon and Breach Science Publishers Inc., London (1994)
6. Fonooni, B., Hellström, T.: Applying a priming mechanism for intention recognition in shared control. In: 2015 IEEE International Multi-Disciplinary Conference on Cognitive Methods in Situation Awareness and Decision Support (CogSIMA), Orlando, FL, USA, March 2015
7. Hellström, T., Bensch, S.: Understandable robots - what, why, and how. Paladyn, J. Behav. Rob. **9**(1), 110–123 (2018)
8. Liscano, R., Manz, A., Stuck, E.R., Fayek, R.E., Tigli, J.: Using a blackboard to integrate multiple activities and achieve strategic reasoning for mobile-robot navigation. IEEE Expert **10**(2), 24–36 (1995). https://doi.org/10.1109/64.395354
9. Ostergaard, E.H., Mataric, M.J., Sukhatme, G.S.: Distributed multi-robot task allocation for emergency handling. In: Proceedings of the 2001 IEEE/RSJ International Conference on Intelligent Robots and Systems, vol. 2, pp. 821–826 (2001). https://doi.org/10.1109/IROS.2001.976270
10. Perera, V., Selvaraj, S.P., Rosenthal, S., Veloso, M.M.: Dynamic generation and refinement of robot verbalization. In: 25th IEEE International Symposium on Robot and Human Interactive Communication. RO-MAN 2016, New York, NY, USA, 26–31 August 2016, pp. 212–218 (2016). https://doi.org/10.1109/ROMAN.2016.7745133
11. Rosenthal, S., Selvaraj, S.P., Veloso, M.M.: Verbalization: narration of autonomous robot experience. In: Proceedings of the Twenty-Fifth International Joint Conference on Artificial Intelligence (IJCAI 2016), New York, NY, USA, 9–15 July 2016, pp. 862–868 (2016). http://www.ijcai.org/Abstract/16/127
12. Zhu, Q., Perera, V., Wächter, M., Asfour, T., Veloso, M.M.: Autonomous narration of humanoid robot kitchen task experience. In: 17th IEEE-RAS International Conference on Humanoid Robotics. Humanoids 2017, Birmingham, United Kingdom, 15–17 November 2017, pp. 390–397 (2017)

Workshop on Decision Support, Recommendation, and Persuasion in Artificial Intelligence (DeRePAI)

Workshop on Decision Support, Recommendation, and Persuasion in Artificial Intelligence (DeRePAI)

Decision support systems are applied in different fields to support individuals and groups, as well as to influence human behaviour and decision-making. Decision support systems are expected to facilitate decision-making while enhancing the quality of that decision, as well as recommender systems are expected to facilitate the choice process in order to maximize the user satisfaction. In decision support and recommendation for groups, it is important to consider the heterogeneity and conflicting preferences of its participants. In addition, decision support and recommendation systems must have strategies for configuring preferences and acquiring user profiles in a non-intrusive (implicit) and time-consuming manner.

On the other hand, the acceptance and effectiveness of the hints and recommendations provided by the system depends on several factors. First, they must be appropriate for the objectives and profile of the user, but also, they must be understandable and supported by evidence (the user must understand why the recommendation is provided and why it is good for him/her). Thus, it is necessary to provide these systems with a mechanism that supports suggestions by means of artificial intelligence. In this way, computational argumentation is a technique that builds upon the natural way humans provide reasons (i.e., arguments) for which a recommendation is suggested and should be accepted. Therefore, a system that uses these technologies must be persuasive in order to obtain the desired results by influencing human behaviour.

In this workshop, we will explore the links between decision-support, recommendation, and persuasion in order to discuss strategies to facilitate the decision/choice process by individuals and groups. This workshop aims to be a discussion forum on the latest trends and ongoing challenges in the application of artificial intelligence technologies in this area.

Organization

Organizing Committee

Jaume Jordán	Universitat Politècnica de València, Spain
João Carneiro	Polytechnic of Porto, Portugal
Stella Heras	Universitat Politècnica de València, Spain
Javier Palanca	Universitat Politècnica de València, Spain
Goreti Marreirosv	Polytechnic of Porto, Portugal
Tiago Oliveira	Tokyo Medical and Dental University, Japan

Program Committee

Grzegorz J. Nalepa	AGH University of Science and Technology, Poland
Vicente Julián	Universitat Politècnica de València, Spain
Víctor Sánchez-Anguix	Florida Universitaria, Spain
Juan Carlos Nieves	Umeå University, Sweden
Paulo Novais	Universidade do Minho, Portugal
Carlos Carrascosa	Universitat Politècnica de València, Spain
Andrés Muñoz	Universidad Católica de Murcia, Spain
Ângelo Costa	Universidade do Minho, Portugal
Paula Andrea Rodríguez Marín	Instituto Tecnológico Metropolitano Medellín, Colombia
Floriana Grasso	The University of Liverpool, UK
Patrícia Alves	Polytechnic of Porto, Portugal
Peter Mikulecky	University of Hradec Kralove, Czech Republic
Eva Hudlicka	Psychometrix Associates Blacksburg, USA
Boon Kiat-Quek	National University of Singapore, Singapore
Florentino Fdez-Riverola	University of Vigo, Spain
Hoon Ko	Chosun University, South Korea
Guillaume Lopez	Aoyama Gakuin University, Japan
Ichiro Satoh	National Institute of Informatics Tokyo, Japan

Trust Model for a Multi-agent Based Simulation of Local Energy Markets

Rui Andrade$^{(\boxtimes)}$ ⓘ, Tiago Pinto$^{(\boxtimes)}$ ⓘ, and Isabel Praça$^{(\boxtimes)}$ ⓘ

GECAD - Knowledge Engineering and Decision Support Research Centre,
School of Engineering Polytechnic of Porto (ISEP/IPP) Porto, Lisbon, Portugal
{rfaar,tcp,icp}@isep.ipp.pt

Abstract. This paper explores the concept of the Local Energy Market and, in particular, the need for Trust in the negotiations necessary for this type of market. A multi-agent system is implemented to simulate the Local Energy Market, and a Trust model is proposed to evaluate the proposals sent by the participants, based on forecasting mechanisms that try to predict the expected behavior of the participant. A case study is carried out with several participants who submit false negotiation proposals to assess the ability of the proposed Trust model to correctly evaluate these participants. The results obtained demonstrate that such an approach has the potential to meet the needs of the local market.

Keywords: Trust · Local Energy Market · Multi-agent system

1 Introduction

The energy market and electric grid play a major role in everyday life. Most areas in modern society require electric energy to operate properly. The electric grid has become indispensable for life in modern society. Due to these reasons, it is important to maintain and improve the stability and reliability of the energy grid.

Currently energy grids tend to follow a very strict and somewhat inefficient structure. A high number of entities, that desire to consume energy, are connected to a single centralized energy supplier entity. Traditional energy markets, such as wholesale or retail markets, were not designed to support the rising in distributed energy generation coming from Renewable Energy Sources (RES) in households, small commerce and small industry. Such facts raise questions about different ways of structuring energy markets to deal with these challenges.

One of the possible proposals to answer to this problem is the creation and implementation of Local Energy Market (LEM). LEM are structured in such a way as to enable small-scale negotiations and energy exchanges between participants, who traditionally would only be final consumers. These markets are

This work has received funding from National Funds through FCT (Fundaçao da Ciencia e Tecnologia) under the project SPET – 29165, call SAICT 2017.

F. De La Prieta et al. (Eds.): PAAMS 2020 Workshops, CCIS 1233, pp. 183–194, 2020.
https://doi.org/10.1007/978-3-030-51999-5_15

designed to operate within a regional area, such as a neighborhood or a city. Participants in this market are the local households, small commerce and small industry, that may be regular consumers or consumers with some type of local energy generation, being referred to as *prosumers*. Furthermore, local small-scale power plants can also participate in the LEM. The LEM is better designed to deal with distributed energy generation from RES because the surplus in generation from local energy producers and *prosumers* can be purchased and utilized by local consumers. This flexibility of response makes LEM an attractive proposition for the future of energy markets.

In order to guarantee the success and desired operation of the LEM, it is necessary to ensure security and trust in negotiations. While security is focused on the traditional measures of cyber-security, such as security in network communications, trust is focused on ensuring that the LEM participants and their proposals in the negotiations are viable and trustworthy.

The objective in this work is to create a LEM simulation, and incorporate a trust model. The trust model should be able to score participants trust level during negotiations, allowing the untrustworthy participants (low trust score) to be prohibited from participating in the LEM.

A MAS is a system that combines several Agents, these are software entities that have the capacity to interact among themselves. For this reason it is ideal to simulate the LEM, as each market participant can be simulated individually, and by the means of their interactions it is possible to simulate a far more complex environment, as is the case of the LEM.

After this introductory Section, the document is organized as follows: Sect. 2 presents the context of the work, describing the concepts of the LEM, and of trust models for MAS. Section 3 describes the proposed solution and its development. Section 4 delineates how the experimentation and evaluation process was performed. Lastly, Sect. 5 presents the conclusions of this work.

2   Local Energy Market

The Local Energy Market (LEM) is a novel energy market model. There is no definite definition on what a LEM is, however many authors have addressed this issue, and among their work a general idea of the LEM begins to emerge. Authors exploring this topic tend to define 3 key aspect: (i) Market structure; (ii) Advantages; (iii) Challenges.

The structure of the LEM is generally defined as a group of local participants (such as a neighborhood) [2–4], which are capable of trading energy among themselves. Participants in the local market are separated into 3 kinds [3,6,12]:

- **Consumers:** who wish to buy energy;
- **Producers:** who wish to sell energy;
- **Prosumers:** (consumers with some source of energy generation) who wish to buy and sell energy;

Both the market participants and the underling electrical grid, that serves as a basis for the LEM, are defined as having a monitoring sensors for consumption, generation, energy storage and other data sources; and network communication technologies to share this information [3, 12]. Such an energy grid is referred to as a Smart-Grid [2].

The LEM brings several potential advantages when compared to traditional energy markets. Some authors [2, 6] claim that the LEM would make a more efficient use of electrical grids. Simultaneously it is believed that the shift to Local Energy Markets could reduce the greenhouse effect [2] and create a more sustainable environment [6, 12]. Participants in the LEM (especially traditional consumers) take a much more involved role in the market when compared to traditional markets. These participants gain the ability to directly negotiate and can achieve cost reductions or even profits with their participation [2, 6, 12]. Lastly, the versatility of the LEM makes it possibly for the coexistence with traditional markets [6, 12], that being the case the local market can adapt to the needs of each specific community.

Currently the LEM is facing some challenges that prevent its adoption at a large scale. Abidin et al. [2] identify security concerns as one of these challenges. The local market, and consequently the underling Smart-Grid, deal with a lot of sensitive information that needs to be properly secured from unauthorized access; and from malicious entities who may tamper with data in order to have some financial gain. The former also emphasizes the need for Trust in negotiations in the Local Energy Market (LEM). Interest from the community and an economic upfront investment by investors are also seen as one of the current challenges to the LEM adoption [4, 6]. From a technical point of view the implementation of Smart-Grids capable of providing the support needed for the LEM is still a challenge that needs further research [6]. Lastly, the support form governments and creation of adequate legislation is a must for the success of the LEM [6].

2.1 Trust in Multi-agent Systems

Trust and Reputation Systems (TRS) are designed with the objective of predicting the reliability in the behavior of an entity by analyzing data from past interactions [9]. By performing such analyzes, TRS are able to associate a reputation to each user. Good reputation indicates that the user is trust worthy in its negotiations, and vice versa.

In [9] several trust models are identified, some of which are specific for the Marketplace area of applicability. Two of these trust models seem interesting for this project since they are targeted at a marketplace but apply different strategies. These models are the e-commerce model and ReGreT [10].

[5] views the e-commerce trust model from the perspective of eBay. eBay operates as an online auction web site. Users of this platform can propose their sale offers and/or place bids on other users' offers. In online auction web sites such as eBay the participants in the transactions are humans and these platforms implement mechanisms for participants to review their experience in the

transaction. This feedback provided by the users is then used to feed the TRS with the data necessary to access the reputation of the users [9].

ReGreT is a trust and reputation model proposed by [10]. This model is different from the eBay model because it does not consider trust as a global value. ReGreT has a focus towards modularity [11]. Modules might be used or not depending on the needs of each context. ReGreT considers three kinds of information for trust: the agent own experiences, information from other agents and the social structure among agents. These types of information coincide with the three dimensions used in ReGreT to calculate trust, which are the following:

- **Individual dimension:** Considers the outcomes observed directly by the agent when in negotiation with another agent.
- **Social dimension:** Considers information provided by other entities. Something can be useful when direct information is not available.
- **Ontological dimension:** Considers the contextual information that can be gained by the reputation.

In another work [7] the authors identify three distinct approaches that can be followed when developing a trust mechanism for a MAS. Each approach considers a different dimension of trust. These approaches are:

- **Security Approach:** Is focused on the traditional security mechanisms [13]: confidentiality, availability, authentication, integrity, non-repudiation. This dimension aims to prevent cyber-security threats;
- **Institutional Approach:** Considers the idea of a centralized entity that acts as an overseer in the MAS. This centralized entity, takes the place of an institution that must evaluate all agents and ensure that each one of them is trustworthy. This is the case for the e-commerce trust model;
- **Social Approach:** Is similar to the way humans interact in the real world. With this trust model each agent decides who it considers trustworthy. Agents can make this decision based on their interactions with other agents, and/or by considering others' opinions. This is the case for the ReGreT trust and reputation model.

3   Proposed MAS and Trust Model

The developed MAS follows the agent structure already proposed in [8]. In that work a computational model of a LEM is separated into three kinds of agents:

- **Market Interactions Manager:** Is at the center of every LEM and is responsible for managing all negotiations within the market. The task of ensuring Trust in the negotiations is also a responsibility of the Market Interaction Manager.
- **Participant agent:** Acts on behalf of consumers, producers or prosumers. This agent assumes the role of a negotiator that seeks to best satisfy the needs of the respective market participants (home owners, local commerce and small

industry owners). The Participant Agent will have Sensor Agents that report to him the information needed for the negotiations. The Participant Agent is then able to make proposals to buy or sell energy in the market;

– **Sensor agent:** Has the single responsibility of acquiring one type of data and reporting said data to his respective Participant Agent. A Sensor agent can be, for example, connected to a meter measuring energy consumption in a household, while another sensor agent can be connected to a web service in order to obtain the weather forecast;

With these 3 kinds of agents it is possible to create a reasonably complete representation of a LEM, which includes: consumers, producers and prosumers. The Sensor Agents allow the cyber-physical system, such as the ones of Smart Houses and other connected environments. A complete representation of the proposed LEM model is presented in Fig. 1.

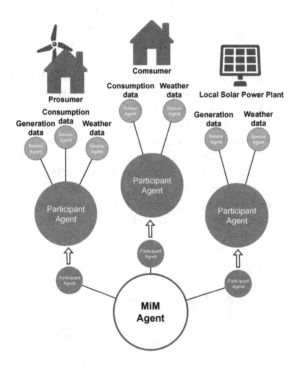

Fig. 1. Proposed LEM model diagram

The LEM is composed of several participants, represented by their respective Participant Agent and all of these agents are connected to the MIM Agent. In Fig. 1 three participants are further detailed as examples of how real participants might be structured in a realistic scenario. These participants are the following:

– **Consumer:** Represents a household without self generation that participates in the market.

– **Prosumer:** Represents an household that participates in the market and has
its own energy generation, with a small wind generator.
– **Local Solar Power Plant:** Exemplifies a small photovoltaic power plant
that is part of the LEM.

3.1   Trust Model

To support the market it is proposed an Institutional based Trust model to
be used by the MIM, capable of evaluating the behavior of participants and
detecting faulty or malicious activities. This Trust model was chosen over the
Social model because with a social model participants might need access to
sensitive (consumption, generation, etc.) data from other participants in order
to make their own Trust evaluation.

The idea for the Trust mechanism is that with information such as weather,
historical consumption and generation data, and other contextual data, it is
possible to use forecasting methods to try to predict what the participant's consumption, generation or proposals should be in the current market negotiation
period.

Using such forecasted values it is possible to obtain an idea if the participant
is trustworthy over time. Since forecasting methods always have a certain degree
of uncertainty a single proposed value that does not match the forecasted value
does not provide a reliable metric. So by using an evaluation over time it is
thought that incorrect forecasted values become negligible.

Figure 2 presents a diagram of the proposed Trust evaluation process. As
shown the trust evaluation process takes three values as input: the participant's
proposed values for the current market negotiation period, the participant's trust
value from the previous negotiation period, and the forecasted value based on
the participants historical and contextual data.

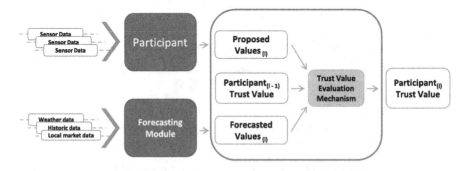

Fig. 2. Trust evaluation process

The definition of the proposed trust model is the following:

The Trust Value ranges from $[0, 1]$ where 1 is the highest trust and 0 lowest trust value. The Trust value for a participant p in negotiation period i is represented as t_{pi}.

The evaluation formula takes several variables into consideration that can be configured to obtain the best possible results, these variables are:

- ar: represents the *acceptance range*, which is a percentage value;
- tiv: represents the *trust increase value*, a value by which the participant's trust is increased;
- tdv: represents the *trust decrease value*, a value by which the participant's trust is decreased;
- sv_{pin}: represents the *submitted value* by participant p, from the data source of sensor n in market negotiation period i;
- fv_{pin}: represents the *forecasted value* for participant p, for sensor n in negotiation period i;
- t_{p0}: represents the *default trust value*, the trust value with which all participants start with.

Equation 1 shows how the trust evaluation is calculated by being combined with either the Eq. 2 for the asymmetric acceptance range or the Eq. 3 for the symmetric acceptance range.

The difference between the asymmetric and the symmetric acceptance range is that the asymmetric has a higher acceptance range when the forecasting mechanism over estimates the value, since a percentage from a higher value results in a higher range.

$$t_{pi} = t_{p(i-1)} + \frac{1}{n} \sum_{i=1}^{n} trust\_eval(sv_{pi}, fv_{pi}) \tag{1}$$

$$asym(sv_{pi}, fv_{pi}) = \begin{cases} tiv & \text{if } sv_{pi} > fv_{pi} * (1 - ar) \text{ AND } sv_{pi} < fv_{pi} * (1 + ar) \\ tdv & \text{otherwise} \end{cases} \tag{2}$$

$$sym(sv_{pi}, fv_{pi}) = \begin{cases} tiv & \text{if } fv_{pi} > sv_{pi} * (1 - ar) \text{ AND } fv_{pi} < sv_{pi} * (1 + ar) \\ tdv & \text{otherwise} \end{cases} \tag{3}$$

There needs to be some consideration of how each participant's trust value is interpreted. Two things need to be taken into account: a participant that always submits real and true values should be fully trustworthy and so should be evaluated with a 1.0 trust value; on the other hand a participant that always submits false values should not be trusted and should have a trust evaluation of 0.0.

There is however some subjectivity in considering these trust evaluations. For example, a participant that always submits real and true values and is evaluated with a 0.9 trust value, or a participant that always submits false values and is evaluated with a 0.1 trust value also seem like acceptable evaluations. Given this subjective nature of the trust evaluation three trust ranges are proposed:

- **Trustworthy**: range where the trust value is $[h_t, 1]$, and any participant in this range is fully trusted;
- **Unsure**: range where the trust value is $[m_t, h_t[$, and any participant in this range is considered to be a possible malicious or faulty participant and should, for example be further evaluated by the market authority;
- **Untrustworthy**: range where the trust value is $[0, m_t[$, and any participant in this range is considered a malicious or faulty participant and should be prevented from participating in the market.

The values of: h_t minimum threshold for high trust and m_t minimum threshold for medium trust, are variable values that can be configured accordingly to the needs of the LEM.

4   Case Study

The idea for this case study is to simulate a LEM with several participants that vary in the amount and intensity of false proposals and observing how the proposed Trust model evaluates these participants. Since the trust model is based on forecasting, forecasting methods are simulated as a Normal Standard Distribution based on what the real proposal value should be, this way forecasting methods with distinct levels of accuracy and precision can be estimated, and it is possible to see how the performance of the forecasting method influences the Trust model performance.

The LEM was simulated for a 24 h period and with 15 min market negotiation period duration, which results in a total of 96 market negotiation periods. Each simulation was performed 10 times and its results were averaged. The 24 h simulated were of a Monday, simulated from 00:00–24:00 h. The LEM aggregates 4 participants using real consumption data from private homes publicly available in [1]. Each participant has his own bias in the proposals it submits:

- **TP** - True Proposer: Is the only who does not have a bias and always sends the real value;
- **LUaUP** - Low Under and Over Proposer: Sends a real value 80% of the times and a value between 30% under to 30% over the real value the rest of the times;
- **MUaOP** - Medium Under and Over Proposer: Sends a real value 50% of the times and a value between 60% under to 60% over the real value the rest of the times;
- **HUaOP** - High Under and Over Proposer: Sends a real value 30% of the times and a value between 90% under to 90% over the real value the rest of the times.

With these participants configurations the expected result is a correlation between the trust value of the participant and the amount of false submissions. The True Proposer acts as a base line showing if trustworthy participants are being correctly identified.

As for the estimated forecasting methods, four were simulated, in decreasing levels of accuracy and precision. The estimated forecasting methods have the following mean $\bar{x}$ and standard deviation σ:

- **Perfect Predictor**: $\bar{x} = 1.0\ \sigma = 0.0$;
- **Low Center Predictor**: $\bar{x} = 1.0\ \sigma = 0.2$;
- **High Center Predictor**: $\bar{x} = 1.0\ \sigma = 0.4$.

The simulations are preformed with both the Symmetric and Asymmetric acceptance methods. Lastly the Trust formula variables are configured as such: $ar = 0.5$, $tiv = 0.01$, $tdv = -0.08$ and $t_{p0} = 0.8$; and the trust ranges are: *Trustworthy* $[0.8, 1]$, *Unsure* $[0.5, 0.8[$ and *Untrustworthy* $[0, 0.5[$.

These values were chosen after some experimentation as they proved to be adequate values for the specific scenario in study.

4.1   Case Study Results and Discussion

To present these results in a clear way, each simulation was divided into 2 graphs showing the trust value for each participant over time, separated by the forecasting method and acceptance method.

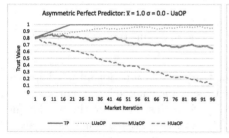
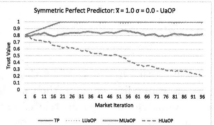

Fig. 3. Asymmetric perfect predictor   **Fig. 4.** Symmetric perfect predictor

Looking at Fig. 3 there is a clear distinction in the trust evaluation of each participant. Analyzing Fig. 4 the results have some changes from the Asymmetric model. All participants obtained a higher trust value compared to the results of the Asymmetric acceptance.

Figures 5 and 6 show different result. In the previous estimator the trust value for the TP participant was always 1.0, but now with the uncertainty in the estimated forecasting method the trust value oscillates, however it remains close to 1.0. In Fig. 6 the results are very similar to the ones obtained with the Perfect Predictor. The biggest difference is in Fig. 5 where the TP and LUaOP participants obtained trust values very similar to the ones obtained with the Perfect Predictor, and the MUaOP and HUaOP participants obtained evaluations significantly lower. This demonstrates that the acceptance formula used can make a big difference in the results.

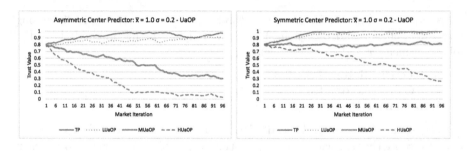

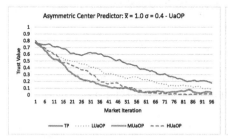

Fig. 5. Asymmetric low predictor

Fig. 6. Symmetric low predictor

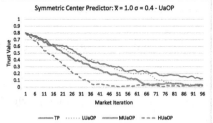

Fig. 7. Asymmetric high predictor

Fig. 8. Symmetric high predictor

Lastly both Fig. 7 and Fig. 8 show low trust evaluations for all participants. There are some differences in the way the trust value changed over time between the Asymmetric and Symmetric acceptance formulas, however the at the end the values are very similar (all below 0.2). Even the TP participants obtained a low trust evaluation, this result shows that with a low performing forecasting method the trust evaluation is also low performing.

Finally these results lead us to conclude that:

1. Using the proposed trust methodology it is possible to dynamically update the trust value of a participant;
2. The MIM agent is able to use the proposed trust methodology to access the trust value of a participant;
3. The performance of forecasting methods has a direct impact on the trust evaluation;
4. The acceptance formula can have an impact on the trust evaluation;
5. The higher the amount of false values a participant submits the lower his trust value will be.

5   Conclusion

The Local Energy Market (LEM) is an emergent market model that is aimed towards solving the challenges currently faced in the energy landscape. One of the requirements for the success of LEM is Trust in its negotiations. The main goals in this work are the development of a Multi-Agent System (MAS) for simulation and modeling LEM; and the proposal of a Trust model capable of ensuring trust the LEM negotiations.

A MAS was developed with three types of agents, namely:(i) the Sensor Agent, (ii) the Participant Agent and (iii) the Market Interaction Manager (MIM) Agent, each with their own responsibilities, thus facilitating, the process of modeling the market.

To give response to the needs of trust in the LEM, a formulation was proposed to calculate a trust value for each participant based on the analysis of the participant's historical data, contextual data, such as weather data, and by using forecasting methods to predict the participants expected behavior. The trust value given to participants evolves over time and takes into consideration its market submissions to the LEM, the forecasting of those submissions and considers the disparity between those values.

A case study was carried out in which several simulations were made with 4 participants using realistic consumption data and with different biases towards submitting false values. Each simulation used a different estimated forecasting mechanism with distinct levels of accuracy and precision.

The LEM was simulated for a 24 h period and 15 min market negotiation period duration, which resulted in a total of 96 market negotiation periods. This case study aim was to evaluate the ability of the proposed trust formulation to respond to market needs by evaluating each participant with an appropriate trust value.

The realization of the case study made it possible to conclude that: (i) The forecasting methodology used has a big impact on the performance of the trust formulation, but the acceptance formula also needs to be considered; (ii) A bad forecasting method, will provide a bad trust evaluation; (iii) The higher the amount of false values a participant submits the lower his trust value will be, which is the desired outcome.

Lastly some ideas need to be considered for future development and exploration: (i) The use of different acceptance methods, such as acceptance with a static value, fuzzy logic, or another acceptance method that provides better results; (ii) There is also a need to establish more concretely which trust values would be the most ideal to assign to participants with different behaviors; (iii) Furthermore, another point of research should be continuing the exploration of trust methods, and combining them with real forecasting methodologies, in order to understand how a trust system works as a whole.

References

1. Open Data Sets IEEE PES Intelligent Systems Subcommittee. https://site.ieee.org/pes-iss/data-sets/
2. Abidin, A., Aly, A., Cleemput, S., Mustafa, M.A.: Towards a local electricity trading market based on secure multiparty computation (2016)

3. Ampatzis, M., Nguyen, P.H., Kling, W.: Local electricity market design for the coordination of distributed energy resources at district level. In: 2014 IEEE PES Innovative Smart Grid Technologies Conference Europe (ISGT-Europe), pp. 1–6. IEEE (2014)
4. Bremdal, B.A., Olivella, P., Rajasekharan, J.: EMPOWER: a network market approach for local energy trade. In: 2017 IEEE Manchester PowerTech, pp. 1–6 (2017). https://doi.org/10.1109/PTC.2017.7981108
5. Houser, D., Wooders, J.: Reputation in auctions: theory, and evidence from eBay. J. Econ. Manag. Strategy 15(2), 353–369 (2006)
6. Mendes, G., Nylund, J., Annala, S., Honkapuro, S., Kilkki, O., Segerstam, J.: Local energy markets: opportunities, benefits, and barriers (2018)
7. Pinyol, I., Sabater-Mir, J.: Computational trust and reputation models for open multi-agent systems: a review. Artif. Intell. Rev. 40(1), 1–25 (2013)
8. Praça, I., Ramos, S., Andrade, R., da Silva, A.S., Sica, E.T.: Analysis and simulation of local energy markets. In: 2019 16th International Conference on the European Energy Market (EEM), pp. 1–5. IEEE (2019)
9. Rahimi, H., Bekkali, H.E.: State of the art of trust and reputation systems in e-commerce context. arXiv preprint arXiv:1710.10061 (2017)
10. Sabater, J., Sierra, C.: REGRET: a reputation model for gregarious societies. In: Fourth Workshop Deception Fraud Trust Agent Societies, vol. 70, pp. 61–69 (2001)
11. Sabater, J., Sierra, C.: Reputation and social network analysis in multi-agent systems. In: Proceedings of the First International Joint Conference on Autonomous Agents and Multiagent Systems: Part 1, AAMAS 2002, pp. 475–482. ACM, New York (2002). https://doi.org/10.1145/544741.544854
12. Teotia, F., Bhakar, R.: Local energy markets: concept, design and operation. In: 2016 National Power Systems Conference (NPSC), pp. 1–6. IEEE (2016)
13. Yan, Y., Qian, Y., Sharif, H., Tipper, D.: A survey on cyber security for smart grid communications. IEEE Commun. Surv. Tutor. 14(4), 998–1010 (2012). https://doi.org/10.1109/SURV.2012.010912.00035

Should You Use a Vote Module for Sentiment Classification of Online Social Text?

Ricardo Barbosa[1,2]($\boxtimes$) (ID), Ricardo Santos[1]($\boxtimes$) (ID), and Paulo Novais[2] (ID)

[1] CIICESI, Escola Superior de Tecnologia e Gestão, Politécnico do Porto,
Porto, Portugal
{rmb,rjs}@estg.ipp.pt

[2] ALGORITMI Center, University of Minho, Braga, Portugal
pjon@di.uminho.pt

Abstract. In this work, we conduct a study where we compare the usage of a single classifier and the usage of a majority vote system composed of multiple classifiers. Each classifier was created using machine learning techniques and trained with real data. For the domain, we considered textual expressions present on online social networks, which can be volatile in characters count. This work seeks to prove two hypothesis: (1) the usage of a vote module that considers the output of an odd number of classifiers, will address the advantages characteristics of each classifier while mitigating their disadvantages; (2) the usage of a vote system will enable classifiers to correctly classify new labels that were not defined in the training process (like classifying neutral sentiment in addition to positive and negative). Our vote module is composed by a Naïve Bayes, a Logistic Regression, and a Support Vector Machine classifier. The tests that we conducted consider the online social textual content that varies in the character counting and our results suggests that there is no need for a vote system when considering the online social content, like comments, that is typically informal and do not surpass the count of 500 characters.

Keywords: Sentiment classification · Machine learning · Online social networks

1 Introduction

Following the definition of the Online Virtual Sensor that extracts data from online social networks [1], we now face the necessity of developing our first module, the sentiment classification. This module is an essential characteristic of our virtual sensor, described as a vital component in the representation of multidimensional interests network, intended to provide organisations and smart environments with insights about an individual (or group of individuals) [2,3].

This work has been supported by FCT - Fundação para a Ciência e Tecnologia within the Project Scope: UIDB/04728/2020.

F. De La Prieta et al. (Eds.): PAAMS 2020 Workshops, CCIS 1233, pp. 195–204, 2020.
https://doi.org/10.1007/978-3-030-51999-5_16

Sentiment classification of written text is not a novel process by itself [13], however, even with more straightforward initial approaches like supervised learning, there is a constant debate of the algorithm to use, which is directly correlated to the task at hand. While support vector machine algorithms tend to outperform others when dealing with multidimensional and continuous features, methods such decision trees or rule-based algorithms tend to perform better when dealing with discrete or nominal data, and Naïve Bayes method may need a relatively small dataset to achieve the maximum prediction accuracy (when compared to others) [6].

Our final goal for this module is to adopt deep learning approaches [19], like convolutional neural networks [10] [16] or recursive neural networks [17] that are known for better results, and consider particular grammatical situations like double negation, and are even able to recognise sarcasm. However, we are interested in testing this implementation on more straightforward techniques, namely supervised learning: the standard way to solve a learning problem when there are labelled datasets available. Before performing any classification tasks, usually, there is a necessity to choose a classifier. While searching and analysing the majority of the most commonly used classifiers, we were interested in a voting system. Vote is a meta algorithm that combines different classifiers, and by using a combination rule (like majority) produces a result. Our interest in this subject leads us to the definition of two hypotheses:

Hypothesis 1. *The usage of a vote module will address the advantages characteristics of each classifier while mitigating their disadvantages.*

Hypothesis 2. *Without training the classifiers for a specific label (in this case, neutral), and by defining a confidence value for each classification result, the vote module would be able to guess if a sentence has neutral sentiment value correctly.*

This work is divided as follows. In Sect. 2, we perform a literature review and analyse similar works that classify sentiment on online social network content. Section 3 is dedicated to materials and methods and contains four subsections, which include the process of data selection, pre-processing, the selection of machine learning classifiers based on a set of metric scores, and the definition of the vote module. In Sect. 4, we present our results contextualised with the theorems previously defined, considering the domain of online social networks content. This work ends with a conclusion where we discuss if the hypotheses can be proven in this context.

2   Related Work

The application of sentiment analysis (or opinion mining) to the content produced on online social network platforms is not a novel concept. The work of Patodkar and Sheikh [14] is focused on the sentiment analysis of short informal texts found on the online social network Twitter. After the examination of commonly used algorithms for text classification like Naïve Bayes, Decision

Trees, Support Vector Machine, and Random Forests, to perform the classification of these commonly called "tweets", they have chosen the Naïve Bayes algorithm "because it is a simple and intuitive method whose performance is similar to other approaches". In their system proposal, the authors have followed a sequence of steps data pre-processing which includes: paragraph splitter; sentence splitter; word tokenization; word ambiguation; and Part of Speech tagging.

In their work [18], Sotiropoulos, Pournarakis, and Giaglis performed sentiment classification using Support Vector Machines. Their corpus consisted of over 9000 sentences randomly collected from the online social network Twitter. Despise their specific context, (Greek Banks) the main characteristic was present: unstructured and typically informal sentences that do not surpass the count of 500 characters. The choice of the classifier was a result of their comparison of classification accuracy between Support Vector Machines and the following state of the art classifiers: linear SVMs; radial basis function neural networks; random forests; multi-layer neural networks; Bayesian networks; Naïve Bayes; and classification via clustering. Their results contradict the affirmation for the superiority of the Naïve Bayes classifier done by Patodkar and Sheikh [14], and leaves us without a definitive answer for "Which is the best classifier?".

With no answer for the previous question, instead of choosing only one algorithm, Catal and Nangir [5] followed a similar approach to the one proposed on this document and have used a vote system for classifying sentiment in Turkish based comments. Their vote module was based on the conjunction of three classifiers: Naïve Bayes; Support Vector Machine; and Bagging, and their result has shown increase performance when using the vote module, instead of the usage of a single classifier. As mentioned by the authors, this approach proved to be beneficial when classifying Turkish based sentences. Despise a lack of clarity regarding their pre-processing steps, and the specific context and language, the results generated by their vote system suggest a positive perspective for our initial hypothesis.

3 Materials and Methods

Although a specific programming language is not required, we used Python since it has most of the functionalities needed to perform simple Natural Language Processing (NLP) tasks. The term Natural Language Processing involves a broad set of techniques for automated generation, manipulation and analysis of natural or human languages. Although most NLP techniques inherit mainly from linguistics and artificial intelligence, they are also influenced by relatively newer areas such as machine learning, computational statistics, and cognitive science.

Most of the times, it does not fulfill the requirements for the most demanding NLP tasks. To cover this problem, we used the Natural Language Toolkit (NLTK)[1]. NLTK is a collection of modules and corpora, released under an open-source license, that not only provides convenient functions and wrappers that

---

[1] https://nltk.org/.

can be used as building blocks for everyday NLP tasks, but it also provides raw and pre-processed versions of standard corpora used in NLP literature and courses.

The overall process can be described as follow: when given an input, the module should generate an output that contains the sentiment classification value of the input (positive, negative, or even neutral), along with a confidence value that indicates a specific value associated with the classification given by the machine learning algorithms.

3.1   Data Selection

Typically, any process related to NLP, or any type of data classification, begins with a selection of data. Regarding the data that will be used, it can be manually or automatically extracted, or we can select and use an existing dataset. In this work, we decided to use a dataset and, as a result, we needed to select a dataset from the desired domain (online social content). One common practice is to use a dataset that is related to film reviews [21], but we also wanted to integrate other subjects. As a result, the data selected consists in the combination of two datasets: the first being a dataset of hand-picked sentences [8], and the second being a combination of opinions of products, films, and restaurants, gathered from three different major online stores [12]. Both datasets contain sentences labelled with positive or negative sentiment, with no neutral sentences present.

Since a human classified the sentences, they are associated with a personal judgement that results in the classification label. However, after a review of the data, we agree that the own judgement on the pre-classified data will not induce bias on the classification process, meaning that we agree with the labelling performed. Therefore, the selected dataset contains close to 7000 entries of sentences, of different lengths, classified with a positive tag, and the same amount for negative (to prevent bias towards one sentiment).

3.2   Pre-processing Data

Each sentence will suffer a pre-processing manipulation that starts with the creation of a bag of words, containing each expression found in the sentence, associated with the correct sentiment label. The classification that we will conduct on this work is performed in uni-grams, despite promising results with n-grams [4], meaning that textual characteristics like double negation, irony, or sarcasm will not be considered by the classifiers which should improve classification result values, but reduce real-world scenarios application. This decision is based on the initial intention of having a more straightforward approach to the problem. This document classification process extracts each word and grammatical features from sentences, disregarding grammar and order, but keeping multiplicity. Since only words that have an impact on the classification are needed for this process, it is possible to discard punctuation or symbols.

There are additional steps that can improve the quality of the data [7]. As a result, we replace contractions with their expanded versions (e.g. "won't" is replaced by "will not"), as well as removing common errors like extra characters (e.g. "loooove" is replaced by "love"). Each word is then attributed to a Part of Speech (POS) tag, and the process ends with another data transforming task, which converts each word to its lower-case form. This process generates as output a list of individual words, with a POS tag and classified as either positive or negative. The POS tag will be necessary since only some grammatical features determine the polarity of a word, and we only considered every variation of nouns, verbs, adverbs, and adjectives.

Like every real-life scenario, some words appear more often than others, and there is the need to exclude some words that appear less frequently, preventing the occurrence of false positives. This task is accomplished by creating a frequency distribution list of all words present in the dataset that contains words tagged with POS and with a sentiment value associated (positive or negative). It would be possible to train our classifiers by using all of this amount of words; however, it may not be useful, and we should implement a limit. Therefore, it is needed a filtering process that contains a determined amount of the most common words. The final step is dedicated to the creation of a training set that will be used to train the classifiers and a testing set that will be used to measure the accuracy value of the classifiers. We selected a 1:3 ration, meaning that 2/3 of the total features set will be used for training the classifiers, while the remaining 1/3 will be used for testing their accuracy. To prevent bias towards one specific sentiment, before the creation of the training and test sets, all features are shuffled.

3.3   Classifier Selection

We have selected three different algorithms: Naïve Bayes algorithm, Logistic Regression, and Support Vector Machines.

The Naïve Bayes classifier is a supervised statistical and classification method for information classification. The classifier is based on the Bayes Theorem with the "naive" assumption of independence between every pair of features, meaning that the presence (or absence) of a particular feature has no effect or relation with the presence (or absence) of any other feature.

Logistic Regression is a technique that derives from the field of statistic. Is highly used in binary classification problems (meaning that we can only have two different class values). Despise being more associated with prediction problems (rather than classification) we have selected it since its model is different from the other two choices.

Support vector machines (SVMs) are a set of supervised learning methods used for classification, regression and outliers detection. This method technique was introduced by Vapnik [20] and optimised, among others, by Platt [15]. SVMs take the set of training data and marking it as part of a category then predicts whether the test document is a member of an existing class. These methods are often used in text classification, image analysis, or bio-informatics (to name a few).

Table 1. Metrics scores (AC - Accuracy; PR - Precision; RE - Recall; F1 - F_Measure), and respective deviations, considering 5 instances of 3 classifiers (NB - Naïve Bayes; LR - Logistic Regression; SVM - Support Vector Machine) across different features count (from 100 to 10000)

	100 Features						500 Features					
	NB		LR		SVM		NB		LR		SVM	
	MEAN	BEST	MEAN	BEST	MEAN	BEST	MEAN	BEST	MEAN	BEST	MEAN	BEST
AC	0.739±0.06	0.818	0.773±0.05	0.818	0.803±0.06	0.894	0.794±0.02	0.815	0.817±0.02	0.842	0.808±0.02	0.839
PR	0.743±0.02	0.809	0.786±0.04	0.823	0.817±0.04	0.887	0.794±0.02	0.815	0.817±0.02	0.842	0.809±0.02	0.840
RE	0.735±0.06	0.816	0.769±0.05	0.818	0.801±0.06	0.899	0.793±0.02	0.816	0.816±0.02	0.842	0.808±0.02	0.838
F1	0.731±0.07	0.812	0.764±0.06	0.818	0.796±0.06	0.891	0.793±0.02	0.815	0.816±0.02	0.842	0.808±0.02	0.839

	1000 Features						5000 Features					
	NB		LR		SVM		NB		LR		SVM	
	MEAN	BEST	MEAN	BEST	MEAN	BEST	MEAN	BEST	MEAN	BEST	MEAN	BEST
AC	0.810±0.02	0.836	0.832±0.02	0.850	0.828±0.01	0.842	0.848±0.01	0.856	0.855±0.01	0.862	0.849±0.01	0.857
PR	0.810±0.02	0.837	0.832±0.02	0.850	0.828±0.01	0.842	0.848±0.01	0.856	0.855±0.01	0.861	0.849±0.01	0.856
RE	0.808±0.02	0.835	0.831±0.02	0.849	0.828±0.01	0.842	0.847±0.01	0.854	0.855±0.01	0.861	0.849±0.01	0.856
F1	0.809±0.02	0.836	0.831±0.02	0.850	0.828±0.01	0.842	0.847±0.01	0.855	0.855±0.01	0.861	0.849±0.01	0.856

	7500 Features						10000 Features					
	NB		LR		SVM		NB		LR		SVM	
	MEAN	BEST	MEAN	BEST	MEAN	BEST	MEAN	BEST	MEAN	BEST	MEAN	BEST
AC	0.842±0.01	0.847	0.845±0.01	0.853	0.840±0.01	0.846	0.841±0.01	0.848	0.842±0.00	0.846	0.837±0.00	0.841
PR	0.842±0.01	0.847	0.845±0.01	0.853	0.840±0.01	0.845	0.841±0.00	0.848	0.842±0.00	0.845	0.837±0.00	0.840
RE	0.841±0.01	0.846	0.844±0.01	0.852	0.840±0.01	0.845	0.841±0.01	0.848	0.841±0.00	0.846	0.837±0.00	0.841
F1	0.842±0.01	0.847	0.845±0.01	0.853	0.840±0.01	0.845	0.841±0.01	0.848	0.841±0.00	0.845	0.837±0.00	0.841

As stated before, we need to select the number of features to be used. This can be a trial and error process since it varies from the type of data used. We have chosen different intervals of features, namely 100, 200, 500, 1000, 5000, 7500, and 10000 features, seeking to understand at what number of features the classifiers best perform. Since the data is shuffled we also train each classifier five times with the same feature number, meaning that in this initial process we will train 90 classifiers. The results of this classification process can be seen on Table 1 that contains the mean value for each classifier across four different metrics (Accuracy, Precision, Recall, and F_Measure), respective deviations, as well as a reference to the best score of that classifier using different amounts of features.

We can observe that despite an extraordinary case regarding an SVM classifier with 100 features, each classifier seems to better perform at 5000 features. To understand if other hidden value could have better performance, we defined two new feature values that correspond to the lower and upper intervals of 5000. We generate 30 new classifiers with a number of 3500 and 6250 features, and the results of this classification process did not outperform the classifiers trained with 5000 features.

3.4 Vote Module

Despise the similarity between metric values, is possible that classifiers with similar values will produce different outputs regarding the sentiment classification of a given sentence (one can determine that the sentence is positive, while the others can determine that is negative).

Of the 120 classifiers previously trained, we will select three of them (one for each algorithm). Since the best scores were found with 5000 features, we will choose the best classifier for each algorithm trained with 5000 features. To prevent a lack of consensuses regarding the classification, the vote module will consider an odd number of classifiers (three). This voting system will include the outputs of the selected three classifiers, and use a statistical implementation of mode to output a classification result. The mode of a sample is the element that occurs with higher frequency in the collection, and since there is present an odd number of classifiers if only one of the classifiers conclude that one sentence is positive, the remaining two conclude that is negative, taking in consideration the confidence values of each classifier, is more likely that the sentence is negative. Theoretically, the voting system also provides a solution to the problem when a classifier has a classification with a low confidence value, by supporting its decision with the outputs of the other classifiers.

4   Results

Different online social networks appeal to different types of people and is only natural that the content is also different. One of those differences is correlated with the number of characters present per sentence, and we want to include those differences in our test. We use the character limit of selected popular networks as a reference to define our length intervals. The social network Twitter is known for its 140 characters restriction, Snapchat is limited to 80, a Reddit title is limited to 300, and Pinterest limits is content to 500 characters. Additionally, ideal character count includes 40–80 for Facebook and 70–110 for Twitter [9].

Based on the character limitations, and recommendations, across the most popular online social networks, we defined the following length intervals for our test: tiny - under 40 characters; small - between 40 and 80; medium - between 80 and 160; and long - between 160 and 500 characters. For each interval, we define ten manually selected real sentences that respect each interval length. Regarding the sentiment of each sentence, we divided each label into 'slight' and 'strong', meaning that we have sentences that are slightly positive, and sentences strong negatives. As a result, our test data is composed of 10 sentences for each length interval, divided into two categories (slight and strong), meaning that we have a small sample consisting of 160 sentences. Since the sentences were manually collected and tagged, their sentiment is subjective to our interpretation. Because the classifiers were not defined to it, we also avoid the usage of double negations and irony.

By testing each sentence using the three selected classifiers and the vote module, we obtained the results present in Table 2. This table represents the number of correct guesses for each classifier, and an additional line that represents the output of the vote module. Overall, each classifier surpasses the 80% mark of correct classifications, with the best results belonging to the Naïve Bayes algorithm

Table 2. Correct classification results of 160 sentences that vary in size (T - tiny; S - small; M - medium; L - long), considering 3 classifiers (NB - Naïve Bayes; LR - Logistic Regression; SVM - Support Vector Machine) and a vote module

	Positive								Negative								Total	
	Slight				Strong				Slight				Strong					
	T	S	M	L	T	S	M	L	T	S	M	L	T	S	M	L	Numeric	Percentage
NB	9	6	8	7	10	9	7	8	8	6	10	8	8	8	10	10	132/160	83%
LR	7	7	8	6	9	8	7	8	9	7	10	9	9	8	10	9	131/160	82%
SVM	7	7	8	6	9	8	8	7	9	7	10	8	9	9	10	9	131/160	82%
VOTE	7	7	8	6	10	8	7	8	9	7	10	9	9	8	10	9	132/160	83%

and the vote module (with 83% each). Also, we do not see a significant difference between the classification of 'slight' and 'strong' positive/negative sentences.

Table 3. Correct classification results of 170 sentences that vary in size (T - tiny; S - small; M - medium; L - long; VAR - various), considering 3 classifiers (NB - Naïve Bayes; LR - Logistic Regression; SVM - Support Vector Machine) and a vote module, and neutral text

	Positive								Negative								Neutral	Total	
	Slight				Strong				Slight				Strong				VAR		
	T	S	M	L	T	S	M	L	T	S	M	L	T	S	M	L		Numeric	Percentage
NB	8	6	8	7	8	9	7	7	7	5	10	8	8	8	10	10	2	128/170	75%
LR	6	5	5	6	7	7	7	8	7	5	9	7	8	8	9	9	9	122/170	72%
SVM	6	5	6	6	8	8	7	6	7	6	10	7	8	8	10	9	9	126/170	74%
VOTE	7	6	6	7	8	8	7	8	7	5	10	7	8	8	10	9	9	130/170	76%

Motivated by the second hypothesis, we conducted a new test. In addition to the previous test data, we include data that is neutral in sentiment. This is a small sample of data that consists of 10 sentences that vary in the character count. In order to predict this new label, we introduced a new rule to our classifiers output: if a confidence value of output is bellow 65%, the sentence is labelled as neutral. Also, since it affects our vote module, we defined that if each classifier outputs a different result (one positive, one neutral, and one negative), the default output of the vote is neutral. By observing the new results, detailed in Table 3, we notice a considerable decrease in the number of correct guesses, and low classifications result for neutral sentences for the Naïve Bayes algorithm. In this test, the vote module has a higher number of correct classifications (76%), surpassing the second-best by 1%. Despite being able to predict the neutral inputs, it is notable that the overall accuracy percentage of the voting module is inferior to the previous scenario where were only considered positive and negative inputs. The results reinforce the importance of having neutral examples when performing sentiment classification [11].

5   Conclusion

Our initial hypothesis states that the usage of a vote module could outperform the usage of a single classifier, especially when taking into consideration different characters count. By analysing the test results, represented in Table 2, this hypothesis was not confirmed. The classification result for each classifier is similar to the others, meaning that the vote module was not able to surpass any of them (being equally matched by the Naïve Bayes classifier). This means that the extra resources for the vote module can, in this context, be avoided since it did not offer better results.

We do believe that one of the main reasons for the hypothesis not being fulfilled resides inside the pre-processing step. The quality of this process leads to an insignificant difference between algorithms, despite their natural differences and sets of strengths and weaknesses. When comparing our results to the result present on the work of Catal and Nangir [5] (where they also used a vote algorithm), we believe that the difference on the dataset domain, the pre-processing steps (which are not sufficiently detailed on their work), and the difference in languages, have been decisive for the clear differences in the results.

Regarding the second hypothesis of this work, we fail to see this hypothesis proved. Despite being able to classify neutral sentences correctly, overall, the results of including neutral classification without neutral entries present on the training set are low. Globally, each classifier, and the vote module, were inferior to the previous results, concluding that if neutral classification is needed, then neutral training entries are vital (which was expected for supervised learning).

References

1. Barbosa, R., Santos, R.: Online social networks as sensors in smart environments. In: 2016 Global Information Infrastructure and Networking Symposium (GIIS). IEEE, October 2016. https://doi.org/10.1109/giis.2016.7814950
2. Barbosa, R., Santos, R.: Layer by layer: a multidimensional approach to online social profiles. In: 2017 Computing Conference. IEEE, July 2017. https://doi.org/10.1109/sai.2017.8252202
3. Barbosa, R., Santos, R.: Multidimensional approach to online interest networks. In: DEStech Transactions on Computer Science and Engineering (CMEE), January 2017. https://doi.org/10.12783/dtcse/cmee2016/5372
4. Bespalov, D., Bai, B., Qi, Y., Shokoufandeh, A.: Sentiment classification based on supervised latent n-gram analysis. In: Proceedings of the 20th ACM International Conference on Information and Knowledge Management. CIKM 2011, pp. 375–382. ACM, New York (2011). https://doi.org/10.1145/2063576.2063635
5. Catal, C., Nangir, M.: A sentiment classification model based on multiple classifiers. Appl. Soft Comput. **50**, 135–141 (2017). https://doi.org/10.1016/j.asoc.2016.11.022

6. Celli, F.: Adaptive Personality Recognition from Text. LAP Lambert Academic Publishing (2013). https://www.ebook.de/de/product/20375194/fabio_celli_adaptive_personality_recognition_from_text.html
7. Chopra, D., Joshi, N., Mathur, I.: Mastering Natural Language Processing with Python. Packt Publishing, Birmingham (2016)
8. Harrison: Positive and negative short reviews dataset, May 2013. https://pythonprogramming.net/static/downloads/short_reviews/
9. Jackson, D.: Know your limit: The ideal length of every social media post. https://sproutsocial.com/insights/social-media-character-counter//
10. Kim, Y.: Convolutional neural networks for sentence classification. arXiv preprint arXiv:1408.5882 (2014)
11. Koppel, M., Schler, J.: The importance of neutral examples for learning sentiment. Comput. Intell. **22**(2), 100–109 (2006). https://doi.org/10.1111/j.1467-8640.2006.00276.x. https://onlinelibrary.wiley.com/doi/abs/10.1111/j.1467-8640.2006.00276.x
12. Kotzias, D., Denil, M., De Freitas, N., Smyth, P.: From group to individual labels using deep features. In: Proceedings of the 21th ACM SIGKDD International Conference on Knowledge Discovery and Data Mining, pp. 597–606. ACM (2015)
13. Pang, B., Lee, L., Vaithyanathan, S.: Thumbs up?: sentiment classification using machine learning techniques. In: Proceedings of the ACL-02 Conference on Empirical Methods in Natural Language Processing. EMNLP 2002, vol. 10, pp. 79–86. Association for Computational Linguistics, Stroudsburg (2002). https://doi.org/10.3115/1118693.1118704
14. Patodkar, V., I.R., S.: Twitter as a corpus for sentiment analysis and opinion mining. IJARCCE **5**, 320–322 (2016). https://doi.org/10.17148/IJARCCE.2016.51274
15. Platt, J.C.: Advances in Kernel Methods: Support Vector Learning. The MIT Press, Cambridge (1998). https://www.amazon.com/Advances-Kernel-Methods-Support-Learning/dp/0262194163?SubscriptionId=0JYN1NVW651KCA56C102&tag=techkie-20&linkCode=xm2&camp=2025&creative=165953&creativeASIN=0262194163
16. Severyn, A., Moschitti, A.: Unitn: training deep convolutional neural network for Twitter sentiment classification. In: Proceedings of the 9th International Workshop on Semantic Evaluation (SemEval 2015), pp. 464–469 (2015)
17. Socher, R.,et al.: Recursive deep models for semantic compositionality over a sentiment treebank. In: Proceedings of the 2013 Conference on Empirical Methods in Natural Language Processing, pp. 1631–1642 (2013)
18. Sotiropoulos, D.N., Pournarakis, D.E., Giaglis, G.M.: SVM-based sentiment classification: a comparative study against state-of-the-art classifiers. Int. J. Comput. Intell. Stud. **6**(1), 52–67 (2017)
19. Tang, D., Wei, F., Qin, B., Liu, T., Zhou, M.: Coooolll: a deep learning system for twitter sentiment classification. In: Proceedings of the 8th International Workshop on Semantic Evaluation (SemEval 2014), pp. 208–212 (2014)
20. Vapnik, V.N.: The Nature of Statistical Learning Theory. Springer, Heidelberg (1998). https://www.amazon.com/Nature-Statistical-Learning-Theory/dp/0387945598?SubscriptionId=0JYN1NVW651KCA56C102&tag=techkie-20&linkCode=xm2&camp=2025&creative=165953&creativeASIN=0387945598
21. Wawre, S.V., Deshmukh, S.N.: Sentiment classification using machine learning techniques. Int. J. Sci. Res. (IJSR) **5**(4), 819–821 (2016)

Strategies in Case-Based Argumentation-Based Negotiation: An Application for the Tourism Domain

Rihab Bouslama[1(✉)], Jaume Jordán[2], Stella Heras[2], and Nahla Ben Amor[1]

[1] LARODEC, ISG, Université de Tunis, Tunis, Tunisia
rihabbouslama@yahoo.fr, nahla.benamor@gmx.fr
[2] Valencian Research Institute for Artificial Intelligence (VRAIN), Universitat Politècnica de València, Camino de Vera s/n, 46022 Valencia, Spain
{jjordan,sheras}@dsic.upv.es
http://vrain.upv.es/

Abstract. Negotiation is a key solution to find an agreement between conflicting parties especially during the purchase journey. This paper treats the negotiations between a travel agency and its customers in the domain of tourism. Both automated negotiation and argumentation are gathered to create a framework for automated agents, presenting a travel agency and its customers, to negotiate a trip and exchange arguments. Agents take advantage of their past experiences and use Case-Based Reasoning to select the best strategy to follow. We represent agents using two types of profiles, *Argumentative profile* that represents agents' ways of reasoning and *Preference profile* that embodies customers' preferences in the domain of tourism.

Keywords: Automated negotiation · Argumentation · Case-Based Reasoning · Strategy · Tourism

1 Introduction

The e-tourism is growing over the last decade [13], implying an increase of the percentage of customers that book a trip online. Hence, it is necessary to have an efficient booking system that takes into account the whole process of booking, including the negotiation between customers and travel agencies. A trip may be negotiated based on different criteria (e.g., destination), where customers try to minimize their costs and get the best offer that matches their preferences, and the travel agency tries to maximize its profits and satisfy its customers.

Automated negotiation is an important sub-field of the Artificial Intelligence (AI) domain. Proposals mainly concern negotiation protocols, negotiation frameworks, and reasoning mechanisms in the context of Multi-Agent Systems (MAS) [12]. Other research works went beyond exchanging offers between agents and proposed the exchange of arguments as additional information to enhance the

© Springer Nature Switzerland AG 2020
F. De La Prieta et al. (Eds.): PAAMS 2020 Workshops, CCIS 1233, pp. 205–217, 2020.
https://doi.org/10.1007/978-3-030-51999-5_17

negotiation process and include persuasion [7,16]. Argumentation is widely studied in MAS as a mean to solve conflicts between agents with positions [14].

Another interesting research area of AI is Case-based Reasoning (CBR) [1], which has been studied in both argumentation and negotiation. Few attempts included CBR in Argumentation-Based Negotiation (ABN) frameworks such as the preliminary work of Sycara [20], where she proposed the PERSUADER system that plays the role of a mediator between a company and its trade union in the domain of labour management. CBR was also used in the domain of resources allocation to select a negotiation strategy from the set of past negotiations of the agents [19]. A generic framework for ABN using CBR was proposed for bilateral settings [5]. Then, an improved version for mediated multilateral negotiations was presented in [6]. Both of these works were based on the work proposed in [10], where authors presented a case-based argumentation approach for MAS.

An important aspect of automated negotiation is agents' strategies. They are influenced by many factors such as the negotiation domain, goals, and agents' profiles. [14] discusses different strategies that are originally studied in the social science in the domain of energy market. In particular, it focuses on two groups of strategies: *concession making* and *problem solving* where agents start from an opening position (extreme, reasonable, or modest) and make a sequence of concessions (large, moderate, or small). In an ABN context, [8] defines a strategy as a set of tactics that are short time moves to pursue a high-level goal. They propose three tactics: *Boulware, Conceder*, and *LastMinuteTactic*. One way to select the best strategy is to use decision trees as proposed in [9]. Another approach uses CBR [11], where strategies are based on agents' profiles that define their attitude towards the generated and received arguments.

Most of the frameworks that include computational argumentation ensure reasoning by applying a set of inference rules, which requires an explicit model of the domain. In fact, in the domain of tourism it is not possible to define the rules in advance. Thus, a case-base representation of agents' reasoning makes the framework more dynamic, and agents' knowledge easier to maintain.

In this work, we propose an ABN system in the domain of tourism. The system is dedicated for travel agencies to help them in the negotiation process with their customers, represented as automated agents. We define *preference profiles* that explain the customers' desires and *argumentative profiles* that illustrate the travel agency's and its customers' ways of arguing. Considering the benefits of using a CBR, both negotiation parties will follow a case-based strategy generation. CBR helps agents to select the argument to put forward at each step of the negotiation and thus, devise the dialogue strategies based on their experiences.

The paper is organized as follows. Section 2 presents the architecture of the proposed framework and its main components. Section 3 discusses the negotiation protocol and the strategical reasoning followed by agents. Finally, Sect. 4 summarises the paper and proposes future work.

2 Case-Based Argumentation-Based Negotiation

This work aims to propose an ABN framework in the domain of tourism to support trip negotiations of a travel agency and its customers where the exchange of arguments between agents is devised by the CBR. Formally, the proposed ABN framework is defined as a tuple $ABN = \langle A_0, A, O, Arg \rangle$ where A_0 is the travel agency agent, A: the set of n customer agents such that $A = \{A_1, \ldots, A_n\}$, $O = \{O_1, \ldots, O_n\}$ is the set of all possible offers for n customer agents. Concretely, for an agent i with m offers, $O_i = \{o_{i1}, \ldots, o_{im}\}$ and $Arg = \{Arg_1, \ldots, Arg_n\}$ is the set of all arguments exchanged between the A_0 and its n customer agents. For an agent i, $Arg_i = \{arg_{i1}, \ldots, arg_{il}\}$, where l is the number of arguments.

The global architecture is depicted in Fig. 1 and its main components (i.e., agents, knowledge resources, arguments) are detailed below.

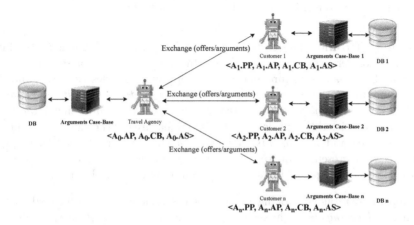

Fig. 1. The global architecture of the proposed framework

2.1 Agents

The framework is conceived for a MAS that supports agents with different behaviours. Agents are defined based on their profiles that rule their behaviour and importantly, their reasons to accept or reject an offer or an argument. Given a travel agency (A_0) and a customer (A_i) we define an argumentative profile $A_0.AP$ (resp. $A_i.AP$) for both agents, that characterizes the way they negotiate and argue. For the customers, we also define a preference profile ($A_i.PP$), which embodies their preferences regarding a trip.

Argumentative Profile. The argumentative profile of an agent defines the way it persuades, accepts or rejects offers and arguments. To define this profile, we adapt the profiles proposed in [3,11] to an ABN setting as follows:

- *Agreeable*: the easiest agent to convince in the negotiation. Prefers short time negotiations. Accepts whenever possible. Agrees on an argument if she does not have an attack argument. When she loses a round (we have at least one round), she accepts the position of the counter party only if it is in her list of potential offers. This type of agent makes big concessions.
- *Open minded*: an average negotiator agent. Not influenced by time. Agrees on an argument if she does not have an attack argument. If she loses a round, she will not accept an offer if it not her current preferred one. She will make small concessions by proposing the next most preferred offer.
- *Argumentative*: the strictest negotiator agent. Prefers long negotiations with a maximum of utility. Agrees on an argument if she does not have an attack argument. If she loses a round and she still have arguments in her case-base, she will insist on her previous offer. Otherwise, she will make small concessions (next most preferred offer). She will not accept an offer if it is not her current preferred one even if it is in her list of preferred offers.

Preference Profile. The preference profile is domain dependent and defines customers' preferences regarding a trip. In fact, a trip has a set of features that may be classified to fundamental and optional. Besides the price and the destination, features as *season, weather, country's safety rank, health and hygiene rank*, and *country's global rank* represent fundamental features that interest all type of agents with different degrees. Optional features as the existence or not of *shopping areas* and *monuments*, depend on agent's preference profile. Inspired from the work presented in [15], we propose the following profiles of customers (using examples of optional features) that embody the travel personae:

1. *Photographer* (agent looking for nice places): she may be influenced by features as *buildings* for sight seeing, *natural parks, monuments*, and *mountains*.
2. *Popular cities seeker* (agent looking for typical holiday destinations): she may be influenced by features as *means of transportation, monuments, museums*, and *local markets*.
3. *Adventure seeker* (agent looking for adventure holidays): she is interested by adventure activities and active tourism possibilities in these places (e.g., *mountains, jungle, desert*).
4. *Parties seeker* (agent looking for parties and fun activities): she may be influenced by features as *concerts, restaurants*, and *coffee shops*.
5. *Fashion seeker* (agent looking for shopping areas): she may be influenced by features as *shopping area* and *local markets*.
6. *Relaxation seeker* (agent looking for relaxation): she may be influenced by features as *hotel's accommodation* and *hotel's number of stars*.
7. *Culture seeker* (agent looking for cultural attractions): she may be influenced by features as *mosques, cathedrals, synagogues, monuments*, and *museums*.
8. *Food seeker* (agent looking to try different food): she may be influenced by features as *local markets, restaurants, coffee shops*, and *hotel accommodation*.

2.2 Knowledge Resources

In our framework we make use of *argument case-bases* and *argumentation schemes* as knowledge resources to generate and manage arguments, following the approach proposed in [5,10]. Case-Based Reasoning (CBR) is a methodology based on the idea that similar cases have similar solutions [1]. This reasoning is so similar to human behaviour during a negotiation where they use their past experiences to justify their positions.

From this perspective, we propose an *Arguments Case-Base* (ACB) to be the main knowledge resource used by agents to make decisions (e.g., generating and selecting a specific argument). The travel agency has its own ACB denoted by $A_0.CB$. Similarly, a customer i has her own ACB denoted by $A_i.CB$. Then, with this resource we can follow a CBR approach and make possible for the agents to learn about different profiles, the type of arguments that they usually accept (resp. reject), and at which time of the dialogue a specific argument was accepted. The ACB is composed of several cases that embody an agent's argumentation experience (store previous arguments in the form of cases). Therefore, each exchanged argument in the dialogue is retained in the case-base. The components of one argument case are:

- *Profile*: both preference profile as well as argumentative profile of the opponent are stored. This information helps agents to learn about their opponents and to know which kind of arguments they accept (resp. reject).
- *Argument Type*: may be any type of arguments that will be further discussed (e.g., explanation, reward). This information helps the agent to learn the type of arguments that is usually accepted by each profile.
- *Argument Conclusion*: the conclusion of the argument (commonly, the outcome of the offer that it supports or attacks).
- *Argument Acceptance*: the final decision (i.e., acceptance or rejection) on each argument is saved to help argument selection.
- *Acceptance Time*: the time of acceptance (e.g., at the beginning, at the end) of the argument is also important. It helps agents to select the appropriate argument at each period of the dialogue, since it can denote patterns, such as that a specific type of argument often results in shorter dialogue.
- *Success Rate*: indicates how many times a given argument was accepted in a given time by a given agent. Indeed, arguments with the highest *Success Rate* are the arguments that have more chance to be accepted.

By storing these information, agents are able to select the best strategy to follow in each situation. Table 1 shows an example of the information stored in an ACB. By the argument case AC1 we can infer that popular cities seekers with an argumentative profile would quickly accept arguments to support offers for Paris at a price of 100€ if the agency includes breakfast for free, even when they commonly engage in large negotiations. However, they would reject the same argument, and hence the underlying offer, if the price increases to 200€.

The second knowledge resource is *Argumentation Schemes* (AS). They represent patterns of common human reasoning. The work of Walton [21] presented

29 different AS taking the form of a set of premises, a conclusion and a set of critical questions (possible ways of attacking the underlying argument). From this set of schemes, we selected a subset which especially captures the usual mode of reasoning in the tourism domain:

- *Argument from Popular Opinion* (APO): captures the fact that humans tend to believe a thing true if the majority hold this opinion. In our travel domain, this stands for the fact that if most customers accept a given offer in a given circumstances then, it is a good reason for other customers to accept it.
- *Argument from Popular Practice* (APP): is a variant of the above, representing the fact that humans are willing to do what most people do. In the travel domain, the travel agency can convince its customers by referring to popular practices. Indeed, similar travellers tend to do similar activities.
- *Argument from Expert Opinion* (AEO): captures the reasoning by which humans accept as true the opinions of an expert. Travel agencies work with experts from different fields. Thus, appealing to their knowledge is a way to convince customers. For example, if the travel agency appeals to information coming from the world economic forum tourism report, customers may trust accepting the offer.
- *Argument from Waste* (AW): captures the behaviour by which humans try not to waste the work done. Spending a long time for the negotiation may be expensive for the travel agency and for the customers. In such cases, accepting a given offer may prevent the negotiation parties from losing money.

Therefore, AS can be combined with the information stored in the ACB to generate arguments that represent the underlying line of reasoning that each scheme captures. For instance, in a negotiation with a popular cities seeker with an argumentative profile, and in view of the AC1 represented in Table 1, by the APP AS we can generate an argument to support an offer (Paris at 100€ per night), since it is common for this type of agents (80% success rate) to quickly accept this type of offer, so the travel agency could speed up the negotiation.

Table 1. Example of an Argument Case-Base

AC ID	Profile	Arg. type	Conclusion	Arg. acceptance	Acceptance time	Success rate
AC1	Argumentative+Popular Cities Seeker	Reward (Ac=Breakfast included for free)	(Paris, 100€)	Accept	Beginning	80%
AC2	Argumentative+Popular Cities Seeker	Reward (Ac=Breakfast included for free)	(Paris, 200€)	Reject	Beginning	90%

2.3   Arguments

Arguments represent the persuasion part of the negotiation which influences agents' initial spaces of acceptance. Several classifications of arguments are evoked in the literature. Arguments may be classified as *practical* arguments expressing facts used to support an offer or *epistemic* arguments presenting agents believes. Overall, arguments may entail different purposes [10,11]:

- *Support*: arguments that support an offer proposed by an agent.
- *Attack*: rebut and undercut arguments where the former attacks the counter party's offer (i.e., the conclusion of an argument) and the latter attacks the premises of the counter parties' arguments.

Another threefold classification highly used in the argumentation community was proposed in [18] where we distinguish *threats*, *rewards* and *appeals*. Amgoud and Prade [4] propose a close variant of this classification by saving *threats* and *rewards* and defining classical ABN arguments, the so-called *explanations*, arguing that the different forms of appeals can be modeled in this class. Following their taxonomy, our framework includes *explanations*, *threats* and *rewards*.

Besides the fact that *explanations*, *threats* and *rewards* are very common in the argumentation field, they illustrate the type of arguments usually exchanged between sellers and buyers. Following the definition of an argument proposed in [11] we define an explanation argument as:

Definition 1 (Explanation argument). *$Arg = \langle \phi, S \rangle$, where ϕ is the conclusion of the argument, and S is the support set of an argument.*

We define threat and reward arguments as follow:

Definition 2 (Threat argument). *$Arg = \langle \phi, S, Ac \rangle$, where ϕ is the conclusion of the argument, S is the support set of an argument, and Ac is an action that threatens the counter party and violates her goals.*

Definition 3 (Reward argument). *$Arg = \langle \phi, S, Ac \rangle$, where ϕ is the conclusion of the argument, S is the support set of an argument, and Ac is an action that promotes a reward for the counter party.*

The *support set* can consist of different elements, depending on the argument purpose. On the one hand, if the argument entails a support, the support set is the set of features (*premises*) that represent the context of the domain where the argument has been proposed (e.g. features of the offer) and optionally, any knowledge resource used by the proponent to generate the argument (*argumentation schemes* and *argument-cases*). On the other hand, if the argumen is an attack argument, the support set can include any of the allowed attacks in our framework (*distinguishing premises* (DP) or *counter-examples* (CE)).

Thus, a DP is a premise that distinguishes two offers (represents a feature with a different value for these offers). A CE in our framework is an offer that includes the same features than another offer, but promote different outcomes.

3   Argumentation-Based Negotiation Protocol

In this section, we present the ABN protocol that governs the negotiation between agents. Although we focus on a bilateral negotiation between the travel agency and each one of its customers, the same process may be executed simultaneously with n customers (i.e., concurrent negotiation [2]). However, the most common operation of a travel agency is to engage in one to one negotiations (even when the booking is for a group, there is usually one representative of the group). The protocol includes two phases: (i) negotiation phase (i.e., exchange of offers) and (ii) argumentation phase (i.e., exchange of arguments).

Algorithm 1. ABN protocol

```
1:  procedure ABNprotocol(A_0, A_i, O_i = {o_{i1}, ..., o_{im}})
2:      agreement ← False
3:      Send(A_0, A_i, O_i)                          ▷ A_0 sends a set of possible offers to A_i
4:      O_{ij} ← SelectMaxUtility(O_i)               ▷ A_i computes and selects max utility offer
5:      AskWhy(A_i, A_0, O_{ij})                      ▷ A_i challenges the offer under discussion
6:      Assert(A_0, A_i, O_{ij})                ▷ A_0 asserts the offer by sending a support argument
7:      if Accept(A_i, O_{ij}) then
8:          agreement ← True
9:          NegotiationOutcome ← O_{ij}              ▷ The negotiation ends with an agreement
10:     else
11:         NegotiationOutcome ← Argue(A_i, A_0, O_{ij}, O_i)
12:     return NegotiationOutcome
```

Algorithm 1 describes an overview of the whole negotiation phase. First, the travel agency (A_0) generates a set of possible offers based on the customer (A_i) preferences (line 3). Then, A_i challenges the offer that she prefers and waits for explanations from A_0 (lines 4–5). In her turn, A_0 sends arguments to support her offer (line 6). In this step, two cases are possible: A_i accepts A_0's offer (lines 7–9), or A_i attacks A_0's offer and enters in the argumentation process (line 11).

Algorithm 2. Argumentation Protocol

```
1:  procedure Argue(A_i, A_0, O_{ij}, O_i, MaxNbRounds)
2:      agreement ← False, NegotiationOutcome ← ∅, round ← 0, Opponent ← A_i    ▷ Agents
        alternate the role of an opponent that attacks the counter party
3:      repeat
4:          if Opponent = A_i then
5:              Arg_i ← GenerateArgument(A_i)           ▷ A_i generates an arg. from its ACB
6:              Attack(A_i, A_0, Arg_i, O_{ij})          ▷ A_i attacks A_0
7:              agreement ← RespondToAttack(A_0)         ▷ A_0 responds agreeing or not
8:              Opponent ← A_0
9:          else
10:             if PossibleAttack() = True then
11:                 Arg_0 ← GenerateArgument(A_0)
12:                 Attack(A_0, A_i, Arg_0, O_{ij})
13:             else
14:                 O_i = Remove(O_{ij}, O_i)             ▷ Removes discussed offer from the set
15:                 O_{ij} ← GenerateNewOffer(O_i)
16:         round ← round + 1
17:     until (agreement = True) OR (round = MaxNbRounds) OR (Arg_i = ∅) OR (Arg_0 = ∅)
        OR (O_i = ∅)
18:     if agreement = True then
19:         NegotiationOutcome ← O_{ij}
20:     return NegotiationOutcome
```

Algorithm 2 outlines the argumentation phase. Agents follow an alternating offers protocol similar to the one proposed in [5] in order to attack or support an argument (resp. an offer), or propose a new offer.

3.1 Offers Generation and Evaluation

As highlighted in Algorithm 1, A_0 is in charge of generating the set of possible offers (O_i) based on A_i's preferences. To do so, she uses a data base that contains a set of features describing different trips.

Definition 4 (Offer). $o = \langle F, \Theta \rangle$, where $F = \{f_1, ..., f_n\}$ is the set of n features characterizing an offer, and Θ is the outcome of the offer.

In Definition 4, an offer is characterised by a set of features F. Each agent distributes a preference order over these features where $f_1 \prec_i f_2$ indicates that the feature f_2 is more preferred than feature f_1 for agent i. For instance, $hotel\_pension \prec_{A_1} safety$ means that for A_1 $safety$ is more important than $hotel\_pension$. Θ represents the features $price$ and $destination$. For example, the first row of Table 2 is an offer where $SafetyRank$, $Period$ and $Weather$ are the set of features, and the outcome is Paris for 100€ per night.

Table 2. Example of data

Destination	Safety rank	Period	Weather	Price per day
Paris, France	5.7	December	Cold/Rainy	100€
Cancun, Mexico	4.2	July	Hot	80€

Agents evaluate offers using their utility functions that embody the preference-based aspect of our framework. In fact, each agent has a different *satisfaction* value that she gets from each feature and thus from a given offer.

Definition 5 (Satisfaction of Offer). The satisfaction *from a feature for an agent* A_i *is defined using a satisfaction function:* $A \times F \rightarrow \mathbb{R}^+$, *where the satisfaction from the whole offer is:* $satisfaction(A_i, o) = \sum_{k=1}^{n} satisfaction(A_i, f_k)$.

The *satisfaction* from a feature represents its worth for an agent. For instance, for a customer A_1 the preference order over features is $concerts <_{A_1} accommodation$. Since, one feature may have different values, then the agent gets different satisfaction such as $satisfaction(A_1, accommodation = allinclusive) = 10.5$ while $satisfaction(A_1, accommodation = breakfastand bed) = 6.1$. This means A_1 is more satisfied with an all inclusive accommodation. However, each offer has a cost for the agent (i.e., price):

Definition 6 (Cost of Offer). *A* cost *of an offer o is defined using a cost function: $A \times o \to \mathbb{R}^+$, where the cost of the offer represents the price to pay for that offer: $cost(A_i, o) = price(o)$.*

As in [17], we define the utility function in terms of satisfaction and cost:

Definition 7 (Utility of Offer). *The* utility *of an offer o for an agent A_i is:* $u(A_i, o) = (satisfaction(A_i, o) - cost(A_i, o)) \times \delta_{A_i}$.

In the above definition, δ is a discount factor that represents the influence of time on agents' utilities. The level of influence differs according to agents' profiles.

3.2 Argument Generation and Evaluation

Agents have a data base with information about several trip destinations. Table 2 depicts an example of these information that concern two destinations, their safety rank, the period of the trip, the weather and the price per day.

At first, arguments are constructed using this knowledge base and by taking into consideration the context of the negotiation. For instance, if agents are negotiating Paris as a destination, an explanation argument as: ⟨ (Paris, 100€), safety rank = 5.7 ⟩ may be generated. After generating the arguments based on the negotiation context, they are stored in case bases. Besides the argument itself, the information stored in the case bases (Sect. 2.2) helps agents to select the best argument to send in new negotiations. Indeed, the selection of a strategy is ensured following the CBR. Actually, A_0 and A_i will challenge each other. More precisely, the persuasion phase is based on two parts:

Challenging the counter party's argument by sending:

- Rebut argument: may be sent to (1) criticize the offer promoted by the attacked argument by sending an explanation (e.g., CE), (2) send a reward or threat to the counter party to change her offer or to accept an offer or (3) send an AS.
- Undercut argument: may be sent to (1) criticize one or many features of the attack argument, (2) ask for more explanations on the offer promoted by the argument, (3) add additional information that were missed (DP). If agents need more explanation about the offer, they will ask for more information from the counter party (will be sent as additional features).

Table 3. Agents' Argument Case-Bases

ACB ID	AC ID	Profile	Arg. type	Conclusion	Arg. acceptance	Acceptance time	Success rate
ACB_0	AC3	Argumentative+Popular Cities Seeker	Explanation (AS= APO)	(Paris, 100€)	Accept	Beginning	80%
ACB_i	AC1	Open minded	Explanation (CE= Madrid, 80€)	(Paris, 100€)	Reject	Beginning	70%
ACB_i	AC2	Open minded	Threat (Ac= see other travel agency)	(Paris, 100€)	Reject	End	90%

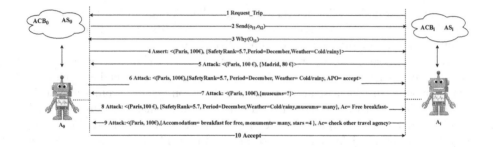

Fig. 2. An example of an ABN dialogue

Responding to a challenge depends on the received argument:

- Response to a rebut: by (1) proposing another offer or (2) sending an AS.
- Response to an undercut: by (1) sending an explanation, (2) proposing another offer, (3) sending an AS or (4) sending Threat or Reward.

The choice of which argument to send from the above list represents the *strategy* that an agent follow which is based on her profile and her ACB.

3.3   Illustrative Example

Figure 2 depicts an ABN dialogue between the travel agency A_0 and a customer A_i. Agents' argumentative profiles are: $A_0.AP = OpenMinded$ while $A_i.AP = Argumentative$. For the customer: $A_i.PP = PopularCitiesSeeker$. ACB_0 (resp. ACB_i) and AS_0 (resp. AS_i) are the travel agency (resp. customer) knowledge resources. Table 3 depicts A_0 and A_i case bases where besides $AC3$, the travel agency has in her CB the cases presented in Table 1. A_i starts by requesting a trip proposition from A_0 indicating that she is looking for a safe country with a good hygiene rank where she can find museums and monuments. A_0 sends two possible offers (presented in Table 2).

Message 4 contains a *Support argument* in which the support set has the features of the offer. A_i computes her utility from this offer, and since she is not satisfied yet, she attacks it by sending a rebut argument (CE) in message 5 generated using her ACB (i.e., case $AC1$). In message 6 the travel agency sends an *Explanation argument* with an AS, more precisely, an APO saying most of customers accept this offer. Message 8 and 9 present a *Reward* and a *Threat* respectively, where A_0 explained the missing feature (museums) and offered a reward. As for A_i she threatened A_0 saying that she also wants a 4 stars hotel, otherwise, she will check another agency.

4   Conclusion

This paper presents an Argumentation-Based Negotiation framework to aid the travel agency and its customers in their trip negotiations. In general, negotiations between a buyer and a seller are very strategic. The domain of tourism is not an exception, the travel agency seeks to maximize its profits and customers try to minimize their costs and maximize their satisfaction.

From this perspective, we presented the framework's architecture and the reasoning process that help agents to select the best argument to send at each part of the dialogue. In fact, a strategy is defined based on agents' profiles and their *Arguments Case-Base*. The travel agency and its customers are characterized by an *Argumentative profile* that presents their ways of reasoning. Customers are also characterized by a *Preference profile* that embodies their preferences regarding a trip. Both negotiation parties have their own *Arguments Case-Base* that they use to select the appropriate argument in a given situation.

Future work will focus on an experimental study in which more refined strategies will be proposed and tested for their impact on the negotiation process.

References

1. Aamodt, A., Plaza, E.: Case-based reasoning: foundational issues, methodological variations, and system approaches. AI Commun. **7**(1), 39–59 (1994)
2. Adnan, M.H.M., Hassan, M.F., Aziz, I., Paputungan, I.V.: Protocols for agent-based autonomous negotiations: a review. In: ICCOINS, pp. 622–626. IEEE (2016)
3. Amgoud, L., Parsons, S.: Agent dialogues with conflicting preferences. In: Meyer, J.-J.C., Tambe, M. (eds.) ATAL 2001. LNCS (LNAI), vol. 2333, pp. 190–205. Springer, Heidelberg (2002). https://doi.org/10.1007/3-540-45448-9_14
4. Amgoud, L., Prade, H.: Generation and evaluation of different types of arguments in negotiation. In: NMR, pp. 10–15 (2004)
5. Bouslama, R., Ayachi, R., Ben Amor, N.: A new generic framework for argumentation-based negotiation using case-based reasoning. In: Medina, J., et al. (eds.) IPMU 2018. CCIS, vol. 854, pp. 633–644. Springer, Cham (2018). https://doi.org/10.1007/978-3-319-91476-3_52
6. Bouslama, R., Ayachi, R., Ben Amor, N.: A new generic framework for mediated multilateral argumentation-based negotiation using case-based reasoning. In: Kern-Isberner, G., Ognjanović, Z. (eds.) ECSQARU 2019. LNCS (LNAI), vol. 11726, pp. 14–26. Springer, Cham (2019). https://doi.org/10.1007/978-3-030-29765-7_2
7. Dimopoulos, Y., Moraitis, P.: Advances in argumentation based negotiation. In: Negotiation and Argumentation in Multi-agent Systems: Fundamentals, Theories, Systems and Applications, pp. 82–125 (2014)
8. Hadidi, N., Dimopoulos, Y., Moraitis, P.: Tactics and concessions for argumentation-based negotiation. In: Computational Models of Argument: Proceedings of COMMA 2012, vol. 245, pp. 285–296 (2012)
9. Hadoux, E., Hunter, A.: Strategic sequences of arguments for persuasion using decision trees. In: AAAI (2017)
10. Heras, S., Jordán, J., Botti, V., Julián, V.: Argue to agree: a case-based argumentation approach. IJAR **54**(1), 82–108 (2013)
11. Heras, S., Jordán, J., Botti, V., Julián, V.: Case-based strategies for argumentation dialogues in agent societies. Inf. Sci. **223**, 1–30 (2013)
12. Jennings, N.R., Faratin, P., Lomuscio, A.R., Parsons, S., Sierra, C., Wooldridge, M.: Automated negotiation: prospects, methods and challenges. Int. J. Group Decis. Negot. **10**(2), 199–215 (2001)

13. Lazar, C.M.: Internet-an aid for e-tourism. Ecoforum J. **8**(1), 1–4 (2019)
14. Lopes, F., Novais, A.Q., Coelho, H.: Bilateral negotiation in a multi-agent energy market. In: Huang, D.-S., Jo, K.-H., Lee, H.-H., Kang, H.-J., Bevilacqua, V. (eds.) ICIC 2009. LNCS, vol. 5754, pp. 655–664. Springer, Heidelberg (2009). https://doi.org/10.1007/978-3-642-04070-2_71
15. Park, S., Tussyadiah, I., Mazanec, J., Fesenmaier, D.: Travel personae of american pleasure travelers: a network analysis. J. Travel Tour. Mark. **27**, 797–811 (2010)
16. Rahwan, I., Ramchurn, S.D., Jennings, N.R., Mcburney, P., Parsons, S., Sonenberg, L.: Argumentation-based negotiation. KER **18**(4), 343–375 (2003)
17. Rahwan, I., Sonenberg, L., McBurney, P.: Bargaining and argument-based negotiation: *some preliminary comparisons*. In: Rahwan, I., Moraïtis, P., Reed, C. (eds.) ArgMAS 2004. LNCS (LNAI), vol. 3366, pp. 176–191. Springer, Heidelberg (2005). https://doi.org/10.1007/978-3-540-32261-0_12
18. Sierra, C., Jennings, N.R., Noriega, P., Parsons, S.: A framework for argumentation-based negotiation. In: Singh, M.P., Rao, A., Wooldridge, M.J. (eds.) ATAL 1997. LNCS, vol. 1365, pp. 177–192. Springer, Heidelberg (1998). https://doi.org/10.1007/BFb0026758
19. Soh, L.K., Tsatsoulis, C.: Agent-based argumentative negotiations with case-based reasoning. In: AAAI Fall Symposium Series on Negotiation Methods for Autonomous Cooperative Systems, pp. 16–25 (2001)
20. Sycara, K.P.: Persuasive argumentation in negotiation. Theory Decis. **28**(3), 203–242 (1990). https://doi.org/10.1007/BF00162699
21. Walton, D.: Argumentation Schemes for Presumptive Reasoning. Routledge, Abingdon (2013)

Towards a Classifier to Recognize Emotions Using Voice to Improve Recommendations

José Manuel Fuentes, Joaquin Taverner[(✉)], Jaime Andres Rincon, and Vicente Botti

Valencian Research Institute for Artificial Intelligence (VRAIN), Universitat Politècnica de València, Valencia, Spain
{jofuelo1,joataap,jrincon,vbotti}@dsic.upv.es

Abstract. The recognition of emotions in tone voice is currently a tool with a high potential when it comes to making recommendations, since it allows to personalize recommendations using the mood of the users as information. However, recognizing emotions using tone of voice is a complex task since it is necessary to pre-process the signal and subsequently recognize the emotion. Most of the current proposals use recurrent networks based on sequences with a temporal relationship. The disadvantage of these networks is that they have a high runtime, which makes it difficult to use in real-time applications. On the other hand, when defining this type of classifier, culture and language must be taken into account, since the tone of voice for the same emotion can vary depending on these cultural factors. In this work we propose a culturally adapted model for recognizing emotions from the voice tone using convolutional neural networks. This type of network has a relatively short execution time allowing its use in real time applications. The results we have obtained improve the current state of the art, reaching 93.6% success over the validation set.

Keywords: Emotion recognition · Voice analysis · Recommendation system

1 Introduction

Emotions play an important role in our social interactions. Our ability to recognize emotions is based on the ability to recognize different verbal and non-verbal communication acts such as gestures or facial expression. The voice tone is one of the non-verbal communications that allows to identify the emotion. When we refer to the recognition of the voice tone we are referring to the set of prosodic characteristics such as the tone, energy, or speech speed, but not the spoken message itself. Depending on the voice tone in which a person speaks different emotions can be expressed. For example, a low voice tone with low frequencies may be related to sadness, while a tone with ups and downs may be identified

© Springer Nature Switzerland AG 2020
F. De La Prieta et al. (Eds.): PAAMS 2020 Workshops, CCIS 1233, pp. 218–225, 2020.
https://doi.org/10.1007/978-3-030-51999-5_18

as joy. The underlying problem that must be faced when analyzing emotions in the voice tone is the dependence of the voice tone on factors such as culture or language [6]. Different cultures may interpret the voice tone differently [4]. In addition, the musicality of the voice tone varies depending on the language. Therefore, when designing models capable of recognising emotion from the voice tone, these cultural and idiomatic factors must be taken into account.

In the area affective computing [8] different models have been proposed to recognize emotions from variations in the voice tone. Currently most of these models are based on the use of Neural Networks (NN). More specifically in the use of Recurrent Neural Networks (RNN). These networks allow the voice tone to be analysed sequentially. However, these networks have a high computing time for classification which makes them not useful in real time applications. In this work we propose a cultural adapted classifier to recognize emotions in real time from the voice tone for Spanish speakers which in future works can be used as input for a recommendation system. Our model uses a Convolutional Neural Network to analyze the characteristics of the voice tone. This type of NN obtain's good results in less time than the RNN. In addition, thanks to the pre-processing of the signal, our model is tolerant to failures.

2 Related Work

Intelligent user-based recommendation systems are commonly based on extracting information about the user to perform a customized recommendation. In recent years, an increasing number of models consider different affective characteristics, such as emotions or mood, to improve the personalization of recommendations. For example, in [15] a model for recommending recipes according to the user's mood is presented. This model is based on tests to consult the user's mood and recommend a recipe that fits that mood. The problem with this model is that the user must enter his mood manually. In contrast, models that are able to recognize emotions or mood automatically are less invasive to the user. For example the model proposed in [9] allows to recommend songs using the emotions expressed by the user. For this, the system captures an image of the face and extracting the emotional state through neural networks. One of the main challenges when generating this type of system is to generate models that allow for real-time emotion recognition. One of the most common ways to capture user emotion in present literature is voice tone analysis. The recognition of emotions through the tone of voice is a difficult challenge. This is due in part to both the cultural and linguistic dependence of the voice tone and to the pre-processing of the audio signal for subsequent analysis. At present there are different techniques that allow to extract characteristics of the voice tone such as the duration or the energy of the signal. *Mel Frequency Cepstral Coefficients* (MFCC) [11] are the most commonly used features in automatic audio recognition. This technique assumes that in short periods of time the characteristics of the audio remain relatively stable. Therefore, by a preprocess, which subdivides the audio signal into smaller fragments, relatively static characteristics can be extracted for each fragment of the audio signal. On the other hand, *Spectral Rolloff* technique [1] allows to obtain characteristics about the relationship between energy and frequency. Its use in conjunction with other features, such as MFCCs, has been shown to improve the overall performance of speech recognition systems [5]. The *Log Filterbank Energies* spectrogram model is also widely used to extract characteristics from the voice tone. This spectrogram is obtained by applying filter banks to the signal periodogram. They are an intermediate step in obtaining MFCCs. Therefore, they have a higher correlation than MFCCs, but in some cases they retain a greater amount of information from the original signal [14].

The characteristics obtained through the different pre-processes are then used to perform the recognition of the audio signal using different machine learning techniques. Within the area of recognition of emotions in the tone of voice, different classification techniques have been used. The first approximations made in the area of the recognition of emotions in the tone of the voice were based on the use of Hidden Markov Models (HMM) or Support Vector Machines (SVM) [12]. At present, with the rise of neural networks, most proposals use models based on Recurrent Neural Networks (RNN). This type of networks allow developers to work with data based on time sequences. Therefore, they are suitable for continuous audio analysis. One of the most used RNNs in this field are the *Long Short Term Memory* (LSTM) [2]. LSTM allow to solve the problem of gradient vanishing or exploding. This type of neural network has proven effective in improving the accuracy of recognition in different tasks. For example, in [3] the authors compare two classical models, *Multivariate Linear Regression* (MLR) and SVM, with a modern LSTM obtaining the best results with the use of the LSTM. However, RNNs have the disadvantage that their processing time is high. Therefore, RNNs are not highly recommended for applications designed to be used in real time. This is why, in recent years, there have been models that propose to use Convolutional Neural Networks (CNN). CNNs are a type of neural networks specialized in image analysis. CNN has also proven to be very effective in the task of recognition patterns in audio. To do this, the network is fed with images of the spectral frequencies of the audio. This type of technique has proven to be effective in recognizing emotions in tone of voice with less compute time than RNN. For example, in [16], a CNN is compared with a classical SVM. The authors tested both models on two types of tasks: image classification and audio emotion recognition. In both tasks the CNN improves the accuracy of the SVM. Specially in the audio task, where the authors get an accuracy of 97.6% with the CNN, which is much higher than the 46.6% obtained with the SVM. On the other hand, in this type of classification task we have to take into account factors such as culture and language. Over the years different authors have theorized about the dementia between emotions, culture and language. Constructivist psychology holds that emotions depend on these cultural and idiomatic factors and that it is therefore impossible to correctly identify an emotion without taking them into account [10]. In the case of emotion analysis based on the tone of voice, cultural and idiomatic factors take on greater importance since substantial differences can appear in the variation of acoustic frequency when expressing emotions [7]. Therefore, this type of recognition systems must be adapted through the use

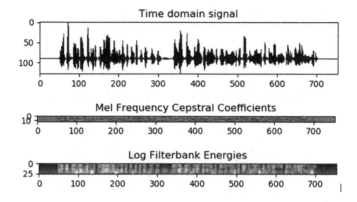

Fig. 1. MFCC and LFE extracted from the signal represented in the time domain

of corpus specialized in the culture and language in which they are going to be used. Using general models or models trained in other languages can lead to errors in predicting emotion [13]. At present, however, most of the proposals in this area are focused on emotion analysis for English speakers.

3 Proposal

The proposal presented in this paper would allow the use of the voice to recognize emotional states. The cues would serve as an input to a recommendation system. However, due to the complexity of performing emotion classification using the voice, in this proposal we focus on how to classify emotions. Because of this complexity and the high dependence that the tone of voice has on language and culture discussed above, we propose a model of emotion recognition in the tone of voice adapted to Spanish speakers. Our proposal is based on CNNs, since, as mentioned above, there are precedents of improving the state of the art by applying the advantages of CNNs to the voice recognition task. However, as CNNs are specialized in the processing of data matrices, it is necessary to pre-process the audio signal. In this pre-process we have extracted two main characteristics of the audio: the *Mel Frequency Cepstral Coefficients* (MFCC) and the *Log Mel-Filterbank Energies* (LFE). Then we fed this two characteristics to the network as individual images. We considered also to use the *Time-domain Signal Representation* and the *Spectral Subband Centroids*, but adding them offered worse results.

An example of the features extracted from an acoustic signal along with the corresponding time domain signal is shown in Fig. 1. On the other hand, when working with audio signals we must consider the time factor since the audio files can have different duration. Therefore, it is not possible to apply padding techniques in a direct way to these type of samples it is necessary to regularize the size. To do that, we have made an split of the samples into fragments of a fixed size (13×200 pixels for the MFCC and 26×200 pixels for the LFE). We

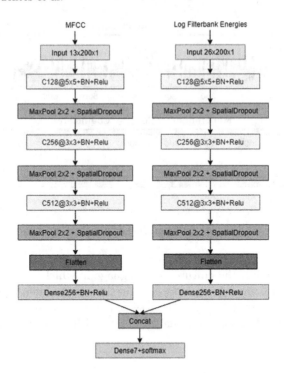

Fig. 2. Proposed convolutional neural network for the audio problem

have applied padding to the last fragment of each audio to adjust it to the same size.

We design a non-sequential CNN with two parallel convolutional branches: one to analyze MFCC audio characteristic and the other to analyze the LFE audio characteristic. We have used the same structure for both branches:

- 1 convolutional layer of 128 5 × 5 sized filters.
- A max pooling layer with 2 × 2 filters and stride 2 followed by a spatial dropout layer.
- 1 convolutional layer of 256 5 × 5 sized filters.
- A max pooling layer with 2 × 2 filters and stride 2 followed by a spatial dropout layer.
- 1 convolutional layer of 512 5 × 5 sized filters.
- A max pooling layer with 2 × 2 filters and stride 2 followed by a spatial dropout layer.
- A flatten layer.
- 1 fully connected layer of 256 neurons.

Then, the results of both fully connected layers are concatenated to a fully connected output layer of 7 neurons one for each emotion including the neutral state. The resulting schema of the CNN is shown in Figs. 2 and 3.

Table 1. Number of samples per class in the voice task

Class	Anger	Disgust	Fear	Happiness	Sadness	Surprise	Neutral
Number of samples	725	732	735	732	728	730	1658

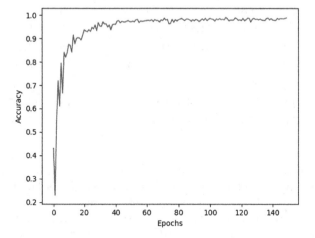

Fig. 3. Accuracy of the CNN throughout iterations for the validation set.

3.1 The Voice Data Set

As mentioned above, as the voice tone is cultural and language dependant, we had to use a corpus adapted to the language in which the model is going to be used that in this case is Spanish. However, despite there are a large number of data sets for voice classification in English, to our knowledge the only data set made for this proposal in Spanish is the *INTER1SP Spanish Emotional Database* [1]. This data set contains 6040 samples of audio pronounced, in a silent studio, by two actors: a man and a woman. Table 1 summarizes the distribution of the samples for the six emotion and the neutral state.

We decided to divide the data set into three parts: training set, validation set, and test set. The percentages assigned follow the classic distribution of 70% for training, 15% for validation, and 15% for test.

3.2 Results

The accuracy obtained by this model is 93.6% for the validation test (see Table 2). The current state of the art for this corpus is at a precision of 90.05%, which corresponds to the work presented in [3]. In that proposal the authors combined melfrequency cepstrum coefficients with modulation spectral features. Comparing our results with the results obtained for the same corpus in the

---

[1] http://catalog.elra.info/en-us/repository/browse/ELRA-S0329/.

Table 2. Confusion matrix for the validation test corresponding to the 15% of the samples.

%	Joy	Surprise	Fear	Anger	Disgust	Sadness	Neutral	Rate
Joy	**97.63**	3.19	0.00	2.00	1.31	0.00	0.87	97.30
Surprise	0.68	**89.36**	1.11	1.00	1.31	0.00	0.00	93.33
Fear	0.00	1.06	**94.44**	0.00	1.31	5.08	0.87	92.39
Anger	0.34	2.13	3.33	**94.00**	2.61	5.08	1.74	86.24
Disgust	0.68	1.06	1.11	3.00	**90.85**	1.69	0.00	94.56
Sadness	0.34	1.06	0.00	0.00	0.65	**81.36**	0.87	92.31
Neutral	0.34	2.13	0.00	0.00	1.96	6.78	**95.65**	91.67
Precision	97.63	89.36	94.44	94.00	90.85	81.36	95.65	

current state of the art we can observe that our model improves the accuracy of emotion recognition for this corpus. This success rate is largely due to the absence of environmental noise in the data set. Therefore, the success rate could be reduced in noisy environments. On the other hand, the pre-process carried out to obtain the characteristics divided each audio fragment into different partitions. This partitioning allows the system to make some mistakes as long as the majority of the fragments that compose the audio are correctly classified.

4   Conclusion and Future Work

In this work we have proposed a model of recognition of emotion in the tone of voice adapted to personal factors such as culture and language which will be used as input for a recommendation system. Our model is weighted to analyze the emotion in the tone of voice in real time. For this we have designed a model based on the use of convolutional neural networks. This type of network makes it possible to recognize emotion in the tone of the voice in less time than recurrent neural networks. In addition, our model is adapted to the culture and language in which it will be used through the use of a Spanish data set. The results we have obtained improve the current state of art on this data set. In addition, the way in which we have pre-processed the signal, dividing each audio fragment into different partitions, allows the system to have a certain tolerance to errors. This is because the resulting emotion is predominant for the set of fragments.

As future work we want to increase the set of samples incorporating another data set. We also want to create another model in a different language to compare cross-cultural variations and to be able to analyze the success rate generated by both classifiers when used in a language different than the language of the data set. Finally, we want to incorporate this model into a recommendation system in order to adapt it to the user's emotion.

Acknowledgements. This work is partially supported by the Spanish Government project TIN2017-89156-R, GVA-CEICE project PROMETEO/2018/002, Generalitat Valenciana and European Social Fund FPI grant ACIF/2017/085, Universitat Politecnica de Valencia research grant (PAID-10-19), and by the Spanish Government (RTI2018-095390-B-C31).

References

1. Balakrishnan, A., Rege, A.: Reading emotions from speech using deep neural networks. Technical report, Stanford University, Computer Science Department (2017)
2. Hochreiter, S., Schmidhuber, J.: Long short-term memory. Neural Comput. **9**, 1735–1780 (1997)
3. Kerkeni, L., Serrestou, Y., Mbarki, M., Raoof, K., Mahjoub, M.: Speech emotion recognition: methods and cases study, pp. 175–182 (2018)
4. McCluskey, K.W., Albas, D.C., Niemi, R.R., Cuevas, C., Ferrer, C.: Cross-cultural differences in the perception of the emotional content of speech: a study of the development of sensitivity in Canadian and Mexican children. Dev. Psychol. **11**(5), 551 (1975)
5. Paliwal, K.K.: Spectral subband centroid features for speech recognition. In: Proceedings of the 1998 IEEE International Conference on Acoustics, Speech and Signal Processing. ICASSP 1998 (Cat. No. 98CH36181), vol. 2, pp. 617–620. IEEE (1998)
6. Paulmann, S., Uskul, A.K.: Cross-cultural emotional prosody recognition: evidence from Chinese and British listeners. Cogn. Emot. **28**(2), 230–244 (2014)
7. Pépiot, E.: Voice, speech and gender: male-female acoustic differences and cross-language variation in English and French speakers. Corela Cogn. Représent. Lang. (HS-16) (2015)
8. Picard, R.W., et al.: Affective computing. Perceptual Computing Section, Media Laboratory, Massachusetts Institute of Technology (1995)
9. Rincon, J., de la Prieta, F., Zanardini, D., Julian, V., Carrascosa, C.: Influencing over people with a social emotional model. Neurocomputing **231**, 47–54 (2017)
10. Russell, J.A., Lewicka, M., Niit, T.: A cross-cultural study of a circumplex model of affect. J. Pers. Soc. Psychol. **57**(5), 848 (1989)
11. Schuller, B., Rigoll, G., Lang, M.: Hidden Markov model-based speech emotion recognition, vol. 2, pp. 401–404 (2003)
12. Schuller, B., Villar, R., Rigoll, G., Lang, M.: Meta-classifiers in acoustic and linguistic feature fusion-based affect recognition, vol. 1, pp. 325–328 (2005)
13. Thompson, W., Balkwill, L.-L.: Decoding speech prosody in five languages. Semiotica **2006**, 407–424 (2006)
14. Tyagi, V., Wellekens, C.: On desensitizing the Mel-cepstrum to spurious spectral components for robust speech recognition. In: Proceedings of the IEEE International Conference on Acoustics, Speech, and Signal Processing. ICASSP 2005, vol. 1, pp. I–529. IEEE (2005)
15. Ueda, M., Morishita, Y., Nakamura, T., Takata, N., Nakajima, S.: A recipe recommendation system that considers user's mood. In: Proceedings of the 18th International Conference on Information Integration and Web-based Applications and Services, pp. 472–476. ACM (2016)
16. Zhang, B., Quan, C., Ren, F.: Study on CNN in the recognition of emotion in audio and images. In: 2016 IEEE/ACIS 15th International Conference on Computer and Information Science (ICIS), pp. 1–5, June 2016

Improving Collaboration in Industry 4.0: The Usage of Blockchain for Knowledge Representation

Pedro Pinheiro, Ricardo Santos$^{(\boxtimes)}$ ⓘ, and Ricardo Barbosa$^{(\boxtimes)}$ ⓘ

CIICESI, Escola Superior de Tecnologia e Gestão, Politécnico do Porto,
Porto, Portugal
{8140403,rjs,rmb}@estg.ipp.pt

Abstract. With the introduction of Industry 4.0 in many industrial environments, many changes are going to take place in the manufacturing processes. Blockchain can help the collaboration between organisations, by improving and leading the way for a decentralised future, where transactions can happen much faster while ensuring that a more knowledgeable and demanding consumer has its expectations fulfilled. In this work we propose a model that uses blockchain and multi-agent systems to help represent an organisation in a network of entities, as well to create a system that is capable of handling entity transactions and provide a way of improving decision-making by enabling decisions to be done faster in a rapidly changing environment.

Keywords: Industry 4.0 · Blockchain · Multi-agent systems · Collaboration

1 Introduction

The industry is facing one of the most significant changes to date, with the introduction of technologies that aim to start a new revolution that will impact the overall performance, quality, and control of the manufacturing processes [16], often called Industry 4.0 (I4.0) [31]. In I4.0, due to the way technological revolutions have shaped society, consumers are going to be much more connected and better informed about products and trends, creating a demand for highly customised products with ever-shortening life cycle [3]. Because of that, organisations, belonging to different kinds of industries have established between them a business process collaboration, that typically operates in a supply chain, to introduce significant benefits into their business activities. Nevertheless, to be able to answer the demands of I4.0, organisations will need to collaborate more efficiently, making faster and reliable decisions, and establishing transactions between the right partners. For this to be possible, a correct representation of

This work has been supported by national funds through FCT - Fundação para a Ciência e Tecnologia through project UIDB/04728/2020.

F. De La Prieta et al. (Eds.): PAAMS 2020 Workshops, CCIS 1233, pp. 226–237, 2020.
https://doi.org/10.1007/978-3-030-51999-5_19

these organisations, and respective transactions, needs to be made, to create a system capable of supporting real-world business transactions in the future.

Our proposal consists of using blockchain and a Multi-Agent System (MAS) to represent an industry in an environment where there is a necessity to collaborate and compete one with each other. The objective is to create a model that can aid decision-making processes, regarding which entity should one rely on to solve existing dependencies. The model will have two components that will allow a representation of the interactions, reasoning, and knowledge of an entity.

This paper is structured as follows: Sect. 2 contains an overview on the basic principles of Industry 4.0 as well as brief description on the principles of Blockchain; Sect. 3 presents our proposal and describe our model in detail. Finally, in the final section we end this work with a small conclusion and an overview of the future work.

2 Overview

2.1 Concepts of Industry 4.0

The 21st century is marked by a digital transformation, with constant innovation in the various fields of technology that affects the way products are manufactured and how services are provided [7]. With the recently emerging technologies, like the Internet of Things (IoT), wireless sensor networks, big data, cloud computing, embedded systems, and mobile Internet, starting to be adopted and brought into the manufacturing environment created a new concept, the concept of I4.0, first introduced by the German industry in 2011 [27]. The main objective of I4.0 is to use the emerging information technologies to implement IoT and services, deeply integrate business and engineering processes, making manufacturing more flexible, efficient, and green, while always searching for high quality and low-cost [31]. Under this concept, consumer's opinions on product manufacturing, personalisation, and delivery have become more demanding, requiring factories to become self-aware, self-maintenance, and capable of making market predictions [18].

Based on I4.0 are the Cyber-Physical Systems (CPS), which are defined as the technology for managing interconnected systems between its physical assets and its computational capabilities [17]. Social Cyber-Physical Systems are an evolution of the CPS model, and combines the production services with the consumer, enabling it to understand consumer demands and offer personalised products and services on valuable time [34].

2.2 Principles of Blockchain

The Blockchain technology was introduced as a solution to the problem of making a database both secure and widely distributed [28], resulting in a technology that combines peer-to-peer networks, cryptographic algorithms, and a decentralisation mechanism [32], enabling trusting interactions between individuals without the need for a trusted intermediary [6]. Blockchain is a peer-to-peer distributed ledger technology that registers all the transactions that happened to all the participants on the network [10]. The blockchain follows a decentralised approach where it is replicated and maintained by every participant, which removes the need for a trusted centralised entity to manage the registry [10]. Blockchain can execute arbitrary tasks, called smart contracts, which are digital contracts that make sure that contractual conditions are met before any transaction is completed, reducing the amount of human involvement required to create, execute, and enforce a contract [1].

3   Proposed Approach

Let us assume a group of organisations where each provides a set of services or products, and to fulfill the production of such elements they rely on services/products provided by other organisations. The decision, regarding which other organisation is going to be selected to buy products from, can become a complicated task. There are always going to exist a set of dependencies established between two or more entities sharing value in a supply chain. Since the processes that compose this type of activity are prone to establish a link and in an extensive supply chain, is hard to have an overall idea of all transactions made [1].

The objective of this proposal is to develop a model that is capable of representing an entity and illustrate how such an entity relates and perceives others. By simplifying how transactions can be established between them and how to make an improvement in decision-making, we can enable any entity to make a better choice when it comes to whom rely on to complement its manufacturing needs.

3.1   Model Breakdown

Our model is represented in Fig. 1 previously introduced in previous works [25,26], was designed to be capable of representing and supporting the complex structure of dependencies created between entities, in the industry environment, to improve decision-making and to facilitate the relationships between them, through collaboration. With the introduction of industry 4.0, industries need to look at the individualisation of customer's requirements, where the goal is to deliver various goods to fulfill small customer groups with specific needs while reducing production costs and focusing in personalisation, flexibility, and responsiveness.

The manufacturing flexibility and the integration of different processes and activities are guaranteed, due to the intelligent manufacturing environment of industry 4.0. The problem is how, besides handling manufacturing and processes flexibility, industries will be able to fulfill personalised demands in the industry 4.0 context. To achieve this, there needs to exists a better collaboration between industrial organisations and other businesses, even if they are competitors, to find success in the demanding environment of industry 4.0. Providing a model to improve collaboration in industry 4.0 is the goal of this proposal.

The model starts by creating a network as suggested by the work of Schuh et al. (2014), where entities can collaborate towards stronger cooperation, and each can achieve their targets. This collaborative network of entities aims at being an entry point for this model, allowing organisations, that already have some form of a relationship established or are looking for new partners [29], to consolidate their goal and objectives. For each entity on this network, there is a recurrent process happening where first interaction is established with other entity. Then, using the data gathered from the interaction, a reasoning process happens from where new information is learnt so that it can be used for future processes.

The second part of this model is formed by: (1) a layer that uses multi-agent systems to handle the reasoning and the interactions between the entities; (2) a blockchain to handle knowledge representation. With these two technologies combined, we can provide empowerment for decision-makers in a decentralised system, which is also a key factor to promote collaboration in the context of industry 4.0 [29]. The combination of MAS and blockchain is not new, as explained in the work of Calveresi et al. (2018), some recent trends rely on the promising idea of integrating MAS and blockchain with the expectation of providing blockchain features in use cases where agent technology might require them. The same work also states that this combination can represent a robust solution if properly managed [10]. One example of the use of this technology, applied to similar topics as this proposal, can be seen in the work of Casado-Vara et al. (2018) that presented a model that uses blockchain, smart contacts, and MAS to coordinate the tracking of food in the agriculture supply chain [11]. This model relies on blockchain to store all the transactions, with the authors pointing out security and decentralisation features as the main reasons why blockchain was applied. To coordinate all the members of the supply chain, the authors use a MAS formed by several layers and agent.

To store data regarding an entity and transactions for all the participants in the network, a consortium blockchain is used, which, in our opinion, is the best fit to represent the current problem, since it provides a shared, immutable, and transparent append-only register of all the actions that have happened to all the participants in the network. A consortium blockchain provides many of the benefits of a private blockchain, such as efficiency and transaction and data access privacy, without consolidating the power in one entity. The unique strategy of the consortium blockchain is highly beneficial for organisational collaboration since it operates under the leadership of a group instead of a single entity.

This group is the one that specifies who are the authorised transaction validators, and who has permissions to participate in the consensus process. Transaction data and general data on the blockchain are also controlled using permissions, that are managed by this group. With these specifications, this partially decentralised distributed ledger can be applied to highly regulated businesses, since it has excellent efficiency in the transactions, with no transaction fees.

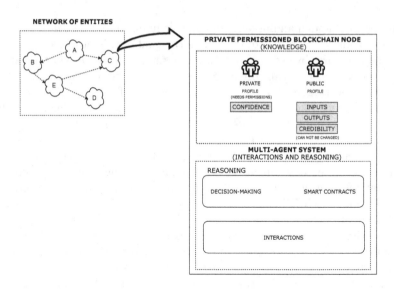

Fig. 1. Multi-Agent System and Blockchain based model representation

The overall system rules are easier to manage and can achieve better protection against external disturbances.

To implement this component, Hyperledger Fabric is going to be used. Fabric is a system for building and operating distributed ledger solutions for running smart contracts on a permissioned blockchain, and it has been used in more than 400 prototypes, proofs-of-concept, and production distributed ledger systems, across multiple industries [4]. Since this is a system for permissioned networks, Fabric uses a portable notion of membership that can be integrated with industry-standard identity management. The membership service provider maintains the identities of all participants in the network, and it is used for issuing credentials that are used for authentication and authorisation. Hyperledger Fabric also supports the execution of arbitrary smart contracts, that are called chaincodes [9], making sure that controlled access to the ledger is provided, as well maintaining information encapsulated and automating aspects of transactions between entities. Another critical component in Hyperledger Fabric is the possibility of creating channels, which allows for a set of entities to create a separated form of communication between them, enabling them to establish private and confidential transactions. This creates a separated ledger from the primary ledger [30], where only the entities associated with the channel can see the transactions data, allowing for competing entities to perform individual business transactions with other entities, without their competitors having access to the information.

Entity's data will be stored on the blockchain using a public and private profile to guarantee that it has information about the network, about the other entities, and about its own profile [21]. This information will get more precise along the time and through interactions done by the entity. The private profile will need permissions to be accessed and will store data that will represent the confidence that the entity has on the overall network and each remaining entity. This is represented by a percentage value ranging from zero to one hundred per cent. This private profile should only be accessed by the entity to which it is associated. Regarding the public profile, it contains mostly accessible information about the entity and how it is perceived by the network, and stores the following variables:

1. Inputs – represent the needs of the entity, namely what it needs from the other entities in the network in order to fulfill its business processes. As an example, these inputs can be raw materials, maintenance needs, shipping services, among others. This value can be read by every one in the network, but only the entity can update this values;
2. Outputs – what it has to offer to the network and to its entities. This will ultimately represent the input of some other entity;
3. Credibility – corresponds to how credible we are to the network and to each entity, meaning that this variable will hold a percentage value ranging from zero to one hundred, that will tell, based on previous interactions, how much the other entities trust a certain entity. Despite being stored in the public part of the profile, so the other entities can see our level of credibility, this value can not be changed even by the entity to whom it refers, setting permissions to only allow the value to be read.

The confidence and credibility values are critical in the context of this model. Both of this values are important to categorise and to create a separation between entities, with confidence being linked only to the corresponding entity and with credibility being linked to all entities in the network, despite referencing only the entity owner of the profile. Credibility is used in the context of this model, to provide a way of an entity to be individually classified by all the others entities in the network. On the other hand, the confidence values have a more simple and direct approach, they are used to provide an entity a way of storing their evaluation for each entity, based on their previous interactions. The way these profiles are setup allow for a scenario where, for instance, an entity B has a low level of credibility in the network. However, because previous interactions with entity A were successful, entity A has a high level of confidence in B, which enables it to rely on this entity to establish future interactions.

The other component of this model is based on a multi-agent system and its purpose is to provide a solution to handle the reasoning and the interactions between entities, achieving its end result that is to decide which is the best entities, from the network of entities, to interact with in each situation. This proposition meets another subject, the supplier selection problem, that is often referenced in the literature [5, 13, 22]. The supplier selection problem considers qualitative and quantitative criteria as influencing factors to perform the selection [14]. But when moving to an industry 4.0 manufacturing environment, organisations cannot rely on the typical entity selection process, since this too will be affected by industry 4.0 [5]. This process needs to be updated and its ideologies transferred into a more sustainable approach, where social measures and influencing factors are incorporated into the selection process [5].

This component uses a MAS, since these systems are suited for modelling distributed problems [20], where multiple agents interact with each other to achieve local and global objectives [12], and is formed by two layers, the interaction layer and the reasoning layer. MAS are intelligent systems, where autonomous agents dwell in a world with no control or persistent knowledge [24]. An agent is any entity that senses its environment and acts over it, performing a task continuously [15], with a strong autonomy [35], in a shifting environment, coexisting with other entities and processes [2]. A MAS are a network of agents that work together to solve problems that a single agent would not be able to solve [15] and can be applied to a variety of operating environments and development platforms [35].

The interaction layer is responsible for the communications between entities [21], gathering any type of interaction established between two entities in the network, creating a history of interactions that can be used as a point of reference to the future. The reasoning layer is formed by the decision-making module and the smart contract module. The decision-making module will provide the intended support to the entity in the choice of the preferable entity to get its inputs. The smart contract module is were predetermined agreements between entities will be created, establishing conditions for completing transactions, before being executed in the blockchain.

To design the multi-agent system in this work we followed the methodology presented by Nikraz et al. (2006). The methodology presented by Nikraz et al. focus on the critical issues of analysing and designing a multi-agent system, with particular emphasis on the analysis and design phases, that are based on the Foundation for Intelligent Physical Agents (FIPA) standards [23]. To design the system, an identification, categorisation, and refinements of agent types are performed during the analysis phase. The multi-agent system proposed in the reasoning and interaction layer is formed by several agents that represent many parties and functions. In this system, three types of agents are defined: Blockchain Agent (BA), Entity Agent (EA), and the Decision Maker Agent (DMA). From this analysis results, an agent diagram (as indicated in the methodology being followed), helps to identify the main agent types and what possible interactions there might exist [23]. As such, for this system, the agent diagram can be seen in Fig. 2. With those agents is possible to create an agent-based system capable of supporting the requirements presented by the problem in question, while assigning responsibilities to each of the agents so that each can, individually, perform their tasks.

3.2   Why Use a Blockchain

In this model, blockchain can act as a catalyst for growth and could provide a core feature for a system where innovative practices will thrive and create a truly

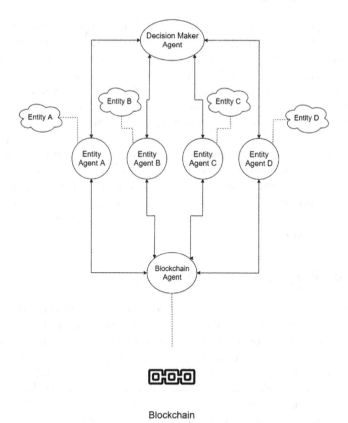

Fig. 2. Representation of the network of agents

collaborative global economy, with shared goals and objectives for the benefit of the entire network of entities [8].

The usage of blockchain aligns with our proposal since there are multiple entities in the same network, which creates an opportunity to run a permissioned blockchain among this set of known, identified participants [4]. A permissioned blockchain provides a way to create interactions among a group of entities that have a common goal but do not fully trust each other, such as industries that exchange funds, goods or information. At the same time, none are willing to agree on a trusted third party [33]. In this exact scenario, the usage of smart contacts in a private permissioned blockchain can simplify trustless protocols between multiple parties, while the details of the contract remain hidden and it only concerns a well-known number of participants. With the support of blockchain, it is possible to create a system that allows for strong interactions to be streamlined in an environment where there is a lack of trust [8] and therefore, provide opportunities for consumers and business, through improved collaboration.

In this proposal the usage of a blockchain allows the removal of a trusted mediator since each entity might operate a node in the network, making sure that a single entity does not have full control over the ledger [36], making this type of blockchain partly decentralised [19]. In addition to transactions, commitments and meta-commitments can be securely stored in the blockchain [10]. In this type of blockchain, participants know and identify each other [30], and anyone can join the network, after proper verification of their entity. Then a set of permissions are given to the entities to only allow them to perform a specific set of writing and reading operations [33]. This can provide guaranty that entities only have access to the appropriated sets of information about the other entities on the network while controlling and updating the shared state of the network and issuing transactions [10]. For instance, if entity A only makes transactions with B and C, there is no need for the rest of the entities to have permission to read the shared data.

4 Discussion and Future Work

This paper presents a new approach for representing multiple industries and their interactions in an environment affected by I4.0 standards. This approach uses a private permissioned blockchain implemented thought Hyperledger Fabric, as a base for knowledge representation, where all the entities data and respective transaction are going to be stored. Aided by the use of a MAS to handle all the reasoning and provide improved decision-making capabilities for the system. With this model, entities can perform faster transactions, without having to rely on a typical third party to validate them. They can assess more dynamically the other entities in the network, establish pre-arranged conditions between them, using smart contracts, and rely on the agent component to perform more efficient management of the network, while providing essential information to help entities with decisions. The features provided by the model improve collaboration, guaranteeing that entities will be ready to fulfilled consumers needs and demands in the future of industrialisation.

Future lines of work include exploring the MAS component, namely, develop the agent's responsibilities and interactions, develop the actions for the decision-maker agent, and how the MAS module and the blockchain will interact.

References

1. Abeyratne, S.A., Monfared, R.P.: Blockchain ready manufacturing supply chain using distributed ledger. Int. J. Res. Eng. Technol. 05(09), 1–10 (2016). https://doi.org/10.15623/ijret.2016.0509001. http://esatjournals.net/ijret/2016v05/i09/IJRET20160509001.pdf
2. Adeyeri, M.K., Mpofu, K., Adenuga, O.T.: Integration of agent technology into manufacturing enterprise: a review and platform for industry 4.0. In: 2015 International Conference on Industrial Engineering and Operations Management (IEOM). IEEE, March 2015. https://doi.org/10.1109/ieom.2015.7093910

3. Ameri, F., McArthur, C.: A multi-agent system for autonomous supply chain configuration. Int. J. Adv. Manuf. Technol. **66**(5–8), 1097–1112 (2012). https://doi.org/10.1007/s00170-012-4392-9

4. Androulaki, E., et al.: Hyperledger fabric: a distributed operating system for permissioned blockchains. In: Proceedings of the Thirteenth EuroSys Conference on - EuroSys 2018. ACM Press (2018). https://doi.org/10.1145/3190508.3190538

5. Azadnia, A.H., Saman, M.Z.M., Wong, K.Y.: Sustainable supplier selection and order lot-sizing: an integrated multi-objective decision-making process. Int. J. Prod. Res. **53**(2), 383–408 (2015). https://doi.org/10.1080/00207543.2014.935827

6. Bahga, A., Madisetti, V.K.: Blockchain platform for industrial internet of things. J. Softw. Eng. Appl. **09**(10), 533–546 (2016). https://doi.org/10.4236/jsea.2016.910036. http://www.scirp.org/journal/jsea

7. Blanchet, M., Rinn, T., Von Thaden, G., De Thieulloy, G.: Industry 4.0: the new industrial revolution-how Europe will succeed. Hg. v. Roland Berger Strategy Consultants GmbH. München. Abgerufen am 11.05. 2014 (2014). http://www.rolandberger.com/media/pdf/Roland_Berger_TAB_Industry_4_0_20140403.pdf

8. Buchanan, B., Naqvi, N.: Building the future of EU: moving forward with international collaboration on blockchain. JBBA **1**(1), 1–4 (2018)

9. Cachin, C., Schubert, S., Vukolić, M.: Architecture of the hyperledger blockchain fabric *. Technical report (2016), www.hyperledger.org

10. Calvaresi, D., Dubovitskaya, A., Calbimonte, J.P., Taveter, K., Schumacher, M.: Multi-Agent systems and blockchain: results from a systematic literature review. In: Demazeau, Y., An, B., Bajo, J., Fernández-Caballero, A. (eds.) PAAMS 2018. LNCS (LNAI), vol. 10978, pp. 110–126. Springer, Cham (2018). https://doi.org/10.1007/978-3-319-94580-4_9

11. Casado-Vara, R., Prieto, J., la Prieta, F.D., Corchado, J.M.: How blockchain improves the supply chain: case study alimentary supply chain. Procedia Comput. Sci. **134**, 393–398 (2018). https://doi.org/10.1016/j.procs.2018.07.193. https://linkinghub.elsevier.com/retrieve/pii/S187705091831158X

12. Eddy, Y.F., Gooi, H.B., Chen, S.X.: Multi-agent system for distributed management of microgrids. IEEE Trans. Power Syst. **30**(1), 24–34 (2014)

13. Fiala, P.: Information sharing in supply chains. Omega **33**(5), 419–423 (2005). https://doi.org/10.1016/j.omega.2004.07.006

14. Ghadimi, P., Ghassemi Toosi, F., Heavey, C.: A multi-agent systems approach for sustainable supplier selection and order allocation in a partnership supply chain. Eur. J. Oper. Res. **269**(1), 286–301 (2018). https://doi.org/10.1016/j.ejor.2017.07.014. https://linkinghub.elsevier.com/retrieve/pii/S0377221717306410

15. Glavic, M.: Agents and multi-agent systems: a short introduction for power engineers, pp. 1–21 (2006)

16. Kang, H.S., et al.: Smart manufacturing: past research, present findings, and future directions. Int. J. Precis. Eng. Manuf.-Green Technol. **3**(1), 111–128 (2016). https://doi.org/10.1007/s40684-016-0015-5

17. Lee, J., Bagheri, B., Kao, H.A.: A cyber-physical systems architecture for industry 4.0-based manufacturing systems. Manuf. Lett. **3**, 18–23 (2015). https://doi.org/10.1016/j.mfglet.2014.12.001

18. Lee, J., Kao, H.A., Yang, S.: Service innovation and smart analytics for industry 4.0 and big data environment. Procedia CIRP **16**, 3–8 (2014). https://doi.org/10.1016/j.procir.2014.02.001. http://www.sciencedirect.com/science/article/pii/S2212827114000857

19. Lin, I.C., Liao, T.C.: A survey of blockchain security issues and challenges. Int. J. Netw. Secur. **19**(5), 653–659 (2017). https://doi.org/10.6633/IJNS.201709.19(5). 01. https://pdfs.semanticscholar.org/f61e/db500c023c4c4ef665bd7ed2423170773 340.pdf

20. Marreiros, G., Santos, R., Ramos, C., Neves, J.: Context-aware emotion-based model for group decision making. IEEE Intell. Syst. Mag. **25**(2), 31–39 (2010)

21. Marreiros, G., Santos, R., Ramos, C., Neves, J., Bulas-Cruz, J.: ABS4GD: a multi-agent system that simulates group decision processes considering emotional and argumentative aspects. In: AAAI Spring Symposium Series, pp. 88–95 (2008)

22. Mettler, T., Rohner, P.: Supplier relationship management: a case study in the context of health care. J. Theoret. Appl. Electron. Commer. Res. **4**(3), 58–71 (2009). https://doi.org/10.4067/S0718-18762009000300006

23. Nikraz, M., Caire, G., Bahri, P.A.: A methodology for the analysis and design of multi-agent systems using JADE. Technical report (2006)

24. Oprea, M.: Applications of multi-agent systems. In: Reis, R. (ed.) Information Technology. IIFIP, vol. 157, pp. 239–270. Springer, Boston, MA (2004). https://doi.org/10.1007/1-4020-8159-6_9

25. Pinheiro, P., Macedo, M., Barbosa, R., Santos, R., Novais, P.: Multi-agent systems approach to industry 4.0: enabling collaboration considering a blockchain for knowledge representation. In: Bajo, J., et al. (eds.) PAAMS 2018. CCIS, vol. 887, pp. 149–160. Springer, Cham (2018). https://doi.org/10.1007/978-3-319-94779-2_14

26. Pinheiro, P., Santos, R., Barbosa, R.: Industry 4.0 multi-agent system based knowledge representation through blockchain. In: Novais, P., et al. (eds.) ISAmI2018 2018. AISC, vol. 806, pp. 331–337. Springer, Cham (2019). https://doi.org/10.1007/978-3-030-01746-0_39

27. Qin, J., Liu, Y., Grosvenor, R.: A categorical framework of manufacturing for industry and beyond. Procedia CIRP **52**, 173–178 (2016). https://doi.org/10.1016/j.procir.2016.08.005. http://www.sciencedirect.com/science/article/pii/S22 1282711630854X?via%3Dihub

28. Rabah, K.: Overview of blockchain as the engine of the 4th industrial revolution. Mara Res. J. Bus. Manag. **1**(1), 125–135 (2016). The Africa Premier Research Publishing Hub www.mrjournals.org Mara Research Journals MR Journal of Business & Management

29. Schuh, G., Potente, T., Wesch-Potente, C., Weber, A.R., Prote, J.P.: Collaboration mechanisms to increase productivity in the context of industrie 4.0. Procedia CIRP **19**, 51–56 (2014). https://doi.org/10.1016/j.procir.2014.05.016. https://linkinghub.elsevier.com/retrieve/pii/S2212827114006453

30. Sukhwani, H., Wang, N., Trivedi, K.S., Rindos, A.: Performance modeling of hyperledger fabric (permissioned blockchain network). In: 2018 IEEE 17th International Symposium on Network Computing and Applications (NCA), pp. 1–8. IEEE, November 2018. https://doi.org/10.1109/nca.2018.8548070

31. Wang, S., Wan, J., Li, D., Zhang, C.: Implementing smart factory of industrie 4.0: an outlook. Int. J. Distrib. Sens. Netw. **12**(1), 3159805 (2016). https://doi.org/10.1155/2016/3159805

32. Wright, A., Filippi, P.D.: Decentralized blockchain technology and the rise of lex cryptographia. SSRN Electron. J. (2015). https://doi.org/10.2139/ssrn.2580664, http://www.ssrn.com/abstract=2580664

33. Wust, K., Gervais, A.: Do you need a blockchain? In: 2018 Crypto Valley Conference on Blockchain Technology (CVCBT), pp. 45–54. no. i. IEEE, June 2018. https://doi.org/10.1109/cvcbt.2018.00011, https://ieeexplore.ieee.org/document/8525392/

34. Zhang, F., Liu, M., Shen, W.: Operation modes of smart factory for high-end equipment manufacturing in the internet and big data era. In: Smc 2017.Org (2017). http://www.smc2017.org/SMC2017_Papers/media/files/0642.pdf

35. Zhao, J.Y., Wang, Y.J., Xi, X.: Simulation of steel production logistics system based on multi-agents. Int. J. Simul. Model. **16**(1), 167–175 (2017). https://doi.org/10.2507/ijsimm16(1)co4, http://www.ijsimm.com/Full_Papers/Fulltext2017/text16-1_167-175.pdf

36. Zheng, Z., Xie, S., Dai, H., Chen, X., Wang, H.: An overview of blockchain technology: architecture, consensus, and future trends. In: 2017 IEEE International Congress on Big Data (BigData Congress), pp. 557–564. IEEE, June 2017. https://doi.org/10.1109/bigdatacongress.2017.85, http://ieeexplore.ieee.org/document/8029379/

Learning to Communicate Proactively in Human-Agent Teaming

Emma M. van Zoelen[1]([✉]), Anita Cremers[1,3], Frank P. M. Dignum[2,4,5], Jurriaan van Diggelen[1], and Marieke M. Peeters[1]

[1] TNO, Kampweg 55, 3769 DE Soesterberg, The Netherlands
{emma.vanzoelen,anita.cremers,jurriaan.vandiggelen,
marieke.peeters}@tno.nl
[2] Utrecht University, Domplein 29, 3512 JE Utrecht, The Netherlands
f.p.m.dignum@uu.nl
[3] University of Applied Sciences,
Heidelberglaan 7, 3584 CS Utrecht, The Netherlands
[4] Umeå University, 901 87 Umeå, Sweden
[5] Czech Technical University, Zikova 1903/4, 166 36 Praha 6, Czech Republic

Abstract. Artificially intelligent agents increasingly collaborate with humans in human-agent teams. Timely proactive sharing of relevant information within the team contributes to the overall team performance. This paper presents a machine learning approach to proactive communication in AI-agents using contextual factors. Proactive communication was learned in two consecutive experimental steps: (a) multi-agent team simulations to learn effective communicative behaviors, and (b) human-agent team experiments to refine communication suitable for a human team member. Results consist of proactive communication policies for communicating both beliefs and goals within human-agent teams. Agents learned to use minimal communication to improve team performance in simulation, while they learned more specific socially desirable behaviors in the human-agent team experiment.

Keywords: Human-agent teaming · Reinforcement Learning · BDI-agent · Human-agent communication · Proactive · Context-sensitive

1 Introduction

As intelligent agents gain more capabilities, responsibilities for the accurate, effective, efficient and safe execution of tasks is handed over from humans to agents. Since humans have their own unique abilities at which they outperform agents, a logical step is for humans and agents to collaborate in human-agent teams, exploiting the strengths of both.

Research on human-agent teaming has existed for about twenty years, especially in safety-critical domains [2,12]. One of the most important aspects of

© Springer Nature Switzerland AG 2020
F. De La Prieta et al. (Eds.): PAAMS 2020 Workshops, CCIS 1233, pp. 238–249, 2020.
https://doi.org/10.1007/978-3-030-51999-5_20

teaming is communication, a necessary skill for collaboration and related aspects such as coordination of tasks and maintaining situational awareness [11]. For successful (human-agent) teamwork it is vital that this communication is **proactive**. Proactive communication can reduce cognitive load of team members by anticipating their information need [3], enabling team members to primarily focus on their own tasks, while communicating when necessary. This paper explores how we might achieve proactive communication in human-agent teams.

In teaming tasks, preferred levels of proactivity for the agent might change over time depending on the context. Therefore, to achieve proactivity, **context-sensitivity** is needed to make sure there is neither communication overload nor a lack of communication as team members **adapt** to the needs of specific team members and situations [11]. As environments and teamwork itself are highly dynamic and at times unpredictable, pre-programming all communication beforehand is unfeasible. Adaptivity and context-sensitivity are more easily achieved through data-driven learning methods. Therefore, we created a simple learning algorithm to enable agents to learn when to communicate proactively and when not to, taking into account the current context. In order to evaluate whether this enabled agents to learn proactive communication behavior suitable for teamwork, we conducted simulation runs as well as human-agent teaming experiments in which the agents continued to learn from humans. The main contribution of this paper is an attempt at creating proactive communication in human-agent teaming, focusing on an evaluation of its dynamics and effects in actual human-agent teaming contexts.

In Sect. 2 we elaborate on related work on agent communication systems, focusing on human-agent teaming and proactivity. We give a description of the task environment used in Sect. 3. The methods used to learn the proactive communication policies are explained in Sect. 4, while the experiment that was conducted to evaluate them and the results obtained are described in Sect. 5.

2   Related Work

2.1   Agent Communication

Existing work on communication systems for human-agent teaming generally does not deal with proactivity and leaves most of the initiative up to the human team member. Work has been done on *context-sensitive* communication systems, e.g. [16], but this serves mostly to incorporate context when replying to human conversational partners, i.e. *reactive* communication. Studies that do look at *proactive* communication focus mostly on conversational information to determine whether initiative should be taken, such as in [3]. If other context factors are taken into account, it is usually used for initiative in ongoing conversations, where communication is the main task and both partners are fully engaged in the conversation, such as in [4]. Initiating conversation is also important in teaming tasks for which conversation is not the main activity. Our work attempts to focus on achieving *proactive communication in general human-agent teaming tasks*, using context-sensitivity to determine whether or not communication of certain information in a given situation is beneficial for the team performance.

Within existing work on proactive communication, a distinction is made between communication of beliefs versus communication of goals. While both have a positive influence on task performance, the effect is larger for the communication of goals [3]. Furthermore, each requires different situational characteristics to decide whether or not to communicate, as communicating about goals is more deliberative whereas communicating about beliefs is more reactive. In our work, we made a distinction between these two types of communication as well.

2.2 Technical Implementation

Most of the research on agent communication uses agent behavior that is either preprogrammed, learned passively and under supervision by exposing the agents to large amounts of dialogue text, or learned within a conversation-related context. Such approaches are unsuitable for capturing the subtle ways in which humans communicate to coordinate in collaborative teaming tasks [13]. A promising approach is to use machine learning methods like *Reinforcement Learning* (RL) to solve tasks modeled as *Markov decision processes* (MDPs), enabling agents to coordinate their actions in collaborative games. Following such methods agents play a coordination game repeatedly and receive utility for each chosen action. Using RL methods, agents learn trade-offs between the costs and values of communicative acts, optimizing a communication policy in a given game [7]. Most of this research uses multi-agent evaluations to train and test the learned behavior, using high numbers of simulation runs. To better accommodate human-agent collaboration, the research presented in this paper used existing machine learning methods to optimize proactive communication, but evaluated the learned behavior in a human-agent context. This allowed for the agents to tweak their policies to enable collaboration with human team members.

3   Blocks World for Teams

We adopted the Blocks World for Teams (BW4T) environment [10] as a task environment to evaluate the developed agents. BW4T is a 2D blocks world environment that offers the possibility of finishing a task in multi-human, human-agent and multi-agent team configurations. Team members work on the same task by controlling an avatar (represented by a large black square) in the environment. This avatar can be controlled by a human through a graphical user interface, or by an agent program. The simple representation offers the opportunity to work on the teaming abilities of intelligent agents as well as to evaluate them with humans. The insights gathered within this environment are a first step towards real-life applications due to this possibility. The BW4T environment consists of rooms containing colored blocks, which are connected by corridors, and a special drop zone. The team's task objective is represented by a sequence of colored blocks in the corner of the screen. The team members can achieve their objective task by searching the rooms for blocks in the appropriate color, and deliver them to the drop zone in the order the objective describes.

Agents can see the environment and the locations of the rooms, but they can only see what blocks are in a room when they are in that room. Agents can only see other team members when they are in the same zone or in neighboring zones, meaning that they usually do not know where their team members are unless they communicate this to each other. They can see when another agent is in a certain room by the color of the door: the door is green when a room is free, and red when a room is occupied.

Team members (humans or agents) could complete the task on their own, but the task can be achieved much quicker when working as a team. The creators of BW4T call this *soft interdependence* [9]. It is therefore useful for agents to communicate their observations and what they are doing. Since performance on the task is measured by the time it takes to deliver all the blocks in the sequence, appropriate communication and collaboration can greatly increase performance.

4 Adaptively Communicating Agents

Using the GOAL agent programming language [15], which is based on the BDI paradigm, we programmed agents to display basic behavior that lets them solve the task, such that the learning of proactive communication could be added. Since BDI-agents reason in anthropomorphic concepts, this provides a basic shared level of understanding that can be used in human-agent teaming. Details of the rules for the basic behavior within one deliberation cycle are shown in Fig. 1. These rules enable agents to solve the task by themselves, but also to deal with communication from team members. The rest of this section describes how the mechanism for learning to communicate proactively was added.

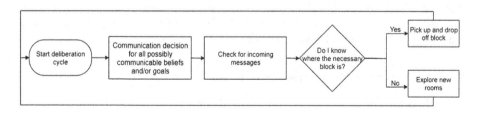

Fig. 1. Basic agent behavior

4.1 General Overview of Method Chosen: RL in Game-Setting

The developed agents learn how to communicate proactively using Q-learning. The learning process of the agents makes use of an existing Q-learning module that has been developed for the GOAL agent programming language [15]. With

Table 1. Three different communication strategies

(a) Belief Communication Strategy	During every cycle c, for all beliefs ϕ^*, evaluate state s and determine action with highest expected reward a from $A_m = \{communicate\ \phi,\ silence\}$
(b) Goal Communication Strategy	During every cycle c, for all goals γ^{**}, evaluate state s and determine action with highest expected reward a from $A_m = \{communicate\ \gamma,\ silence\}$
(c) Combined Communication Strategy	During every cycle c, for all goals γ and beliefs ϕ, evaluate state s and determine action with highest expected reward a from $A_m = \{communicate\ (\phi\ or\ \gamma),\ silence\}$

$^*\phi$: block(Block, Color, Room)
$^{**}\gamma$: see Table 2

this adaptive functionality, agents can learn preferences across a set of communicative acts. This was modeled for three different communication strategies (Table 1).

During every deliberation cycle, an agent considers each of its beliefs about a block or goal, and chooses to either communicate that information or remain silent. This decision is based on the expected rewards for that particular communicative act in the state that the agent is currently in, which is determined from previously obtained rewards. The state consists of all beliefs and goals of the agent. Agents received a penalty of -1 for every message they sent, to make sure they would not communicate too many messages. At the end of a run, agents received a reward based on the time it took to achieve the objective. With r_{max} being the maximum reward and t the time it took achieve the objective in seconds or in simulation steps, this reward was calculated as $R = r_{max} - t * 20$. The height of the cost and the value of r_{max} were determined by looking at how often the Q-learning module was run, to make sure that below-par completion time would yield a cumulative reward of zero.

4.2 Filtering the State Representation

Using Reinforcement Learning has a disadvantage; in order to learn how to communicate and optimize their policy, agents will have to play the game a large number of times. When moving to the context of human-agent teaming, agents might have to train with humans, for which it would be a laborious effort to train the agent in communication from scratch. We solved this by creating a smaller state representation using aggregated state factors. An added advantage is that this allows for qualitative explanations about why an agent learned certain behavior by looking at the aggregated state-action pairs after training.

Rules in the BDI program can be used to incorporate reasoning steps before initiating the learning process to aggregate state factors. In order to decide whether information about a block should be communicated, it is for example relevant to consider two features: whether the information has been communicated before and whether the block is part of the task currently at hand. This translates to two aggregated factors that should be considered when deciding about communication: (a) redundancy and (b) relevance to the task. These two factors describe (a) whether a message about a belief has been communicated before ($communicated(a)$, $a \in \{true, false\}$) and (b) whether a block is needed to finish the task and the position of the observed block in the task objective's sequence ($inTask(a)$, $a \in \{false, 0, 1, 2, 3, 4, 5\}$). By using these two factors as the state representation instead of all beliefs of the agent, the state space is greatly reduced. For other communication strategies, such as goal communication, other state factors can be determined to create a similarly small and general state representation. For the agents described here, a redundancy factor has been implemented ($communicated(a)$, $a \in \{true, false\}$), as well as a factor describing how many steps a specific goal is removed from the main goal of finishing the sequence (($abstraction(a)$, $a \in \{1, 2, 3, 4, 5\}$), see Table 2) and a factor about whether an agent is pursuing a block, and how many distance units that block is currently removed from the agent ($pursuingBlock(a)$, $a \in \{false, 1, 2, 3, 4, 5, 6, 7, 8, 9\}$).

Table 2. The different abstraction level goals

Abstraction	
1	A goal to be in the drop zone
2	A goal to hold a block while being in a room with that block
3	A goal to be near a block while being in a room with that block (in order to pick it up)
4	A goal to be in a room of which the agent knows it has the necessary block
5	A goal to be in a room while not knowing where the necessary block is

5   Experimentation

The developed agents were evaluated in two experimental steps: (a) multi-agent team simulations to train the basic communicative behaviors of the agents, and (b) human-agent team experiments to refine communication suitable for a human team member. This enabled us to see the difference between the behaviors learned from simulation and the behaviors learned from human team partners.

5.1   Simulation Runs

Experimental simulation runs were done with agent-only teams using two communication strategies: (a) communicating beliefs and (b) communicating goals.

Table 3. Results of simulation runs with means (and standard deviations) of time, the number of messages and the p-value after comparing to the 'Always Silent' strategy

Communication strategy	Time (s)	Nr of messages	p-value
(a) Belief	59.25 (7.20)	54.71 (58.43)	0.0014
(b) Goal	58.92 (12.35)	12.09 (16.25)	0.0084
Always silent	61.64 (7.62)	0	

Experimental series of 200 runs per condition were evaluated with an exploration rate of 0.001. The speed of the BW4T environment was set to 100 fps and the task sequence changed randomly every run.

Results and Discussion. For both communication strategies, agents are able to increase their performance by drastically decreasing the time it takes to finish the sequence after about five runs. The number of messages sent drops as well, and although there is a high variety between runs, on average the decrease is maintained. Both communication strategies are able to perform significantly better than an 'always silent' communication strategy (see Table 3). The most important learned behavior for both communication strategies was based on the redundancy state factor. There was no clear learned behavior for the other state factors. This behavior stabilized after about 50 runs for the belief communication strategy, and after about 80 runs for the goal communication strategy.

While it seems like the agents use a higher number of messages than necessary, this can be attributed to the exploration rate being greater than 0 (i.e. 0.001). Taking this into account, we observe that agents learn to communicate mostly the necessary messages. Due to the randomized task sequence there is a high variety in task performance, but on average both communication strategies improve on the 'always silent' strategy. The fact that no clear behavior is learned on the other state factors suggests that these are not relevant for the simulated agents. While the simplified state representation causes the learned behavior to be trivial, we can still say that some level of proactive behavior is achieved.

5.2   Human-Agent Experiment

An experiment with humans was conducted to test how results obtained in agent-agent communication experiments transfer to human-agent communication, as well as to compare the performance of human-agent teams working with agents using all three communication strategies as presented in Table 1. Human communication was limited to the same strategy as that of the agent. In the experiment, humans solve the BW4T task together with an agent that has been trained in simulation, to enable further learning from the human. Each participant played the game for 3 practice rounds, after which they played 10 times, with a randomized task sequence for every new round.

Participants. Thirty people participated (14 male, 16 female), consisting of students from Eindhoven University of Technology and interns from the Dutch applied research institute TNO, with an average age of 22 (SD = 2.3). Participants were randomly allocated to one of the three groups. In both the belief communication and goal communication condition there were 4 males and 6 females, while in the combined communication condition there were 6 males and 4 females. In each condition the participants with the highest task performance received a gift voucher of €10 to make sure they performed to their best abilities.

Process. During the experiment, the agent continued its learning process, and the learned model of the human-agent teams was compared qualitatively with that of the agent-only teams. Based on convergence rates observed in the agent-only experiments, the agents were pre-trained in 50 runs for the belief-communicating condition and in 80 runs for the other conditions. The agents used an exploration rate of 0.1 with a decay of 0.05 during training, and an exploration rate of 0.001 during the experiment. The three groups of human-agent teams were compared on task performance, qualitative team experience, usability and trust. Qualitative team experience was measured by asking participants halfway and at the end of the experiment to grade the extent to which they collaborated as a team on a scale from 1 to 10. Usability and trust were measured through a questionnaire at the end of the experiment, which was based on existing questionnaires [1,5,8,14], but adapted to fit the context at hand. The questions were evaluated on a Visual Analogue Scale of 10 cm.

Results and Discussion. Results are presented in Table 4. Trust and usability scores were analyzed for differences between the conditions using a One-Way ANOVA. The scores for qualitative team experience and task performance were analyzed using a Repeated Measure ANOVA. If a significant difference was found, a post-hoc analysis was done using a Tukey HSD test. A significant effect was found between the three conditions for qualitative team experience ($F(2,27)$ = 4.72, p = .018), as well as for usability ($F(2,27)$ = 5.017, p = .014). For qualitative team experience, the mean score for the belief communication strategy is significantly different from the goal communication strategy (p = .044) and the combined communication strategy (p = .014). For usability, a significant difference was found between the belief communication strategy and the goal

Table 4. Results quantitative measures: means (and standard deviations)

	(a) Belief	(b) Goal	(c) Combined
Task performance	127.26(12.58)	141.52(17.37)	134.74(10.87)
Qualitative team experience	5.78(1.35)	7.01(0.65)	7.01(0.65)
Usability	58.92(12.35)	12.09(16.25)	0.0084
Trust	5.13(1.23)	6.97(1.26)	6.92(0.72)

communication strategy (p = .025). No significant differences were found for task performance or trust.

Unlike in previous studies, no difference in task performance was found. This is probably due to the complexity of the agent behavior: participants could more easily predict the behavior of the agents in the belief communication strategy. Interestingly, the other two strategies were still valued significantly higher in qualitative team performance and usability, meaning that this is not directly related to objective task performance. The lack of differences for trust might be attributed to the questionnaire being unsuitable for human-agent teams, as the original questionnaire was made for human teams. The outcomes of the learning model after playing with humans are provided in the next sections.

Belief Communication Strategy. After playing with humans, agents maintain to only communicate when a message has not been communicated before and when the block is present in the task sequence at location 2, 3, 4 or 5. It differs per person which of these locations is preferred, although communicating when it exists in position 2 appears in half of the participants. The only newly learned behavior is that agents no longer communicate a block that is the current next block in the sequence (in position 0).

The fact that the agents learn to communicate a block that is the current next block in the sequence in simulation, but lose this behavior when playing with humans, can easily be explained: when communicating this to an agent, it does not matter much for the task performance if the receiver of the message will pick up the block. However, if this receiving agent is a human, this human will likely be slower than the agent. It is therefore better for the agent to not let the human interfere with this block and not communicate it.

Goal Communication Strategy. After playing with humans, from each participant, agents learn to communicate their goal when: (1) the goal they are pursuing is of abstraction level 3, (2) the goal has not been communicated before, and (3) they are pursuing a block that is 4 to 8 steps away, or they are not pursuing a block. Also, the agents learn from each participant that a level 4 goal must be communicated if it has not been communicated before and if they are pursuing a block that is 7 steps away. Last, the agents learn that it should communicate a goal of abstraction level 5 most of the time.

These results can be logically explained from a human point of view. The learned behavior for a goal of abstraction level 3 can be explained as always communicating about a block when an agent will pick up a certain block if it is in the room containing that block, to let their team member know that they have it. Being in a room with a block sets the distance of that block to 0, so the other distances are other blocks of the same color existing in the environment: distance 4 until 8 are basically all possible distances. The learned behavior for a level 4 goal means that agents should communicate that they are picking up a certain block if they are still quite far away from that block. If they are closer by, it is better to wait until they are in the room with the block before communicating.

Last, communicating a level 5 goal is letting your team members know where you are going, to make sure you are not occupying each other's rooms.

Combined Communication Strategy. For the combined communication strategy, the belief and goal communication were looked at separately. For belief communication, similar to in the belief-communication condition, the agents learn to communicate the location of blocks at different moments for different participants. Communicating about a block that is the next one in the sequence (inTask(0)), however, appears most often. For goal communication, the results of the learning model are similar to those in the goal-communication condition.

The most interesting result is the communication of a block that is the next one in the sequence. Apparently agents should do this when it is combined with goal communication, while they should remain silent when it is not. A possible explanation for this is that when combined with goal communication, agents can let their human team members know that they know where a block is, and that they will pick it up. This way, the human knows that they should not interfere.

6   Discussion

Our work is an attempt at achieving proactive communication in teaming tasks where communication is not the main activity, making use of context and adaptivity to determine communication decisions. While we have used mostly existing methods in terms of technical implementation, we used these algorithms to show that it is possible to achieve a working form of proactive communication. Our main contribution is that we compared behavior learned in simulation with behavior learned from actual human-agent teaming experiments.

In existing work on communication in human-agent teaming, agents are often only evaluated in simulation [6], which is mostly the case when learning is involved, or human-agent teams are only evaluated on task performance [3], which is mostly the case when there are fixed communication strategies. We managed to evaluate learning agents in an experiment with humans, showing that these agents learned different and more sophisticated behavior after learning from humans as compared to learning in simulation. Also, the type of communication that agents use influence the extent to which people feel they collaborate with the agent as a team. Such subjective evaluations give interesting insights on the development of proactively communicating agents, that can be used to improve algorithms in the future.

We used the BDI paradigm to define the state space to enable learning of proactive communication. While the integration of RL in BDI-agents has been used before [15], using it for communication or for learning from humans has not been done before. While we do not necessarily propose this as a new method for the implementation of intelligent agents, it does make online learning of communication feasible, especially for research into how learning is affected by interaction with humans. There is a lot of control over what can be learned, which helps to use smaller numbers of learning runs. It also helps researchers and programmers to analyze the learned behavior in a qualitative manner, to increase understanding of why the agents learn certain behavior.

The evaluations were, however, conducted in the simplified environment of BW4T, and while this makes it easy to program agents, it makes it hard to determine how this scales to real world scenarios. It will be relevant to look into more complex and realistic environments to see if (online) learning mechanisms as presented still work in such environments. Moreover, it will be interesting to let agents learn more complete communication strategies, as the results of the combined communication strategy in the human-agent teaming experiment showed that interaction between different communication strategies can influence the results. Overall, our results help to set an example for how we might let agents learn proactive communication behavior in teaming contexts with humans.

7   Conclusion

The aim of this study was to take a first step towards creating agents that learn to communicate proactively to enable fluent and successful-human-agent teaming, as well as to see what value learning from humans real-time brings. As a task environment, the BW4T environment was chosen in order to evaluate agent- as well as human-agent teams on their collaboration and communication.

The results from simulations show that agents can learn proactive communication strategies that lets them perform better than without communication on a team task. Moreover, we showed that learned behavior can be transferred from a simulation context to a context where agents learn with humans, as the most important learned factors stayed the same after learning from humans. The agents continued to adapt their behavior to those humans, as extra relevant learned behaviors could be observed. Our work therefore paves the path for future research into the development of agents using more complex learning algorithms in more complex environments than were used in this study, while keeping the needs of the human team members in mind.

References

1. Bernsen, N.O., Dybkjær, L.: Building usable spoken dialogue systems: some approaches. Sprache und Datenverarbeitung **28**(2), 111–131 (2004)
2. Bradshaw, J.M., et al.: Adjustable autonomy and human-agent teamwork in practice: an interim report on space applications. In: Weiss, G., Hexmoor, H., Castelfranchi, C., Falcone, R. (eds.) Agent Autonomy, vol. 7, pp. 243–280. Kluwer Academic Press, Boston (2003). https://doi.org/10.1007/978-1-4419-9198-0_11. http://link.springer.com/10.1007/978-1-4419-9198-011
3. Butchibabu, A.: Anticipatory Communication Strategies for Human Robot Team Coordination (2016)
4. Chu-Carroll, J.: MIMIC: an adaptive mixed initiative spoken dialogue system for information queries. In: Proceedings of the Sixth Conference on Applied Natural Language Processing, pp. 97–104. Association for Computational Linguistics, Seattle (2000). https://doi.org/10.3115/974147.974161, http://portal.acm.org/citation.cfm?doid=974147.974161

5. Costa, A.C., Anderson, N.: Measuring trust in teams: development and validation of a multifaceted measure of formative and reflective indicators of team trust. Eur. J. Work Organ. Psychol. **20**(1), 119–154 (2011). https://doi.org/10.1080/13594320903272083, http://www.tandfonline.com/doi/abs/10.1080/13594320903272083

6. Foerster, J., Assael, I.A., de Freitas, N., Whiteson, S.: Learning to communicate with deep multi-agent reinforcement learning. In: Lee, D.D., Sugiyama, M., Luxburg, U.V., Guyon, I., Garnett, R. (eds.) Advances in Neural Information Processing Systems 29, pp. 2137–2145. Curran Associates, Inc. (2016). http://papers.nips.cc/paper/6042-learning-to-communicate-with-deep-multi-agent-reinforcement-learning.pdf

7. Goldman, C.V., Zilberstein, S.: Optimizing information exchange in cooperative multi-agent systems. In: Proceedings of the Second International Joint Conference on Autonomous Agents and Multi Agent Systems, pp. 137–144. ACM Press, Melbourne (2003)

8. Jarvenpaa, S.L., Leidner, D.E.: Communication and trust in global virtual teams. Organ. Sci. **10**(6), 791–815 (1999). https://doi.org/10.1287/orsc.10.6.791, http://pubsonline.informs.org/doi/abs/10.1287/orsc.10.6.791

9. Johnson, M., Bradshaw, J.M., Feltovich, P.J., Jonker, C.M., van Riemsdijk, B., Sierhuis, M.: The fundamental principle of coactive design: interdependence must shape autonomy. In: De Vos, M., Fornara, N., Pitt, J.V., Vouros, G. (eds.) COIN -2010. LNCS (LNAI), vol. 6541, pp. 172–191. Springer, Heidelberg (2011). https://doi.org/10.1007/978-3-642-21268-0_10. http://link.springer.com/10.1007/978-3-642-21268-0 10

10. Johnson, M., Jonker, C., van Riemsdijk, B., Feltovich, P.J., Bradshaw, J.M.: Joint activity testbed: blocks world for teams (BW4T). In: Aldewereld, H., Dignum, V., Picard, G. (eds.) ESAW 2009. LNCS (LNAI), vol. 5881, pp. 254–256. Springer, Heidelberg (2009). https://doi.org/10.1007/978-3-642-10203-5_26. http://link.springer.com/10.1007/978-3-642-10203-5 26

11. Klein, G., Woods, D.D., Bradshaw, J.M., Hoffman, R.R., Feltovich, P.J.: Ten challenges for making automation a "team player" in joint human-agent activity. IEEE Intell. Syst. **19**(6), 91–95 (2004). https://doi.org/10.1109/MIS.2004.74

12. Kruijff, G.J.M., Janıcek, M., Keshavdas, S., Larochelle, B., Zender, H.: Experience in system design for human-robot teaming in urban search & rescue. In: 8th International Conference on Field and Service Robotics, Matsushima, Japan, pp. 1–14 (2012)

13. Lazaridou, A., Peysakhovich, A., Baroni, M.: Multi-agent cooperation and the emergence of (natural) language. arXiv:1612.07182 [cs], December 2016

14. Lewis, J.R.: IBM computer usability satisfaction questionnaires: psychometric evaluation and instructions for use. Int. J. Hum.-Comput. Interact. **7**, 57–78 (1995)

15. Singh, D., Hindriks, K.V.: Learning to improve agent behaviours in GOAL. In: Dastani, M., Hübner, J.F., Logan, B. (eds.) ProMAS 2012. LNCS (LNAI), vol. 7837, pp. 158–173. Springer, Heidelberg (2013). https://doi.org/10.1007/978-3-642-38700-5_10. http://link.springer.com/10.1007/978-3-642-38700-5 10

16. Sordoni, A., et al.: A neural network approach to context-sensitive generation of conversational responses. arXiv:1506.06714 [cs], June 2015

Workshop on Multi-agent Systems
and Simulation (MAS&S)

Workshop on Multi-agent Systems and Simulation (MAS&S)

Multi-agent systems (MASs) provide powerful models for representing both real-world systems and applications with an appropriate degree of complexity and dynamics. MASs are designed for representing systems at different levels of complexity. They use agents as autonomous, goal-driven, and interacting entities, which are organized into societies that exhibit emergent properties The agent-based model of a system can then be executed to simulate the behavior of the complete system, so that knowledge of the behaviors of the entities (micro-level) produces an understanding of the overall outcome at the system-level (macro-level).

Several research and industrial experiences have already shown that the use of MASs offers advantages in a wide range of application domains (e.g. financial, economic, social, logistic, chemical, engineering, or Internet of Things). When MASs represent software applications, they need to be validated and evaluated before their deployment and execution. Thus, methodologies that support these processes through simulation of the MASs under development are highly required. In both cases (MASs as software applications and MASs as models for the analysis of complex systems), simulation plays a crucial role that needs to be further investigated.

Organization

Organizing Committee

Fuentes-Fernández, Rubén	Universidad Complutense de Madrid, Spain
Migeon, Frédéric	Institut de Recherche en Informatique de Toulouse, France
Seidita, Valeria	Università degli Studi di Palermo, Italy

Program Committee

Antunes, Luis	Universidade de Lisboa, Portugal
Azar, Ahmad Taher	Benha University, Egypt
Bernon, Carole	Université Paul Sabatier, France
Cipresso, Pietro	Istituto Auxologico Italiano - IRCCS, Italy
Davidsson, Paul	Malmö University, Sweden
Garro, Alfredo	University of Calabria, Italy
Guerrieri, Antonio	University of Calabria, Italy
Molesini, Ambra	Università di Bologna, Italy
Petta, Paolo	OFAI, Austria

Ribino, Patrizia   ICAR-CNR, Italy
Savaglio, Claudio   University of Calabria, Italy
Vizzari, Giuseppe   Università di Milano-Bicocca, Italy
Zia, Kashif   Sohar University, Oman

An Agent-Based Simulation to Study the Effect of Consumer Panic Buying on Supply Chain

Rithika Dulam[1(✉)], Kazuo Furuta[1], and Taro Kanno[2]

[1] Department of Technology Management for Innovation,
The Graduate School of Engineering, The University of Tokyo, Tokyo, Japan
`rithika.dulam@gmail.com`
[2] Department of Systems Innovation, The Graduate School of Engineering,
The University of Tokyo, Tokyo, Japan

Abstract. This paper presents the development of an agent-based model to study the response of a supply chain of bottled water due to consumer panic buying, triggered by a large-scale disaster, by modelling the consumers and the supply chain stakeholders as autonomous agents. Consumer panic buying increases the demand of product which proves difficult for the stores to handle. The model helps in understanding the performance of the supply chain due to the sudden rise in demand and the strategies applied to control it. A preliminary study to show the effectiveness of the consumer quota policy, used by the retailers, in handling the supply chain disruption and in fulfilling essential consumer needs is presented here.

Keywords: Consumer panic buying · Supply chain · Agent-based model · Disaster

1 Introduction

Natural disasters, nowadays, are far from rare events, causing extensive damage to life and property. The number of natural disasters has been increasing by the year, with growing intensity and damage [3]. A disaster, irrespective of the type, affects every aspect of human life and creates an atmosphere of fear and anxiety. People tend to take precautionary actions of survival to mitigate future risks such as stockpiling of essentials to avoid a possible stockout.

The Great East Japan Earthquake, which occurred in 2011, was one of the most destructive disasters in recent times. The tsunami which followed had cost countless human lives and huge economic loss. The failure of the Fukushima Daichi nuclear plant had intensified the already heightened crisis manifold. Panic buying was prevalent in all sectors from food and beverage industry to the auto component market [1]. People shopped for basic supplies excessively, especially Tokyo, due to the fear of radiation contamination. Bottled water, processed food,

© Springer Nature Switzerland AG 2020
F. De La Prieta et al. (Eds.): PAAMS 2020 Workshops, CCIS 1233, pp. 255–266, 2020.
https://doi.org/10.1007/978-3-030-51999-5_21

bread and instant meals were among the top-selling list [2], during the long aftermath. On 23rd March 2011, the Tokyo water department released a notice that the tap water must not be fed to infants due to the increased radioactive iodine levels [4]. This instigated people to panic buy on bottled water in unprecedented quantities which has led to necessitous people without access to bottled water. The media articles, during that time, have reported the stockout of food and drinking water in stores across the capital city. Bottled water manufacturers were at a loss to meet the demand and millions of stock had been imported [5]. While the government has urged the people against panic buying, the effect it had was minimal. This situation hampered the circulation of bottled water within the metropolis and also in the affected areas [2].

Panic buying leads to a sudden increase in demand, which has the potential to disrupt an entire supply chain. This disruption leads to supply shortage leading to more panic buying forming a vicious circle. Research on understanding consumer panic buying is conducted by sociologists and psychologists but is mostly limited to statistical analysis. Kurihara [2], from a survey conducted after the Great East Japan Earthquake, found that unpreparedness of disaster and excessive media coverage had caused excessive buying of essential goods. Liren et al. [6] have put forward the evolution mechanism and development tendency of panic purchase and suggested that the government involvement controls panic purchase. Cavallo et al. [7] have reported that the disaster impacted product availability directly from the analysis of online data collected from retailers.

The supply chain performance is becoming critical to business success; hence, supply chain disturbances could have a significant effect. With a focus on the causes, effects, and mitigation of the disruptions, a substantial amount of literature is available on supply chain disturbances by the specialists, mostly ignoring the impact of consumer behaviour [1]. Inoue et al. [8] have simulated nationwide supply chains of Japan and have calculated the indirect damage and its propagation during the 2011 triple disaster. Ivanov et al. [9] discussed the difficulties in managing the emergency logistics in disaster situations by analysing existing quantitative methods and have made suggestions for best practices during disruptions. Yoon et al. [1] studied the retailer's sourcing strategy under consumer stockpiling due to supply disruptions and compared single and multiple sourcing from a retailer's perspective. Shou et al. [10] have studied consumer panic buying with supply disturbances and found that consumers stockpile when the price or holding cost is low or when they carry risk-averse behaviour. However, the available literature has not included the human behaviour in the analysis. There is a lack of research in the area of understanding the effect of consumer panic behaviour on supply chain and vice versa. The question of how the strategies used by the businesses affect the consumer's cognition has not been answered. Hence, there is an immense requirement to bridge the gap between consumer behaviour and supply chain management for better functionality. This effort is a novel approach to developing an agent-based model of consumer panic behaviour and supply chain together.

The objective of this research is to develop a model to study the effects of consumer behaviour and the supply chain on each other in disaster aftermath using an agent-based model. Precisely, to analyse the panic buying of bottled water and to identify the reasons leading to the disruption of supply chain and to examine strategies to control panic buying such as limiting sales per person, sourcing strategy, agent communication etc. The rest of the paper is divided into three parts, where the second part deals with the explanation of the methodology used to develop the model. The results would be explained in the third part, along with its analysis and discussion. Finally, the last part would deal with conclusions and future work.

2 Model Description

The methodology to model the scenarios described in the previous section is aptly an agent-based approach, as it allows an autonomous design of the characteristics and actions of the agents involved. Hence, it is very effective to assign heterogeneous properties to individual agent. The structure of the model consists of, a supply chain model and a consumer purchase model, which are explained in the following subsections. The model comprises of the supply chain agents and consumer agents, which are modeled to resemble their behavior and actions in reality. The agents decide their actions depending on their respective circumstances at any given point of time.

2.1 Supply Chain Model

A supply chain is a network of organizations, individuals, resources involved from the manufacture to sale of a product. The model is built on the assumption that the price, profits, costs do not play a role in a disaster situation, as price gouging during emergencies is a violation in many places. A 3-tiered hierarchical supply chain of bottled water (Fig. 1) has been considered, with the assumption that the raw materials required are available or produced, near the facility itself.

The model has five types of supply chain agents (SCA) which includes manufacturers, distributors, individual retailers, chain heads, and chain stores, with four supply chain levels, which are the manufacturer level, the distributor level, chain head level and retailer level. The manufacturer sells the product to the distributors, who in turn sell to the chain heads and individual retailers. The chain head distributes the product among all its chain stores. The consumers can interact and purchase from the retail level SCAs only. The communication among the SCAs is restricted to the exchange of information related to buying and selling of the product. Single sourcing of the product, based on the distance to the seller's location, is considered for this model.

The SCA attributes, such as the economic order quantity, safety stock, have been considered from the traditional inventory management studies [11]. The service level, a factor which affects the parameters used in the calculations, is the probability that the amount of inventory on hand is sufficient to meet expected

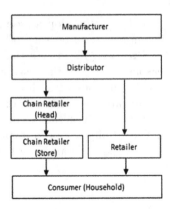

Fig. 1. Supply chain hierarchy.

demand or in other words the probability that a stockout will not occur. It is considered to be 95% for all the SCAs. Lead time inventory is the inventory held by the SCA for sale during lead time, which is the time lag between placing an order and receiving the order. It is given by Eq. (1). The lead time of each SCA is dependent on the SCA's level.

$$Lead\ Time\ Inventory = d * L \qquad (1)$$

where,

L – Lead time
d – Average sales

Safety stock is a buffer held above the normal inventory level, which is used during emergencies, given by Eq. (2).

$$Safety\ Stock = z * \sigma_d * \sqrt{L} \qquad (2)$$

where,

σ_d – Standard deviation of average sales
z – Number of standard deviations based on the service level probability

Reorder point is the inventory level at which a new order is to be placed in order to sustain until the time inventory is replenished, given by Eq. (3).

$$Reorder\ Point = d * L + z * \sigma_d * \sqrt{L} \qquad (3)$$

The economic order quantity (EOQ) is a formula for determining the optimal order size that minimises the costs to the SCA. It is one of the critical elements as it directly affects the performance of the SCA. EOQ, in this model, is considered assuming the demand during each interval of lead time is uncertain, independent, and can be described by a normal distribution, given by Eq. (4).

$$Order\ Quantity = d * (t_b + L) + z * \sigma_d * \sqrt{t_b + L} - I \qquad (4)$$

where,

t_b – Time between the placing of two orders

I – Current inventory

The values for lead time, average sales and its standard deviation in the above methods have been assumed based on the information obtained from the reports [12,13] of convenience stores and manufacturers. When a stockout occurs due to uncertain demand, a lost sale is considered. A lost sale is defined as the selling opportunity lost due to the stockout of product. The lost sales are accommodated into the model by adding it to the order quantity. But, as the consumer moves to all the stores to make a purchase, there is a high probability of lost sales being duplicated. Hence, a factor of 0.1 is multiplied to the lost sales before adding and modifying the EOQ, in case of a stockout. (Several factors between 0 and 1 were tried for various simulations with same initial conditions, but 0.1 was found to be optimal to modify the EOQ, as increased demand was satisfied without holding excess inventory compared to the average sales.) The average sale (d) and the standard deviation of average sales (σ_d) are calculated in regular intervals with a refresh period of 7 to 10 intervals. The SCA action algorithm, where the actions are indicated in blue (dotted symbol), can be seen in Fig. 2.

2.2   Consumer Purchase Model

The consumer purchase model is the decision-making process leading to the purchase of the product, using its available resources influenced by the emotional, behavioural factors of the consumer. The consumer agent of the current model is the 'Household'. The decision-maker and the buyer of the household is the 'head' (eldest member of the household), while the other members are considered to be the influencers. The size of a household varies from 1 to 4 members, as an average Japanese household size is 2.5 [14]. The age of a member is considered between 0–80 years. Every member has their selection on whether they can consume tap water or not. The average and daily household water consumption is a cumulative value over its members. The current consumer decision making is modelled to be rational where the purchase quantity and the purchase interval are decided based on the available inventory. If a consumer agent meets a stockout at a store, it heads to the next nearest store until it can make a purchase. In case, all the stores in its vicinity are out of stock, the consumer increases its purchase quantity for the next interval, assuming the consumer is panicked due to the stockouts. The factor of increase is considered as 1.5, as a trail value, which would be improved to be based on the psychological characteristics in future. The consumer decision-making algorithm is shown in Fig. 2, with the consumer actions indicated in red (dashed symbols).

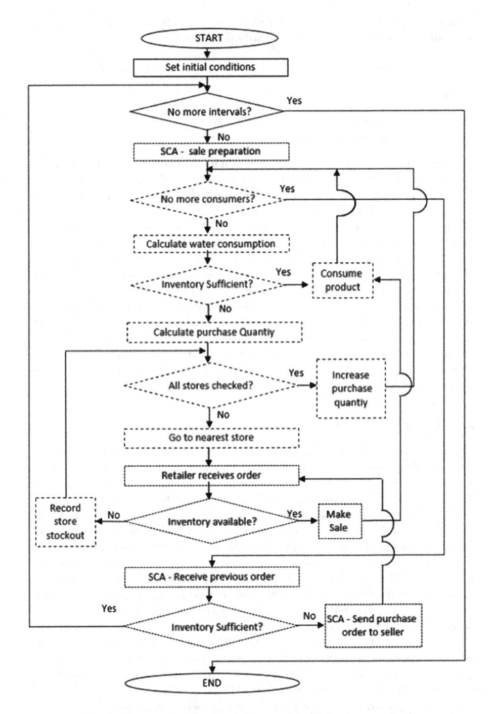

Fig. 2. Flowchart of the simulation model. (Color figure online)

Water Consumption. The average water consumption of each agent is calculated based on the data obtained from a survey conducted by Yano et al. [15]. The average of the normally distributed data of daily water consumption for men and women is 1553 ml and 1360 ml respectively. A standard deviation of the average water consumption has been calculated from the binned values, by applying Sheppard's corrections to be unbiased, which are obtained to be 572.65 ml for men and 555.16 ml for women. The water consumption is calculated as a Gaussian random number with reference to the above values. Water consumption for infants (0–5 years) is randomly generated between a minimum of 300 ml to a maximum of 1500 ml [16].

2.3   Time Sequence of Simulation

The time interval of the model is fixed and is considered as one day. The flow of the simulation is divided into 3 phases. Phase 1 is a pre-disaster phase with regular sales, where all the agents try to maximize their utility. The consumers place orders depending solely on their requirement. The supply meets the demand for all the intervals in Phase 1. Consumers consume both tap and bottled water. A disaster occurs after a few intervals of the start of the simulation. With the trigger of the disaster, Phase 2 is initialised. Due to the fear of radiation contamination, people stop the consumption of tap water. Some households, for example, households with young children, resort to stockpiling. Hence, the demand for bottled water increases unusually, causing a supply chain disturbance, which cascades through the hierarchy leading to a supply chain disruption. Phase 3 begins when an SCA employs a strategy to mitigate the supply chain disruption. A popular approach to control consumer demand is the quota policy, which is used in the current model. The retailers limit the quantity of sale to each consumer, to cut down large sales. The reaction of the consumer to the quota policy is also included in the model, where all the members of the household visit the store to make a purchase.

3   Results and Analysis

3.1   Initial Conditions

The environment for the test simulation is a virtual grid of 100×100 size in which the agents are generated randomly, as shown in Fig. 3. Currently, two test cases are considered to understand the output of the simulation. One with 200 households and 6 SCAs, with a maximum manufacturing capacity of 1500 units/interval and the second one with 2000 households and 12 SCAs, with a manufacturing capacity of 15000 units/interval, where one unit is one litre. The location of the consumer agents and store agents are in blue, red and pink dots respectively. Each consumer accesses the nearest store, hence the selection of the store depends on the spatial distribution. In Phase 3, sale quantity is restricted to 2 units per person. The scope of the simulation is currently small, considering its initial stages. The simulation is run for 50 intervals in which the disaster is set to occur in the 25th interval. The strategy of limiting sales, to control the demand is applied from the 26th interval.

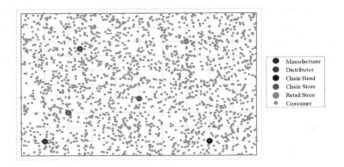

Fig. 3. Example of agent spatial distribution in the environment (Color figure online)

The initial inventories and the average sale values of the SCAs are set such that the transient period for the model is considerably low. The initial values of all SCAs have been considered such that they adapt to the customer demand and obtain a stable initial state of the system in a shorter time. The initial average sale of the retail level SCAs is calculated based on the possible number of consumers in its vicinity, while the same for the higher tier SCAs is the sum of average sale of all its customers. The initial opening inventories of each SCA is twice the average sale multiplied with the lead time intervals. The stabilized system is where all SCAs manage their stocks and sales without hurdles, which can be seen in the initial intervals of Fig. 4 and 5. The simulation is coded using Java language on eclipse development environment.

3.2   Results - Analysis

A supply chain disturbance is an occurrence which has a negative impact even from the optimized regular operations of the SCA. The disturbance when continues for a number of continuous intervals and for more than two supply chain tiers is considered as a disruption in this model. The negative impact of the disturbance is measured by the performance of a SCA, which is detailed in the next section.

Performance of SCA. A measure to understand the performance of the SCA is the Inventory-Sale(IS) ratio, given by Eq. (5). It is obtained by dividing the inventory by the total demand, which is the sum of sale and lost sale. The lost sale appears in the equation only if a stockout occurs.

$$Inventory - Sale\ ratio\ = \frac{Inventory}{Sale\ +\ Lost\ Sale} \tag{5}$$

If the IS ratio > 1, the white region in Fig. 4, it means that the SCA is in a safe condition and has sufficient inventory to meet its demand. If this ratio < 1, the red region in Fig. 4, the SCA falls into the stockout zone and is seen as a disturbance. In order to focus on the stockout zone, the y-axis, indicating the inventory-sale ratio has been shown from 0 to 2.0. The value moves way above 2.0 but, as the SCA is already safe, the entire graph has not been shown in the figure.

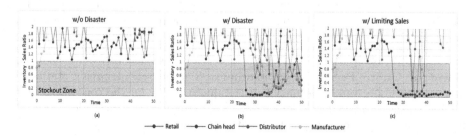

Fig. 4. Inventory-sale ratio for 200 households

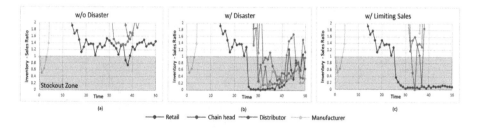

Fig. 5. Inventory-sale ratio for 2000 households

The Fig. 4 shows the tier level IS ratio for all the SCAs. Every line in the graph shows the combined IS ratio of all the agents in a supply chain level. The first part of each graph in Fig. 4 and 5, 0–25th intervals, shows Phase 1. Figure 4(a) shows the case without a disaster. It can be seen that no SCA is in the stockout zone, indicating complete demand satisfaction. After the disaster triggers in the 25th interval, it can be seen in Fig. 4(b) that the demand is so high that all the SCAs are in the stockout zone for consistently more than 10 intervals. This indicates a crash in the supply chain, in line with our expectations, as all the stakeholders in the supply of the product would be at a loss to satisfy the demand at every tier level. The Fig. 4(c) shows the supply chain performance with the quota policy. It can be seen clearly that the supply chain disruption was avoided with the help of the strategy. The retail level graph would continue to remain in the stockout zone as the consumer demand is far greater than the available inventory.

The result of 2000 households case is shown in Fig. 5. An outcome similar to the 200 households case can be seen. In Fig. 5(a) it can be seen that the ratio for the retail level has gone into the stockout zone once. This was due to an increased demand than the expected sale of a particular store, but there was no cumulative stockout as the consumer could purchase at another store. Hence, it can be said to be a minor disruption. In Fig. 5(b), the disaster had disrupted the supply chain as the demand surge has effected the SCAs at all levels. In Fig. 5(c), the limiting sales strategy has effectively avoided the crash by cutting down large sale volumes to consumers.

Effect of Quota Policy on Consumers. The household buying status is analysed to understand the impact of the quota policy on the consumer. The buying status is divided into four categories. Category 0 - household needs to make a purchase and could make a sufficient (as much quantity as required) purchase. The consumer was able to purchase as much as required. Category 1 - household needs to make a purchase and could make an insufficient (less than required quantity) purchase. Category 2 - household needs to make a purchase and could not make a purchase. Category 3 - household decided not to make a purchase.

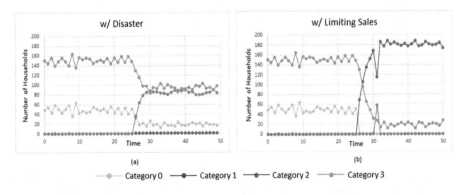

Fig. 6. Household buying status in disaster case and limiting sales case

Figure 6a and 6b show the household buying status in disaster and quota policy cases, respectively, for the instance of 200 households. Phase 1 of both the graphs shows that the households hold only category 0 and 3, indicating that households who made a purchase could make a full purchase. Once the disaster occurs, the number of category 2 households rises rapidly, indicating the increase in the number of households without the bottled water. The number of Category 1 households is still zero, indicating households who could make a purchase, made a full purchase. In limiting sales case, the rise in the number of category 1 households can be seen. Most of the households could make a minimum purchase, with a condition where all the household members move to the store to make a purchase. The number of category 0 households is nearly 0, as the demand of consumer over the set limit was not satisfied, while the number of category 2 households can be seen to be 0 for most of the intervals, indicating that no household was left without stock.

3.3 Discussion

The results show the effect of the panic buying and the consumer quota policy on the supply chain. Panic buying does have a negative effect on each SCA and the supply chain overall. The quota policy had proved effective by curtailing the demand surge from propagating up the hierarchy and saving the SCAs from the damage due to supply chain disruption. The effect of quota policy on the households can be said to have both a positive and negative effect. While the individual consumer demand was not satisfied, a larger number of consumer's minimum needs have been fulfilled, which is the main target of limiting sales. Hence, an overall positive effect is established on a societal level, as the target of reaching out to as many consumers as possible has been achieved.

The validation of the model is a difficult task for agent-based models. The primary method of validation of this model can be performed by comparing the obtained results with the actual data of the supply chain stakeholders. But, procurement of such information is quite difficult. Another method to validate the model could be by using the consumption and demand distributions of the consumers, which would be tested in future.

4 Conclusions

A simulation model is being developed to understand the response of the supply chain due to consumer panic buying and vice-versa in the aftermath of a large-scale disaster. A simplistic model of the same along with the preliminary reactions of the supply chain due to the disaster and quota policy has been presented in the paper. The strategy of limiting sales was found to be effective in avoiding the supply chain disruption and in increasing the availability of the product to more consumers. Such tools would help the government to identify the people resorting to excessive buying and work on reducing the panic among the people and are quite useful for the industries to take measures to mitigate the disruptions after the disaster.

Future Work. In the future, the supply chain model needs to be improved to include a more intelligent model. The consumer purchase model would be developed to accommodate the factors affecting the decision-making process such as the number of children, the experience of disaster, quality of tap water, etc., making it a more complex process. The scope of the model needs to be increased to obtain more realistic results in a bigger scenario.

References

1. Yoon, J., Narasimhan, R., Kim, M.: Retailer's sourcing strategy under consumer stockpiling in anticipation of supply disruptions. Int. J. Prod. Res. **56**(10), 3615–3635 (2018)
2. Kurihara, S., Maruyama, A., Luloff, A.: Analysis of consumer behavior in the Tokyo metropolitan area after the great East Japan earthquake. J. Food Sys. Res. **18**(4), 415–426 (2012)
3. Increasing Disasters, Munich Re, Geo Risks Research, NatCatSERVICE, March 2019. https://www.iii.org/graph-archive/96424. Accessed 16 Jan 2020
4. Ministry of Health: Labour and Welfare, Increase of radioactive iodine in City tap water. https://www.mhlw.go.jp/stf/houdou/2r985200000167kd.html. Accessed 16 Jan 2020
5. Bottled water import by manufacturers. http://www.promarconsulting.com/company-news/special-report-impact-of-japans-disasters/. Accessed 16 Jan 2020
6. Liren, X., Junmei, C., Mingqin, Z.: Research on panic purchase's behavior mechanism. In: Proceedings of the 9th International Conference on Innovation and Management, pp. 1332–1335 (2012)
7. Cavallo, A., Cavallo, E., Rigobon, R.: Prices and supply disruptions during natural disasters. Rev. Income Wealth **60**, S449–S471 (2014)
8. Inoue, H., Todo, Y.: Firm-level simulation of supply chain disruption triggered by actual and predicted earthquakes. In: RIETI Discussion Paper Series (2018). 18-E-013
9. Ivanov, D., Wendler, E.: Natural disasters and supply chain disruption management. In: Handbook of Disaster Risk Reduction and Management. World Scientific (2017)
10. Shou, B., Xiong, H., Shen, X.: Consumer panic buying and quota policy under supply disruptions. Working Paper. City University of Hong Kong, Hong Kong (2013)
11. Russell and Taylor: Operations Management, 7th. edn. John Wiley, Hoboken (2011)
12. Seven-Eleven Japan's business model. http://www.7andi.com/library/dbps_data/_template_/_res/ir/library/ar/pdf/2012_11.pdf. Accessed 16 Jan 2020
13. Suntory R&D, production market report. https://www.suntory.com/softdrink/news/pr/article/SBF0557E.html. Accessed 16 Jan 2020
14. Ministry of Foreign affairs of Japan (2018). https://www.mofa.go.jp/policy/human/women_rep5/010.html. Accessed 16 Jan 2020
15. Yano, et al.: Water consumption survey, March 2007. https://unit.aist.go.jp/riss/crm/exposurefactors/documents/factor/food_intake/intake_water.pdf. Accessed 16 Jan 2020
16. National health and nutrition examination survey, National center for health statistics, CDC, United States of America. https://www.cdc.gov/nchs/nhanes/index.htm. Accessed 16 Jan 2020

Multi-agents Ultimatum Game
with Reinforcement Learning

Tangui Le Gléau[1,2]([⊠]), Xavier Marjou[1], Tayeb Lemlouma[2], and Benoit Radier[1]

[1] Orange Labs, Lannion, France
{tangui.legleau,xavier.marjou,benoit.radier}@orange.com
[2] IRISA, Rennes, France
tayeb.lemlouma@irisa.fr

Abstract. *The Ultimatum Game* is an experimental economics game in which an agent has to propose a sharing partition of a limited amount of resources to other agents who have to accept it or not. If the offer is rejected per consensus, the process of sharing is abandoned. So all agents have to guess what are the best decisions (offer and vote) to optimise their respective gain. We focus on an iterated multi-agent version of Ultimatum Game also known as the Pirate Game, a riddle in which pirates have to share coins according to specific rules. To solve such game, we employ a multi-agent model. In particular, we design a new kind of Artificial Neural Network model able to output an integer partition of discrete finite resources, trained by a Reinforcement Learning agent to identify an acceptable offer to the voting agents. We take an interest in evaluating the performances against several kinds of voting behaviours. The results are close to theoretical optima for all tested scenarios thus demonstrating the flexibility of our method.

Keywords: Multi-agents systems · Ultimatum game · Reinforcement Learning · Game theory

1 Introduction

Numerous use-cases involve resource sharing between multiple actors in multi-agents systems (MAS) where the involved actors try to gain a common quantity of interest and reach consensus [1]. For instance, in the context of telecommunication, one given Mobile Network Operator (MNO) can share 5G network resources with vertical industries [2], thereby allowing them to request the reservation of a network slice in the MNO infrastructure [3].

As modern networks (e.g. IoT and UAV) become more decentralized and autonomous, network agents entities often incorporate Artificial Intelligence (AI) strategies to achieve local decisions and maximize the network performance [4]. Some approaches like [5] propose to solve such network resource management with the application of the Reinforcement Learning (RL) approach [6], which is a trial and error process where an agent can identify the best sequence of actions

© Springer Nature Switzerland AG 2020
F. De La Prieta et al. (Eds.): PAAMS 2020 Workshops, CCIS 1233, pp. 267–278, 2020.
https://doi.org/10.1007/978-3-030-51999-5_22

to maximise its cumulative reward. In such approaches, resources management depends solely on the MNO sharing of its infrastructure. In several use-cases, the demanding agents can accept or refuse an offer (i.e. a sharing distribution), which is a critical assumption for the MNO in case the total demand exceeds its available resource capacity.

Obviously, for an offerer agent, the design of sharing strategies is crucial as failing to satisfy the demands of other agents could result in excluding the offerer from the business. For dynamic and unpredictable environments (e.g. in hybrid human-agent groups [7]), it is extremely difficult to completely specify the offerer strategy at the time of its design and before runtime applications [8]. Indeed, the design of a MAS based on the understanding of actions and interactions within artificial agents remains a challenging task. In this respect, the Ultimatum Game (UG) paradigm can be considered as a viable candidate to capture such complex interactions in a dynamic and heterogeneous environment [7]. In this context, we investigate a multi-agent version of UG.

UG had already been studied in particular with a multi-agent setting [9–13]. In this paper, we tackle the problem of UG with discrete finite resources which is a rather interesting hypothesis of the game. We focus on the application of a Reinforcement Learning approach to model the behaviour of a given proposer (i.e. offerer) and voter agents in the multi-agents version of UG with discrete resources.

From a more complex and more attractive perspective, we focus on a particularly interesting version of the UG, which is inspired by a curious riddle called the *Pirate Game* where several agents are hierarchically ranked. The principle of this riddle is as follows: n_P pirates have to share n_C coins. There is a hierarchy among pirates: $P_1, P_2, ..., P_{n_P}$ and the proposer is the Highest Rank Pirate (HRP) who initiates the offer of coins partition. Then, all pirates (including the proposer) vote for or against the partition. If the partition is accepted, the game is over and the coins are distributed; if it is rejected, the HRP is eliminated and the next HRP has to propose a new partition; and so forth. It is worth noting that all the pirates are considered as rational players (meaning that they prefer one coin rather than zero regardless of any feeling of injustice, fairness, etc.). Moreover, each pirate knows his rank in the hierarchy and prioritises to survive then to maximise its profit. The PG can be summarised as an iterated game of maximum n_P rounds in each of which the remaining pirates play an ultimatum game. The rationality of agents leads to one interesting equilibrium that is demonstrated in Appendix A. The Pirate Game (PG) presents many motivating properties as in many real-world applications, it involves multiple agents (the pirates) trying to share a pool of common finite resources (the coins); it has a well-defined set of rules; it benefits from a mathematical modelling, which is a perfect baseline for evaluating the obtained results. In this work, in order to model such MAS, we propose an Artificial Neural Network (ANN) base model able to output a discrete partition. Thanks to an Reinforcement Learning (RL) algorithm (REINFORCE algorithm described of Sect. 2), the ANN is trained to have the highest chances to generate a partition that will be accepted by most rational players involved in the sharing.

The paper is structured as follows: after a brief background on Reinforcement Learning methods (Sect. 2), we present our model in Sect. 3, in particular, a method to generate a stochastic integer partition. Then, after introducing some scenarios of behaviours that we experiment (Sect. 4), we show the results of the RL agent learning in Sect. 5. Finally, we discuss our results and provide some perspectives in Sect. 6.

2   Background on Reinforcement Learning

RL is a trial and error process that generates an optimal policy $\pi(a|s)$ which relates the best action a to a current state s (each action delivers a single reward r_t) so that the cumulated reward R_t is maximal.

2.1   Value-Based Methods

A popular category of value-based algorithms is *Temporal-Difference* learning (TD-Learning) [6] which consists, for each state s, to evaluate a function value $V(s)$ representing the reward expectancy from the state s and according to a policy π: $V(s) = \mathbb{E}[R_t|s_t = s]$. The principle of TD-learning is to evaluate the mean of value at each state. The update is computed at each step t of episodes:

$$V(s_t) \leftarrow V(s_t) + \alpha(r_{t+1} + \gamma V(s_{t+1}) - V(s_t))$$

where $0 < \alpha < 1$ is a learning rate and $0 < \gamma \leq 1$ is a discount-rate which attenuates the importance of future rewards.

2.2   Policy-Based Methods

The core idea of such methods is to directly determine a policy that relates the optimal actions to the states (e.g. REINFORCE algorithm [14]). The principle is to find an optimal policy $\pi^*(a|s)$ modelised with parameters θ: π_θ, the problem consists in finding optimal parameters θ^* such as:

$$\theta^* = \underset{\theta}{\text{argmax}}\ J(\theta), \quad \text{where } J(\theta) = \sum_\tau P(\tau|\theta)R(\tau)$$

with τ a sequence of states and actions (called a trajectory) and $R(\tau)$ the cumulative reward of trajectory τ. Then, the gradient is computed:

$$\nabla_\theta J(\theta) \approx \frac{1}{N} \sum_{i=1}^{N} \nabla_\theta \log(\pi_\theta(\tau_i))R(\tau_i)$$

Then, the algorithm consists of sampling trajectories thanks to current stochastic policy π_θ in order to compute the gradient $\nabla_\theta J(\theta)$ to finally update the parameters with gradient descent.

3   Model

As presented previously at the outset of this paper, we implement a model using RL to solve the riddle. This means that our proposed model learns the best decisions to fulfil priorities induced by the game rules: survive first, then earn coins.

3.1   Players

In order to solve the PG with our proposed model, we introduce two functions: a *proposer* function to propose a partition and a *voter* function allowing each agent to vote for or against the offer. Both functions are shared by all pirates because every pirate's goal is to find out his optimal behaviour whatever his rank. Then, at any time during the learning process, any pirate is able to compute an offer according to his hierarchical situation or vote according to the proposed partition, the proposer's rank and his own.

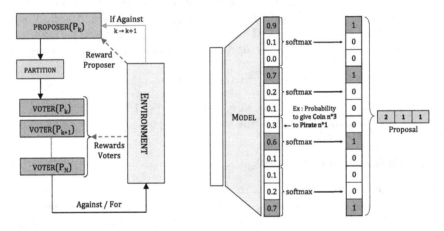

(a) The models of proposer and voter are trained together toward the equilibrium

(b) Model of Proposer: neural network outputting a distribution of integer partition ($n_P = 3$, $n_C = 4$)

Fig. 1. Architecture of algorithm

Proposer. As mentioned above, the *proposer* function is generic, therefore it takes as input at least the rank of the proposer. The use of a neural network which is a priori not necessary is motivated by the possibility to use a more complex input to represent the state (for example, the history of previous behaviours using recurrent hidden state or communication protocols between agents of different hierarchy, see Sect. 6). The output is an integer partition describing the number of coins n_C with a maximum number of pirates n_P terms. Several techniques can be considered: first, we can use a network output of n_P neurons in each of which there would be the number of coins assigned to each pirate. The problem of this method is that neurons values must be integers where the total sum is a specific integer equals to the number of resources. Hence, there are major constraints which are technically difficult to impose. Another possibility would be to normalise the output of n_P neurons, multiply it by n_C and take the closest integer for each neuron. Unfortunately, this method can lead to an issue of rounded values as the sum would differ from expected n_C with a difference up to 50% in the worst cases, which would be difficult to adjust. To overcome this problem, we propose a new encoding of the integer partition. We use an output Y of $n_P n_C$ neurons, and we apply one softmax every n_P neurons in such a way that we obtain n_C vectors of probabilities (of n_P values). We can formally link the output Y and $f(c, p)$ the probability to give coin c to pirate p :

$$Y[i] = f(\lfloor \frac{i}{n_P} \rfloor, \ i \bmod n_P) \Leftrightarrow f(c, p) = Y[n_P c + p]$$

Then, the partition P of integer n_C with n_P terms can be formally written as follows:

$$P[i] = Card\{c, \ i = \underset{x}{\mathrm{argmax}} \ f(c, x)\} \ \forall i \in [0, n_P - 1]$$

The proposed model ensures that every coin is attributed to one and only one pirate, which is the definition of a partition. Moreover, the model provides stochasticity which is interesting for training and allows to use the REINFORCE algorithm.

Figure 1b depicts an example of the model used for the partition proposal when $n_C = 4$ coins and $n_P = 3$ pirates.

Voters. To model and train the voter function, we use a value-based algorithm (simple Monte-Carlo) which evaluates the mean score of coins for each state proposer id and voter id). Thanks to this baseline, each voter can compare the number of coins proposed to the number of coins he could get in the next step. Then he can choose to accept or to reject the offer. When at least 50% of the voters accept the offer, the offer is declared accepted, otherwise, the offer is declared rejected.

3.2   Training

Both the proposer and voter functions are trained simultaneously. For the proposer, we use the REINFORCE algorithm with deep learning. The environment provides a reward of $+\exp(c)$ with c the number of coins when the offer is accepted and a reward of -1 for death (elimination) when the offer is rejected. We use the exponential function to insist on the greediness of pirates, which somehow corresponds to an increasing marginal utility.

4   Experimented Scenarios

In this section, we present the scenarios we want to study in addition to the Pirate Game (version with hierarchical ranks as mentioned in the introduction). For reproducibility, the code has been made available[1].

4.1   Selfish and Rational Vote

In this scenario, all pirates vote according to the rules of the original PG [15]. Each pirate is purely rational and only considers its interests, hence voting selfishly. As mentioned in the introduction, the rationality of agents leads to an equilibrium (demonstrated in Appendix A).

4.2   Prosocial Votes

In this scenario, we ignore the assumption of rationality. Each pirate (except the proposer who remains selfish) votes for a proposal if and only if the partition looks equally fair to all pirates, otherwise votes against it. Hence, the pirates' vote becomes a prosocial vote.

To this purpose, the voters decide according to the result of a Jain's index calculation [16]. If a system allocates resources to n contenting users, such that the ith user receives an allocation x_i, then the index for the system is:

$$J(x_1, x_2, ...x_n) = \frac{\left(\sum_{i=1}^n x_i\right)^2}{\left(n \sum_{i=1}^n x_i^2\right)}$$

When this index approaches 1, a distribution is considered equally fair to all parties; when this index approaches $1/n$, a distribution is considered completely unfair. For our work, we decided arbitrarily that when the Jain's index of the distribution proposal is equal to the theoretical maximum possible Jain's index (provided in Appendix B), a voter accepts the proposed partition, otherwise it votes against it. We can easily guess that the optimal strategy will converge towards a partition where each integer of coins distribution will differ from maximum one coin.

4.3   Prosocial Vote with Partial Observation

In this scenario, we extend the previous scenario with a partial observation of the proposal: we suppose that each pirate knows only what he received. So the proposer who has to guarantee only a majority of votes can adapt more easily his offer.

---

[1] https://github.com/tlgleo/Pirate_Riddle/blob/master/pirates_riddle.ipynb.

5   Results

For each behaviour of voters, our REINFORCE training algorithm provides the proposer with a policy which is a probabilities distribution over possible partitions.

The results are presented using tables displaying the number of coins received by each pirate according to his rank and the number of living pirates. The upper row of a table represents the distribution when n_P pirates are alive with the first pirate P_1 being the HRP. The second row represents the distribution when $n_P - 1$ pirates are alive with P_2 being the HRP; and so forth. A white bin represents a case where a HRP is eliminated, meaning that this dead pirate will not receive any coins.

The learning graphs represent two curves: the orange one is the reward of RL algorithm which is the mean number of coins received by the proposer. The blue one shows the evolution of the euclidean distance between the predicted TD-learning of voter function and theoretical solutions (when a deterministic optimal solution exists).

5.1   Selfish Votes only

This sub-section presents the results obtained when all pirates vote according to the original rules of the PG. Figure 2a shows that the proposer's reward grows quickly and is close to the optimal solution as soon as the training reaches 2000 episodes[2]. As mentioned previously, the results may seem counter-intuitive but we demonstrated in Appendix A that this is the best strategy for the proposer being faced with rational agents.

Figure 2b shows that the proposed distribution is close to the optimal solution.

5.2   Prosocial Vote

In this part, we present the evaluation results obtained when only the HRP votes selfishly and when all the other agents vote prosocially by accepting the partition plan if and only if Jain's index is maximal. Figure 3b shows that the new behaviour of the voters leads to a distribution which is fairer for the different pirates.

As expected, the only cases where the selfish vote of the proposer is enough to win most resources are when there are only one or two pirates in the MAS (represented by the last two rows in Fig. 3b). In all other cases, the selfish vote of the proposer agent is thwarted by the prosocial votes of the other agents.

---

[2] The training of REINFORCE algorithm can be seen here: https://youtu.be/gh4USNJVWuw.

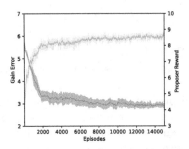

Pirate rank					
P1	**P2**	**P3**	**P4**	**P5**	
8.0±0.1	0.0±0.0	1.0±0.1	0.0±0.0	1.0±0.0	♙♙♙♙♙
	9.0±0.0	0.0±0.0	1.0±0.0	0.0±0.0	♙♙♙♙
		9.0±0.0	0.0±0.0	1.0±0.0	♙♙♙
			9,9±0.3	0,1±0.3	♙♙
				10.0±0.0	♙

(a) Learning curves of RL agents, shaded areas represent confidence intervals (95% over 10 runs). The orange curve is the reward of the proposer and the blue one shows the voter TD-learning error (with theoretical equilibrium).

(b) The number of coins for each situation (one to five players). The table shows the means and standard deviations from probabilities distribution learned by our proposer RL agent in 15 000 episodes.

Fig. 2. Results with the PG original behaviour (i.e. with purely rational players) with $n_P = 5$ pirates and $n_C = 10$ coins. Our RL agent is looking for the best probabilities distribution to earn the highest score. (Color figure online)

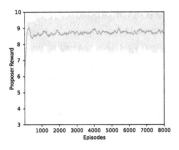

Pirate rank					
P1	**P2**	**P3**	**P4**	**P5**	
2.0±0.0	2.0±0.0	2.0±0.0	2.0±0.0	2.0±0.0	♙♙♙♙♙
	3.0±0.2	2.2±0.5	2.8±0.6	2.0±0.3	♙♙♙♙
		4.0±0.3	3.0±0.2	3.0±0.2	♙♙♙
			10.0±0.1	0.0±0.1	♙♙
				10.0±0.0	♙

(a) Learning curves

(b) Learned distribution

Fig. 3. Results in mixed mode (highest rank is selfish, the voters are prosocial with $n_P = 5$ pirates, $n_C = 10$ coins

5.3 Partial Observation

In this scenario, each voter knows only his part of the plan. We can see that our agent succeeds to achieve a good strategy. The best one consists in selecting enough pirates and convince them to vote for his sharing. Since the observation is partial which means that they only know their part, the proposer only has to concentrate the resources on the minimal number of agents, for example with two of the five pirates and give the minimal number that requires the optimal value of Jain's index. Figure 4 shows the results of the distribution. Thought the choice of voters doesn't change the optimal strategy, we can notice that the learning algorithm deterministically selects the same pirates to give them the minimum number of coins.

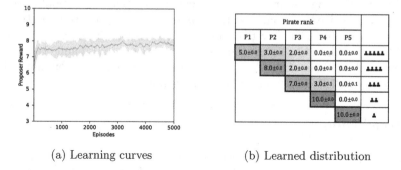

(a) Learning curves   (b) Learned distribution

Fig. 4. Results in prosocial mode with partial observation ($n_P = 5$ pirates, $n_C = 10$ coins)

6   Discussion and Next Steps

In this section, we discuss the salient technical aspects of our proposed model and some perspectives raised.

6.1   Adaptability of the Model

The empiric work shows that the same ANN model can predict near to optimal offers in different scenarios without knowing a priori the voting criteria of the other players, which demonstrates a great deal of flexibility.

The results also illustrate the divide and conquer proverb: the proposer generally obtains a bigger reward when all other agents vote selfishly than when all other agents vote prosocially. In the selfish scenario, the proposer earns $n_C - \lfloor (n_P - 1)/2 \rfloor$ coins whereas in the prosocial scenario, he wins $\lfloor n_C/n_P \rfloor \pm 1$ coins. In other words, the lesson learned by the players is that they gain more rewards by collaborating than by acting selfishly.

One of the most outstanding results is the one of Sect. 5.2: an HRP willing to act selfishly is forced to propose a prosocial offer when two or more lower-rank pirates vote prosocially, otherwise the offer is rejected. In other words, the adaptability of the model also leads to a high influenceability.

6.2   Communication Between Players

In the experimented scenarios, the agents do not communicate and their behaviour is assumed to be purely rational. This means that the decisions of agents are based on their unique personal interest without communicating with other agents before voting. Thanks to this rationality, their behaviour can be predicted therefore allowing proposers to adapt the offers. It could be interesting to introduce a communication canal directly linked to a specific action such as voting against the next offer. This canal should be binary and would be used as an implicit message addressed to a specific agent. The agent would learn to interpret the received message and then change his vote to encourage the proposer to modify his offer. For this purpose, it would be interesting to use an LSTM layer to take into account the previous messages [17,18] and observe how the agents adapt their offers. As described in [19], introducing communication can leads to implicit collaboration between agents.

7 Conclusion

In this work, we addressed a multi-agent version of Ultimatum Game, an economics game in which a proposer offers a partition of resources and voters accept it or not. In the version called the Pirate Game, the players are hierarchically ranked. If the vote is rejected, the proposer is eliminated from the game leaving his role to his successor. We showed that a Reinforcement Learning agent can solve such UG, which means that the agent gains the ability to decide optimally when processing a given offer of resources sharing so it earns enough and stays "alive".

For technical conclusions, we succeeded to implement a learning algorithm able to solve a discrete problem where the solution is represented by an integer partition which is not trivial. This same proposed approach can address similar real-world problems such as resource affectation, allocation, sharing, etc. Finally, we showed empirically that the reinforcement learning paradigm was a robust mean to address these problems. Specifically, it converges to an equilibrium even in a case where several adversary agents try to earn payoff with a different hierarchical situation.

A Proof of Optimal Selfish partition

For n_P pirates and n_C coins, the optimal proposal P following the game rules and satisfying the rational priorities of pirates is:

$$P_{n_P}[i] = \begin{cases} n_C - \lfloor (n_P - 1)/2 \rfloor, & \text{if } i = 0 \\ 1, & \text{if } i = 2(k+1) \\ 0, & \text{if } i = 2k+1 \end{cases}$$

with $\lfloor \ \rfloor$ denoting the floor function.

We can show this by backward induction on the number of pirates n_P:

- **Base Case:** for $n_P = 1$, there is only one possible partition: $P[0] = n_C$
- **Induction step:** let us assume the assertion is valid for n_P, let us show the assertion is valid for $n_P + 1$.

The proposer (decision maker) who will naturally vote for himself needs to convince only $\lfloor n_P/2 \rfloor$ other pirates to guarantee the majority of acceptance ie his survival. Then to fulfil the priority of maximal gain, it is optimal to choose the $\lfloor n_P/2 \rfloor$ lowest gains in the partition P_{n_P} and to offer them only one coin more (this will convince them thanks to their rationality) and offer zero coins to others. In the partition P_{n_P}, there are $\lfloor n_P/2 \rfloor$ null gains, so we choose to offer one coin to them and zero to others. In the new partition P_{n_P+1}, it doesn't change the explicitation since the incrementation of index (highest rank is always 0) compensates the parity modification. Finally, the decision maker takes for him the remaining coins: $P_{n_P+1}[0] = n_C - \lfloor n_P/2 \rfloor$. Therefore, the propriety is verified for $n_P + 1$.

B   Maximal Jain's index of an integer partition

We can show that the maximal value of the Jain's index of any partition of the integer n_C in n_P terms is given by:

$$\overline{J(n_P, n_C)} = \left[1 + \frac{d(1-d)}{x^2}\right]^{-1}$$

where

- x is the ratio $x = n_C/n_P$
- d the decimal part of x: $d = x - \lfloor x \rfloor$

When n_C is divisible by n_P, $d = 0$, so $\overline{J(n_P, n_C)} = 1$. If not, $\overline{J(n_P, n_C)} < 1$. For example, $\overline{J(4, 10)} \approx 0.962$ with for example the optimal partition [4 4 3 3].

References

1. Ding, L., Han, Q., Ge, X., Zhang, X.: An overview of recent advances in event-triggered consensus of multiagent systems. IEEE Trans. Cybern. **48**(4), 1110–1123 (2018)
2. White Paper 5G for Connected Industries and Automation. 5G ACIA, 2nd edn. February 2019
3. White paper ETSI GANA model in 5g network slicing: Programmable monitoring, GANA knowledge planes. ETSI (2019)
4. Luong, N.C., et al.: Applications of deep reinforcement learning in communications and networking: a survey. IEEE Commun. Surv. Tutor. **21**(4), 3133–3174 (2019). Fourthquarterdd
5. Li, R., et al.: Deep reinforcement learning for resource management in network slicing. IEEE Access **6**, 74429–74441 (2018)
6. Sutton, R.S., Barto, A.G.: Reinforcement learning: An introduction (2018)
7. Santos, F.P., Pacheco, J.M., Paiva, A., Santos, F.C.: Evolution of collective fairness in hybrid populations of humans and agents. In: AAAI Technical Track: Multiagent Systems, pp. 6146–6153 (2019)

8. Sen, S., Weiss, G.: learning in multiagent systems. In: Multiagent Systems: A Modern Approach to Distributed Artificial Intelligence, pp. 259–298 (1999)

9. De Jong, S., Tuyls, K., Verbeeck, K.: Artificial agents learning human fairness. In Proceedings of the 7th International Joint Conference on Autonomous Agents and Multiagent Systems-Volume 2, pp. 863–870. International Foundation for Autonomous Agents and Multiagent Systems (2008)

10. Chang, Y.H., Maheswaran, R.: The social ultimatum game and adaptive agents. In: The 10th International Conference on Autonomous Agents and Multiagent Systems-Volume 3, pp. 1313–1314 (2011)

11. De Jong, S., Uyttendaele, S. and Tuyls, K.: Learning to reach agreement in a continuous ultimatum game. J. Artif. Intell. Res. **33**, 551–574 (2008)

12. Zhong, F., Kimbrough, S.O., Wu, D.J.: Cooperative agent systems: artificial agents play the ultimatum game. In: Proceedings of the 35th Annual Hawaii International Conference on System Sciences, pp. 2207–2215. IEEE (2002)

13. Santos, F.P., Santos, F.C., Melo, F., Paiva, A. and Pacheco, J.M.: Learning to be fair in multiplayer ultimatum games. In: Proceedings of the 2016 International Conference on Autonomous Agents & Multiagent Systems, pp. 1381–1382 (2016)

14. Williams, R.J.: Simple statistical gradient-following algorithms for connectionist reinforcement learning. Mach. Learn. **8**(3), 229–256 (1992)

15. Stewart, I.: A puzzle for pirates. Sci. Am. **280**(5), 98–99 (1999)

16. Jain, R.K., Chiu, D.M.W., Hawe, W.R.: A Quantitative Measure Of Fairness And Discrimination For Resource Allocation In Shared Computer Systems. Technical report, Digital Equipment Corporation, September 1984

17. Foerster, J., Assael, I.A., De Freitas, N., Whiteson, S.: Learning to communicate with deep multi-agent reinforcement learning. In: Advances in Neural Information Processing Systems, pp. 2137–2145 (2016)

18. Foerster, J.N., Assael, Y.M., de Freitas, N., Whiteson, S.: Learning to communicate to solve riddles with deep distributed recurrent q-networks. arXiv preprint arXiv:1602.02672 (2016)

19. Cao, K., Lazaridou, A., Lanctot, M., Leibo, J.Z., Tuyls, K., Clark, S.: Emergent communication through negotiation. CoRR, abs/1804.03980 (2018)

BDI Multi-agent Based Simulation Model for Social Ecological Systems

Tito Julio Muto[1], Elias Buitrago Bolivar[2], and Enrique González[1(✉)]

[1] Pontificia Universidad Javeriana, Bogota, Colombia
{tmuto, egonzal}@javeriana.edu.co
[2] Corporacion Universitaria Republicana, Bogota, Colombia
elias.buitrago@javeriana.edu.co

Abstract. This paper presents the design of a simulation model for social ecological systems based on multi-agent systems. The multi-agent system incorporates subsets of intelligent agents that make decisions according to their environment and productive activity, resulting on a human-like behavior. A BDI model is proposed to model the behavior of agents simulating human entities. This allows to have a tool for decision making that can be adjusted to real data, as well as a behavior not only statistical but emergent, self-organized and adaptive. The proposed simulation model involves, in the same context, social, environmental, economic and spatial variables, i.e. social-ecological systems. Therefore, it has the potential to support decision makers in the country (mayors, governors, ministers, among others), allowing them to have a tool that shows the interaction between different entities with results in territorial planning processes.

Keywords: Complex-environmental systems · Multi-agent systems · Cellular automata · Simulation model · Multi-agent simulation · BDI agent

1 Introduction

The Socioecological Systems (SES) or Coupled Human and Natural Systems (CHANS), allow an approach to the understanding of the complexity of human interactions with the natural territory through an integrated transdisciplinary vision, integrating concepts from the ecological and the social sciences, with the support of mathematics and computing [1, 2]. The application of the SES concept in empirical studies conducted in different ecosystems of the five continents, has shown common characteristics that these systems exhibit: nonlinear dynamics with thresholds, reciprocal feedback loops, delays, resilience, heterogeneity, surprises, and coupling that have effects on the present conditions of the system [2]. That systemic approach allows to determine the interaction between its components at different temporal and spatial scales. Likewise, lets study the different factors involved in the use of the ecosystem services (ES) immersed in particular SES, incorporating the knowledge of the surrounding communities. The ES show how the resource of natural capital of the country can be affected by endogenous or exogenous variables, putting them in many cases at risk when they do not have clear policies in their use and regulation [3].

© Springer Nature Switzerland AG 2020
F. De La Prieta et al. (Eds.): PAAMS 2020 Workshops, CCIS 1233, pp. 279–288, 2020.
https://doi.org/10.1007/978-3-030-51999-5_23

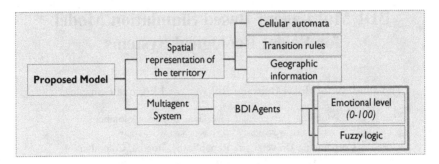

Fig. 1. Schematic design of the proposed model.

Although the literature shows advances in computer modeling and simulation of environmental tasks, some research topics remain open. For instance, the modeling of the different agents involved (human, biophysical, government entities, and the ecosystem itself) and their respective interactions at different temporal and spatial scales [4]. Therefore, SES computational simulation seeks to understand and predict these dynamics, as Schlueter et al. refers: "by analyzing and simulating the possible development pathways and expected results, SES models contribute to increasing our understanding of SES as adaptive complex systems, as well as our ability to manage them effectively" [5]. As a result, research in agent-based models (ABM) oriented to describe and predict land use in communities immersed in productive processes has been gaining momentum [7].

Filavitova et al. [6] points out four major research directions considered as priorities about how to maximize ABM effectiveness in the SES simulation context: modeling of agent behavior, design and parameterization of the agents' decision models; sensitivity analysis, verification and validation of ABMs; coupling of sociodemographic, ecological and biophysical models; and special representation. In addition, a series of operational criteria regarding ABM implementation phase have been highlighted recently: types of models, method of describing the model, programming language used in the implementation, verification of the output of the simulations, model analysis, evaluation and validation of results [4].

The objective of the model presented in this work, is to build an interrelationship between the different components of a SES simulation system and how they interact with the BESA and BDI agents, and also with the cellular automata that represents the territory; topic not covered in this paper. In addition, how their decisions influence the processes of land use and territory planning, based on a set of productive activities such as: agricultural, livestock, mining and ecosystem services. The latter being of vital importance to determine the influences that a farmer would have based on a production system scheme for supply and demand, purchase and sale of products; as raw materials in some cases and in others as manufactured products. The simulation model was designed using the AOPOA methodology for the development of multi-agent systems, which is based on construction of artifacts throughout the model cycle [8].

2 Structure of the Multi-agent Model

The proposed simulation model seeks to support decision making based on an environmental and social context. In this context, a farmer agent can develop productive activities such as: agriculture, livestock, mining or SE. Likewise, the types of agents that can interact with other agents, as well as the reception of messages or requests between agents, must be considered in the model. The model incorporates the concept of cellular automaton, in a way that permits to simulate entities that, due to their neighborhood behavior, interact with others and can change their status according to a set of simple transition rules (environmental entities). Figure 1 introduces the schematic design of the proposed model.

The proposed model was developed based on the AOPOA methodology for the construction of multi-agent systems. The role of each agent was defined as goal oriented in the design phase. These goals are defined by disaggregation into smaller ones that will lead to the fulfillment of the general objective. The main objective is to determine the behavior and characteristics that a farmer must have in his decision processes. Defining the roles of agents and their description in the context of the simulation model, as well as their roles and skills is essential (Table 1). Therefore, the model takes into account consumer-type entities of products such as: raw material or goods manufactured by another or other entities defined as industry-type agents.

Table 1. Agent roles and their descriptions. AOPOA methodology.

Role	Description
Farmer (FA)	Entity that shows decision-making behavior, based on their needs and productive activity, which can be (agricultural, livestock, mining or ecosystem services)
Market (MA)	It is the entity responsible for regulating the prices of products that are marketed by farmers and also allows consumers and industry to buy or sell them
Consumer (CA)	The consumer of raw material or manufactured goods in the model
Industrial (IndA)	Interacts by buying and selling products as raw material that are produced by the farmers and sells the products it produces
Associations (AA)	Associations are entities that interact with farmers and the market; they allow to have associations in which they can market their products
Bank (BA)	The banks interact with the farmers as a money lending entity so that the farmer, if necessary, go to that entity to obtain money and develop his productive activity
Property (PrA)	Ecosystem services are developed on the site, such as those based on plant cover and development of productive activity (agriculture, livestock, mining or ecosystem services)
Training Institution (TA)	It plays a fundamental role in the model as it allows farmers to know and acquire knowledge of their activity, being more productive in many cases and more aware of the environmental implications of their activity
Perturbation (PA)	The disturbances are of three types: climatic, strike or intermediation. Each of these perturbation influences negatively the normal course of events, production, and market exchanges

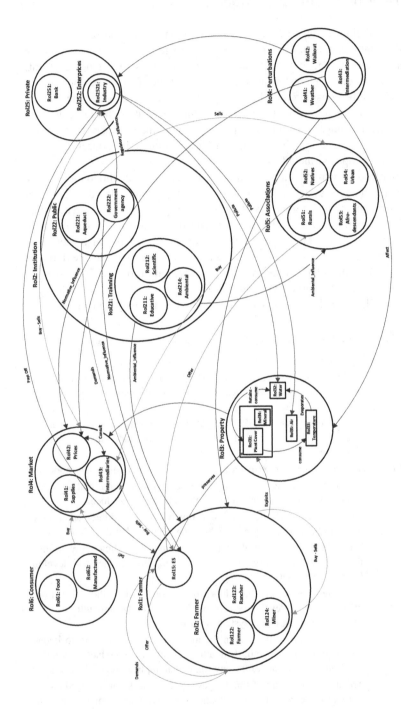

Fig. 2. Agent roles and interactions obtained using the AOPOA methodology.

Figure 2 presents the agent's goal-based decomposition model and the interaction scheme of the final proposed multi-agent model. The BDI farmer agents interact with the MA market for processes of purchase and sale of products (raw material in other manufactured goods) and input products for their productive activities. The FA BDI farmer has a direct interaction between the AP property which allows him to develop his productive activity in his farm, defined the behavior of the latter with a cellular automaton behavior, which has horizontal neighborhood interactions with automata of the same type and vertical interactions with other automata such as: precipitation, drainage (rivers) and sun radiation.

Within the interaction that an FA BDI farmer has with the BESA basic agents, the exchange he makes with the training agent can be highlighted, which can increase his knowledge of productive activities. Thus, the FA farmer can change his expectations and enable the development of his activities more productively or even change his main productive activity. This is achieved based on information dissemination processes, in principle, for a farmer agent to make the decision to attend and increase their knowledge, which will influence his decision making process.

3   BDI Concurrent Agent Model

A BDI agent model is well suited for the simulation of human-like entities, for instance the behavior of a farmer. This an approach is inspired on the way the human beings reason, taking into account the agent's resources and capacities, and choosing what specific goals the agent should fulfill in order to achieve its global objectives [12]. The agent's beliefs, desires and intentions define an action plan that can achieve a specific goal selected based on a reasoning deliberative process. In this section a brief introduction to the proposed BDI model [10] is made. This model is characterized for managing several concurrent threads: to process incoming information that modified the agent beliefs, to evaluate simultaneously the potential goals that can become agent desires, to select the intentions taking into account their contribution to the global objectives of the agent, and finally to execute the action plan associated to the agent intentions.

A BDI agent starts the process with the perception of its environment; in order to obtain information, sensor requests must send by the agent, or in other cases the environment sends automatically information as a consequence of the execution of an action. Besides, an agent can also acquire information thanks to the message sent by other agents. The perceived and received information is stocked on the agent's beliefs.

Then, the decision-making model for the simulation model is based on the agent beliefs and the use of fuzzy logic for the reasoning process. The agent evaluates, taking into account the information of its beliefs, all the specific potential goals by calculating their contribution, a value that indicates the expected gain of achieving a goal. The desires are the viable specific goals that have a high contribution value. The BDI model is characterized by incorporating a pyramid of goals (Fig. 3). This hierarchical structure organizes the agent desires according to their priorities; desires that belong to the same hierarchical level are ordered by their contribution values. The desires that are placed higher in the pyramid are selected as intentions; several intentions can be instantiated at the same time, only if they do not require the same agent's resources or abilities.

Finally, an action plan is executed in order to achieve each instantiated intention. The execution process is continuously supervised in order detect when a goal intention must be stopped or replaced by another one. The action plan specifies the actions that the action must perform, but also the messages that it should sent to other agents. Thus, the interaction rules are triggered according to the agent's BDI control mechanism and context.

This proposed BDI architecture applies the concepts of goals, desires, beliefs and intentions, which together model the structure of a rational human-like agent, allowing a complex decision-making process. Multiple concurrent potential goals are considered and evaluated concurrently. In the proposed architecture, for this BDI flow to be fully functional, four processes must be instantiated: 1. Data management and training, allows to control all the sensory information of the agent and controls the activities of updating beliefs; 2. Instance of desires to intentions, allows to evaluate the goals received from the previous process and decide which ones become intentions; 3. Mapping dominant goals, take the current intention, assign the associated role and generate the agent's action plan; 4. Garbage collection, collects the goals that due to environmental circumstances were already executed by agent, and should not be part of the current desires and intentions.

4   BDI Farmer Agent Model

Specifically, for the proposed simulation model, there are only one BDI agent, the Farmer Agent; the others are either BESA agents or are cellular automata agents. The behavior of the BDI farmer agent is determined by its main goal: to develop a productive activity that maximizes its well-being. Additionally, the BDI farmer agent must assume a set of responsibilities according to a specific role. The goals are triggered based on actions that the BDI farmer must execute to meet them; from a perception that the agent receives from the environment (BDI goals).

Beliefs in the BDI farmer agent define their mental state and are modified by communicating with other agents or the environment. In this model, the agent's capabilities are contemplated as knowledge in economic activity, energy, proactivity, productivity, among others. The cause-effect model of the actions depends on their capabilities and the internal state of each of them. Likewise, it must be indicated with whom the agent interacts and if there are other beliefs that the agent has according to his perception of the environment. The desires of the agent define what goals he can execute. Thus, a deliberative process is generated to select the intention goals, seeking to choose the ones that maximizes the overall agent's objective. Therefore, a goal may become a current intention of the agent; where intentions represent the last step in the flow that lead to the execution of actions. Through this process, it is ensured that the agent's behavior is guided by goals. Thus, the intentions are focused on actions to achieve a general goal. Intentions become reality through actions which are defined in an action plan. Thus, the intentions become actions after verifying their viability.

Fig. 3. Hierarchy pyramid of BDI goals.

The priority of the goals in a BDI farmer agent is based on a hierarchical pyramid (see Fig. 3). The priority of goals is structured as follows: survival, obligation, opportunity, requirements, needs. For example, if the BDI farm agent has a role as a farmer without energy, they must be prepared to eat, an action classified as a survival goal. If there is another goal such as that the farmer must work, it's less important of eating because he cannot work without energy. The five categories of the goal pyramid have specific goals and roles mapped, as shown in Table 2. The agent role specifies the behavior of the agent in order to achieve the associated goal.

Table 2. BDI farmer agent roles classified according to the BDI pyramid of goals.

Goal type	Id.	Associated goal	Agent role
Survival	Ms-1	Farmer agent must eat	Farmer agent without energy
	Ms-2	Farmer agent must work to earn money	Farmer agent worker
Obligation	Mob-3	Farmer agent must pay bank obligations	Farmer agent debtor
	Mob-4	Farmer agent must take care of his productive activities	Farmer agent monitor
	Mob-51	Farmer agent must cultivate the property	Farmer agent
	Mob-52	Farmer agent must work his cattle	Farmer agent worker rancher
	Mob-53	Farmer agent must work his mine	Farmer agent worker miner
	Mob-54	Farmer agent must take care of his ES	Farmer agent worker ES
	Mob-6	Farmer agent must consult the market price system, demand and supply of products	Farmer agent information consultant
Opportunity	Mop-7	Farmer agent must attend the trainings offered by the training entity	Farmer agent student
	Mop-8	Farmer agent must review the opportunity for assistance in the development of sustainable projects	Farmer agent worker ES
	Mop-9	Farmer agent must partner with others to sell their products	Farmer agent community
Requirements	Mr-10	Farmer agent must apply for a loan in order to have money and develop his activity	Farmer agent debtor
Needs	Mn-11	Farmer agent must sell his products	Farmer agent businessman

BDI farmer agent behavior modulating variables

The behavioral modulating variables [10] define the characteristics of the BDI agent and are fundamental in the processes; to determine the agent's dominant goal (intention) in a specific moment of simulation process. Besides, the actions that must be executed are parametrized according to the value of these variables. These variables are part of the agent's beliefs. In the case of the BDI farm agent in the simulator, the more important ones are: knowledge of a productive activity, being proactive or not, the level of energy, the emotional situation of the agent, well-being, and the amount of money he has to meet his basic needs and to develop a productive activity.

The modulating variables are introduced for the decision-making process based on the BDI of the farm agent, in order to quantify the status of the agent and that the system can read the status of the agent. Based on them, it is then possible to validate the type of decision that an agent could opt for, taking into account the structure of the goal pyramid. The modulatory variables for the farm agent are the following: (i) *variables for the type of activity:* the farmer agent will always have the option to change his productive activity, according to the influence of the trainer and the market values that maximize his investment and improve his living conditions and that of his family; (ii) *variables of a personal nature:* the farmer agent must have the capacity, among many ways to use his property, take into account the environment and what it means to make one or the other decision; (iii) t*errain-dependent variables:* the farmer agent is influenced by the activity of his neighbors and also by the basic needs met.

5 Validation

The programming framework used for the implementation of the multi-agent system is BESA, developed by the SIDRe research group at the Pontificia Universidad Javeriana [11]. The programming of agents is based on three type of entities: BESA basic agents (limited reasoning structure), cellular automatons property agents and BDI famer agents.

The property agents simulate the territory using a model based on multilayer cellular automata, whose behavior is associated with its environment and its neighborhood. They use a set of transition rules, which can modify the status of each land cell, either by the action of an agent that performs actions on any of the automatons (plant cover-trees-cultivation, precipitation, radiation, drainage) or by the interaction between several layers. A more detailed explanation of this agent is out of the scope of this paper.

The proposed model was validated using real data of the Rancheria river region in Colombia. The Rancheria river basin is an area with high richness in hydrological environmental services, provided by its ecosystems and a high tree density area. The characteristics and data of this territory and the development of the first environmental services project make it attractive to develop the validation study; since it was possible to access the information generated. The validation study was centered on analyzing the deforestation effects while different capacitation and incentives are provided to the farmers in order to motivate them to provide ecosystem services.

The behavior of the simulator was consistent with the expert expectations as different conditions were included in the configuration variables of the simulations (training sessions, number of agents, economic level, welfare, knowledge). A factorial design was used for the number of repetitions of the validation experiment, taking into account that an incremental number of agents was taken to see the response and the use of resources. Thus, with groups of 20 agents that increased in a factor of 20 to reach a number of 156. Number of repetitions was fixed in 160.

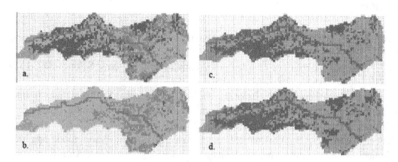

Fig. 4. Result of validation experiment (change of land coverage based on extreme conditions of the agents). Above original coverage image (a and c). Below image of the territory after the interaction of the agents (b and d). Dark points represent forest coverage.

The result of the validation experiment shows a tendency of extreme soil change for extreme conditions of the agents. When the rules are identified as of high welfare and a high economic level, the agents do not make many modifications of the land (right side in Fig. 4). However, under other conditions, the deforestation process is triggered; highly influenced by poor knowledge of farmer agents (left side in Fig. 4). Also, it can be seen that changes in coverage can occur due to extreme conditions of precipitation, temperature and changes derived from production activities by farmer agent, which are given by the influence of the environment in their perceptions (modifying their beliefs, desires or intentions) and the change in their diffuse variables of well-being.

6 Conclusions

In the contemporary world, the study and analysis of complex systems through engineering, has given humanity endless knowledge and has marked milestones in the history of our civilization. The objective of this research work was to model complex systems, specifically ecological and social systems, to support decision-making in territorial planning processes. It was shown that environmental systems can be approached from the point of view of complexity, exploring engineering techniques that combine cellular automata and agent-based models, to build predictive simulation processes. In these, different scenarios, environmental systems, and variables such as climate change, land planning and use, microeconomics, ecosystems and particularly ecosystem services can be included.

In Colombia, it can be seen how environmental authorities, research institutions and companies in the productive sector need instruments that support their decision-making and are based on information that helps them be consistent with the plans and proposals they make. Therefore, the proposed model has the potential to support decision makers (mayors, governors, ministers, among others), allowing them to have a tool that shows the interaction between different entities with results in territorial planning processes.

References

1. Ostrom, E.: A general framework for analyzing sustainability of social-ecological systems. Science **325**, 419–422 (2009)
2. Liu, J., et al.: Complexity of coupled human and natural systems. Science **317**, 1513–1516 (2007)
3. de Groot, R.S., Alkemade, R., Braat, L., Hein, L., Willemen, L.: Challenges in integrating the concept of ecosystem services and values in landscape planning, management and decision making. Ecol. Complex **7**(3), 260–272 (2010)
4. Schulze, J., Müller, B., Groeneveld, J., Grimm, V.: Agent-based modelling of social-ecological systems: achievements, challenges, and a way forward. J. Artif. Soc. Soc. Simul. **20**, 2 (2017)
5. Schlueter, M., Mueller, B.: New horizons for managing the environment: a review of coupled social-ecological systems modeling. Nat. Resour. Model. **25**, 219–272 (2012)
6. An, L., Zvoleff, A., Liu, J., Axinn, W.: Agent-based modeling in coupled human and natural systems (CHANS): lessons from a comparative analysis. Ann. Assoc. Am. Geograph. **104**, 723–745 (2014)
7. Matthews, R.B., Gilbert, N.G., Roach, A., Polhill, J.G., Gotts, N.M.: Agent-based land-use models: a review of applications. Landscape Ecol. **22**, 1447–1459 (2007). https://doi.org/10.1007/s10980-007-9135-1
8. González, E., Torres, M., Rodriguez, J.: La Metodologia AOPOA. Rev. Av. Eng Sist. E Inform. **4**, 8 (2007)
9. de Senna Carneiro, T.G., de Andrade, P.R., Camara, G., Vieira Monteiro, A.M., Pereira, R.R.: An extensible toolbox for modeling nature-society interactions. Environ. Model Softw. **46**, 104–117 (2013)
10. Ángel, R.S.: MSSIN: Modelo de Simulación Social basado en Agentes con un Enfoque Inteligente. Universidad Javeriana, Systems Engeniering PI113-01 (2012)
11. Enrique, G., Cesar, B., Jamir, A.: Agents for Concurrent Programming. CPA 2003, pp 157–166. Enschende-Holanda, IOS Press, September 2003
12. Wooldridge, M.: Reasoning about Rational Agents. The MIT Press, Cambridge (2000)

Workshop on Multi-agent based Applications for Energy Markets, Smart Grids and Sustainable Energy Systems (MASGES)

Workshop on Multi-agent based Applications for Energy Markets, Smart Grids and Sustainable Energy Systems (MASGES)

The electrical power industry has evolved into a distributed and competitive industry in which market forces drive the price of energy. Deregulation led to the establishment of wholesale markets, where competing generators can offer their electricity output to retailers, and retail markets, where end-use customers can choose their suppliers. Electricity markets are indeed a complex and evolving reality, meaning that researchers lack insight into numerous open problems that are being raised. Chief among these is the need of new market designs to manage the variability and uncertainty of the increasing levels of renewable generation.

Also, future power systems will integrate a large number of distributed energy resources and new players. Smart grids are intrinsically linked to the challenges raised by new power systems and are expected to improve their efficiency and effectiveness, while ensuring reliability and a secure delivery of electricity to end-users. They should be capable of autonomously and intelligently configuring themselves to make the most efficient use of the available resources, to be robust to different kinds of failures and energy production deviations, and to be extendable and adaptable in the face of the rapidly changing technologies and requirements.

The distributed nature of all these systems, and the autonomous behavior expected for them, points towards software agents and multi-agent systems as a foundation for their realization and deployment. Accordingly, the focus of this workshop is on the application of software agents and multi-agent systems to electricity markets for integrating variable renewable energy and emerging technologies, such as smart grids, distributed generation, demand response, storage, smart homes, and electrical vehicles.

Organization

Organizing Committee

Fernando Lopes — LNEG - National Laboratory of Energy and Geology, Portugal

Isabel Praça — Polytechnic Institute of Porto, Portugal

Roozbeh Morsali — Swinburne University, Australia

Rainer Unland — University of Duisburg-Essen, Germany

Program Committee

Renewable Energy Support Policy Based on Contracts for Difference and Bilateral Negotiation

Hugo Algarvio[1,2], Fernando Lopes[1(✉)], and João Santana[2,3]

[1] LNEG–National Laboratory of Energy and Geology,
Est. Paço do Lumiar 22, Lisbon, Portugal
`fernando.lopes@lneg.pt`
[2] Instituto Superior Técnico, Avenida Rovisco Pais 1, Lisbon, Portugal
[3] INESC-ID, Rua Alves Redol 9, Lisbon, Portugal
`{hugo.algarvio,jsantana}@tecnico.ulisboa.pt`

Abstract. The European Union has been one of the major drivers of the development of renewable energy. The energy policies of most European countries have involved subsidized tariffs, such as the feed-in tariff in Portugal, the regulated tariff and the market price plus premium in Spain, and the Renewables Obligation in UK, that came into effect in 2002. Recently, UK has made some reforms and started to consider contracts for difference (CfDs) as a key element of the energy policy. This paper presents a support policy based on CfDs and bilateral negotiation. The first phase consists in a CfD auction and the second phase involves a bilateral negotiation between a Government and each of the selected investors. The paper also presents a case-study to analyze the potential benefits of the support policy. It was performed with the help of the MATREM system. The preliminary results indicate some advantages for the Government (and, in some cases, for the investors as well).

Keywords: Energy markets · Renewable energy · Contracts for difference · Feed-in tariffs · Price risk · MATREM system

1 Introduction

The energy industry has evolved into a liberalized industry in which market forces drive the price of electricity. Three markets models have been distinguished [1,2]: pools, bilateral contracts and hybrid models. A pool is defined as a centralized marketplace that clears the market for buyers and sellers. Market entities submit offers for the quantities of power that they are willing to trade.

J. Santana—This work was supported by "Fundação para a Ciência e Tecnologia" with reference UID/CEC/50021/2019.

F. De La Prieta et al. (Eds.): PAAMS 2020 Workshops, CCIS 1233, pp. 293–301, 2020.
https://doi.org/10.1007/978-3-030-51999-5_24

These offers are handled by a market operator, whose function is to coordinate and manage the transactions between market entities. Bilateral contracts are agreement between two parties to trade electrical energy. The hybrid model combines several features of the previous two models.

There are various types of contractual arrangements that fall under the broad heading of bilateral contracts, notably contracts for difference (CfDs). Such contracts are bilateral agreements to provide a specific amount of energy for a fixed price, referred to as the strike price. Also, CfDs are typically indexed to a reference price, which is often the centralized market-clearing price. In some cases, CfDs can be one way contracts, when the difference payments are made by one of the parties only [3,4].

The evolution of renewable energy has increased substantially over the past decade. Europe has been at the forefront of the renewable energy policy design and deployment [5,6]. In particular, Portugal has benefited from a feed-in tariff [7]. In Spain, two different types of retribution have been considered: the regulated or feed-in tariff and the market price plus premium. In UK, there have been two main policy instruments: the Non-Fossil Fuel Order, a centralized bidding system that ran from 1990 to 1998, and the Renewables Obligation, that came into effect in 2002. Recently, UK has made some reforms to meet the challenges of the electricity sector. Contracts for difference are a key element of such reforms—they are essentially private law contracts between low carbon electricity generators and a Government-owned company. CfDs provide long-term price stabilisation to low carbon plants, allowing investment to come forward at a lower cost of capital and therefore at a lower cost to consumers [8,9].

Renewable generation is characterized by high fixed capital costs but near-zero variable production costs, and a great dependence on weather conditions. These characteristics may significantly influence the behavior and outcomes of energy markets. In particular, high levels of renewable generation may reduce market prices due to their low-bid costs, and increase price volatility because of their increased variability and uncertainty [11].

Against this background, this paper presents a study to investigate the potential benefits of both contracts for difference and bilateral negotiation as a basis of a renewable energy support policy. It considers a particular Government (e.g., the Portugal or Spain Governments) that makes a public announcement of new investment in wind energy involving two phases. The first phase consists in a CfD auction, like the UK CfD auctions [8,10], when the investors make their offers. This phase is simulated by considering a contract net protocol. The Government selects all the offers that provide a specific level of benefit and comply with the requirements. In the second phase, there is a bilateral negotiation between the Government and each of the selected investors, where the parties negotiate a mutually acceptable value for the strike price. Negotiation involves an iterative exchange of proposals and counter-proposals. The study is conducted with the help of an agent-based tool, called MATREM [12,13].

The remainder of the paper is structured as follows. Section 2 presents an overview of the markets supported by the MATREM system, placing emphasis on the bilateral marketplace for negotiating long-term contracts (notably contracts for difference). Section 3 discusses some aspects of the formalization of bilateral negotiation involving CfDs. Section 4 presents the case-study and discusses the experimental results. Finally, concluding remarks are presented in Sect. 5.

2 MATREM: Overview of the Bilateral Marketplace

MATREM (for Multi-Agent TRading in Electricity Markets) is an energy management tool for simulating liberalized electricity markets. The tool supports a day-ahead market, a shorter-term market (an intra-day market), a balancing market, a futures market, and a bilateral marketplace. Market entities are modeled as software agents equipped with models of individual and social behaviour, enabling them to be pro-active (i.e., capable of exhibiting goal-directed behaviour) and social (i.e., able to communicate and negotiate with other agents in order to complete their design objectives). Currently, the tool supports generating companies, retailers, aggregators, coalitions of consumers, traditional consumers, market operators and system operators. A detailed description of the tool is presented in [12]. A classification of the tool according to various dimensions associated with both energy markets and software agents can be found in [13]. This section gives an overview of the markets supported by the tool, particularly the bilateral marketplace.

The day-ahead market is a central market where generation and demand can be traded on an hourly basis [14]. The intra-day market is a short-term market and involves several auction sessions. Both markets are based on the marginal pricing theory. The balancing market is a market for primary, secondary and tertiary reserve. For the particular case of tertiary reserve, two computer simulations are performed, one for determining the price for up-regulation, and another for computing the price for down-regulation.

The futures market is an organized market for standardized financial and physical contracts. Such contracts may span from days to years and typically hedge against the price risk inherent to day-ahead and intra-day markets. Players enter orders involving either bids to sell or buy energy in an electronic trading platform that supports anonymous operation. The platform automatically and continuously matches the bids likely to interfere with each other.

The bilateral marketplace allows market participants to negotiate all the details of two different types of tailored (or customized) long-term bilateral contracts, namely forward contracts and contracts for difference (see, e.g., [15]). Forward bilateral contracts are agreements between two agents to exchange a specific energy quantity at a certain future time for a particular price. Contracts for difference are agreements in which each agent ensures the other against discrepancies between the contract price (or strike price) and the market-clearing price. The terms and conditions of both types of contracts are flexible and can be negotiated privately to meet the objectives of two parties. To this end, market agents are equipped with a model that handles two-party and multi-issue negotiation [16,17]. Negotiation proceeds by an iterative exchange of offers and counter-offers. An offer is a set of issue-value pairs, such as "energy price = 50 €/MWh", "contract duration = 6 months", and so on. A counter-offer is an offer made in response to a previous offer. The bilateral marketplace and the associated negotiation of long-term contracts represents a novel and powerful tool. Accordingly, some details about the negotiation process follow.

Let $A = \{a_1, a_2\}$ be the set of software agents participating in negotiation. The agent interact according to the rules of an alternating offers protocol [18]. This means that one offer (or proposal) is submitted per time period, with an agent $a_i \in A$ offering in odd periods $\{1, 3, \dots\}$, and the other agent $a_j \in A$ offering in even periods $\{2, 4, \dots\}$. The negotiation process starts with a_i submitting a proposal $p_{i \to j}^1$ to a_j at time period $t = 1$. The agent a_j receives $p_{i \to j}^1$ and can either accept it, reject it and opt out of the negotiation, or reject it and continue bargaining. In the first two cases, negotiation comes to an end. Specifically, if the proposal is accepted, negotiation ends successfully. Conversely, if the proposal is rejected and a_j decides to opt out, negotiation terminates with no agreement. In the last case, negotiation proceeds to the next time period $t = 2$, in which a_j makes a counter-proposal $p_{j \to i}^2$. The agent a_i receives the counter-proposal $p_{j \to i}^2$ and the tasks just described are repeated, i.e., a_i may either accept the counter-proposal, reject it and opt out of the negotiation, or reject it and continue bargaining. Negotiation may end with either agreement or no agreement.

Negotiation strategies are computationally tractable functions that define the negotiation tactics to be used during the course of negotiation. Concession tactics are functions that generate new values for each issue at stake throughout negotiation. Let X designate an issue and denote its value at time t by x. Formally, a concession tactic for X is a function with the following general form:

$$Y(x) = x + (-1)^m C_f(x - lim) \tag{1}$$

where $m = 0$ if an agent a_i wants to minimize X or $m = 1$ if a_i wants to maximize X, $C_f \in [0, 1]$ is the concession factor, and lim is the limit for X (i.e., the point where a_i decides to stop the negotiation rather than to continue, because any agreement beyond this point is not minimally acceptable). The concession factor C_f can be a positive constant independent of any objective criteria. Also, C_f can be modelled as a function of a single criterion. Useful criterion include the total concession made on each issue throughout negotiation as well as the amount or quantity of energy for a specific trading period [19].

3   Bilateral Negotiation and Contracts for Difference

As noted, contracts for difference are agreements in which the purchaser pays the seller the difference between the contract price (or strike price) and some reference price, usually the market-clearing price. Concretely, CfDs are settled as follows [1]:

- if the strike price is higher than the market-clearing price, the buyer pays the seller the difference between these two prices times the energy quantity agreed;

- conversely, if the strike price is lower than the clearing price, the seller pays the buyer the difference between these two prices times the quantity of energy agreed.

In this section, we consider that CfDs may specify the provision of different quantities of energy for different periods of time, at different prices (see also [19]). Thus, we consider that the set of negotiating issues includes n strike prices and n energy quantities. Let P_k be a strike price and Q_k an energy quantity (for $k = 1, \ldots, n$). Let p_k denote the value of P_k for quantity q_k of Q_k. Also, let rp_k be the value of a reference price RP_k associated with a specific period of a day. The financial compensation associated with CfDs can now be formalized. Specifically, when the strike prices are smaller than the reference prices, the amount to pay is as follows:

$$C_s = \sum_{k=1}^{n} (rp_k - p_k) \times q_k \tag{2}$$

And the amount to pay by buyers to sellers is as follows:

$$C_b = \sum_{k=1}^{n} (p_k - rp_k) \times q_k \tag{3}$$

4 Case-Study

This section analyzes the potential benefits of a renewable energy support policy involving two phases. The agents are a Government of a particular country (e.g., Portugal or Spain) and various investors (or renewable energy producers). The first phase consists in a CfD auction, like the UK CfD auctions, where investors can make offers, and the Government select the best ones according to pre-defined requirements. The second phase consists in a private bilateral negotiation between the Government and each of the selected investors, to obtain a mutually acceptable value for the strike price. Since each selected investor knows the first proposal of the other investors, there is the possibility to make a more competitive offer in this phase. Accordingly, this support policy could be advantageous for the Government (and, in some cases, for the investors as well).

First Phase: CfD Auction. The public announcement involves the investment in wind energy in a maximum of 100 MW of installed capacity (per investor). The investors can propose projects involving less than 100 MW, but only in group with investors in a similar situation. Joint projects involving more than 100 MW of installed capacity can be accepted, in case they are advantageous for the Government. All investors should submit the following: strike price (SP), average expected power factor (PF) of the project, and (iii) installed capacity (IC). The power factor consists in the average number of hours that wind farms will be operating at the installed capacity/nominal power.

The points (P) attributed to each proposal are computed by considering the relation between the strike price and the average expected power factor, as well as the installed capacity (see Eq. 4). The power factor and the strike price have weights k_1 and k_2, respectively (such that $k_1 + k_2 = 1$). Since SP is often the most important factor, in this work we consider $k_1 = 0.3$ and $k_2 = 0.7$.

$$P = 100 \times \left(\frac{k_1\, PF}{k_2\, SP} \times (1.05 - \frac{1 - \frac{IC}{100}}{10}) \right) \tag{4}$$

Table 1. CfD auction results: projects accepted for the next phase.

Project Id	Strike price (€/MWh)	Power factor (%)	Installed capacity (MW)	Points
9	74.20	31.90	100.00	18.84
2	73.85	31.90	30.00	18.14
3	75.80	31.30	80.00	18.05
1	73.90	29.50	100.00	17.96
11	75.70	30.20	100.00	17.95

The CfD auction involved a total of 15 proposals, but only 5 were accepted for the next phase. Specifically, projects 1, 9 and 11 were accepted as individual projects, while projects 2 and 3 were accepted as a joint project. This means that investors of projects 2 and 3 make a strategic alliance to be awarded a CfD (although their companies remain separated). Table 1 shows the CfD allocation auction round outcome, with the 5 projects delivering 410 MW of renewable energy. Several potential projects for the next delivery years did not get awarded a CfD, which may to some extent raise questions about the viability of the CfD regime for small and medium enterprises. Probably, a strike price of around 80 € is acceptable, but lower than this could be not workable. Furthermore, the importance of interest rates in relation to the strike price should not be ignored in future work, given that the project time line will likely extend into periods of possible interest rate change which could impact on the viability of any strike prices.

Second Phase: Private Bilateral Negotiation. After announcing the results of the CfD auction, the Government starts private bilateral negotiations with the investors. For projects 1, 9 and 11, negotiation involves the Government and each of the corresponding investors. Projects 2 and 3 are a joint project, meaning that negotiation involves the Government and the agent representing the joint project. A detailed description of the negotiation process between the Government and the investor responsible for project 9 follows.

Negotiation proceeds through two main phases: a beginning or initiation phase (pre-negotiation) and a middle or problem-solving phase (actual negotiation). Pre-negotiation involves the creation of a well-conceived plan specifying the issues at stake, the limits and targets, the attitude toward risk and an appropriate strategy. In this work, the negotiating agenda involves mainly the strike price. The limit or resistance point is the point where each party decides to stop the negotiation rather than to continue. The target point is the point where each negotiator realistically expects to achieve an agreement. We consider that the Government adopts a risk-seeking attitude. Thus, assuming the existence of a number of interested investors, the Government can adopt an aggressive position throughout negotiation in searching for a good deal. The investor adopts a risk-averse attitude, acting carefully to achieve a deal and award a CfD. Both parties adopt concession strategies, meaning that they are willing to partially reduce their demands to accommodate the opponent.

Actual negotiation involves an iterative exchange of offers and counter-offers. The investor makes an opening offer involving the strike price shown in Table 1 (74.20 €/MWh). The Government may be pleased with such an offer, but might still believe that there is room for a few concessions. Accordingly, the Government responds with an offer involving a strike price lower than the received price, lets say 72.50 €/MWh. After these two offers, the parties may argue for what they want, but at a certain point they recognize the importance of moving toward agreement. Thus, and despite the fact of being reluctant to make any concession, the investor slightly reduces the strike price. The Government decides to respond in kind and mirror the concession of the investor. And the agents enter into a negotiation dance, exchanging proposals and counter-proposals, until they reach the final price of 73.37 €/MWh. This price represents a good deal for the Government and an acceptable deal for the investor, who will be awarded with a contract for difference for the next 15 years.

5   Conclusion

This article has presented an energy support policy based on contracts for difference and bilateral negotiation. The support policy involves two phases. The first consists in a CfD auction, like the UK auctions, and the second involves a private bilateral negotiation between each of the selected investors and a particular Government.

Preliminary results from a case-study indicate some advantageous for the Government (and, in some cases, for the investors as well). In the future, we intend to perform a number experiments, using controlled experimentation as the experimental method, to evaluate the effectiveness of the support policy in a number of different situations.

References

1. Kirschen, D., Strbac, G.: Fundamentals of Power System Economics. John Wiley, Chichester (2018)
2. Lopes, F., Coelho, H.: Electricity Markets with Increasing Levels of Renewable Generation: Structure Operation, Agent-based Simulation and Emerging Designs. Springer, Heidelberg (2018). https://doi.org/10.1007/978-3-319-74263-2

3. Stoft, S.: Power Systyem Economis: Designing Markets for Electricity. IEEE Press and Wiley Interscience (2002)
4. Lopes, F.: Electricity markets and intelligent agents part I: market architecture and structure. In: Lopes, F., Coelho, H. (eds.) Electricity Markets with Increasing Levels of Renewable Generation: Structure, Operation, Agent-based Simulation, and Emerging Designs. SSDC, vol. 144, pp. 23–48. Springer, Cham (2018). https://doi.org/10.1007/978-3-319-74263-2_2
5. European Union: Directive 2009/28/EC of the European Parliament and of the Council on the promotion of the use of energy from renewable sources and amending and subsequently repealing Directives 2001/77/EC and 2003/30/EC, 23 April 2009. http://eur-lex.europa.eu/legal-content/EN/TXT/?uri=CELEX:32009L0028. Accessed Feb 2020
6. European Union: The Promotion of the use of Energy from Renewable Sources, Directive (EU) 2018/2001, 11 December 2018. http://data.europa.eu/eli/dir/2018/2001/oj. Accessed Feb 2020
7. Lopes, F., Sá, J., Santana, J.: Renewable generation, support policies and the merit order effect: a comprehensive overview and the case of wind power in Portugal. In: Lopes, F., Coelho, H. (eds.) Electricity Markets with Increasing Levels of Renewable Generation: Structure, Operation, Agent-based Simulation, and Emerging Designs. SSDC, vol. 144, pp. 227–263. Springer, Cham (2018). https://doi.org/10.1007/978-3-319-74263-2_9
8. Department for Energy and Climate Change: Implementing Electricity Market Reform, June 2014. https://www.gov.uk/government/publications/implementing-electricity-market-reform-emr. Accessed Feb 2020
9. Grubb, M., Newbery, D.: UK Electricity Market Reform and the Energy Transition: Emerging Lessons, Working Paper Series CEEPR WP 2018–004, Massachusetts Institute of Technology, February 2018
10. Eversheds: First Contract for Difference (CfD) auction results announced, Eversheds Sutherland International. https://www.eversheds-sutherland.com/global/en/what/articles/index.page?ArticleID=en/Energy/first-cfd-auction-results-announced-150226. Accessed Feb 2020
11. Ela, E., et al.: Overview of wholesale electricity markets. In: Lopes, F., Coelho, H. (eds.) Electricity Markets with Increasing Levels of Renewable Generation: Structure, Operation, Agent-based Simulation, and Emerging Designs. SSDC, vol. 144, pp. 3–21. Springer, Cham (2018). https://doi.org/10.1007/978-3-319-74263-2_1
12. Lopes, F.: MATREM: an agent-based simulation tool for electricity markets. In: Lopes, F., Coelho, H. (eds.) Electricity Markets with Increasing Levels of Renewable Generation: Structure, Operation, Agent-based Simulation, and Emerging Designs. SSDC, vol. 144, pp. 189–225. Springer, Cham (2018). https://doi.org/10.1007/978-3-319-74263-2_8
13. Lopes, F., Coelho, H.: Electricity markets and intelligent agents Part II: agent architectures and capabilities. In: Lopes, F., Coelho, H. (eds.) Electricity Markets with Increasing Levels of Renewable Generation: Structure, Operation, Agent-based Simulation, and Emerging Designs. SSDC, vol. 144, pp. 49–77. Springer, Cham (2018). https://doi.org/10.1007/978-3-319-74263-2_3
14. Algarvio, H., Couto, A., Lopes, F., Estanqueiro, A., Santana, J.: Multi-agent energy markets with high levels of renewable generation: a case-study on forecast uncertainty and market closing time. Distributed Computing and Artificial Intelligence, 13th International Conference. AISC, vol. 474, pp. 339–347. Springer, Cham (2016). https://doi.org/10.1007/978-3-319-40162-1_37

15. Sousa, F., Lopes, F., Santana, J.: Contracts for difference and risk management in multi-agent energy markets. In: Demazeau, Y., Decker, K.S., Bajo Pérez, J., de la Prieta, F. (eds.) PAAMS 2015. LNCS (LNAI), vol. 9086, pp. 155–164. Springer, Cham (2015). https://doi.org/10.1007/978-3-319-18944-4_13

16. Lopes, F., Mamede, N., Novais, A.Q., Coelho, H.: A negotiation model for autonomous computational agents: formal description and empirical evaluation. J. Intell. Fuzzy Syst. **12**, 195–212 (2002)

17. Lopes, F., Mamede, N., Novais, A.Q., Coelho, H.: Negotiation in a multi-agent supply chain system, In: 3rd International Workshop of the IFIP WG 5.7 Special Interest Group on "Advanced Techniques in Production Planning & Control", pp. 153–168. Firenze University Press (2002)

18. Osborne, M., Rubinstein, A.: Bargaining and Markets. Academic Press Inc., New York (1990)

19. Lopes, F., Algarvio, H., Santana, J.: Agent-based simulation of electricity markets: risk management and contracts for difference. In: Alonso-Betanzos, A., et al. (eds.) Agent-Based Modeling of Sustainable Behaviors. UCS, pp. 207–225. Springer, Cham (2017). https://doi.org/10.1007/978-3-319-46331-5_10

A Two Tier Architecture for Local Energy Market Simulation and Control

Rui Andrade[1]([⊠]) [iD], Sandra Garcia-Rodriguez[2] [iD], Isabel Praca[1] [iD], and Zita Vale[1] [iD]

[1] ISEP/GECAD, Porto, Portugal
{rfaar,icp,zav}@isep.ipp.pt
[2] CEA, LIST, Data Analysis and Systems Intelligence Laboratory,
91191 Gif Sur Yvette, France
sandra.garciarodriguez@cea.fr

Abstract. This paper addresses energy management and security having as basis sensing and monitoring of cyber-physical infrastructure of consumers and prosumers, and their participation in the Local Energy Market (LEM). The vision is to create a layered multi-agent framework that brings a complete view of the cyber-physical system of LEM participants, and provides optimization and control of energy for said participants. The proposed system is separated into a Market layer and a Cyber-Physical layer, each of them providing different services. The cyber-physical layer, represented by SMARTERCtrol system, provides Data Monitoring and Optimized Energy Control of individual building resources. The Market layer, represented by LEM Multi-Agent System, provides Negotiation, Forecasting, and Trust Evaluation. Both systems work together to provide and integrate a tool for simulation and control of LEM.

Keywords: Multi-agent systems · Energy · Optimization · Forecasting

1 Introduction

According to European Commission [4] the share of renewables in Power and Energy Systems (PES) could reach 50% by 2030 with an important contribution from variable sources. This sets significant challenges to distribution grids since large part of the renewables will be implemented at household level. Furthermore, the European parliament proposal for the regulation of the internal Energy Market (EM) suggests that the role of consumers in future PES will be central [7]. The developed solutions and technology should encourage and enable consumers to take part in the energy transition and participate in EM transactions. One of the main reasons for the need of an active participation from consumers and prosumers is the current inaccuracies in the balance settlement,

This work has received funding from National Funds through FCT (Fundaçao da Ciencia e Tecnologia) under the project SPET – 29165, call SAICT 2017.

F. De La Prieta et al. (Eds.): PAAMS 2020 Workshops, CCIS 1233, pp. 302–313, 2020.
https://doi.org/10.1007/978-3-030-51999-5_25

as it happens in most European countries, since much of the load is profiled because the smart meters roll out is not completed yet [20]. While smart meters facilitate accurate and efficient balance settlement, the development of metering and control opportunities needs to be addressed carefully in regulatory rules. For example, the handling of imbalances caused by control actions made by non-balance responsible parties is one of these issues [24].

Information exchange structures and models to enable interaction between local, retail and wholesale EM are urgently needed, including effective proposals on how local markets should be taken into account by regulatory aspects. In this context, the use of simulation tools and the study of the different market mechanisms and the relationships among their stakeholders, becomes essential.

A local market can be seen as a place where individual consumers and prosumers meet to trade energy in a neighborhood environment [12]. A major goal for local EM is to contribute in a decentralized PES [25]. Distributed Energy Resources (DER) have increased the complexity of PES radically and therefore flexibility is emerging as the most crucial element in the system. Advantage of local markets is not only that self-generation can be consumed locally but it also strengthens local distribution networks and provides new opportunities for local industry and regional businesses.

The practical implementation and widespread of local EM is, however, highly dependent on the available physical structure. One of the main drivers in this scope is the development already achieved in Smart Grid (SG) technology. Sensor networks are one of the most suitable technologies for SG due to their low-cost, collaborative and longstanding nature. Wireless sensor Networks (WSNs) can enable both utilities and customers to transfer, monitor, predict, measure, and manage energy usage effectively. Thus, WSN can revolutionize the current electric power infrastructure by integrating information and communication technologies (ICT) [11,27]. Such a heavy dependence on ICT networking inevitably surrenders SG to potential vulnerabilities. Thus, security emerges as a critical issue because millions of heterogeneous devices (e.g., sensors, meters) are interconnected via communication networks.

Multi-Agent Systems (MAS) [28] are particularly well suited for the analysis of complex interactions in dynamic systems, such as energy market [10]. Some of the key advantages of MAS are the facilitated inclusion of new models, market mechanisms, and types of participants, as well as the ability to resolve problems in a distributed way [28]. Several modeling tools for simulating EM have emerged, such as AMES [16], EMCAS [14], ABEMS [8] and MASCEM [22].

In this paper we present a two layer approach to model the LEM. These layers are the MAS energy management system (SMARTERCtrol) that performs data collecting and optimized control of the grid resources, and the Local Energy Market Multi-Agent System (LEMMAS) that performs energy negotiating among local participants, provides energy forecasting and trust evaluation for the negotiations.

The remain of the paper is organized as follows. Section 2 describes the Local Energy Market; and presents the LEMMAS simulation model and its integration with the SMARTERCtrol systems. Section 3 details the LEMMAS services and their importance fore the system. Section 4 details the SMARTERCtrol for control and optimization. Section 5 presents the conclusions of this work.

2   Local Energy Market

The energy landscape is changing at a rapid rate, renewable energy sources created the opportunity for traditional consumers to become producers of part, or in some cases all, of their energy needs. However this increase in what is called Distributed Energy Resources (DER) can create large and unpredictable fluctuation of energy loads in the electric grid.

The Local Energy Market (LEM) [17] is an emergent market model that is aimed at solving the problems inherent to the Renewable and DER, such as unpredictability of energy generation. Participants in the LEM who are generating energy but not consuming it can chose to sell it in the LEM.

The key features of the LEM are the flexibility it provides in terms of creating distributed and efficient energy consumption, and the opportunity, created for traditional consumers, to participant in a kind of energy market. In this section, we present an overview of the LEMMAS simulation model and detail how it can benefit from the integration with the multi-agent optimization and control system (SMARTERCtrol).

In a previous work [19], the authors present a MAS model to simulate and study the LEM. This model is composed of three kinds of agents:

- Sensor agent: Representing the cyber-physical system;
- Participant agent: Representing participants in the negotiation;
- Market Interactions Manager (MIM): Representing the negotiation manager.

Participants in the LEM can be either consumers, producers or *prosumers* (consumers with some form of generation, e.g. an household with solar panels). Each participant is modeled accordingly to its role with the corresponding sensor agents representing its cyber-physical system.

In the LEMMAS simulation model the agents follow an hierarchical structure in their communication. The sensor agents only communicate with their respective participant agent, sending updated values for consumption, generation, battery charge, etc. The participant agents sends a proposal to the MIM. And the MIM acts as central authority in the negotiation: sends messages to all participants in other to enable the negotiation process. Each participant agent would have the necessary number of sensor agents to model its cyber-physical system.

Figure 1 illustrates the architecture proposed in this article. Two layers are evidenced in this architecture, the Local Market Layer and the Cyber-Physical Layer. These layers should have independent responsibilities but be complementary to each other. On the Cyber-Physical Layer each household or building is represented and supported by the SMARTERCtrol system. The SMARTER-Ctrol system is responsible for providing the services of Data Monitoring, in

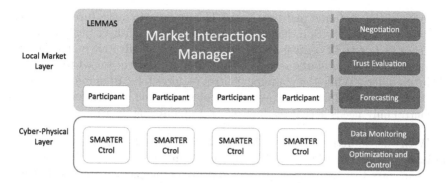

Fig. 1. Local Market two layer architecture

terms of consumption, generation, and other data sources like energy storage (if available); and the optimized control of energy resources. The Market Layer is represented by the LEMMAS system, composed of the group of Participants and the Market Interactions Manager. The LEMMAS provides the services of Negotiation, Trust Evaluation, and Forecasting.

The household or building is represented in both layers but in different ways, in the Local Market layer this representation is made by the participant agent that is able to submit proposals to buy or sell energy in the LEM. The proposals, as well as the forecasting service, are integrated with the SMARTERCtrol of each participant in order to make use of the current and historical data collected by the SMARTERCtrol. Lastly, the integration with the SMARTERCtrol system can also happen as a result of the negotiation. That is, after an energy transaction is agreed upon in the Local Market, this information must be sent to the SMARTERCtrol system of the participants involved in said transaction. With the obtained information the SMARTERCtrol system must perform the necessary optimization and control operations in order to allow the desired energy transaction.

The SMARTERCtrol system brings improvements to the LEM's performance, reliability and resilience, by performing two different kinds of control:

1. Scheduling control based on forecasted data: these forecasts are related to the microgrid devices (such as consumption schedules of home appliances, battery levels, etc.) or other forecasted information for generation (e.g. solar radiation, wind speed, etc.) to plan the use of the generated flexibility, based on the result of the MAS optimization. This type of control may handle uncertainties in forecasts. It can also adapt itself to possible changes in grid topology by applying receding horizon control along the time in which the planning activity is undertaken; for instance, in case control relies on forecasted information, initial planning can be done with great advance (e.g. the day ahead) and then refined when getting closer to real-time.
2. Real-time control: It is based on real-time information provided by sensors (e.g. power quality analysers, voltage sensors, etc.) to monitor the status of all

nodes of the grid on a real-time basis. The scope is to make sure grid parameters are always within statutory limits and cope with critical conditions. These two types of control are both required for an effective management of the smart-building, but the type of information that they need to fulfil their duties differs. While the planning control requires forecasted information and data about scheduled or expected use of smart grid technologies, real-time control only needs actual readings of grid monitoring devices.

With the addiction of the SMARTERCtrol system, the sensor agents are no longer used. The SMARTERCtrol acts as an aggregator of all sensor data that can pass this information to the corresponding participant agent, this is evidenced in Fig. 1.

In turn the participant agent sends information detailing the result of the negotiations in the LeM to the SMARTERCtrol. Thus allowing the SMARTERCtrol to make the necessary control adjustments and optimizations to enable the desired outcome. For example, a participant agent might agree to sell energy to another LEM participant. In this scenario the SMARTERCtrol system should adjust the necessary control flow to make that transaction happen.

3   LEMMAS Services

The Local Energy Market Multi-Agent System (LEMMAS) takes the responsibility of providing the platform necessary for the negotiation between the participants. However the negotiation needs to be supported with other functionalities. For this reason the LEMMAS provides two complementary services to the negotiation, then being forecasting, and trust evaluation.

3.1   Negotiation

The main service provided by the LEMMAS is the service of negotiation. The negotiation in LEMMAS is made in Mediated Contracts, that is, there is a third-party that plays the role of a mediator and manages the negotiation. These Mediated Contracts follow a Double Sided Auction model that defines the Market Clearing price, and is performed regular intervals in order to keep up with the market needs.

In the LEMMAS this mediator is the Market Interactions Manager (MIM) agent. When performing the negotiation, this agent also takes advantage of the Trust Evaluation service in order to only allow trusted participants in the negotiation.

3.2   Forecasting

The forecasting service provided by the LEMMAS is used internally by the Trust Evaluation Service and by the SMARTERCtrol system as well. The forecasting module includes several methods and a set of strategies for day-ahead and hour-ahead forecasting. Indeed, one of the most important targets of the energy operators is to be able to have a better control on the energy consumption and also being prepared for the amount of energy demand in the following hours or days. In order to provide consumption and generation forecasting for different short and long terms, this service should make use of various forecasting methods: Artificial Neural Networks [5], Support Vector Machines [26], Fuzzy Rule Based Systems [13], Reinforcement Learning [2], Time Series Analysis [6] and Ensemble Methods [23]. Ensemble Methods, in particular, have already shown a good performance in a precious work [23].

3.3   Trust Evaluation

In any kind of negotiation trust is a crucial factor. Negotiating with an non trusted party may jeopardize the negotiation. The Trust Evaluation service provides an important security layer for the participants. The idea for the trust mechanism, dynamic profiles of each participant are defined, based on previous market negotiations and using the forecasting service. These profiles are then used according to the context, current weather conditions, time, date, etc., to support the analysis of the feasibility of submitted proposals. LEMMAS follows what is called an Institutional Trust model [18], that means there exists a centralized entity responsible for applying the trust model. In the case of LEMMAS this role is played by the MIM agent that acts as the centralized institution, and enforces the Trust model [1].

4   Multi-agent Optimization and Control

This section presents a multi-agent optimization and control system (SMARTERCtrol) for microgrids. Taking into account the constraints, limitations and user preferences, its goal is to perform an optimized management of the self-controlled resources of a microgrid. Furthermore, this system is connected to the forecasting service described previous Sect. 3.2. This way SMARTERCtrol enriches the quality of decisions by also considering some consumption/generation forecasts in the decision making.

SMARTERCtrol is composed by two main modules, the optimization module and the control one. Each of them counts with a different multi-agent system model and deploys their own agents which are continuously communicating to coordinate:

- **Control** module: agents are in charge of controlling the existing devices. This module deploys one agent(*Control Device*) per device of the microgrid plus a central coordinator one (*Control Node*). Their main tasks are collecting the forecasts or actual observations, communicate with the optimization module and get the optimized schedules, and convert the optimized schedules received from the optimization module into orders that are then sent to the self controlled devices. It makes sure that the devices follow such schedules. Note that in case of real time control, schedules would have just one instant period of time (no planning needed).

– **Optimization**: optimization agents collaborate to implement a distributed optimization algorithm based on message passing [15]. Relying on the information (forecasts, observations, etc.) provided by the control module, this module computes the best schedules and sends them to it. Two kind of agents are used in this module, *Optimization Node* and *Optimization Device*. The number of agents deployed will depend on the microgrid scenario.

Figure 2 shows a schema of both modules as well as the main interactions among their agents. The concrete algorithms that each module follows are described below.

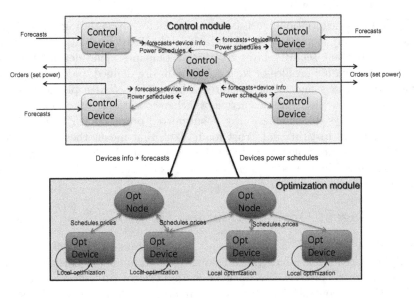

Fig. 2. SMARTERCtrol optimization and control modules, interactions

4.1 Control Module Algorithm

This module connects the platform with the external microgrid. As Algorithm 1 shows, this module runs a continuous loop in which every T time the same steps from 2 to 12 are repeated. T is set a priori according to user preferences and microgrid definition. Algorithm 1 also shows the interactions between agents and modules, where "$A -> B$" means that A sends the message msg to B.

4.2 Optimization Module

Implemented with an agent oriented architecture already described in [9], this module performs the optimization task. It is based on the message passing algorithm adapted to energy management, and proposed by [15]. Such approach

---

Algorithm 1. Control module algorithm

1: **for** every T time **do**
2:    [Control] Node agent $->$ [Control] Device agents
       msg: *initial time stamp* (number)
       Real Devices $->$ [Control] Device agents
       msg: *device properties & constraints* (object)
       Forecast service $->$ [Control] Device agents
       msg: *forecasts* (when applicable) (data set)
3:    [Control] Device agents:
       action: Compose device model from info received
4:    [Control] Device agents $->$ [Control] Node agent
       msg: *device model* (object)
5:    [Control] Node agent
       action: Compose scenario model (object)
6:    [Control] Node agent $->$ [Optimization Module]
       msg: *scenario model* (object)
7:    [Optimization Module]
       action: runs distributed optimization
8:    [Optimization Module] $->$ [Control] Node agent
       msg: *devices power schedules* (object)
9:    [Control] Node agent $->$ [Control] Device agents
       msg: *new time stamp, Power Schedule* (number, vector of real numbers)
10:   [Control] Device agents $->$ **Real Devices**
       msg: *power setup for instant t* (real number)
11:   [Control] Node agent $->$ [Control] Device agents
       msg: *new time stamp* (variable)
       msg: *power schedule* (vector of real numbers)
12:   [Control] Device agents $->$ **Real Devices**
       msg: *power setup for current time instant t* (real number)
13: **end for**

---

relies on the alternating direction method of multipliers (ADMM), which is an algorithm that solves convex optimization problems by breaking them into smaller pieces so that they will be then easier to handle [3]. [15]'s model considers two types of elements in a given grid, namely: the *devices* and the *nets* (called *optimization devices* and *optimization nodes* respectively in our approach). The devices D (i.e. generators, fixed loads, deferrable loads, alternate direct current transmission lines, storages, etc.) have their own constraints and objectives. Devices are connected to each other by means of a net (i.e. bus), which also has its own objectives. In the same way, nets are connected through double terminal devices, such as transmission lines. The model tries to minimize the global network objective subject to the device and net constraints, over a given time horizon.

[15] use a proximal message passing algorithm to resolve this optimization problem. It is an iterative algorithm where at each step, each device: (i) exchanges simple messages with its neighbours in the network; and then (ii) it solves its own optimization problem by minimising a local objective function,

augmented by the messages it has received. The authors showed that their approach converges to a solution when the devices objective and constraints are
convex. The method is completely decentralized and needs no global coordination other than synchronizing iterations; the problems to be solved by each
device can be typically solved efficiently and in parallel according to the authors.

In this work, we considered evolutionary optimization algorithms [29] to solve
such local optimization. The using of this kind of algorithms is recurrent in literature since they are proved to be good approaches to solve microgrid problems [21]. For instance, their flexibility allows to handle the most hard constraints
in the optimization process. Moreover, their operators can be easily modified to
improve the algorithm performance in the specific problem to solve.

4.3 Systems Connection

Lastly the two systems, LEMMAS and SMARTERCtrol, are connected at the
Forecasting level. The Control nodes in SMARTERCtrol make use of the Forecasting values obtained from LEMMAS' Forecasting Module, as shown in Fig. 3.
This architecture brings advantages at the level of separation of concerns into:
Simulation, Control and Optimization. The two domains can be developed separately, but have the advantage of working together, taking advantages of each
others strengths. The SMARTERCtrol taking Control of real devices gains access
to a Simulation environment that uses the Real-time monitoring data with strategies optimized for the context, and provides SMARTERCtrol with the forecasts
necessary.

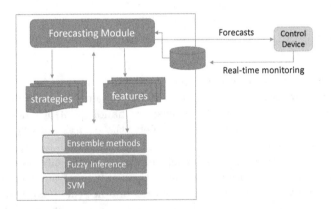

Fig. 3. Forecasting-Module with SMARTERCtrol

5 Conclusion

As it was discussed in this article energy markets are going through a shift of
paradigm, from centralized production to distributed production of energy. This

changes bring benefits in terms of flexibility, for consumers who can afford sell generation, as well as possible benefits to the environment with the increased use of renewable energy sources. However this benefits come with some negative aspects: the increase of distributed production makes the energy grid more complex and hard to manage. The ever increasing usage of renewable energy sources, e.g. solar, creates unpredictable energy fluctuation, and the moments of higher production do not always correspond with the moments of higher consumption needs. Fore these reasons, having systems capable of simulating and controlling the energy grids will always be needed.

In this article we proposed a two tier architecture to simulate and control the Local Energy Market (LEM). The two layers in this architecture are the Local Market Layer and the Cyber-Physical Layer. Such separation of concerns brings benefits in terns of development by dividing systems in smaller more specialized components, but the system remain tightly integrated as a full stack solution for LEM simulation and control. This was possible due to the usage of services in each layer that can integrate with services from the other layer whenever necessary.

The Cyber-Physical Layer corresponds to the SMARTERCtrol system, representing a single household or building. The SMARTERCtrol system provides the services of Data Monitoring in terms of consumption, generation, and other data sources (if available); and for the optimized energy control.

The Market Layer corresponds to the LEMMAS system. It represents the LEM as a whole with several participants, each one connected with its own SMARTERCtrol system and Market Interactions Manager agent, acting as the central authority of these market. The LEMMAS system provides the services of Negotiation, Trust Evaluation, and Forecasting.

The integration between the two layers is as follows. The Negotiation service gives each participant the opportunity to make proposals to buy or sell energy in the market. Such proposals are made taking into consideration the participant needs reported by the Data Monitoring service. The Negotiation service uses the Trust Evaluation service to verify which participants should be allowed in to participant in the market. The Trust Evaluation takes into consideration the values forecasted by the Forecasting service considering data from the Data Monitoring service.

Lastly, the Negotiation service communicates its results to the Optimization and control service so that this service can make the necessary changes in the grind to make the energy transactions agreed in the Local Market.

With this new approach the LEMMAS sensor agents are replaced by the SMARTERCtrol. The benefits of this new approach are twofold. First, the SMARTERCtrol system acts a central point that aggregates the data from all sensor readings and makes it available for other services. And second, the SMARTERCtrol system can perform the necessary control and optimization operations to realize the energy transactions agreed the local energy Market negotiation process.

References

1. Andrade, R., Pinto, T., Praça, I.: A Multi-Agent System Simulation Model for Trusted Local Energy Markets (2019)
2. Andrade, R., Pinto, T., Praça, I., Vale, Z.: UCB1 based reinforcement learning model for adaptive energy management in buildings. In: Rodríguez, S., et al. (eds.) DCAI 2018. AISC, vol. 801, pp. 3–11. Springer, Cham (2019). https://doi.org/10.1007/978-3-319-99608-0_1
3. Boyd, S., Parikh, N., Chu, E., Peleato, B., Eckstein, J.: Distributed optimization and statistical learning via the alternating direction method of multipliers. Found. Trends Mach. Learn. **3**(1), 1–122 (2011)
4. European Commission: Horizon 2020 Work Programme 2018–2020. Secure, clean and efficient energy, vol. 2020 (2018). http://ec.europa.eu/research/participants/data/ref/h2020/wp/2018-2020/main/h2020-wp1820-energy_en.pdf
5. Deb, C., Eang, L.S., Yang, J., Santamouris, M.: Forecasting diurnal cooling energy load for institutional buildings using artificial neural networks. Energy Build. **121**, 284–297 (2016)
6. Ediger, V.Ş., Akar, S.: Arima forecasting of primary energy demand by fuel in turkey. Energy Policy **35**(3), 1701–1708 (2007)
7. European Comission: Regulation on the internal market for electricity 0379(2016) (2016). https://ec.europa.eu/energy/sites/ener/files/documents/1_en_act_part1_v9.pdf
8. Garcia-Rodriguez, S., Gomez-Sanz, J.J.: Robust decentralised agent based approach for microgrid energy management. In: Proceedings of the 18th International Conference on Autonomous Agents and MultiAgent Systems, pp. 772–780. International Foundation for Autonomous Agents and Multiagent Systems (2019)
9. Garcia-Rodriguez, S., Sleiman, H.A., Nguyen, V.-Q.-A.: A multi-agent system architecture for microgrid management. Trends in Practical Applications of Scalable Multi-Agent Systems, the PAAMS Collection. AISC, vol. 473, pp. 55–67. Springer, Cham (2016). https://doi.org/10.1007/978-3-319-40159-1_5
10. Gomez-Sanz, J.J., Garcia-Rodriguez, S., Cuartero-Soler, N., Hernandez-Callejo, L.: Reviewing microgrids from a multi-agent systems perspective. Energies **7**(5), 3355–3382 (2014)
11. Grilo, A., et al.: A wireless sensors suite for smart grid applications. In: 1st International Workshop on Information Technology for Energy Applications (2012)
12. Ilic, D., Da Silva, P.G., Karnouskos, S., Griesemer, M.: An energy market for trading electricity in smart grid neighbourhoods. In: 2012 6th IEEE International Conference on Digital Ecosystems and Technologies (DEST), pp. 1–6. IEEE (2012)
13. Jozi, A., Pinto, T., Praça, I., Silva, F., Teixeira, B., Vale, Z.: Energy consumption forecasting based on hybrid neural fuzzy inference system. In: 2016 IEEE Symposium Series on Computational Intelligence (SSCI), pp. 1–5 (2016). https://doi.org/10.1109/SSCI.2016.7849859
14. Koritarov, V.S.: Real-world market representation with agents. IEEE Power Energy Mag. **2**(4), 39–46 (2004)
15. Kraning, M., Chu, E., Lavaei, J., Boyd, S.: Dynamic network energy management via proximal message passing. Found. Trends Optim. **1**(2), 73–126 (2014)
16. Li, H., Tesfatsion, L.: Development of Open Source Software for Power Market Research: The AMES Test Bed. Iowa State University, Department of Economics, Staff General Research Papers 2 (2009)

17. Mengelkamp, E., Diesing, J., Weinhardt, C.: Tracing local energy markets: a literature review. IT-Inf. Technol. **61**(2–3), 101–110 (2019)

18. Pinyol, I., Sabater-Mir, J.: Computational trust and reputation models for open multi-agent systems: a review. Artif. Intell. Rev. **40**(1), 1–25 (2013)

19. Praça, I., Ramos, S., Andrade, R., d. Silva, A.S., Sica, E.T.: Analysis and simulation of local energy markets. In: 2019 16th International Conference on the European Energy Market (EEM), pp. 1–5 (2019). https://doi.org/10.1109/EEM. 2019.8916524

20. Ramos, S., Duarte, J.M., Duarte, F.J., Vale, Z.: A data-mining-based methodology to support mv electricity customers characterization. Energy Build. **91**, 16–25 (2015)

21. Sanseverino, E.R., Di Silvestre, M.L., Ippolito, M.G., De Paola, A., Re, G.L.: An execution, monitoring and replanning approach for optimal energy management in microgrids. Energy **36**(5), 3429–3436 (2011)

22. Santos, G., Pinto, T., Praça, I., Vale, Z.: MASCEM: optimizing the performance of a multi-agent system. Energy **111**, 513–524 (2016). https://doi.org/10.1016/j. energy.2016.05.127

23. Silva, J., Praça, I., Pinto, T., Vale, Z.: Energy consumption forecasting using ensemble learning algorithms. In: Herrera-Viedma, E., Vale, Z., Nielsen, P., Martin Del Rey, A., Casado Vara, R. (eds.) DCAI 2019. AISC, vol. 1004, pp. 5–13. Springer, Cham (2020). https://doi.org/10.1007/978-3-030-23946-6_1

24. Smart Grid Task Force: Regulatory Recommendations for the Deployment of Flexibility - EG3 REPORT. Policy Report by Smart Grid Task Force, European Commission pp. 1–94, January 2015. https://ec.europa.eu/energy/sites/ener/files/ documents/EG3Final-January2015.pdf

25. Van Der Schoor, T., Scholtens, B.: Power to the people: local community initiatives and the transition to sustainable energy. Renew. Sustain. Energy Rev. **43**, 666–675 (2015)

26. Vinagre, E., Pinto, T., Ramos, S., Vale, Z., Corchado, J.M.: Electrical energy consumption forecast using support vector machines. In: 2016 27th International Workshop on Database and Expert Systems Applications (DEXA), pp. 171–175. IEEE (2016)

27. Wang, W., Lu, Z.: Cyber security in the smart grid: survey and challenges. Comput. Netw. **57**(5), 1344–1371 (2013)

28. Wooldridge, M.: An Introduction to Multiagent Systems. John Wiley, Hoboken (2009)

29. Zhang, J., et al.: Evolutionary computation meets machine learning: a survey. IEEE Comput. Intell. Mag. **6**(4), 68–75 (2011)

Controlled Self-organization for Steering Local Multi-objective Optimization in Virtual Power Plants

Jörg Bremer$^{(\boxtimes)}$ and Sebastian Lehnhoff

University of Oldenburge, 26129 Oldenburg, Germany
{joerg.bremer,sebastian.lehnhoff}@uni-oldenburg.de

Abstract. The future smart grid has to be operated by rather small and hardly flexible energy resources. Such duty comprises different planning tasks. Virtual power plants powered by multi-agent control are seen as a promising aggregation scheme for coping with problem size and for gaining flexibility for distributed load planning. If agents are allowed to freely include local preferences into decision making the overall solution quality deteriorates significantly if no control mechanism is installed. We scrutinized this deterioration and propose an approach based on controlled self-organization to achieve an overall maximization of integrated local preferences while at the same time preserving global solution quality for grid control as much as possible. Some first results prove the applicability of the general approach. Further research directions and questions for future work are derived from these first results.

Keywords: Controlled self-organization · Smart grid · Decentralized multi-objective optimization

1 Introduction

The structure of the energy supply within the power grid is constantly changing. The future smart grid will basically consist of small, volatile and hardly controllable renewable decentralized energy resources (DER). In the long run, these small generation units will have to assume responsibility for all daily grid operation tasks and ancillary services. This can only be achieved when units pool together (most likely with controllable load and batteries) to gain flexibility and potential.

Virtual power plants (VPP) are a well-known instrument for aggregating and controlling DER [2]. A VPP comprises individually operated DER loosely coupled by some communication means and jointly orchestrated by some (decentralized) control algorithm [6]. Integration into current market structures recently also led to VPP systems that frequently re-configure themselves for a market and product specific alignment [27]. In general, VPP concepts for several purposes (commercial as well as technical) have already been developed. A use case

© Springer Nature Switzerland AG 2020
F. De La Prieta et al. (Eds.): PAAMS 2020 Workshops, CCIS 1233, pp. 314–325, 2020.
https://doi.org/10.1007/978-3-030-51999-5_26

commonly emerging within VPP control is the need for scheduling the participating DER. Independently of the specific objective at hand, a schedule (course of energy generation) for each DER has to be found such that the schedule that finally is assigned to a DER is operable without violating any technical constraint [7]. For this paper we go with the example of scheduling for active power planning in day-ahead scenarios (not necessarily 24 h but for some given future time horizon). For large scale problems, distributed (usually agent based) approaches are currently discussed not least due to further advantages like ensured privacy issues. Some recent implementations are [13,16,32]. Distributed organization and self-organized control is also especially a characteristic of dynamic virtual power plants (DVPP) [27].

Some types of VPP specialize in predictive scheduling as operational service [26]. The goal of predictive scheduling is to select a schedule for each energy unit – with respect to a given search space of feasible schedules with respect to a future planning horizon – such that a global objective function (e. g. a target power profile for the VPP) is optimized. This target profile may be a schedule that is assigned to a VPP as a result of some trading action on an energy market. We consider this target schedule as already given for the rest of this contribution.

For solving this problem in a decentralized way, agent-based solutions have been developed. One approach based on a gossiping type of algorithm is given by COHDA – the combinatorial optimization heuristic for decentralized agents [3,15].

The key concept of COHDA is an asynchronous iterative approximate best-response behavior, where each agent – representing a decentralized energy unit – reacts to updated information from other agents by adapting its own selected schedule with respect to local and global objectives. Different objectives are handled by scalarization into a single objective as weighted sum of objectives. As the global (main) goal is achieving a consensus on operation modes such that the market given energy schedule is delivered as agreed on (small deviations are acceptable), attention has to be paid to the result quality of this specific objective. In order to ensure a minimum solution quality for the main goal, control of the weighting of local objectives is needed.

From the perspective of individually operated decentralized energy resources it is desirable to maximize the weight of local preferences. As different participants in the VPP have different characteristics in their flexibilities and thus have different importance in achieving the main goal, individual maximum weight are possible for different participants. On the other hand, the maximum local weights should be assigned in a fair way, at least in the long run.

We propose to use the concept of controlled self-organization to steer the individual use of local preferences based on the current composition (individual flexibilities based on current operational state of different energy units) of the VPP and formulate the optimization problem that has to be solved for finding a set of best local weights.

The rest of the paper is organized as follows. We start with a recap of decentralized algorithms for the scrutinized problem and controlled self-organization in general. We derive an architecture for controlling the local weights and present a first solution for the emerging optimization problem based on evolution strategies. Some results from a simulation study conclude the paper.

2 Related Work

In order to cope with the growing load planning and control complexity in the future smart grid, agent-based and self-organization approaches for problem solving are most promising [36]. Examples can already be found in [1,9,10,30,32]. As a use case for this paper we use the example of decentralized predictive scheduling [15].

The task of predictive scheduling is to plan energy production (e. g. for the next day) of a group of generators. In the future smart grid instead a large group of small distributed energy resources will have to be planned for appropriate dispatch instead – probably pooled together with controllable load and batteries for higher flexibility. Such group is commonly referred to as virtual power plant. In many scenarios such a group trades its flexibility on some energy market and is assigned a schedule from market that has to be operated. The target schedule usually comprises 96 time intervals of 15 min each with a given amount of energy (or equivalently mean active power) for each time interval, but might also be constituted for a shorter time frame by a given energy product that the VPP has to deliver. A schedule in this context is a real valued vector x with each element x_i denoting the respective amount of energy generated or consumed during the i-th time interval. It is the goal of the predictive scheduling to find then exactly one schedule for each energy unit such that

1. each schedule that is assigned to a specific energy resource can be operated by the respective energy unit without violating any hard technical constraint, and
2. the difference between the sum of all targets and a desired given market schedule is minimized.

A basic formulation of the scheduling problem is given by

$$\delta\left(\sum_{i=1}^{m} x_i, \zeta\right) \to \min; \text{ s.t. } x_i \in \mathcal{F}_i \; \forall U_i \in \mathcal{U}. \tag{1}$$

In Eq. (1) δ denotes an (in general) arbitrary distance measure for evaluating the difference between the aggregated schedule of the group and the desired target schedule ζ. [14] for example uses the Manhattan distance; in [4] also measures like excess supply minimization [11] have for example been integrated and tested. Throughout this paper, we will use the Euclidean distance $|\cdot|_2$.

$\mathcal{F}_i$ denotes the feasible region of energy unit U_i. Feasibility of solution can be assured by using a decoder as constraint-handling technique. Such a decoder learns the individual set of feasible schedules of an energy unit and repairs infeasible solutions during optimization [8].

For solving this optimization tasks the fully decentralized combinatorial optimization heuristics for distributed agents (COHDA) has been developed [13,15,27]. An agent in COHDA does not represent a complete solution as it is the case for instance in population-based approaches. Each agent represents a class within a multiple choice knapsack combinatorial problem [20]. Applied to predictive scheduling, each class refers to the feasible region in the solution space of the respective energy unit. Each agent chooses schedules as solution candidate only from the set of feasible schedules that belongs to the DER controlled by this agent. Each agent is connected with a rather small subset of other agents from the multi-agent system and may only communicate with agents from this limited neighborhood. The neighborhood (communication network) is defined by a small world graph [35]. As long as this graph is at least simply connected, each agent collects information from the direct neighborhood and as each received message also contains (not necessarily up-to-date) information from the transitive neighborhood, each agent may accumulate information about the choices of other agents and thus gains his own local belief of the aggregated schedule that the other agents are going to operate. With this belief each agent may choose a schedule for the own controlled energy unit in a way that the coalition is put forward best while at the same time own constraints are obeyed and own interests are pursued; what in turn – if not controlled – may lead to worse main goal quality.

A broadly used model for implementing intelligent agents has been developed by the Rational Agent Project at the Stanford Research Institute (https://www.sri.com/). In this architecture, each agent possesses beliefs about his environment, has a desired goal and access to a database with plans to achieve the goal. Due to the interplay of these beliefs, desires and intentions the architecture is known as BDI architecture.

Without a concrete database with plans, sometimes self-organization is the goal within multi-agent systems. Organic computing systems are highly dynamic and bundle a huge number of changing components; not necessarily agents [23]. Orchestration is not induced from the outside or by central control, but arises as emergent behavior [22]. This trait results in self-configuring, -adapting, and -healing and autonomous systems. Consequently, traditional tools and methods for design and analysis do no longer apply to such systems [34]. In order to introduce the advantages of classical closed loop control systems into the control of emergent systems, a specific observer/ controller architecture has been developed [33]. In this architecture the actual system is under observation of one or more observer components. These observers scrutinize and evaluate emergent behavior patterns inside the controlled system, aggregate information, and report to a controller component that decides based on user allowances and machine learning analysis of report history. In this way, a controlled self-organization is achieved by embedding the actual system into a control loop [25,28].

Examples for implemented controlled self-organization for computer-based applications are given in [19,29], but can also be found in chemistry [18] or quantum physics [31].

We want to use the concept of controlled self-organization to induce a control entity into the multi-agent systems that may observe and keep track of the impact of local optimization preferences and is capable to intervene by providing a vector for individually max values for the weights that the agents may use.

3 Controlling Local Objectives

Optimization problems with different (opposing) objectives constitute a multi-objective problem. In this case, optimality has to be defined by Pareto optimality; i.e. improvement on one objective cannot be achieved without deterioration on the other [24].

Thus, is seems immediately clear that in the case of predictive scheduling the solution quality for the main goal (objective of resembling the market schedule as close as possible) deteriorates if the agents give a too strong weighting to the local objectives (their local preferences).

We created a simulation of different co-generation plants [21] and a multi-agent system with one agent associated to each co-generation plant. The agents capable of using the COHDA algorithm to conduct load planning in a decentralized way. Differing from the original algorithm the agents were allowed to use a weighted sum of two objectives for evaluating the solutions. One objective was for the global goal of achieving a close as possible resemblance of the sum of schedules to the wanted market schedule. The second objective allowed integrating local preferences. We use the example of maximizing the remaining flexibility of the energy unit for trading at the market later. For this purpose we defined

$$E_{\mathcal{S}_d}(\boldsymbol{x}) = \frac{(0.5(\vartheta_{min} + \vartheta_{max}) - \vartheta_d)^2}{(\vartheta_{max} - \vartheta_{min})^2}. \tag{2}$$

$E_{\mathcal{S}_d}$ denotes the state of charge (SoC) error of the buffer store after operating d intervals of the schedule by taking into account the squared deviation of the resulting buffer temperature ϑ_d from the mean of the allowed temperature range $[\vartheta_{min}, \vartheta_{max}]$. In this way the remaining flexibility (to trade on some future market) for the controlled co-generation plant is maximized [5]. To this end, COHDA in the multi-agent system was equipped with an aggregated objective

$$w_j \cdot E_{\mathcal{S}_d}(\boldsymbol{x}_j) + (1 - w_j) \cdot \delta \left(\sum_{i=0}^{n} \boldsymbol{x}_i, \zeta \right) \to \min \tag{3}$$

for optimizing the global objective of minimizing the deviation of the sum of all schedules $\sum_{i=0}^{n} \boldsymbol{x}_i$ (from agents 1 to n) from the desired market schedule ζ and the local goal of minimizing the deviation from the local mean buffer charge $E_{\mathcal{S}_d}$ at the same time. Each agent a_j may individually set the weight w_j for the own local objective individually.

First we tested the impact of different weights on the achieved resemblance to the market schedule. The mean absolute percentage error measure (MAPE) was

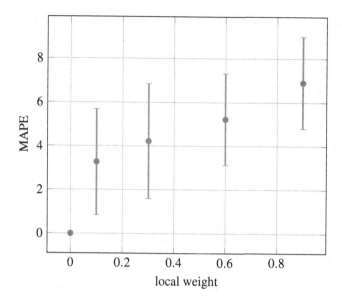

Fig. 1. Deterioration of the primary goal with varying (but identical for all agents) weights for the local (private) objective.

Table 1. Mean and best results for randomly sampled weights (different for all agents) for different normal distributions of w.

$\mathcal{N}(\mu, \sigma)$	Mean		Min.
(0.3,0.15)	7.246	1.738	6.378×10^{-8}
(0.6,0.3)	3.805	0.922	7.973×10^{-3}

used in order to guarantee comparability between different scenarios. Figure 1 shows the result for a scenario with 10 co-generation plants and the same weight for all agents.

As expected the achieved main goal deteriorates if agents are allowed to concurrently include local (opposing) objectives. With a growing weight the result gets worse for the main goal. On the other hand, we scrutinized different weights and consider that different agents with different co-generation plants have different importance for the result within the group. Table 1 shows the result for two different spreads of the weights within the group. We tested 1000 different random combinations of weights for each group. As can be seen (by the growing standard deviation and the minimum results), there are combinations of weights that still result in good primary goal results. Thus, we can conclude that there is potential for finding good combinations of weights by an optimization approach.

To achieve this, we propose the architecture depicted in Fig. 2. Following the approach of controlled self-organization, a control entity will be responsible to interfere the self-organization process if agents choose local weights that lead to deteriorated results when trying to achieve the global goal of jointly operating a generation schedule that has been agreed on at some market. if the result quality falls below some given threshold, the weights are adjusted. In our case, we chose a mean absolute percentage error of 1%, meaning a mean deviation of 1% from the agreed energy delivery.

4   Results

For our evaluation, we use the famous co-variance matrix adaption evolution strategy (CMA-ES). CMA-ES is a well-known evolution strategy for solving black box problems and aims at learning lessons from previous successful evolution steps. New solution candidates are sampled from a multi variate normal distribution $\mathcal{N}(0, C)$ with covariance matrix C which is adapted in a way that maximizes the occurrence of improving steps according to previously seen distributions for good steps. Sampling is weighted by a selection of solutions of the parent generation. In a way, a second order model of the objective function is exploited for structure information. A comprehensive introduction can for example be found in [12]. CMA-ES has a set of parameters that can be tweaked to some degree for a problem specific adaption. Nevertheless, default values applicable for a wide range of problems are available. We have chosen to set these values after [12] for our experiments.

For optimizing the weight vector w we defined the following objective:

$$v \cdot \frac{|w| - \sum_{i=1\ldots|w|} w_i}{|w|} + (1 - v) \cdot \overline{c(w)} + p(w) \to \min \qquad (4)$$

with

$$p(w) = \sum \begin{cases} w_i^2, \ w_i < 0 \\ (w_i - 1)^2, \ w_i > 1 \\ 0, \ 0 \le w_i \le 1 \end{cases} \qquad (5)$$

and $c(w)$ denoting the mean error of COHDA simulations runs conducted with weight vector w measured in MAPE. Function $p(w)$ introduces a penalty for weight values not in $[0, 1]$. In our simulation we set the weight v that balances minimization of 1-weight (thus maximizing the local weights) and minimization of the load scheduling error resulting from the weights to $v = 0.5$.

We used the simulation and multi-agent system presented in Sect. 3 and the architecture from Fig. 2. The control entity has access to the agents to set individual weights for the agents via a control interface. A COHDA optimization run can be started by the control entity. The multi-agent system then conducts COHDA autonomously, but the result again can be observed by the control entity (by subscribing to an observer interface).

Overall, the following control loop is established. The controller conducts CMA-ES with the objective of finding a good weight vector w. During each iteration CMA-ES samples new candidates of w. These candidates are evaluated

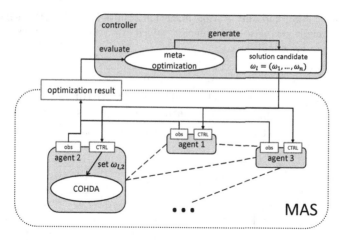

Fig. 2. Architecture for adjusting local weights in controlled self-organized global/local multi-objective energy scheduling.

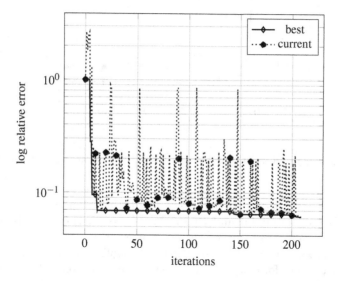

Fig. 3. Example convergence profile for a scenario with 5 co-generation plants.

by sending the respective weight values to the respective agents and starting COHDA. The result schedules of COHDA are collected, summed up and compared with the market schedule ζ (this is repeated 5 times for each candidate w). The mean error from COHDA serves for evaluating the candidate weights w. In this way, good combinations of weights can be found for individually steering the weighting of local preferences in the self-organizing load planning process of the agents.

Figure 3 shows the convergence behavior of a first result for a scenario with 5 co-generation plants. Figure 3 shows another example with 10 units. Please note

Table 2. Mean, min., and and best optimization results (mean MAPE achieved with the resulting weight vector w) for different values of ϵ (threshold for result improvements as termination condition).

ϵ	Mean		Min	Max
0.1	1.7311	1.0840	0.0043	3.6410
0.01	1.3607	1.1656	0.0029	3.5628
0.001	0.9803	0.8854	0.00079	2.9657

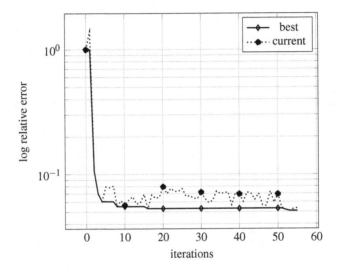

Fig. 4. Example convergence profile for a scenario with 10 co-generation plants.

that the primary axis denotes iterations. In each iteration a population of size 8 (for the 5 units scenario) and 10 for the large scenario has to be evaluated respectively. Nevertheless, convergence is promising.

Table 2 shows some statistics on the result quality for the 10 units scenario for different ϵ-values for convergence checks (mean improvement of two succeeding iterations). A moderate ϵ seems to be sufficient to push the quality of the main goal back below 1%, what is rather small compared with forecast error e. g. in photovoltaics production as a prerequisite for the initial market trading [17]. Overall, the results are promising enough to justify further research and improvements (Fig. 4).

5   Conclusion

Integrating local intentions and preferences into distributed scheduling as local objectives inevitably deteriorates the global solution quality of the primary goal. Examples were given using the predictive scheduling use case in the smart grid domain. We demonstrated that depending on the current situation this deterioration can be mitigated by an appropriate distribution of weights for local objectives. This task constitutes a meta-optimization problem that can be solved by an architecture for controlled self-organization that is introduced into the multi-agent system responsible for planning. First results are promising. Nevertheless, for a quick reaction of the proposed system further research regarding better performance and convergence behavior of the used meta-optimization algorithm are necessary.

References

1. Awad, A., German, R.: Self-organizing smart grid services. In: 2012 Sixth International Conference on Next Generation Mobile Applications, Services and Technologies, pp. 205–210. IEEE (2012)
2. Awerbuch, S., Preston, A.M. (eds.): The Virtual Utility: Accounting, Technology & Competitive Aspects of the Emerging Industry, Topics in Regulatory Economics and Policy, vol. 26. Kluwer Academic Publishers, Berlin (1997)
3. Boyd, S.P., Ghosh, A., Prabhakar, B., Shah, D.: Gossip algorithms: design, analysis and applications. In: Proceedings IEEE 24th Annual Joint Conference of the IEEE Computer and Communications Societies, vol. 3, pp. 1653–1664 (2005)
4. Bremer, J., Rapp, B., Jellinghaus, F., Sonnenschein, M.: Tools for teaching demand-side management. In: Wohlgemuth, V., Page, B., Voigt, K. (eds.) Environmental Informatics and Industrial Environmental Protection - 23rd International Conference on Informatics for Environmental Protection, EnviroInfo2009, pp. 455–463 (2009)
5. Bremer, J.: Constraint-Handling mit Supportvektor-Dekodern in der verteilten Optimierung. Ph.D. thesis (2015). http://oops.uni-oldenburg.de/2336/
6. Bremer, J., Lehnhoff, S.: A decentralized PSO with decoder for scheduling distributed electricity generation. In: Squillero, G., Burelli, P. (eds.) EvoApplications 2016. LNCS, vol. 9597, pp. 427–442. Springer, Cham (2016). https://doi.org/10.1007/978-3-319-31204-0_28
7. Bremer, J., Rapp, B., Sonnenschein, M.: Encoding distributed search spaces for virtual power plants. In: IEEE Symposium Series on Computational Intelligence 2011 (SSCI 2011), Paris, France, April 2011
8. Bremer, J., Sonnenschein, M.: Constraint-handling for optimization with support vector surrogate models - a novel decoder approach. In: Filipe, J., Fred, A.L.N. (eds.) Proceedings of the 5th International Conference on Agents and Artificial Intelligence (ICAART 2013), 15–18 February 2013, Barcelona, Spain, vol. 2, pp. 91–100. SciTePress (2013)
9. Coll-Mayor, D., Picos, R., Garciá-Moreno, E.: State of the art of the virtual utility: the smart distributed generation network. Int. J. Energy Res. 28(1), 65–80 (2004)
10. Wedde, H.F., Lehnhoff, S., Rehtanz, C., Krause, O.: Intelligent agents under collaborative control in emerging power systems. Int. J. Eng. Sci. Technol. 2, 45–59 (2010)
11. Futia, C.A.: Excess supply equilibria. J. Econ. Theory 14(1), 200–220 (1977)
12. Hansen, N.: The CMA evolution strategy: a tutorial. Technical report (2011). www.lri.fr/~hansen/cmatutorial.pdf

13. Hinrichs, C., Bremer, J., Sonnenschein, M.: Distributed hybrid constraint handling in large scale virtual power plants. In: IEEE PES Conference on Innovative Smart Grid Technologies Europe (ISGT Europe 2013). IEEE Power & Energy Society (2013)
14. Hinrichs, C., Lehnhoff, S., Sonnenschein, M.: A decentralized heuristic for multiple-choice combinatorial optimization problems. In: Helber, S., et al. (eds.) Operations Research Proceedings 2012. ORP, pp. 297–302. Springer, Cham (2014). https://doi.org/10.1007/978-3-319-00795-3_43
15. Hinrichs, C., Sonnenschein, M.: A distributed combinatorial optimisation heuristic for the scheduling of energy resources represented by self-interested agents. Int. J. Bio-Inspired Comput. **10**, 69 (2017)
16. Kamphuis, R., Warmer, C., Hommelberg, M., Kok, K.: Massive coordination of dispersed generation using powermatcher based software agents. In: 19th International Conference on Electricity Distribution, May 2007
17. Kramer, O., Gieseke, F.: Short-term wind energy forecasting using support vector regression. In: Corchado, E., Snášel, V., Sedano, J., Hassanien, A.E., Calvo, J.L., Ślęzak, D. (eds.) SOCO 2011. AINSC, pp. 271–280. Springer, Berlin Heidelberg, Berlin, Heidelberg (2011). https://doi.org/10.1007/978-3-642-19644-7_29
18. Lehn, J.M.: Towards complex matter: supramolecular chemistry and self-organization. Eur. Rev. **17**(2), 263–280 (2009)
19. Liu, L., Thanheiser, S., Schmeck, H.: A reference architecture for self-organizing service-oriented computing. In: Brinkschulte, U., Ungerer, T., Hochberger, C., Spallek, R.G. (eds.) ARCS 2008. LNCS, vol. 4934, pp. 205–219. Springer, Heidelberg (2008). https://doi.org/10.1007/978-3-540-78153-0_16
20. Lust, T., Teghem, J.: The multiobjective multidimensional knapsack problem: a survey and a new approach. CoRR abs/1007.4063 (2010)
21. Meunier, F.: Co-and tri-generation contribution to climate change control. Appl. Thermal Eng. **22**(6), 703–718 (2002)
22. Mittal, S., Rainey, L.: Harnessing emergence: the control and design of emergent behavior in system of systems engineering. In: Proceedings of the Conference on Summer Computer Simulation, pp. 1–10. Society for Computer Simulation International (2015)
23. Müller-Schloer, C., Schmeck, H., Ungerer, T.: Organic Computing–A Paradigm Shift for Complex Systems. Springer Science & Business Media, Heidelberg (2011)
24. Ngatchou, P., Zarei, A., El-Sharkawi, A.: Pareto multi objective optimization. In: Proceedings of the 13th International Conference on, Intelligent Systems Application to Power Systems, pp. 84–91. IEEE (2005)
25. Nieße, A.: Verteilte kontinuierliche Einsatzplanung in Dynamischen Virtuellen Kraftwerken. Dissertation, Carl v. Ossietzky Universität, Oldenburg (2015)
26. Nieße, A., Beer, S., Bremer, J., Hinrichs, C., Lünsdorf, O., Sonnenschein, M.: Conjoint dynamic aggregation and scheduling methods for dynamic virtual power plants. In: Ganzha, M., Maciaszek, L.A., Paprzycki, M. (eds.) Proceedings of the 2014 Federated Conference on Computer Science and Information Systems. Annals of Computer Science and Information Systems, vol. 2, pp. 1505–1514. IEEE (2014)
27. Nieße, A., Beer, S., Bremer, J., Hinrichs, C., Lünsdorf, O., Sonnenschein, M.: Conjoint dynamic aggrgation and scheduling for dynamic virtual power plants. In: Ganzha, M., Maciaszek, L.A., Paprzycki, M. (eds.) Federated Conference on Computer Science and Information Systems - FedCSIS September 2014, Warsaw, Poland (2014)
28. Nieße, A., Bremer, J., Sonnenschein, M.: Continuous scheduling. In: Smart Nord - Final Report, pp. 69–76. Hartmann GmbH, Hannover (2015)

29. Nieße, A., Tröschel, M.: Controlled self-organization in smart grids. In: Proceedings of the 2016 IEEE International Symposium on Systems Engineering (ISSE), pp. 1–6. IEEE (2016)

30. Nikonowicz, Ł.B., Milewski, J.: Virtual power plants - general review: structure, application and optimization. J. Power Technol. **92**(3) (2012). http://papers.itc.pw.edu.pl/index.php/JPT/article/view/284/492

31. Percec, V., et al.: Transformation from kinetically into thermodynamically controlled self-organization of complex helical columns with 3D periodicity assembled from dendronized perylene bisimides. J. Am. Chem. Soc. **135**(10), 4129–4148 (2013)

32. Ramchurn, S.D., Vytelingum, P., Rogers, A., Jennings, N.R.: Agent-based homeostatic control for green energy in the smart grid. ACM Trans. Intell. Syst. Technol. **2**(4), 35:1–35:28 (2011)

33. Richter, U., Mnif, M., Branke, J., Müller-Schloer, C., Schmeck, H.: Towards a generic observer/controller architecture for organic computing. In: Jahrestagung, G.I. (1) LNI, vol. 93, pp. 112–119. GI (2006)

34. Steghöfer, J.-P., et al.: Trustworthy organic computing systems: challenges and perspectives. In: Xie, B., Branke, J., Sadjadi, S.M., Zhang, D., Zhou, X. (eds.) ATC 2010. LNCS, vol. 6407, pp. 62–76. Springer, Heidelberg (2010). https://doi.org/10.1007/978-3-642-16576-4_5

35. Watts, D., Strogatz, S.: Collective dynamics of 'small-world' networks. Nature **393**(6684), 440–442 (1998)

36. Wu, F., Moslehi, K., Bose, A.: Power system control centers: past, present, and future. Proc. IEEE **93**(11), 1890–1908 (2005)

Data Mining for Remuneration of Consumers Demand Response Participation

Catarina Ribeiro[1,2,3], Tiago Pinto[1,2(✉)], Zita Vale[2],
and José Baptista[3,4]

[1] GECAD – Research Group on Intelligent Engineering and Computing for
Advanced Innovation and Development, Vila Real, Portugal
[2] Polytechnic of Porto (ISEP/IPP), Porto, Portugal
{acrib,tcp,zav}@isep.ipp.pt
[3] UTAD – Universidade de Trás-os-Montes e Alto-Douro, Vila Real, Portugal
baptista@utad.pt
[4] CPES – INESCTEC, Porto, Portugal

Abstract. With the implementation of micro grids and smart grids, new business models able to cope with the new opportunities are being developed. Virtual Power Players are a player that allows aggregating a diversity of entities, to facilitate their participation in the electricity markets and to provide a set of new services promoting generation and consumption efficiency, while improving players' benefits. The elastic behavior of the demand consumption jointly used with other available resources such as distributed generation (DG) can play a crucial role for the success of smart grids. This paper proposes methodologies to develop strategic remuneration of aggregated consumers with demand response participation, this model uses a clustering algorithm, applied on values that were obtained from a scheduling methodology of a real Portuguese distribution network with 937 buses, 20310 consumers and 548 distributed generators. The normalization methods and clustering methodologies were applied to several variables of different consumers, which creates sub-groups of data according to their correlations. The clustering process is evaluated so that the number of data sub-groups that brings the most added value for the decision-making process is found, according to players characteristics.

Keywords: Clustering · Distributed generation · Smart grid · Demand response

1 Introduction

The energy system paradigm has changed completely with the massive introduction of renewable energy sources and the introduction of free competition [1]. The uncertainty brought by renewable energy sources' dependency on natural factors, requires the system to use consumers' flexibility to balance the generation variability [2]. However, adequate remuneration schemes for consumers' flexibility are lacking, hence delaying the widespread implementation of demand response programs to incentivize consumers participation. Consumers central role in future power systems, sustained by an active

© Springer Nature Switzerland AG 2020
F. De La Prieta et al. (Eds.): PAAMS 2020 Workshops, CCIS 1233, pp. 326–338, 2020.
https://doi.org/10.1007/978-3-030-51999-5_27

Table 1. Nomenclature

CDR_{calc}	Consumers remuneration
$CDR_{calc}Max$	Maximum remuneration value obtained in a cluster
$CDR_{calc}Med$	Medium remuneration value obtained in a cluster
$CDR_{calc}Min$	Minimum remuneration value obtained in a cluster
$CDR_{calc}Rem$	Remuneration value when affected by a factor
L_c	Consumption value
ML_c	Largest consumption value
$N_{c,h}$	Common normalized load
$P_{RTPDR\,intial}$	Initial consumption of each load
$P_{RTPDRmax}$	Maximum value of reduced energy per consumer
$Product_{RTPMAX}$	Maximum value of reduced energy per consumer
SML_h	Largest consumption value with customized normalization
$SN_{c,h}$	Customized normalized load
μ_i	Object value
CDI	Cluster Dispersion Index
CDR	Cost of reduction
co	Set of all considered consumers
d	Euclidian distance between two points
Elast	Consumers elasticity
Factor	Influence variable
Gen	System production
h	Hour
Income	Recipe for consumer
J	K-means objective function value
MIA	Mean Index Adequacy
R	Load profile of all consumers
w, x, y, z	Influence variables with specific weights
x	Centroid of the cluster

participation in energy markets is therefore, dependent on the models to attract both consumers and aggregators to market transactions.

Important developments concerning market players modelling and simulation including decision-support capabilities can be widely found in the literature [3]; however, these are mostly directed to players participation in the market, and energy resources management, while neglecting the development of flexibility remuneration models that are fair to both consumers and aggregators, while considering the needs from system. Aggregation of small-scale distributed resources, as well as their operation, in a competitive environment leads to the creation of Virtual Power Players (VPP). VPP can aggregate diversity of players and of energy resources, including demand response (DR), making them profitable [4]. The aggregation of players allows the creation of groups (clusters), aiming the capture of common characteristics that better define the resources in a specific context [5, 6].

This paper introduces a methodology for dynamic definition of consumers remuneration for demand response participation. An optimize remuneration method is proposed, considering the potential economic benefit for both the aggregators and the consumers. The proposed model also considers the consumers characteristics (consumption, elasticity, participation in demand response programs) and the needs from the system, such as the volume of generation from renewable sources. The proposed model is applied to a set of consumers, using a data mining process. The case study considers several variables of different consumers of a real smart grid. In this way dynamic remuneration schemes are defined, which contribute to reduce consumption peaks, increase the use of renewable energy and reflect the wholesale market price on consumers.

2 Proposed Methodology

The proposed model is directed to the demand response management from an aggregator that may participate in energy markets. Initially, the aggregator identifies the aggregated consumers and creates groups of consumers according to their similarity, so that the remuneration process may be facilitated depending on players' characteristics, such as consumption, elasticity and energy cost. Clustering methodologies are used in this work to determine the optimal consumer groups to be considered for the application of these methodologies. Although a wide variety of clustering algorithms can be found in the literature, there is no single algorithm that can, by itself, discover all sorts of cluster shapes and structure [7]. K-means clustering algorithm [8] has been used, as it proves to be a robust model for distinct applications: K-means minimizes the distance from each point to the centre of the respective cluster, as defined in (1).

$$J = \min \sum_{i=1}^{k} \sum_{x \in C_i} ||x - \mu_i||^2 \tag{1}$$

where μi is the mean of points in Ci, i.e. the cluster centroid. To determine the quality of partition of players into different clusters, the clusters validity indices MIA and CDI [9] have been used, as formalized in (2) and (3) respectively.

$$MIA = \sqrt{\frac{1}{K} \sum_{k=1}^{K} d^2\left(x^{(k)}, \mu^{(k)}\right)} \tag{2}$$

$$CDI = \frac{\sqrt{\frac{1}{K} \sum_{k=1}^{K} \left[\frac{1}{2 \cdot n^{(k)}} \sum_{n=1}^{n^{(k)}} d^2\left(x^{(m)}, \mu^{(k)}\right) \right]}}{\sqrt{\frac{1}{2K} \sum_{k=1}^{K} d^2\left(x^{(k)}, R\right)}} \tag{3}$$

The K-means algorithm has been used to normalized and non-normalized values of several different consumers' characteristics, in order to allow taking conclusions on the quality of partition. The considered normalization methods are defined in (4) and (5) for Regular Normalization and (6) and (7) for Customized Normalization. The Regular Normalization process is defined as:

$$N_{c,h} = \frac{L_{c,h}}{ML_c}, \forall_{c \in co} \tag{4}$$

$$ML_c = \max(L_c), \forall_{c \in co} \tag{5}$$

The Customized Normalization method normalizes data using each consumers' load value at each period divided by the largest recorded value of all loads in all periods, it is formalized in (6) and (7).

$$SN_{c,h} = \frac{L_{c,h}}{SML_h}, \forall_{c \in co} \tag{6}$$

$$SML_h = \max(L_{co,h}), \forall_{c \in co} \tag{7}$$

The remuneration method is based on different consumers' characteristics. The calculated value of the remuneration associated with demand response is influenced by a factor that comprises the different variables that influence the remuneration calculation. The formulation is summarized as follows.

Equations presented in (8) and (9) are used to represent the remuneration calculation for each consumer.

$$CDR_{calc} = CDR \times Factor \tag{8}$$

$$Factor = w \times P_{RTPR_{MAX}} + x \times P_{RTP_{initial}} - y \times Gen - z \times Elast \tag{9}$$

The parameters w, x, y, z influence variables with different weights and different combinations, represented in Table 2, in order to represent the relative importance of each variable to the remuneration calculation; where $w + x + y + z = 1$.

Table 2. Factors different values, defined by the author

Combination	w	x	y	z
C1	0.25	0.25	0.25	0.25
C2	0.7	0.1	0.1	0.1
C3	0.1	0.7	0.1	0.1
C4	0.1	0.1	0.7	0.1
C5	0.1	0.1	0.1	0.7

Once the remuneration calculation is made, the evaluation of the income that results for the consumer is made. Following are the different approaches to evaluate the income, associated to the application of each of the remuneration methods.

Approach 1 - based on the value of the demand response remuneration of all the players that make up a particular cluster, which will be the cost of reduction when the consumer is paid to reduce consumption. The methods are formalized in (10), (11), (12) and (13).

$$DMax\ Income_{(\text{€})} = CDR_{calc}MAX_{(u.m./kWh)} \times Product\_RTPMAX_{(kWh)} \qquad (10)$$

$$DMin\ Income_{(\text{€})} = CDR_{calc}MIN_{(u.m./kWh)} \times Product\_RTPMAX_{(kWh)} \qquad (11)$$

$$DMed\ Income_{(\text{€})} = CDR_{calc}MED_{(u.m./kWh)} \times Product\_RTPMAX_{(kWh)} \qquad (12)$$

$$DRem\ Income_{(\text{€})} =$$
$$CDR_{calc}Rem_{(u.m./kWh)}\left(Product\_RTPMAX_{(kWh)} \times \frac{CDR_{calc}\ Rem_{(u.m./k\,Wh)}}{CDR_{(u.m./k\,Wh)}}\right) \qquad (13)$$

In methods DMax, DMin and DMed, CDR_{calc}. represents the remuneration value (max, min or med) obtained in a certain cluster. *Preduct_RTPMAX*. represents the reduction of maximum individual consumption of each cluster, to participate in real-time pricing program. The DRem method considers that the value of the remuneration $CDR_{calc}Rem$, is calculated considering that the value of the remuneration associated to the demand response is affected by a factor.

Approach 2 - is based on remuneration processes (13), but now adjusted according to elasticity on a proportional base. Again, this calculation is performed for all players that form each cluster. The methods are formalized in (14), (15), (16) and (17).

$$EMax\ Income_{(\text{€})} =$$
$$CDR_{calc}MAX_{(u.m./kWh)} \times \left(ProductRTPMAX_{(kWh)} \times \left(\frac{CDR_{calc}MAX_{(u.m/kWh)}}{CDR_{8u.m/kWh)}}\right)\right) \qquad (14)$$

$$EMin\ Income_{(\text{€})} =$$
$$CDR_{calc}Min_{(u.m./kWh)} \times \left(ProductRTPMAX_{(kWh)} \times \left(\frac{CDR_{calc}Min_{(u.m/kWh)}}{CDR_{8u.m/kWh)}}\right)\right) \qquad (15)$$

$$EMed\ Income_{(\text{€})} =$$
$$CDR_{calc}Med_{(u.m./kWh)} \times \left(ProductRTPMAX_{(kWh)} \times \left(\frac{CDR_{calc}Med_{(u.m/kWh)}}{CDR_{8u.m/kWh)}}\right)\right) \qquad (16)$$

ERem $Income_{(\text{€})} =$

$$CDR_{calc}Rem_{(u.m./kWh)} \times \left(PreductRTPMAX_{(kWh)} \times \left(\frac{CDR_{calc}Rem_{(u.m/kWh)}}{CDR_{8u.m/kWh)}} \right) \right) \qquad (17)$$

3 Case Study

This case study shows the suitability of the proposed clustering methodology and normalization approaches to solve the problem of players remuneration, considering players with heterogeneous technologies and behaviors. In order to test the adequacy of the method the clustering algorithm has been applied to values obtained from a scheduling methodology of a real network with 30 buses, supplied by one high voltage substation (60/30 kV) with a total number of 937 buses and 464 MV/LV transformers, with 20310 consumers and 548 distributed generators. Figure 1 shows the summarized scheme of the distribution network [10].

The K-means algorithm has been used to perform the clustering process using non-normalized values of load and also normalized values, using both the regular normalization and customized normalization, for k = 3 and 4 for a total of five different groups. Other tests carried out in previous studies, [9, 10], have revealed that the use of the clustering methodology associated to the Customization methodology allows for relevant results to be obtained. In this case study, the lower indices values of MIA/CDI, were achieved with customized normalization for k = 3 in group G5_Elast, as it is possible to see in Fig. 2.

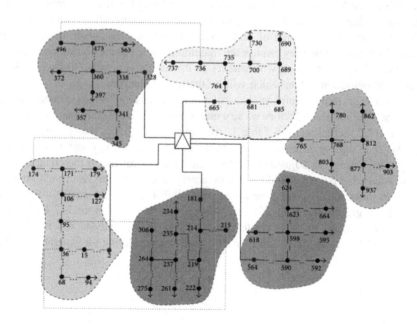

Fig. 1. Distribution network used for the SG simulation.

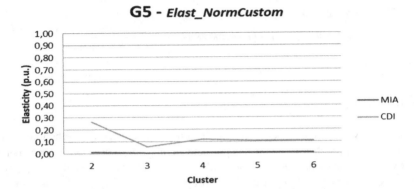

Fig. 2. MIA/CDI indices for G5_elast with customized normalization.

Remuneration Analysis

The methodologies for the definition of the remuneration value of consumers have been tested and the results are now analysed.

Figure 3 A) shows that the results of new CDRcalc have the expected behavior when compared to the base CDR values. When the remuneration is calculated through the minimum value, it is smaller than the base CDR, when it is calculated by the maximum value it is greater, and when we use the average of the values it will be equal to the base CDR.

From a practical point of view, these results are useful for the aggregator (or the entity that defines the remuneration), since allows to manage the overall remuneration to be defined for the group, depending on its strategy and objectives. To maximize their own profits, they can use the minimum amount of remuneration (with consumers having a higher starting value of remuneration); but to attract more customers and increase competitiveness they can use the maximum value (where consumers who have a lower value of remuneration will benefit). In the base it is possible to simply use the average compensation value, which will be the most balanced.

In graph B) a more careful analysis of the compensation values obtained is necessary since the influence factors w, x, y and z in the different combinations (C1, C2, C3, C4 and C5) represented in Table 1, are considered to affect the system in several ways. When assigning different weights to the components w, x, y and z, we intend to analyse how there is an adjustment in the remuneration, related to the changes in the system. Analysing B), we would have to do a very extensive analysis in each group, so in order to make the analysis more assertive we will focus on the results obtained for the G5_Elast group, k = 3. In this case, allocated to cluster 1 were 147 loads, 9312 loads in cluster 2 and 10250 in cluster 3. In order to do this analysis, it is necessary to bear in mind the values that in this case study we are considering for generation and for

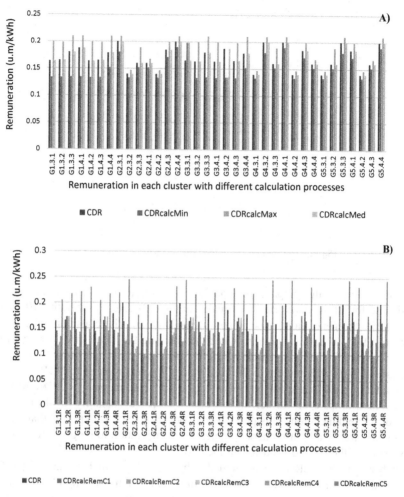

Fig. 3. Remuneration values obtained with methods Min, Max, Med in grafic A) and method Rem in grafic B).

consumption. For the generation we have a value considered high in relation to what is normal, total daily production = 1.2303 p.u, in the case of consumption we are considering a total daily value that corresponds to the total average of each cluster, in the different scenarios.

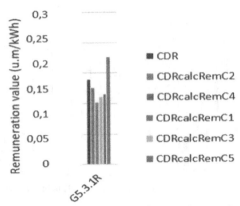

Remuneration values obtained in each
cluster with different calculation processes

Fig. 4. Remuneration values obtained with method Rem.

In the result of the graph corresponding to G5.3.1R, Fig. 4, an equal weight is considered for all the parameters that make up the CDRcalc remuneration (0.25, 0.25, 0.25, 0.25), the generation value is considered high and the consumption has a low value, 0,13995pu. In this situation, when we compare the value of CDRcalc with the average value of CDR base in cluster 1, we find that the value of the remuneration decreases slightly with respect to the base value. When compared to CDRcalcRemC2, where a fairly high weight was attributed to the initial reduction P_RTPDR_MAX, the remuneration drops even further. In this case it drops substantially to1/4 of the initial value of the remuneration. This phenomenon occurs since it is expected that when the system has already a high reduction value, the remuneration to be given to consumers is lower since there is no need for an incentive.

Analysing CDRcalcRemC3 we find that by assigning a high weight to the factor associated with consumption (x), the value of remuneration rises slightly in relation to CDRcalcRemC2 although it remains lower when compared to the initial remuneration, since the initial value considered for consumption was low, although the factor makes it rise slightly, the value of the remuneration remains low. In the case of the CDRcalcRemC4 scenario, a greater weight is attributed to the generation, which already has a high value and will increase the value of the remuneration. In the case of CDRcalcRemC5 it is verified that the value of the remuneration goes up considerably, here a higher weight is attributed to the component of the elasticity.

When we analyse the CDRcalcRem5 result, we find that by increasing the elasticity component (z) in the different scenarios, the value of the remuneration increases considerably compared to the base CDR. In the other groups represented in the graph this trend is maintained for all the results obtained in this simulation.

After calculating the remuneration and respective analysis of results, the income results for the consumer is evaluated. The following are the different approaches to revenue evaluation, associated to the application of each of the remuneration methods.

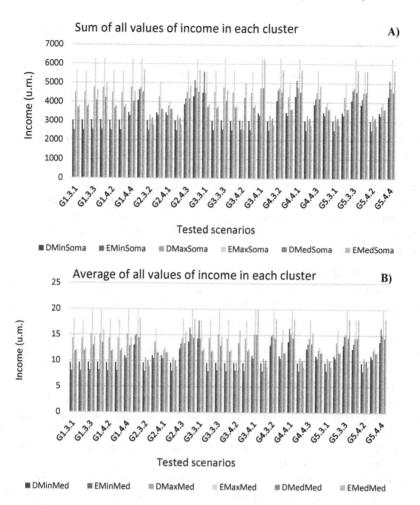

Fig. 5. Results for Sum A) and Average B) of income in each cluster, considering the scenarios defined for methods D and E, Min, Max and Med.

Income Results of Methods Max, Min e Med (D and E)

The graphs in Fig. 5 show the results obtained for the different scenarios considering the sum and the total average of the cluster, in graphs C) and D), respectively.

Analysing the graphs A) and B), is visible that in general, regardless of the scenario considered, the results tend to assume a very similar behavior within the same method. Taking the analysis in detail, we focus on the results of the G5_Elast group, the group already selected in the previous study and for example, in the graph A) of the sum, since the behavior of the results is very similar in both graphs. Thus in graph A) we can verify that: with the DMin and EMin, in the scenarios G5.3.1, G5.3.2, G5.4.2 and G5.4.3 the results of the revenue are larger when the elasticity is not considered, whereas in the other scenarios the opposite is true. From a practical point of view, it should be remembered that the elasticity corresponds to the value that the consumer can reduce or increase the reduction. If there is no elasticity it will always reduce the same at whatever price. But with elasticity, if the price is good (higher than the base CDR), it will reduce more, and then make more money, but if the price is low, it will reduce less because it no longer interests you so much to be having the disadvantage of reducing consumption for a less good price, and consequently having less income. In the mentioned scenarios it is verified that the value of CDRcalc is smaller than the CDRbase. Regarding the results of DMax and EMax, it is verified that in G5.3.1 and G5.4.2 the value of the revenue is higher when the elasticity is not considered, in the remaining scenario the revenue is always greater in method E, when compared to the method D. Being significantly larger in scenarios G5.3.3, G5.4.1 and G5.4.4. In the case of DMed and EMed results, similar to what happened in the Max method only in scenario G5.3.1 and G5.4.2, the remuneration without elasticity 'is higher than the remuneration that considers the elasticity. In the other scenarios value is always higher when considering Method E, and in scenarios G5.3.2 and G5.4.3 the values are very similar, with greater discrepancy in scenarios G5.3.3, G5.4.1 and G5.4.4.

Income Results of Method Rem (D and E)
Since we have a large number of data to the graphics are too large to present in this paper. Analysing the results, we find that in general, regardless of the scenario considered, the results tend to assume a very similar behaviour within the same method. Now, let's focus on the results of the G5_Elast group, the group already selected in the previous study, we can thus verify that: when analysing the results obtained with DSomaC1 and ESomaC1, in the scenarios G5.3.1, G5.3.2, G5.4.2 and G5.4.3 the results of the revenue are higher when the elasticity is not considered, while in the other scenarios the contrary. In this scenario C1 is assigned the same weight to all the parameters that make up the revenue calculation. This phenomenon may explain the fact that the results are similar to the previous methods; when we analyse scenario C2, where a much larger weight is applied in the initial participation or initial value of the reduction, we find that the results obtained for the compensation through method D are higher than with the use of method F in all groups tested; the previous phenomenon occurs again in scenario C3, when a much higher weight is attributed to the value of consumption; for scenario C4, the component y is assigned a very high weight, which affects the generation parameter. In this case, earnings without elasticity will be higher, although in G5.3.3 G5.4.1 and G54.4 the difference is minimal, obtaining very similar values through the two methods; in scenario C5 a high weight is attributed to the component that affects the elasticity parameter. In this scenario, in all the groups considered, the value of the remuneration is always greater in the method E, in relation to the method D.

4   Conclusions

The decision support model proposed in this paper enables attracting consumers to assume an active role in the system, through fairer remuneration strategies. The best clustering results occur for k = 3, in any of the groups relative to the five variables. With MIA and CDI validation was verified that the lowest errors were verified for 3 clusters. When applied to the data, the Customized Normalization was verified that

MIA/CDI error is lower when compared to the results obtained with Regular Normalization process.

The application of the remuneration methodologies allowed to show that it is possible to define remuneration values with different natures for the aggregator. It is possible to group consumers according to their similarity, to identify the basic values of remuneration taking into account the a priori values of each consumer and to calculate average minimum and maximum values of remuneration, appropriate for each group of consumers. It is also possible to verify that by the proposed methodology it is possible to define dynamic remuneration values, which depend not only on the preferences of the aggregator and the consumer in terms of prices, but also on the variation of the generation in each moment, and the incentive to participate in programs of taking into account the basic elasticity of each consumer. It allowed evaluate the impact from the dynamic remuneration schemes by assessing the potential incomes of each consumer when providing consumption flexibility. From the presented results it is possible to verify that the value of remuneration decreases when the elasticity increases and decreases when the generation also increases, being an automatic way to stimulate the participation of the consumers and at the same time to guarantee a fair remuneration for both the participants and the aggregators.

Acknowledgements. This work has received funding from the EU Horizon 2020 research and innovation program under project DOMINOES (grant agreement No 771066) and from FEDER Funds through COMPETE program and from National Funds through FCT under projects CEECIND/01811/2017 and UIDB/00760/2020.

References

1. Ciarreta, et al.: Has renewable energy induced competitive behavior in the Spanish electricity market?" Energy Policy **104**, 171–182 (2017)
2. Tjørring, L., et al.: Increasing the flexibility of electricity consumption in private households: does gender matter? Energy Policy **118**, 9–18 (2018)
3. Ringler, P., Keles, D., Fichtner, W.: Agent-based modelling and simulation of smart electricity grids and markets - a literature review. Renew. Sustain. Energy Rev. **57**, 205–215 (2016)
4. Pinto, T., Vale, Z.A., Morais, H., Praça, I., Ramos, C.: Multi-agent based electricity market simulator with VPP: conceptual and implementation issues. In: Proceedings of the IEEE Power & Energy Society General Meeting, 26–30 July 2009, pp. 1–9 (2009)
5. Kaufman, L., Roussesseeuw, P.: Finding Groups in Data: An Introduction to Cluster Analysis. Wiley, New York (1990)
6. Figueiredo, V., et al.: An electric energy consumer characterization framework based on data mining techniques. IEEE Trans. Power Syst. **20**(2), 596–602 (2005)
7. Jain, A.K., et al.: Data clustering: a review. ACM Comput. Surv. **31**(3), 264–323 (1999)
8. Jain, A.K.: Data clustering: 50 years beyond K-Means. Pattern Recogn. Lett. **31**(8), 651–666 (2010)
9. Chicco, G., et al.: Support vector clustering of electrical load pattern data. IEEE Trans. Power Syst. **24**(3), 1619–1628 (2009)

10. Faria, P., Soares, J., Vale, Z., et al.: Modified particle swarm optimization applied to integrated demand response and DG resources scheduling. IEEE Trans. Smart Grid **4**(1), 606–616 (2013)

11. Ribeiro, C., Pinto, T., Vale, Z.: Customized normalization method to enhance the clustering process of consumption profiles. In: Lindgren, H., et al. (eds) Ambient Intelligence- Software and Applications – 7th International Symposium on Ambient Intelligence (ISAmI 2016). ISAmI 2016. Advances in Intelligent Systems and Computing, vol. 476. Springer, Cham (2016). ISSN 2194-5357. https://doi.org/10.1007/978-3-319-40114-0_8

12. Ribeiro, C., Pinto, T., Vale, Z., Baptista, J.: Data mining for prosumers aggregation considering the self-generation. DCAI 2017. AISC, vol. 620, pp. 96–103. Springer, Cham (2018). https://doi.org/10.1007/978-3-319-62410-5_12

Averaging Emulated Time-Series Data Using Approximate Histograms in Peer to Peer Networks

Saptadi Nugroho[1,2,3](✉), Alexander Weinmann[1], Christian Schindelhauer[1], and Andreas Christ[2]

[1] Albert-Ludwigs-Universität Freiburg,
Georges-Koehler-Allee 51, 79110 Freiburg, Germany
{snugroho,schindel}@informatik.uni-freiburg.de,
saptadinugroho@gmail.com, uni@aweinmann.de
[2] Offenburg University of Applied Sciences,
Badstraße 24, 77652 Offenburg, Germany
{saptadi.nugroho,christ}@hs-offenburg.de
[3] Universitas Kristen Satya Wacana,
Jl. Diponegoro 52-60, Salatiga 50711, Indonesia

Abstract. The interaction between agents in multiagent-based control systems requires peer to peer communication between agents avoiding central control. The sensor nodes represent agents and produce measurement data every time step. The nodes exchange time series data by using the peer to peer network in order to calculate an aggregation function for solving a problem cooperatively. We investigate the aggregation process of averaging data for time series data of nodes in a peer to peer network by using the grouping algorithm of Cichon et al. 2018. Nodes communicate whether data is new and map data values according to their sizes into a histogram. This map message consists of the subintervals and vectors for estimating the node joining and leaving the subinterval. At each time step, the nodes communicate with each other in synchronous rounds to exchange map messages until the network converges to a common map message. The node calculates the average value of time series data produced by all nodes in the network by using the histogram algorithm. We perform simulations which show that the approximate histograms method provides a reasonable approximation of time series data.

Keywords: Agent · Sensor node · Time series data · Approximate histograms · Peer to peer network

1 Introduction

In terms of conceptualization of agent-based framework [1], sensor nodes take data value from a dynamic environment while software agents collect data from sensors and return actions output to the actuators [2,3]. Multiagent systems

© Springer Nature Switzerland AG 2020
F. De La Prieta et al. (Eds.): PAAMS 2020 Workshops, CCIS 1233, pp. 339–346, 2020.
https://doi.org/10.1007/978-3-030-51999-5_28

(MAS) based voltage control systems in [4] constitute autonomous distributed control systems applied in Smart Grids. The communication between the sensor nodes represented by software agents for exchanging messages can be established by using a peer to peer network. A sensor node produces time series data value used as input to a software agent, which has a function for generating the output value. Suppose agents are represented by n nodes and connected by a communication graph G_t established by random connections [5]. Each node has time series values x_t updated over indefinite time. At each time t, nodes exchange the updated values in parallel communication and compute an aggregation function in r rounds. Global system statistic information about the participating nodes in a peer to peer networks could be evaluated using aggregation functions classified into distributive (*count, sum, max, mint*), algebraic (*average, variance*), and holistic (*median*) [6].

As the number of agents in the network increases, the need to compute an approximation of aggregate time series values is more important because the aggregation process involving all nodes in the network can be too expensive. For some applications, a good approximation of an aggregation process is sufficient. However, the aggregation of data streams and the growing number of reporting nodes scalability may become an issue. The aggregation process involving only a few nodes in a peer to peer network can affect the accuracy of the result of a target function.

In this paper, we investigate the concept of time series data aggregation using peer to peer networks by grouping the number of messages exchanged while guaranteeing a relative precision of the approximated result of the aggregation target function. The important challenge is to design a technique for computing an aggregation function while the messages are updated frequently. In this scheme, the designed algorithm will be analyzed, and the approximation error resulted from aggregation calculation will be estimated.

2   Related Works

R. Karp et al. [5] proposed the random phone calls model that has the push and the pull schemes for exchanging the messages among nodes using randomized communication in every round. In the communication graph $G_t = (V, E_t \subseteq V \times V)$ of round $r \geq 1$ obtained by a randomized process, each node $u \in V$ chooses node $v \in V$ independently and uniformly at random from V [5]. The number of neighbors of node u is $d_u = |E_t(u)|$. The node communicates with a randomly selected communication partner in parallel rounds in each time $t \geq 1$ to exchange the messages and calculate an aggregation function. The sender node sends the message to its neighbors by applying the push algorithm. On the other hand, the receiver nodes receive the message using the pull algorithm. The algorithm designed in [5] has $O(n \ln \ln n)$ transmissions and $O(\ln n)$ rounds in communication overhead and needs to send $\Omega(n \ln \ln n)$ messages for each rumor.

Data aggregation using uniform epidemic protocols such as the push-sum protocol, the push-vector protocol, the push-synopses protocol, and the push-random protocol designed by D. Kempe et al. [7] have the rate of convergence exponentially to the result of aggregation functions. However, the push-sum protocol is not suited for time series data where nodes can change their value over time. That is because when a node changes its value, the whole protocol has to start from scratch and any knowledge gained before that is outdated. Even though only one node changed its value, all other nodes have to send their unchanged value to the other nodes again. Thus increasing message complexity. The gossip algorithm designed by D. Shah [8] has the mixing time at most $O(d_u$ log $n)$. The properties of underlying network topologies can affect the performance of the aggregation process using a rumor-based approach. Furthermore, R.V.D. Bovenkamp et al. [9] proposed the Gossipico protocol, a rumor protocol providing a continuous estimation of data aggregation in a churn network, which has $O(\log n)$ convergence. The Gossipico has count and beacon mechanisms to combine the message from every node and speed up the counting process [9].

M. Bawa et al. [10] proposed a tree-based approach to aggregation in which parent nodes send the messages to their children and then afterwards receive the result of the aggregation function calculated from their children. The messages can be propagated through many different paths using spanning trees approach [10]. In the Propagate2All algorithm [10], a node broadcasts the messages to all its neighbors connected to a path of length at most h-hops defined at the beginning of the query process. The Propagate2All algorithm guarantees the approximation of the aggregation function result under a churn network. The approximation number of distinct messages and the size of the network in Propagate2All are estimated using the Flajolet and Martin algorithm [10,11] and the BirthdayParadox algorithm [10] respectively. Data aggregation techniques using a tree-based approach need additional mechanisms to overcome the nodes which fail to contribute the messages during the aggregation process. The single tree algorithm, the multiple tree algorithm, and the Propagate2All algorithm have the time cost of $O(D)$ where D is the network diameter [10].

A histogram of the observed data consisting of the interval value of data and the approximate counter to count the number of nodes could be used to get the average estimation of data in a network [10]. The method proposed by J. Cichon et al. needs time cost of $O(D)$ and message complexity of $O(\log n)$ [12]. Our proposed algorithm of time series data aggregation is based on approximate histograms approach [12].

3   Methods

Let an agent-based sensor represented by a node produces a time series data value of $x_t \in \mathbb{R}_0^+$ obtained by a distributed, randomized process. All the continuous stream of data from nodes are collected using management protocols of peer to peer network and calculated using an aggregation target function. At each time of $t \geq 1$, nodes exchange the data value of x_t collected by applying parallel communication in the communication graph of $G_t = (V, E_t \subseteq V \times V)$ and compute an aggregation function of f in r rounds. The communication graph chosen by an algorithm is built on top of the overlay network. Each node may update and change the data value of x_t at each time step t. The aggregation process yields the actual result streams of y_t continuously.

In this paper, we investigate the relative error of averaging time series data value of x_t using a grouping value algorithm. There are different algorithms that aggregate time series data of nodes in the network. First, the naive algorithm is using a probabilistic method in which each node decides to send the message independently with a constant probability, e.g., tossing a fair coin. Second, we give a grouping value algorithm which collects nodes into sets of peers using a grouping function of $f_g(x)$. A node will not send the data to its neighbor if the difference between the current data value of x_t and the previous data value of x_{t-1} is smaller than some constant c generated by a grouping function.

3.1   Estimation of Number of Nodes

A random variable X is a function that maps the set Ω into $\mathbb{R}$. An exponentially distributed random variable is needed for estimating the number of nodes n [12] in the network. Each node has a collection of L minimum independent random variables [13] distributed exponentially. The unbiased estimator for n when L grows to infinity is given by [12,13]

$$n = \frac{L-1}{\sum_{i=1}^{L} x_i} \tag{1}$$

The algorithm described in Algorithm 1 is run by a node for estimating the number of nodes in the network.

Algorithm 1. Approximating The Number Of Nodes In The Network

1:   ▷ The algorithm of a node
2: **procedure** EXCHANGEMESSAGE(x_{this}, $x_{received}$)
3:     **for** $i \leftarrow 1, L$ **do**
4:         $x_{this}[i] = min\,(x_{this}[i], x_{received}[i])$
5:     **end for**
6: **end procedure**
7:
8: **procedure** ESTIMATOR(x_{this})
9:     **for** $i \leftarrow 1, L$ **do**
10:         $S_{this} = S_{this} + x_{this}[i]$
11:     **end for**
12:     **if** $S_{this} > 0$ **then**
13:         $n = (L-1)/S_{this}$
14:     **else**
15:         $n = 0$
16:     **end if**
17: **end procedure**

3.2   Grouping Time Series Data

We propose a method of grouping the time series data value of nodes using the histogram in the network. Let $x_{min} \in \mathbb{R}_0^+$ and $x_{max} \in \mathbb{R}_0^+$ are the minimal and the maximal values of time series data, and suppose that $x_{min} < x_{max}$ and $x_{min} \le x_t \le x_{max}$. Each node has a histogram that consists of an interval $I = [x_{min}, x_{max}]$. The interval of I has $N \in \mathbb{N}^+$ disjoint subintervals I_j where $j \in \mathbb{N}^+$ and $1 \le j \le N$. We define I_j as follows [12]:

$$I_j = \left[\frac{N-j+1}{N} x_{min} + \frac{j-1}{N} x_{max}, \frac{N-j}{N} x_{min} + \frac{j}{N} x_{max} \right] \tag{2}$$

Each subinterval I_j has two sets of independent random variables with exponential distribution to estimate the number of nodes for which the time series data values are joining and leaving the jth subinterval. A node stores the sets of independent random variables in an array of floating-point numbers. The number of nodes n can be estimated by calculating the difference between the number of nodes joining in n_{join} and the number of nodes leaving n_{leave}. The middle point of subinterval I_j can be calculated as follows [12]:

$$I_j^{Midpoint} = \frac{NX_{min} + (X_{max} - X_{min}) \left(j - \frac{1}{2} \right)}{N} \tag{3}$$

The approximation of the average value of time series data value is defined as follows [12]:

$$\hat{f}_{avg} = \frac{\sum_{j=1}^{N} n_j I_j^{Midpoint}}{\sum_{j=1}^{N} n_j} \tag{4}$$

It is compared with the ground truth, which is defined as the average value of inputs of all nodes in the network at time t as follows

$$f_{avgGT} = \frac{\sum_{i=1}^{n} x_t \left(i \right)}{n} \tag{5}$$

The relative error of the average value at time t can be calculated as follows:

$$\eta = \left| 1 - \frac{\hat{f}_{avg}}{f_{avgGT}} \right| \tag{6}$$

Each node has an active flag of $r_{flag} \in \{0, 1\}$ and a map message of the histogram. The initial value of r_{flag} of a node that joins the network is 1. The node u chooses the node v randomly and communicates with it at each round r. If both active flags are equal to one, then both nodes will exchange and update the message. After updating the message, one of the nodes has to change the value of r_{flag} to zero [9]. However, the two nodes will not update their message during the communication process if both nodes have the active flags that are equal to zero. If both active flags of the nodes which communicate with each other have different values, then the message of the node that has $r_{flag} = 0$ will be erased and replaced by the message of the node that has $r_{flag} = 1$.

At every time t, each node produces a value x_t and identifies a subinterval I_j. All nodes have the same length K of the subinterval, which is determined during the initialization process. Each subinterval I_j has connections with the vector $X_{I_j}^{join}[i \in L]$ and the vector $X_{I_j}^{leave}[i \in L]$ for estimating the node joining and leaving the jth subinterval. The node will store the subinterval I_j and both of $X_{I_j}^{join}$ and $X_{I_j}^{leave}$ in a map message.

At time $t = 1$ and round $r = 0$, each node creates one subinterval I_j which is connected with $X_{I_j}^{join}$ and $X_{I_j}^{leave}$ in a map message. Independent exponential random samples of real values will be generated as input of $X_{I_j}^{join}$. $X_{I_j}^{leave}$ will be set to $+\infty$ [12]. At time $t \geq 1$ and round $r \geq 1$, if the node u and node v have the same subinterval I_j and active flags of both nodes are equal to one, then they will save the result of $f_{min}\left(X_{u,I_j}^{join}, X_{v,I_j}^{join}\right)$ and $f_{min}\left(X_{u,I_j}^{leave}, X_{v,I_j}^{leave}\right)$ into $X_{I_j}^{join}$ and $X_{I_j}^{leave}$. If $I_{v,j}$, X_{v,I_j}^{join} and X_{v,I_j}^{leave} received from the node v do not exist in the node u, then the node u will add them to the map messages of the node u, and vice versa.

All nodes will generate a new value of x_t and determine the subinterval $I_{j,t}$ every time step t. At time step $t+1$, the node u produces a new value of x_{t+1} and identifies the subinterval $I_{u,j,t+1}$. If there is difference between $I_{u,j,t}$ and $I_{u,j,t+1}$, then the node u will update $X_{u,I_{j,t}}^{leave}$ and $X_{u,I_{j,t+1}}^{join}$. If $X_{u,I_{j,t+1}}^{join}$ does not exist in the map message of the node u, then the node u will create a new subinterval $I_{j,t+1}$ which is connected with $X_{u,I_{j,t+1}}^{join}$ and $X_{u,I_{j,t+1}}^{leave}$. The active flag r_{flag} of node u will be set to one if there is difference between $I_{j,t}$ and $I_{j,t+1}$ when the node u produces a new value of x_{t+1}. The active flag r_{flag} of node u will not be changed if $I_{j,t}$ is equal to $I_{j,t+1}$.

4   Experimental Results

We evaluated the time series data averaging algorithm described in the previous section. The network topology used in the simulation is a fully connected network. All nodes generate a random real value between x_{min} and x_{max} in synchronous time t. At the time t, the nodes send and receive map messages in synchronous r rounds until the network converges to a result value of the aggregation function. An observer will calculate the ground truth of the average value and determine whether or not the nodes converged to the average value calculated using the time series data averaging algorithm.

The simulation has networks of size 10, 100, 1000, and 5000 nodes, which all have a uniform distribution of the range from 0 to 100 as their data generator. The data generator generates x_t. The size of the minimum independent random variable L and the number of disjoint subintervals N are set to 20. The simulation is run for 10000 time steps t with r rounds for each time step. Simulations were repeated independently ten times. We assume that the network is not a churned network. Figure 1 shows a box plot of the relative error of the output

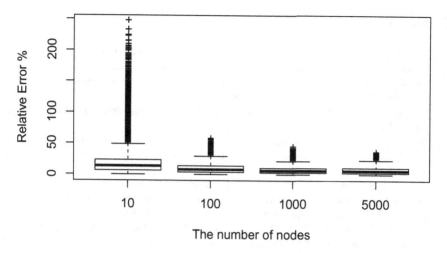

Fig. 1. Box plot of the relative error of the output of time series data averaging algorithm. $L = 20$, $T := 1, 2, 3, ..., 10000$, $n := 10, 100, 1000, 5000$.

of the averaging function. The networks of size 10, 100, 1000, and 5000 have the mean relative errors η of 17.64%, 9.82%, 7.41%, 7.30% respectively. The maximal relative errors of the network size 10, 100, 1000, and 5000 are 245.89%, 55.96%, 43.29%, 34.87% respectively. The plot shows that the relative errors of the output decrease as the number of nodes increase. The size of subintervals and the approximate counter of a node leaving and joining the subinterval contribute to the error of the output.

5   Conclusions

We investigated the design of the time series data grouping and averaging algorithm in a peer to peer network. All nodes in the network generate a new value and update the active flag r_{flag} and the map messages every time t. The map message consists of the subintervals, the vectors X^{join}, and the vectors X^{leave}. The nodes communicate with each other for exchanging the map messages in synchronous r rounds at a time t until all nodes in the network have the same map messages. The average value calculated from the map messages is compared to the ground truth of average value by the observer in the simulation process.

Acknowledgments. This work was supported by the Indonesian Endowment Fund for Education (LPDP) under the BUDI-LPDP scholarship program. The authors acknowledge support from Offenburg University of Applied Sciences and Albert-Ludwigs-Universität Freiburg.

References

1. Sahli, N., Jabeura, N., Badra, M.: Agent-based framework for sensor-to-sensor personalization. J. Comput. Syst. Sci. **81**(3), 487–495 (2015)
2. Russell, S.-J., Norvig, P.: Artificial Intelligence: A Modern Approach, 3rd edn. Pearson Education Inc., Upper Saddle River (2010)
3. Wooldridge, M.: An Introduction to MultiAgent Systems, 2nd edn. Wiley, Chichester (2009)
4. Rohbogner, G., Fey, S., Benoit, P., Wittwer, C., Christ, A.: Design of a multiagent-based voltage control system in peer-to-peer networks for smart grids. Energy Technol. **2**(1), 107–120 (2014)
5. Karp, R., Schindelhauer, C., Shenker, S., Vöcking, B.: Randomized rumor spreading. In: Proceedings 41st Annual Symposium on Foundations of Computer Science, pp. 565–574. IEEE Computer Society, United States (2000)
6. Kuhn, F., Locher, T., Wattenhofer, R.: Tight bounds for distributed selection. In: Proceedings of 19th ACM Annual Symposium on Parallelism in Algorithms and Architectures (SPAA 2007), pp. 145–153. Association for Computing Machinery, New York (2007)
7. Kempe, D., Dobra, A., Gehrke, J.: Gossip-based computation of aggregate information. In: Proceedings of the 44th Annual IEEE Symposium on Foundations of Computer Science (FOCS 2003), pp. 482–491. IEEE Computer Society, Washington (2003)
8. Shah, D.: Network gossip algorithms. In: IEEE International Conference on Acoustics, Speech and Signal Processing Proceedings (ICASSP 2009), pp. 3673–3676. IEEE, Taipei (2009) https://doi.org/10.1109/ICASSP.2009.4960423
9. van de Bovenkamp, R., Kuipers, F., Van Mieghem, P.: Gossip-based counting in dynamic networks. In: Bestak, R., Kencl, L., Li, L.E., Widmer, J., Yin, H. (eds.) NETWORKING 2012. LNCS, vol. 7290, pp. 404–417. Springer, Heidelberg (2012). https://doi.org/10.1007/978-3-642-30054-7_32
10. Bawa, M., Garcia-Molina, H., Gionis, A., Motwani, R.: Estimating aggregates on a peer-to-peer network. Technical report TR-2003-24. Stanford University (2003). http://ilpubs.stanford.edu:8090/586/. Accessed 1 Oct 2018
11. Flajolet, P., Martin, G.-N.: Probabilistic counting. In: Proceedings of the 24th Annual Symposium on Foundations of Computer Science (SFCS 1983), pp. 76–82. IEEE, United States (1983)
12. Cichon, J., Gotfryd, K.: Average counting via approximate histograms. J. ACM Trans. Sens. Netw. (TOSN) **14**(2), 8.1–8.32 (2018)
13. Baquero, C., Almeida, P.-S., Menezes, R., Jesus, P.: Extrema propagation: fast distributed estimation of sums and network sizes. J. IEEE Trans. Parallel Distrib. Syst. **23**(4), 668–675 (2012)

Participation of Wind Power Producers in Intra-day Markets: A Case-Study

Tomás Rocha[1], Hugo Algarvio[2,3], Fernando Lopes[2(✉)], Anabela Pronto[1], and João Santana[3,4]

[1] Faculdade de Ciências e Tecnologia, Universidade Nova de Lisboa, Caparica, Portugal
tg.rocha@campus.fct.unl.pt,
amg1@fct.unl.pt
[2] LNEG-National Laboratory of Energy and Geology, Est. Paço do Lumiar 22, Lisbon, Portugal
fernando.lopes@lneg.pt
[3] Instituto Superior Técnico, Avenida Rovisco Pais 1, Lisbon, Portugal
{hugo.algarvio,jsantana}@tecnico.ulisboa.pt
[4] INESC-ID, Rua Alves Redol 9, Lisbon, Portugal

Abstract. The evolution of renewable energy has increased substantially over the past decade. Wind power producers (WPPs) can submit bids to energy markets, making short-term commitments to produce specific quantities of energy. This article presents a case-study to analyze the benefits of the active participation of wind power producers in energy markets, particularly intra-day markets. The case-study is carried out with the help of the MATREM system. The preliminary results indicate a reduction of the deviations of WPPs, but also a decreasing in their remuneration. Thus, the results highlight to some extent the importance of new market mechanisms to enable the active participation of WPPs in markets, without support policies.

Keywords: Electricity markets · Variable renewable energy · Wind power producers · Intra-day markets · MATREM system

1 Introduction

Electricity markets are a complex evolving reality—there is now a significant number of market participants, each one with their own set of objectives and strategies [1,2]. In Europe, day-ahead markets (DAMs) are the most liquid markets, closing at 12:00 p.m., and using EUPHEMIA, an algorithm based on the marginal pricing theory (see, e.g., [3]). Intraday markets (IDMs) may consider

---

J. Santana—This work was supported by "Fundação para a Ciência e Tecnologia" with reference UID/CEC/50021/2019.

F. De La Prieta et al. (Eds.): PAAMS 2020 Workshops, CCIS 1233, pp. 347–356, 2020.
https://doi.org/10.1007/978-3-030-51999-5_29

auctions or operate continuously. Forward markets trade bilateral contracts to hedge against pool price volatility. Balancing markets (BMs) allow to compensate deviations from the programming schedules committed in other markets.

Most existing market designs were developed without considering the active participation of wind power producers and variable renewable energy (VRE) producers generally. Recently, the European Commission published new rules that establish the general principles and technical details on energy market participation, as well as specify rights and responsibilities among market participants [4,5]. The new rules touch upon a variety of technical aspects, including short term markets, more efficient dispatch, removal of price caps, and a better demand participation. Also, day-ahead and intra-day markets should be organized as being non-discriminatory, transparent, and mainly ensuring that all participants will be able to access the market individually or through aggregation. By 1 January 2021, the imbalance settlement period shall be 15 min in all scheduling areas. Balancing markets should respect the need to accommodate the increasing share of variable generation and the advent of new technologies. Market participants shall be allowed to bid as close to real time as possible, and balancing energy gate closure times shall not be before the intra-day cross-zonal gate closure time.

High shares of variable generation lead typically to a decrease in market prices [6,7]. Intra-day markets have low liquidity in the majority of the European countries, probably because they are not the only option to trade electricity in a particular period of time. Continuous intra-day markets seem to be not very attractive to the participation of VRE producers, since the variable cost of these producers is near-zero, and thus they will trade energy at very low prices in these markets. However, intra-day markets based on auctions, with several sessions, such as the Iberian market (MIBEL), are markets with a relative high liquidity. Accordingly, this paper presents a case-study to analyze the benefits of the participation of wind power producers (WPPs) in intra-day markets. The case-study is conducted with the help of an agent-based tool, called MATREM [8,9]. It considers seven energy scenarios involving the participation of WPPs in the day-ahead market and mainly in different sessions of the intra-day market. Also, it considers data from the Iberian market and REN (The Portuguese Transmission System Operator).

The work presented here builds on our previous work in the areas of market design and the trade of wind power in energy markets [10,11]. In [10], we investigated the benefits of the participation of wind power producers in day-ahead and balancing markets. In [11], we analyzed the impact of the forecast uncertainty and the day-ahead market gate closure on market prices, price volatility and balancing reserve requirements. In this paper, as noted, we investigate the benefits of the participation of WPPS in intra-day markets, in terms of the deviations in reductions and the final revenue.

The remainder of the paper is structured as follows. Section 2 presents a brief overview of electricity markets. Section 3 describes the strategic behavior of wind producers in energy markets. Section 4 presents an overview of the markets supported by the MATREM system. Section 5 presents the case-study and discusses the experimental results. Finally, concluding remarks are presented in Sect. 6.

2   Electricity Markets

The main European markets include the Nordic market (Nordpool), the European central market (EPEX) and the Iberian market (MIBEL). The trading occurs in day-ahead markets through implicit auctions, where clearing prices and equilibrium quantities are computed for every hour of the next day, using the system marginal pricing theory. Intra-day markets may involve auctions, like DAMs, but with several sessions, or can operate continuously, using the pay-as-bid scheme and bilateral contracts.

Transmission system operators consider the commitments made in DAMs and IDMs, and the deviations need to be balanced in balancing markets. There are three key types of load-frequency control products negotiated in European BMs. During real-time operation, primary or frequency controlled reserve (FCR) is the first product to be activated. Secondary or automatic-activated frequency restoration reserve (aFRR) should be activated in 30 s, taking a maximum of 15 min to be completed, replacing FCR. Tertiary or manually-activated FRR (mFRR) should be fully activated in 15 min, and can continue active for hours, freeing up FCR and aFRR.

Forward markets are commonly used to hedge against pool price volatility. However, if derivative products are inappropriately chosen, they may actually reduce the benefit, since market-clearing prices may end up being either too high or too low when compared with contracted prices. Customized (or tailored) forward contracts are essentially long-term contracts, designed to cover the delivery of large amounts of power over longs periods of time.

The participants in electricity markets are heterogeneous and autonomous, and typically follow their own goals and negotiation strategies. Production companies seek to adopt strategies that maximize profit, while consumers adopt strategies that minimize the electricity cost. Also, retailers seek to maximize profit by selling energy to customers. Profit margins are usually narrow as retailers should provide their clients with the lowest possible prices to avoid them to change supplier.

3   Participation of Wind Power Producers in Markets

Wind power producers can submit (wind power) forecasts to the day-ahead market during day $d-1$, thus making commitments to produce specific quantities of wind energy during day d. They can also submit bids to the intra-day market, which are essentially deviations, computed by taking into account the commitments previously made and the updates of wind power forecasts.

WPPs can adopt a strategic behavior to "optimize" their deviations. In the case of large excess deviations from the DAM commitments, it may be favourable to bid such deviations in the intra-day market. Concretely, WPPs can submit the excess deviations from the DAM commitments to the intra-day market at a price near $0 €/$MWh, thus receiving the clearing price (instead of paying penalties by participating in BMs). This strategic behaviour is essentially a deviation-reduction behaviour, not a profit-seeking one.

Accordingly, the following seven scenarios are considered in this work (see also Sect. 5):

- Baseline: wind power producers participate in the day-ahead market only;
- S1: WPPs participate in the DAM and the IDM (2nd session: 0–6 h, 3rd session: 6–12 h, 4th session: 12–18 h, and 5th session: 18–24 h);
- S2: WPPs participate in the DAM and IDM (2nd session: 0–6 h, 3rd session: 6–12 h and 4th session: 12–24 h);
- S3: WPPs participate in the DAM and the IDM (2nd session: 0–6 h, 3rd session: 6–18 h and 4th session: 18–24 h);
- S4: WPPs participate in the DAM and the IDM (2nd session: 0–12 h, and 4th session: 12–24 h);
- S5: WPPs participate in the DAM and the IDM (2nd session: 0–18 h, and 5th session: 18–24 h);
- S6: WPPs participate in the DAM and the IDM (2nd session: 0–24 h).

4   MATREM: Overview of the Supported Markets

MATREM (for Multi-Agent TRading in Electricity Markets) is an agent-based simulation tool for analyzing the behavior and outcomes of electricity markets. The tool supports a day-ahead market, an intra-day market, a balancing market, and a futures market. It also supports a marketplace for negotiating tailored (or customized) bilateral contracts. A detailed description of the system is presented in [8]. A classification of the system according to various dimensions associated with both electricity markets and intelligent agents can be found in [9].

The day-ahead market is a central market where generation and demand can be traded on an hourly basis [12]. The intra-day market is a short-term market and involves several auction sessions. It is used to make adjustments in the positions of participants as delivery time approaches. Both the day-ahead and the intra-day markets are based on the marginal pricing theory. Two pricing mechanisms are supported: system marginal pricing and locational marginal pricing.

The balancing market is a market for primary reserve (or frequency control reserve), secondary reserve (or fast active disturbance reserve), and tertiary reserve (or slow active disturbance reserve). The futures market is an organized market for both financial and physical products conditioned on delivery at a specific time and place. Such products may span from days to years and typically hedge against the financial risk (i.e., price volatility) inherent to day-ahead and intra-day markets.

Especially noteworthy is the possibility to negotiate tailored (or customized) long-term bilateral contracts, specifically forward contracts and contracts for

Table 1. Key features of the producer agents.

Agent	Country	Type	Maximum Capacity (MW)	Marginal Cost (€/MWh)
P_1	Portugal	Wind aggregator	2490	0
P_2	Portugal	Renewable mix	2000	0
P_3	Spain	Renewable mix	30000	0
P_4	Spain	Nuclear	7500	≈35
P_5	Portugal	Hydroelectricity	4500	[30; 60]
P_6	Portugal	Coal	1800	≈30
P_7	Portugal	Combined cycled gas	3000	≈100
P_8	Portugal	Fuel oil	2000	≈170
P_9	Spain	Hydroelectricity	16500	[30; 60]
P_{10}	Spain	Coal	10000	≈30
P_{11}	Spain	Combined cycled gas	22000	≈100
P_{12}	Spain	Fuel oil	4000	≈170

difference (see, e.g., [13]). The terms and conditions of such contracts are flexible and can be negotiated privately to meet the objectives of two parties. To this end, market agents are equipped with a model that handles two-party and multi-issue negotiation. The negotiation process involves basically an iterative exchange of proposals and counter-proposals [14,15].

Market entities are modeled as software agents equipped with models of individual and social behaviour, enabling them to be pro-active (i.e., capable of exhibiting goal-directed behaviour) and social (i.e., able to communicate and negotiate with other agents in order to complete their design objectives). The system supports generating companies, retailers, aggregators, coalitions of consumers, traditional consumers, market operators and system operators.

5   A Case-Study on the Iberian Market

This section presents a case-study to analyse the potential benefits of the participation of wind power producers in the intra-day market. The time period of the study ranges from January 1, 2009 to December 31, 2010. To reduce the number of computational simulations, 31 representative days were selected according to a K-medoids clustering algorithm [16]). The average wind power penetration in Portugal was 16.18%.

The agents are 12 producers (representing the supply-side) and four retailers (representing the demand-side). Several key features of the producer agents are shown in Table 1, including the maximum capacity of the producer P1, repre-

Table 2. Deviations and remuneration of the wind aggregator agent.

Energy scenario	Average deviation (MWh)	Reduction in deviation (%)	Remuneration (€/MWh)
Baseline	322.83	0%	32.87
1	211.20	35%	32.04
2	226.62	30%	
3	226.32	30%	
4	232.11	28%	
5	246.91	24%	
6	271.42	16%	32.64

senting the aggregator of wind power producers, and the corresponding energy price to submit to the day-ahead market.[1]

The wind power generation data was achieved from a set of eight distributed WPPs situated in Portugal (involving the installed capacity of 249 MW, around 10% of the Portuguese installed capacity). To get meaningful results, the data is scaled to 2490 MW (of installed capacity), by multiplying all values by a constant factor.

The following sources of data are considered in the analysis: (i) hourly prices and quantities submitted to the day-ahead and intra-day Iberian markets [17], (ii) hourly requirements of the Portuguese balancing market, and (iii) hourly imbalances and prices of the imbalances (data reported by REN, the Portuguese Transmission System Operator [18]).

The day-ahead and intra-day Iberian markets are simulated by using the MATREM system. The results are presented in Table 2 and Figs. 1, 2 and 3. Specifically, Table 2 presents the reductions in the deviations of the wind aggregator by considering the seven aforementioned energy scenarios. The baseline scenario involves the wind aggregator participation in the DAM only. Scenario S1 presents slightly better results (in terms of deviations) than scenarios S2 and S3, which in turn present better results than scenarios S4, S5 and S6. Figure 1 presents the results for the 31 representative days by considering the baseline and the S1 scenarios. For the majority of days, scenario S1 results in a reduction of the deviations.

Figure 2 presents the relative profit of the wind aggregator in scenario S1 (when compared with the baseline). In most of the 31 representative days, the profit is "negative" (i.e., below the reference profit). A possible explanation is as follows: a significant share of wind power in the intra-day market results in a decrease of the market-clearing price, thus reducing the remuneration of the wind producers. This seems to be a direct effect of the lack of liquidity of the

---

[1] Agent P_1 results from the aggregation of eight WPPs situated in the center of Portugal (henceforth, each WPP is referred to as WPP_j, j = 1,...,8).

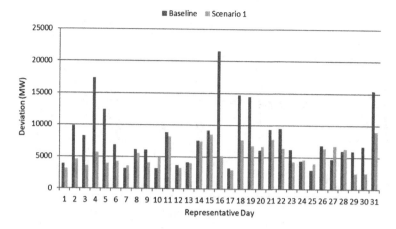

Fig. 1. Baseline and scenario S1: deviations in the 31 representative days

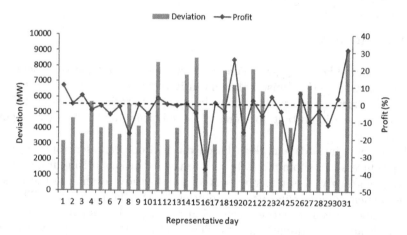

Fig. 2. Scenario S1: profit of the wind aggregator (in relation to the baseline).

intra-day market, since the marginal technology in certain periods of time is a technology with a low marginal cost.

Figure 2 also presents the deviations of the wind aggregator agent. Apparently, there is not a correlation between the deviations and the profit of this agent. Probably, this happens because of the bids that the wind aggregator submits to the intra-day market—that is, bids based on forecast updates when an excess of energy is predicted (in relation to the day-ahead commitments).

Figure 3 depicts the profit of the wind aggregator in scenario S1 (when compared with the baseline) and the bids submitted to the intra-day market. As shown in the Figure, when the bids are significant, the remuneration of the wind aggregator decreases. Overall, the actual intra-day market seems to be not very attractive for the participation of wind power producers.

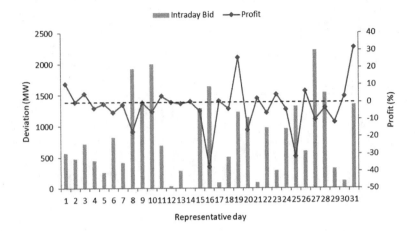

Fig. 3. Scenario S1: relative profit and bids submitted to the intra-day market.

6   Conclusion

Variable renewable energy producers represent a significant source of deviations in energy markets. Mechanisms that incentivize the participation of VRE producers in energy markets without considering feed-in tariffs or other energy support policies are important to increase the efficiency and reliability of power systems.

At present, intra-day markets based on auctions represent options where VRE producers can submit bids to reduce the deviations arising from forecast errors. Accordingly, this paper presented a case-study to analyze the benefits of the participation of wind power producers in the Iberian market. The case-study involved seven scenarios where wind power producers may participate in the day-ahead and intra-day markets. The preliminary results allow to conclude that the participation of a wind aggregator in these markets, mainly in the intra-day market, lead to a reduction in the forecast deviations, but also in the final remuneration. Thus, the results highlight the importance of new market mechanisms to enable the active participation of VRE in electricity markets without support policies.

References

1. Lopes, F., Coelho, H. (eds.): Electricity Markets with Increasing Levels of Renewable Generation: Structure, Operation, Agent-based Simulation, and Emerging Designs. SSDC, vol. 144. Springer, Cham (2018). https://doi.org/10.1007/978-3-319-74263-2
2. Kirschen, D., Strbac, G.: Fundamentals of Power System Economics. Wiley, Chichester (2018)

3. Sleisz, A., Sores, P., Raisz, D.: Algorithmic properties of the all-European day-ahead electricity market. In: 11th International Conference on the European Energy Market (EEM), pp. 1–5. IEEE Computer Society (2014)
4. European Commission, Regulation (EU) 2019/943 of the European parliament and of the Council on the Internal Market for Electricity, 5 June 2019. http://data.europa.eu/eli/reg/2019/943/oj. Accessed Feb 2020
5. European Commission, Common Rules for the Internal Market for Electricity (amending Directive 2012/27/EU), Directive 2019/944, 5 June 2019. http://data.europa.eu/eli/dir/2019/944/oj. Accessed Feb 2020
6. Azofra, D., Martínez, E., Jiménez, E., Blanco, J., Azofra, F., Saenz-Díez, J.: Comparison of the influence of photovoltaic and wind power on the Spanish electricity prices by means of artificial intelligence techniques. Renew. Sustain. Energy Rev. **42**, 532–542 (2015)
7. Ela, E., et al.: Overview of wholesale electricity markets. In: Lopes, F., Coelho, H. (eds.) Electricity Markets with Increasing Levels of Renewable Generation: Structure, Operation, Agent-based Simulation, and Emerging Designs. SSDC, vol. 144, pp. 3–21. Springer, Cham (2018). https://doi.org/10.1007/978-3-319-74263-2_1
8. Lopes, F.: MATREM: an agent-based simulation tool for electricity markets. In: Lopes, F., Coelho, H. (eds.) Electricity Markets with Increasing Levels of Renewable Generation: Structure, Operation, Agent-based Simulation, and Emerging Designs. SSDC, vol. 144, pp. 189–225. Springer, Cham (2018). https://doi.org/10.1007/978-3-319-74263-2_8
9. Lopes, F., Coelho, H.: Electricity markets and intelligent agents part II: agent architectures and capabilities. In: Lopes, F., Coelho, H. (eds.) Electricity Markets with Increasing Levels of Renewable Generation: Structure, Operation, Agent-based Simulation, and Emerging Designs. SSDC, vol. 144, pp. 49–77. Springer, Cham (2018). https://doi.org/10.1007/978-3-319-74263-2_3
10. Algarvio, H., Lopes, F., Couto, A., Estanqueiro, A.: Participation of wind power producers in day-ahead and balancing markets: an overview and a simulation-based study. WIREs Energy Environ. **8**(5), e343 (2019)
11. Algarvio, H., Couto, A., Lopes, F., Estanqueiro, A.: Changing the day-ahead gate closure to wind power integration: a simulation-based study. Energies **12**(14), 2765 (2019)
12. Vidigal, D., Lopes, F., Pronto, A., Santana, J.: Agent-based simulation of wholesale energy markets: a case study on renewable generation. In: Spies, M., Wagner, R., Tjoa, A. (eds.) 26th Database and Expert Systems Applications (DEXA 2015), pp. 81–85. IEEE (2015)
13. Sousa, F., Lopes, F., Santana, J.: Contracts for difference and risk management in multi-agent energy markets. In: Demazeau, Y., Decker, K.S., Bajo Pérez, J., de la Prieta, F. (eds.) PAAMS 2015. LNCS (LNAI), vol. 9086, pp. 155–164. Springer, Cham (2015). https://doi.org/10.1007/978-3-319-18944-4_13
14. Lopes, F., Mamede, N., Novais, A.Q., Coelho, H.: A negotiation model for autonomous computational agents: formal description and empirical evaluation. J. Intell. Fuzzy Syst. **12**, 195–212 (2002)
15. Lopes, F., Mamede, N., Novais, A.Q., Coelho, H.: Negotiation in a multi-agent supply chain system, In: 3rd International Workshop of the IFIP WG 5.7 Special Interest Group on "Advanced Techniques in Production Planning & Control", pp. 153–168. Firenze University Press (2002)
16. Park, H., Jun, C.: A simple and fast algorithm for K-medoids clustering. Expert Syst. Appl. **36**(2), 3336–3341 (2009)

17. OMIE: Operador del Mercado Ibérico de Energía (Spanish Electricity Market Operator). Market Results. http://www.omie.es/files/flash/ResultadosMercado. swf. Accessed Feb 2020
18. REN: Redes Energéticas Nacionais, Daily Summary. http://www.centrodeinform acao.ren.pt/PT/InformacaoExploracao/Páginas/EstatisticaDiariaDiagrama.aspx. Accessed Feb 2020

Workshop on Smart Cities
and Intelligent Agents (SCIA)

Workshop on Smart Cities and Intelligent Agents (SCIA)

Smart cities represent a new way of thinking about urban space by shaping a model that integrates aspects like energy efficiency, sustainable mobility, protection of the environment, and economic sustainability. These aspects represent the goals for future software developments. Current cities provide potentially unlimited settings for intelligent agents to display their ability to react, act proactively, interact between themselves, or otherwise plan, learn, etc. in an intelligent, or rather human, manner.

Therefore, the objective of this workshop is to discuss the use of agent technology in the area of smart cities with the goal of provide intelligence to the cities. We welcome any paper about experiences on the use of agents in smart cities tackling issues related to smart architectures, urban simulations, intelligent infrastructure, smart transport, open data, etc. We also intend to address specific methodological and technological issues raised by the real deployment of agents in rich environments such as smart cities.

Organization

Organizing Committee

Vicente Julián	Universitat Politècnica de València, Spain
Adriana Giret	Universitat Politècnica de València, Spain
Juan Manuel Corchado	Universidad de Salamanca, Spain
Alberto Fernández	Universidad Rey Juan Carlos, Spain
Holger Billhardt	Universidad Rey Juan Carlos, Spain
Javier Bajo	Universidad Politécnica de Madrid, Spain

Program Committee

Adriana Giret	Universitat Politècnica de València, Spain
Alberto Fernandez	Universidad Rey Juan Carlos, Spain
Angelo Costa	University of Minho, Portugal
Carlos A. Iglesias	Universidad Politécnica de Madrid, Spain
Carlos Carrascosa	GTI-IA DSIC Universidad Politecnica de Valencia, Spain
Gabriel Villarrubia	Universidad de Salamanca, Spain
Holger Billhardt	Universidad Rey Juan Carlos, Spain

Javier Bajo	Universidad Politécnica de Madrid, Spain
Javier Palanca	Universitat Politècnica de València, Spain
José Antonio Castellanos	Universidad de Salamanca, Spain
Juan Francisco De Paz	Universidad de Salamanca, Spain
María Navarro	Universidad de Salamanca, Spain
Juan Manuel Corchado	Universidad de Salamanca, Spain
Marin Lujak	IMT Lille Douai, France
Pablo Chamoso	Universidad de Salamanca, Spain
Ramon Hermoso	University of Zaragoza, Spain
Roberto Centeno	Universidad Nacional de Educacion a Distancia, Spain
Sara Rodríguez	Universidad de Salamanca, Spain
Sascha Ossowski	Universidad Rey Juan Carlos, Spain
Vicente Julian	Universitat Politècnica de València, Spain

Legal Implications of Novel Taxi Assignment Strategies

Holger Billhardt, José-Antonio Santos, Alberto Fernández$^{(\boxtimes)}$,
Mar Moreno-Rebato, Sascha Ossowski,
and José A. Rodríguez-García

Universidad Rey Juan Carlos, Madrid, Spain
{holger.billhardt,joseantonio.santos,
alberto.fernandez,mar.rebato,sascha.ossowski,
joseantonio.rodriguez}@urjc.es

Abstract. In the last years, many novel applications have appeared that promote the provision of services or activities in a collaborative way. Examples of such proposals are collaborative transportation services (uber, glovo, amazon flex, etc.), crowdsourcing, exchange help services among citizens, and others. The intrinsic idea behind such systems is to take advantage of existing "capacities" for providing new services or incrementing the efficiency of daily tasks of people at a low cost. Also, many researchers have focused and are analysing novel ideas and approaches in this direction. The concept of Smart Cities is a clear representation of this hype and provides a playground for novel approaches where the aim is to provide a high level of services to citizens in an optimized and thus, more efficient way. As a result of this research effort, many proposals have been and are suggested that could be deployed in the real world. However, such proposals also bring up multiple non-technical issues that need to be tackled before they can be actually implemented in practice. In this sense, in this paper we analyse legal implications of a proposal for collaborative service provision. In particular, we analyse the legal issues related to a recent work on taxi assignments with compensation from the standpoint of the Spanish legislation. From this exercise, we extract a set of topics and requirements, which need to be addressed so as to pave the way for the potential real-world deployment of such a system in a future.

Keywords: Taxi fleet management · Legal analysis · Spanish law · Collaborative economy

1 Introduction

In the last decades and supported by the development of new Information and Communication Technologies (ICT), new economic models have emerged that are based on sharing or exchanging underused assets or services among customers. Terms like "sharing economy", "collaborative economy" or "collaborative consumption" [1], refer to such models. Many of the systems and applications in this field, even though technically solved, present regulatory challenges that allow for their smooth integration into our societies.

© Springer Nature Switzerland AG 2020
F. De La Prieta et al. (Eds.): PAAMS 2020 Workshops, CCIS 1233, pp. 361–372, 2020.
https://doi.org/10.1007/978-3-030-51999-5_30

In this paper, we present an example of such a system, in particular a proposal for a taxi coordination service that mediates between individual (and autonomous) taxies and potential customers [2], and analyse its viability from the viewpoint of current legal restrictions and constraints. From the analysis, we point out some technical issues that can or should be changed in the coordinator proposal, as well as some aspects that we consider need a change in terms of legal regulation.

The remainder of the manuscript is organised as follows: in the next section, we will briefly introduce the taxi assignment approach presented in [2]. Then, we follow the steps proposed in [3] to analyse the taxi assignment approach and we describe the system operation at a high level and from a perspective of possible legal implications. In Sect. 3, we analyse the different operational principals and argue on their legal compliance. As a result of this analysis, Sect. 4 presents and discusses required and possible changes on the technical and the regulatory side in order to make the proposed system compliant with legal requirements and, thus, are essential for putting it into practice. Finally, Sect. 5 concludes this paper.

2   Reassignment of Customers Among Taxis

Urban mobility is one of the main concerns in big cities and one of the main actors involved in the daily traffic activity in urban areas are taxi fleets. They consist of several thousands of vehicles in big cities (e.g. about 15,000 taxis in Madrid, Spain).

Two of the main goals of a taxi fleet are (i) to reduce the response time (e.g., the time between a customer call and the moment a taxi arrives at the customer's location) and (ii) reduce costs of empty movements (e.g., movements taxis have to make in order to get to the location of customers). The provision of efficient methods for taxi assignment to customers is a challenge that can contribute to reducing distances of empty trips with the resulting decrease of traffic flow, pollution and time. Typically, taxi fleet coordination companies apply a *first-come first-served (FCFS)* strategy to assign taxis to customers, that is customers are assigned to available taxis in the order of their appearance. Once the taxi accepts the passenger, the dispatching is irreversible. This method is known to be inefficient [4].

In [2] the authors propose an alternative strategy in which taxies can dynamically interchange already accepted or assigned customers among them. The approach is based on a reassignment of customers if this may lead to globally better solutions, e.g. to an assignment that reduces the overall distance to be traveled by the involved taxis in order to serve the existing clients. As in such reassignments, some drivers may benefit by changing their customers and others may be worse of, the authors propose a compensation schema based on a monetary exchange that goes along with an interchange of customers and assures that all taxi drivers would benefit from participating in such exchanges.

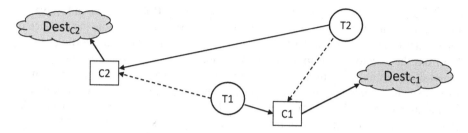

Fig. 1. Example of cost reduction through re-assignment.

2.1 Assignment and Compensation

The idea underlining the approach proposed in [2] is that in certain moments, a reassignment of customers among taxis may be beneficial from a global (cost) perspective. Figure 1 shows an example. The figure shows two customers (C1 and C2) and two taxis (T1 and T2) in a geographic area. Both customers want to go to some destination point ($Dest_{C1}$ and $Dest_{C2}$).

Now let's suppose that customer T1 is assigned to C1 and T2 to C2 (shown by the solid lines). In this case, the overall cost for serving both customers is determined by the driving distances $dist(T1,C1) + dist(C1,Dest_{C1}) + dist(T2,C2) + dist(C2,Dest_{C2})$. As shown schematically in the figure, this overall cost is higher than in the alternative assignment (doted lines): $dist(T1,C2) + dist(C2,Dest_{C2}) + dist(T2,C1) + dist(C1, Dest_{C1})$. In particular, the difference is due to the different distances from the taxies to the customers. Thus, a reassignment of C1 from T1 to T2 and of C2 from T2 to T1 would improve (reduce) the overall cost.

Let's suppose a quite typical price schema of the taxi service where a customer only pays a fare for the distance/time she is moving in the taxi, and maybe some additional fixed price for entering the taxi. That is, the customers do not pay for the distance the taxies have to travel to reach their initial locations. Instead, the cost of this movement is afforded by the taxi drivers. In this case, an agreement between both taxis to simply exchange their customers will probably not be reached, because one taxi (in this case T1) would not like to change, since the distance (and thus, the cost) for attending the new customer (C2) would be higher (we assume for the moment that destinations of customers are not known). In order to convince T1 to accept the exchange of customers, we would need to compensate her (at least) for the additional cost and the extra time spent. On the other hand, T2 would benefit from the exchange, both, in service time and cost. Thus, in comparison to attending customer C2, T2 should be willing to pay for the exchange. In particular, T2 should be willing to pay the travel cost it saves by attending C1 instead of C2 (then still T2 would earn in service time).

The situation described in the example is just one of many other possible situations where the overall service cost may be reduced by exchanging assigned customers among two or more taxies. In many such situations the compensations needed in order to convince taxi drivers that will be worse off after the exchange can be balanced by the amount of money other drivers would be willing to pay for the exchange.

To summarize the compensation schema proposed by Billhardt et al. in [2], we use the following notations. Let t be a taxi and k a customer. Let d_{tk} denote the distance or time units for taxi t to reach the location of customer k, d_{kD} the distance (time) of the trip from the location of customer k her destination, and $d_{tkD} = d_{tk} + d_{kD}$ the distance (time) of the entire trip. Furthermore, assume a price schema as described previously, where *cost* represents the operational cost of moving the car per distance or time unit (including fuel, and other costs), *fcost* is a fixed cost the customer pays for any taxi trip, and *fare* is the fare per distance or time unit a customer pays for the trip from her origin to her destination. Then, the revenue of a trip for taxi t attending customer k is calculated as follows:

$Revenue(t,k) = fcost + fare \cdot d_{kD} - cost \cdot d_{tkD}$

Assuming some compensation c when taxi t is proposed to change customer k for customer i the new revenue will be:

$Revenue'(t,i) = Revenue(t,i) + c,$

On the other hand, in order to accept a reassignment, two different situations should be considered:

(a) If $d_{tkD} < d_{tiD}$: The total new distance is higher. We assume that an economically rational taxi driver would accept this new assignments if she earns the same as before plus the normal fare for the extra distance, that is if:

$Revenue'(t,i) = Revenue(t,k) + (d_{tiD} - d_{tkD}) \cdot (fare - cost)$, and thus,
$c = Revenue(t,k) - Revenue(t,i) + (d_{tiD} - d_{tkD}) \cdot (fare - cost)$

(b) If $d_{tkD} \geq d_{tiD}$: The total new distance is the same or lower. In this case a driver should accept the reassignment if she earns the same as before (still, she would have to spend less time for the same income):

$Revenue'(t,i) = Revenue(t,k)$, and thus,
$c = Revenue(t,k) - Revenue(t,i)$

Note that, depending on the different distances the compensation c may be positive or negative (i.e., is received or has to be paid by taxi drivers). Based on the explained compensation schema, a taxi coordination service can be defined that mediates between potential customers and taxies, assigns (re-assigns) customers to taxies and pays/receives the corresponding compensations. The service implements the following assignment algorithm:

Step 1. New customers are assigned to available taxis using a FCFS method
Step 2. An optimal global assignment is calculated considering only assigned (not occupied) taxis and assigned or unassigned customers.
Step 3. For each new assignment, i.e. a customer is proposed to be assigned to a different taxi, calculate the corresponding compensation c.
Step 4. If the sum of all compensations is negative, and all involved taxies agree to the reassignment, then implement the new assignment. Otherwise, continue with the current assignment.

In this algorithm, a new assignment is only implemented, if the overall benefit of the mediator service is positive (i.e., taxies pay more compensations than they receive). Thus, the mediator service does not incur in additional cost. Instead, it may have some benefit. With respect to step 2, different optimization strategies have been proposed that minimize either the global distances, maximize the economic benefit of the mediator, or combine both ideas.

In the evaluation experiments (with different generated taxi and customer distributions) the proposed reassignment mechanisms shows better performance in all parametrizations than classical assignment strategies (e.g., FCFS and NTNR[1]) with respect to overall cost reduction (and thus, an increment in the global income adding taxi and coordinator service revenues) and average customer waiting times. The improvements depend strongly on the demand. For example, with 1000 taxies and a rate of customer per hour of 2500 customers and using the mixed optimization (optimizing global distance and economic benefit of the mediator service), the average waiting time has been 1.98 min as compared to 3.83 for the NTNR strategy and 39.02 for the FCFS strategy. In the case of taxi and mediator revenue (normalized to 1000 taxi trips in monetary units), the reassignment method obtains a taxi revenue of 6357.12 and a mediator revenue of 20.2, as compared to 6290.53 and 0 for NTNR and 5896.59 and 0 for FCFS.

2.2 High Level Description of System Operation

Upon the description of the proposed taxi coordination system, here we summarise the key aspects of the operation that may be subject to special legal considerations. As proposed by Santos et al. [3] the objective of this summary is to provide a specification of the operation of the proposed system that is easily understandable by legal experts, hiding away pure technical details. We present: the affected domain, subdomain and entities, as well as definitions and operational facts.

- Domain: Traffic.
- Subdomain: regulation of taxi operation.
- Affected entities: taxi services, customers of taxi services, taxi coordination services
- Definitions: see Table 1
- Operational facts: see Table 2
- Assumptions: see Table 3
- Affected general issues:
  - Responsibility of service provision.
  - Data protection.
  - Transparency and accountability.

---

[1] The *NTNR* strategy, like the FCFS strategy, assigns customers to the closest available taxies if there are more available taxies than customers, but it assigns each available taxi to the closest waiting customer if there are less taxies than customers.

Table 1. Definitions.

Term	Description
Taxi coordination services	A private or public service that coordinates the assignment of taxis to customers. It can be freely used by customers to request taxi services. Taxi drivers can freely join a coordination service, which implies that they can be assigned through the coordination service to available customers
Taxi	Vehicle (with driver) that offers transportation services with specific regulations (and price schemas)
Taxi states	*Available* (the taxi in not carrying a customer nor has committed to carry a particular customer), *assigned* (the taxi has committed to carry a customer but is not carrying her yet), or *busy* (the taxi is carrying a customer)
Customer states	*Unassigned* (not yet assigned to any taxi), *assigned* (assigned to a taxi, but still waiting for the taxi to arrive), *served* (currently in a taxi towards her destination location)

Table 2. Operational facts of the taxi reassignment system.

Fact	Description
F-1	The taxi coordination service just assigns customers to taxies. It is not itself a transportation company. New customer requests are assigned to the closest available taxi
F-2	A taxi assigned to a customer may be reassigned to any other customer who is either closer or further away from the taxi's current location
F-3	If a taxi is reassigned to a customer that is closer to its current position than the previous customer, the taxi driver has to pay the estimated amount of cost of the extra driving cost he is saving by moving towards the closer customer instead of the customer that he was originally assigned to
F-4	If a taxi is reassigned to a customer that is farther away to the taxi's current position than the previous customer, the taxi driver receives a compensation for the extra arrival distance that is equal to the fare per kilometres times the extra distance (in kilometres)
F-5	When the coordination service proposes a reassignment to a taxi driver, the taxi driver can accept or reject the proposed reassignment
F-6	If all affected taxi drivers accept a reassignment, it is implemented
F-7	The coordination service makes benefit through the surplus taxis pay when they are reassigned to a closer customer
F-8	Taxi customers pay the regular fare to the driver who is providing the taxi service.
F-9	For each trip, a taxi driver receives the fare paid by the customer. In addition, the driver may receive or may have to pay a compensation to the coordination service (as specified in facts 3 and 4)

Table 3. Assumptions

ID	Description
A-1	The fare schema of the taxi service is based on a fixed rate that customers have to pay and that depends on the distance (and/or time) of the taxi ride from the initial position of the customer to its destination location. Additionally, there may be a fixed amount for starting a taxi trip
A-2	The cost for a taxi to move to the customers initial location is covered by the taxi driver
A-3	Customers cannot select the particular taxi (and driver) they want to use

3 Legal Analysis

In Spain, like in many other countries, the legal-administrative regime of taxi services is usually regulated at the municipality level [5]. It has been defined that "the taxi does not properly constitute a public transport service, but an activity of general interest whose promotion, within the framework of the autonomous legislation, corresponds to the municipality" [6]. This transport activity is intervened and regulated by the Public Administration, but there is no public ownership of it. In the case of Madrid, which we use as a reference, The Ordinance of the City Council regulating the taxi sector continues to define this means of transport as a public service. A public service that could only be understood as an "improper" public service; in other words, an activity of general interest that an individual provides by administrative authorization [7].

The main question, in the legal scope, is whether the proposal contained in this paper conforms to Law, in particular to regulations of the Autonomous Community of Madrid and the City Council of Madrid. This proposal would fit in section no. 66 of the Decree of the Community of Madrid, No. 74/2005, of July 28, which approves the Regulation of Urban Public Transport Services in Passenger Vehicles where it is urged to promote the research, development and implementation of new communication technologies in the taxi sector. Also, this proposal favors the environmental, energy efficiency and efficiency objectives of the sector (such as minimizing the waiting time) principles set by taxi regulations.

A key aspect of the proposal is the legality of a taxi mediation service (F-1). In this regard, the current regulations facilitate the establishment of intermediation companies through computer applications. An intermediation company could perfectly use this system of reassignment as long as it complies with the official rates, established by the City Council of Madrid, that is, no surcharges can be established that increase the price to be paid by customers (F-8). Mediation services can establish their own internal operation (e.g. taxi assignment method) as long as they fulfill this requirement. Therefore, there is no direct incompatibility between the proposed functioning of the taxi coordination service (operational facts F-2, F-3, F-4, F-5 and F-6) and the current taxi regulations. In fact, intermediation companies could even perfectly contemplate to establish that taxi drivers have to accept any proposed (re)assignments as a condition to participate in the platform.

Mediation companies can be public or private entities and thus generate benefit (F-7). Furthermore, they can establish discounts for customers for using their platform. They may include price reductions or bonuses for customers without them being considered as a violation of free and fair competition as indicated in judgment no. 956 of the Provincial Court of Barcelona, of 21 May 2019. The reductions or bonuses for customers do not imply, currently, a position of dominance in the taxi sector nor there are anticompetitive behaviors because the mediation companies subsidize customers.

With regards to taxi fares, they are usually regulated by the municipalities and typically are based on a basic fee plus a rate that depends on distances and/or time traveled, among other factors. Thus, assumption A-1 is compatible.

There are two options for customers to get a taxi: hailing a taxi on the street where the customer is located (or a taxi stop) or booking one to pick up the customer at a specific location. In the latter case, the cost of moving to the pick-up location can be either covered by the taxi driver or the customer. Both options are allowed, thus the one assumed by the proposed system (A-2) is feasible. In particular, the Ordinance no. 8546/2407 of the City Council of Madrid, from December 17th, 2019, establishes a maximum amount that can be charged in case a taxi has been booked in advance. It also establishes that, since January 1st, 2020, pre-contracting with a maximum closed price is allowed: according to the instructions approved by the City Council of Madrid, the client is favored by knowing already the maximum amount to be paid. Since the reassignment decision is based on the fare the customer pays (F-8 and A-1) and cost, our method is also compatible with establishing a closed price agreement with the customer. In case of a closed price schema, the mediation service would still be interested in (re)assigning the closest taxi to each customer, which is the same base of our current approach.

In relation to customers' rights, the Ordinance of the City Council (article 52) establishes that customers can request specific types of taxis (regular, accessible, kids, ...). The mediation service must keep this vehicle requirement in any reassignment. However, customers do not have the right to choose a particular driver (A-3) as long as the vehicle fulfills their requirements.

In the European legal field, it is necessary to talk about the Regulation (EU) 2019/1150 of the European Parliament and of the Council of 20 June 2019 on promoting fairness and transparency for business users of online intermediation services. The taxi assignment approach should promote the fairness and transparency principles (article 1) among professional users of the application, which is a benefit of consumers. In this regard, it must also be taken into account the rights of consumers and users included in the Royal Legislative Decree 1/2007, of 16 November, approving the consolidated text of the General Consumer and User Protection Act and other complementary laws.

According to the European regulation, the principle of transparency is crucial to promoting sustainable business relationships and to preventing unfair behavior to the detriment of business users. The regulation seeks to ensure adequate transparency and the possibility of effective claim for this online platform service and build trust between other similar companies and consumers, creating a fair, predictable, sustainable and trusted online business environment. The freedom of enterprise (art. 38 Spanish

Constitution) should favor, as provided in the European regulation, a competitive, fair and transparent online ecosystem where companies behave responsibly. This is essential for consumer welfare. However, it is important the application of the contractual law between suppliers and professional users who offer services to consumers, so the contractual relationship will exist if both parties concerned express their intention to be bound in an unequivocal manner on a durable medium, without an express written agreement necessarily being required. The general conditions must be easily accessible to professional users, be written in plain and intelligible language, easily available to professional users in the pre-contractual and contractual stage of the online intermediation relationship with the provider. To avoid unequal treatment, must be indicated in their terms and conditions a description of any differentiated treatment which they give, or might give, in relation to services offered to consumers. That description shall refer to the main economic, commercial or legal considerations for such differentiated treatment.

4   Discussion

In general, according to the description in Sect. 3, there are no strong legal limitations that would make the application of the proposed taxi re-assignment approach or the creation of the described taxi service coordinator infeasible. Still, from the legal compliance analysis, there are some particular issues that affect the proposed coordination service and that are worth discussing.

First, regarding the **types of taxis** customers can select, as mentioned in Sect. 3, the mediation service has to assure that the customer is served with the requested type. However, the proposed assignment method does not deal with different types of vehicles. This aspect can be included in steps 1 and 2 of the algorithm, by considering only compatible vehicles for each particular customer request, i.e. incompatible taxis are considered unavailable (or busy) for that specific user. Note that different types of vehicles are not necessarily incompatible (e.g. an "Accessible taxi" can also act as a regular one).

Second, the regulation states that it has to be clear **who has provided a certain service**. That is, the provider of a service must be identifiable in order to establish liabilities due to possible service failure. In this sense, means for registering the assignments of taxis to customers have to be integrated in the deployed platform. However, it is out of the scope of the assignment algorithm.

Third, the taxi driver who participates in the platform does it with all its consequences. In particular, it is possible to oblige her to **accept any assignment/ reassignment.** The taxi driver's freedom is essentially to decide whether or not to use the computer application. So, the proposed coordination service could directly impose any identified (beneficial) reassignment, what would clearly simplify the approach assuring its full efficiency increase. Even in this case, from an economically rational perspective, taxi drivers should be willing to accept any reassignment (with its corresponding compensations), as it has been discussed in Sect. 2. Thus, taxi drivers will have a clear incentive to participate in the coordination platform.

In addition, the proposed application reduces the overall distance that needs to be driven by the taxi fleet. This means that the use of our platform, by means of the dynamic reassignment of customers, generates an economic surplus which can be used in several ways. Usually, we expect it to be shared in some way between the platform owners and the taxi drivers. One particularly compelling option would be to subsidize taxi drivers by lowering (or even abolishing) the commission that each of them must pay for the use of the computer application (currently, in Madrid, up to 12%, in existing platforms such as Uber).

Finally, the local administration may want to encourage the integration of the largest number of taxi drivers into the application to promote infrastructures of this type in the production apparatus according to the Smart Cities model. The City Councils can carry out promotion mechanisms by establishing special rates to finance the different mediation platforms. The local administration must act with equity and avoid excessive damage to taxi drivers against private hire drivers (e.g. Uber and Cabify), for example in unfair competition cases. However, notice that it is obviously acceptable to create economic incentives in the form of fiscal and/or financial aids for vehicles that do not contaminate, and also for platforms that reduce the overall amount of distances travelled and thus sustain urban mobility while reducing traffic jams and contamination.

5 Conclusions

The area of Smart Cities is advancing at fast pace. The development of ICT, connectivity, Internet of Things, smart handheld devices, etc. has given rise to a huge number of developments that aim at facilitating the life of inhabitants of modern cities. Also, the increase of population in big cities is provoking a demand for efficient and sustainable solutions to problems such as traffic jams, $CO2$ emissions, energy consumption, etc.

A lot of research effort is being carried out in order to propose smart approaches to tackle the aforementioned needs. However, scientific solutions are not always applicable in real-life due to legal constraints, which can be different depending on the potential location in which the system is expected to be deployed. Closing the gap between law and a scientific solution may require adapting the solution, modifying the law or a trade-off between both.

In this paper, we have studied the legal implications of deploying collaborative taxi assignment strategies in a city. In particular, we set out from a proposal of a system that foster collaboration among taxi drivers that exchange assigned customers, before they have been picked up, so as to get a better global benefit. We analyse how that proposal fits with the current legislation of the city of Madrid and Spain.

Even though different municipalities may have different directives with regard to taxi services, the regulation of Madrid is among the most complex ones, so we consider it to be sufficiently representative enough to draw interesting conclusions. In Madrid, the regulation of the taxi sector has been incorporating legal regulations for companies that run fleets of passenger vehicles with driver. The ultimate goals is to establish a fair framework in which such companies (e.g. Uber, Cabify) can co-exist and compete with traditional taxi services.

Our main conclusion is that the proposal presented in [2] is ready to be deployed without a need for modifications in existing laws and ordinances. However, small adaptations of the algorithm are required: the type of vehicle the customer requests must be considered in the reassignment, and the taxi drivers cannot reject a reassignment proposed by the coordination system. Furthermore, we have identified several possible improvements to the systems, e.g. through different means of the sharing of surplus obtained, or the option of setting a closed fare with the customer before the trip starts.

It should be noted that the proposed method does not solve the problem occurring under service saturation (the number of customers is higher than the available taxis). In such cases, it may happen that a customer waits for a long time to get a taxi. In the proposed algorithm, it is possible that a customer is unassigned after being assigned a taxi. If the customer is aware of that process the quality of service perception may be low. This can be easily dealt with by means of ad hoc solutions, like giving preference to customers who have been waiting for more than some predefined time limit.

In the following, we propose several lines of further research.

- In a scenario in which several service mediation entities coexist and compete for taxi drivers to join the platform and customers to hire their services, still some cooperation among them can be interesting. For example, it might be interesting for both entities to subcontract services. This would be the case of scarcity of taxis while a high demand exists, but also as an improvement of global assignment as if all taxis were managed by a global coordinator. It is important for such solutions to keep the rights and obligations of each participant in the original platform. For example, customers cannot pay more than they would pay without any reassignment. We think that multiagent systems and agreement technologies are the main research areas for creating a meta-platform that coordinates the different existing platforms.
- Ride sharing is becoming popular, so it is natural to think that a taxi service and a coordination platform could be refined to admit taxi sharing, including the possibility of picking up users during the journey. This possibility is allowed by section 37 of the Decree of the Community of Madrid, No. 74/2005, of July 28, which approves the Regulation of Urban Public Transport Services in Passenger Vehicles as amended by Decree 35/2019. This possibility would mean lowering the price to be paid by the user, a better efficiency of the taxi sector and reduction of traffic congestion and air pollution.
- Our taxi assignment proposal reduces the overall distance traveled by a fleet of taxis, i.e. it reduces costs and thus improves economic benefits. However, it may be interesting to explore other options with focus on different objectives/mobility policies. For example, minimize the number of trips, minimize the number of vehicles in an area, etc. Public administrations can award grants to encourage the implementation of this or similar types of computer applications based on the reassignment idea presented in this paper.

Acknowledgments. This work has been partially supported by the Spanish Ministry of Science, Innovation and Universities, co-funded by EU FEDER Funds, through project grant InEDGEMobility RTI2018-095390-B-C33 (MCIU/AEI/FEDER, UE).

References

1. Botsman, R.: Defining the Sharing Economy: What is Collaborative consumption-and What isn't?, fastcoexist.com (2015). http://www.fastcoexist.com/3046119/defining-the-sharing-economywhat-is-collaborative-consumption-and-what-isnt
2. Billhardt, H., Fernández, A., Ossowski, S., Palanca, J., Bajo, J.: Taxi dispatching strategies with compensations. Expert Syst. Appl. **122**, 173–182 (2019)
3. Santos, J.A., Fernández, A., Moreno-Rebato, M., et al.: Legal and ethical implications of applications based on agreement technologies: the case of auction-based road intersections. Artif. Intell. Law (2019). https://doi.org/10.1007/s10506-019-09259-8
4. Egbelu, P.J., Tanchoco, J.M.A.: Characterization of automatic guided vehicle dispatching rules. Int. J. Prod. Res. **22**(3), 359–374 (1984)
5. Doménech Pascual, G., Soriano Arnanz, A.: Taxi regulation in spain under the pressure of the sharing economy. In: Noguellou, R., Renders, D. (eds.) Uber & Taxis Comparative Law Studies, Bruylant, p. 357 (2018)
6. Tarrés Vives, M.: La regulación del taxi, Atelier, pp. 38–43 (2006)
7. Entrena Cuesta, R.: El servicio del taxi. Rev. Adm. Públ. **27**, 29–62 (1958)

Agent-Based Platform for Monitoring the Pressure Status of Fire Extinguishers in a Building

Alfonso González-Briones[1,2,3(✉)], Roberto Garcia-Martin[4],
Francisco Lecumberri de Alba[2], and Juan M. Corchado[1,2,5,6]

[1] Research Group on Agent-Based, Social and Interdisciplinary Applications
(GRASIA), Complutense University of Madrid, 28040 Madrid, Spain
alfonsogb@ucm.es
[2] BISITE Research Group, University of Salamanca. Edificio I+D+i,
Calle Espejo 2, 37007 Salamanca, Spain
{fcolecumberri,corchado}@usal.es
[3] Air Institute, IoT Digital Innovation Hub (Spain),
Carbajosa de la Sagrada, 37188 Salamanca, Spain
[4] Mechanical Engineering Department, University of Salamanca,
49022 Zamora, Spain
toles@usal.es
[5] Department of Electronics, Information and Communication,
Faculty of Engineering, Osaka Institute of Technology,
Osaka 535-8585, Japan
[6] Pusat Komputeran dan Informatik, Universiti Malaysia Kelantan,
Karung Berkunci 36, Pengkaan Chepa, 16100 Kota Bharu, Kelantan, Malaysia

Abstract. Current European regulations require a minimum number of
fire extinguishers in buildings according to the surface area of the building. The revision of fire extinguishers is a manual process that requires
technicians to visit the place where they are located. This not only
requires time and costs but also importantly the time period between
the fire extinguisher no longer being in optimal condition, the review
being performed and the problems detected. Therefore, it is necessary
to develop a system to register the information on pressure of the extinguisher, transfer the information to a central database where it will be
stored and display it on a web server. For this reason, this article presents
a multi-agent system that allows you to monitor the status of fire extinguishers through the developed prototype, evaluate their status against
other fire extinguishers, collect a history of status and environmental
factors and send notifications if any parameter is not within the range
of normal values. In addition, the system has learning techniques that
allow you to predict changes in the state of the fire extinguisher so that
the incident can be solved before it occurs, as well as evaluating the
behaviour of users in a fire.

© Springer Nature Switzerland AG 2020
F. De La Prieta et al. (Eds.): PAAMS 2020 Workshops, CCIS 1233, pp. 373–384, 2020.
https://doi.org/10.1007/978-3-030-51999-5_31

1   Introduction

Extinguishers, as the name suggests, exist with the purpose of extinguishing fires in case of emergency. Hence, extinguishers are being periodically monitored in order to be refilled when needed.

Fire extinguishers are pressure vessels that contain some elements that allow fires to be extinguished. There are two types of fire extinguishers: stored-pressure and cartridge-operated. In stored pressure units, the expellant is stored in the same chamber as the firefighting agent itself. Within the first type there is a classification according to the type of fire (according to the type of fuel). Depending on the type of fire there are various types of fire extinguishers that contain different types of elements so that they focus on a different type of fire.

As pressurized elements, the review of fire extinguishers require a check of all their mechanical elements and the state of charge of the extinguisher. These reviews are carried out by a specialized operator and undertaken periodically. This could be avoided with a real-time review system, which will also contribute to economic savings.

To do this, it would is necessary to place a series of sensors that measure pressure, temperature and humidity cite [4]. Devices with high pressure levels, such as CO_2 units, require sensors that are more expensive than the extinguisher itself, and therefore the proposed system provides an economical solution.

The aim of the work presented in this article, is to provide a novel system for the analysis of parameters that influence the pressure of fire extinguishers, such as temperature, humidity, etc. On the basis of the data collected by the system, the platform will communicate with the rest of the extinguishers to verify the information. If the information indicates any incidence or if any value is outside its normal range of values, an alert is sent. It should also serve as a platform for analysing how the fire originated, the conditions in which it occurred and the behaviour of people in the event of a fire.

2   Related Work

This section presents a review on the state of the art of the main works, the main technologies used and what should be taken into account when developing the proposal. The advantages and disadvantages of the proposed methods are presented in this article.

There are other similar developments in real-time fire extinguisher monitoring. A [6] system focused on monitoring older people indoors was developed. Here the system used an indoors localization and an environmental measurement using a combination of devices that communicate using Bluetooth low energy (BLE) systems and report the information using Android and web applications.

In another article [9], a security and safety monitor was developed using General Packet Radio Service (GPRS) communication. The system consists of a single chip microcomputer, GPRS wireless communication and a sensor function module realizing data monitoring and short message warning. The system checks for fire risk taking humidity and temperature measurement. It also monitors the light intensity, personal access at unused time and if something goes wrong, it sends a real time alarm. Another example [2] is where a solar radiation monitoring system was developed using photovoltaic sensors using a ESP8266 with WiFi communication.

This development was focused on achieving a low cost system. In the fire extinguishers field, we have analyzed the variables that affect the pressure under which the internal composition of fire extinguishers is stored and we also performed an in-depth study of how to correctly measure the pressure of a fire extinguisher from its outside. Moreover, we have looked into different technologies used in the literature, examining their advantages and disadvantages for the development of our platform.

We must highlight however, that the current literature does not present any type of platform that would be capable of analyzing the parameters that affect the pressure in fire extinguishers. This emphasizes the contribution of our platform which collects data autonomously, controls if the parameters of all fire extinguishers are similar and then detects and notifies of any possible incidents.

An industrial reference we cite [7], does not show any detail on the functioning of the system or its potential.

3   Proposal

We therefore developed a system to monitor the pressure of fire extinguishers and send the data via the internet to a server which receives, stores and displays information so that the monitoring of several extinguishers can be done in real-time. The prototype is also focused on predicting possible fires by detecting abnormal temperature patterns, and motion detection of fire extinguishers with a motion sensor.

The system is essentially a sensor managed through a micro-controller that has IEEE 802.11 capabilities (WiFi) so it can wireless code the information in a JavaScript Object Notation format (JSON). This format is one of the must used and supported data coding notations, and sends the information of the sensor through the internet to the server using Message Queuing Telemetry Transport protocol (MQTT). The server also has a MQTT client that receives the JSON data and decodes it to store it in a database using a Structured Query Language (SQL).

The server also offer a web service so inspectors of extinguishers may access through any web browser and get the information in essentially real-time. This can be observed in Fig. 1.

3.1   Sensorization

It is important to specify in this state of the art system, what are the variables which affect to the extinguishers' internal pressure. This is particularly important when we are dealing with CO_2 extinguishers, which are more sensitive than the

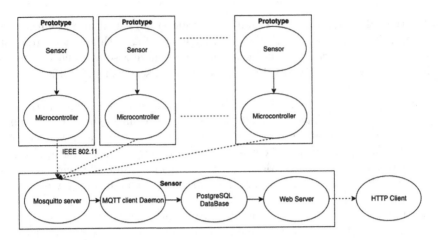

Fig. 1. System main architecture

other types of extinguisher propellers. Also we must work on how to get accurate values with a system without affecting the performance of the device, nor the manufacturing process of it.

The measurement of pressure is usually carried out directly by means of pressure gauges. The basis of a manometer is to measure the displacement generated by pressure. For this task there are different technologies and a common application used in the determination of stresses are strain gauges(SG) [1].

The measurement of pressure is usually made directly by placing the sensor in contact with the pressurized gas.,In our case it is complex to perform because the sensor cannot be introduced into the container, because you need to extract the communication cables in some way and also the sensor can be blocked by the extinguisher agent. On the other hand, to place it externally means to perforate the surface of the extinguisher, which assumes a possible point of failure, and to place a bulky sensor in the valve is not viable due to the space limitation. Finally due to the different pressure ranges we cannot find a universal sensor in the market to cover all the ranges. Due to all these restrictions, wedecided to measure the pressure indirectly, by means of a system that hardly interferes with the use of the extinguisher itself, with the advantage that you don't need to use destructive methods to incorporate it.

Due to the aforementioned restrictions we decided to measure the pressure through the evaluation of the tensions generated by the same method [3]. We know that the container is pressurized, and this will cause a deformation in the geometry of the extinguisher, if we are able to measure these deformations and relate these to the pressures, our problem will be solved.

With regard to pressurized vessels, there are two theories [8], depending on the relationship between the diameter of the element and its thickness, which provide the stress state as a function of the internal pressure.

If its thickness is small compared to its diameter, it is considered thin-walled, the limit is set at do/e >40 where d is the diameter, otherwise it means that the do/e <40 where do is the external diameter, which means that the thickness is more relevant than the diameter. Thus, a different formulation must be used in each case.

In the case of fire extinguishers, in order to optimize the volumen, they are usually manufactured with large diameters, so as a general rule we deal with thin-walled cases. whose correct formulation is well known.

Expression of thin-walled stresses

$$\sigma_\theta = \frac{PD}{2e} \tag{1}$$

Tangential stress

$$\sigma_z = \frac{PD}{4e} \tag{2}$$

Axial stress

$$\sigma_r = \theta \tag{3}$$

Radial stress

Where internal pressure (P) is related to diameter (d) and thickness (e), where the geometry of the extinguisher is also perfectly known.

In our case we can measure deformations and not stresses, but through Hooke's Law, which easily relates tensions and deformations within the linear elastic regime, it is possible to relate the deformation caused by the internal pressure of the gauge because our extinguisher works in this regime due to the material used. So by the application of Hooke's law [5], tensions with deformations can be related.

$$\sigma_{ij} = E\epsilon_{ij} \tag{4}$$

In radial systems, the spatial directions x,y,z are replaced by the radial direction (r), tangential (θ) and z is maintained.

$$\sigma_{r,\theta,z} = E\epsilon_{r,\theta,z} \tag{5}$$

The objective of this work is to relate the internal pressure (P) with the deformation (ϵ) which it is produced by. Since we know the stress values as functions of pressure (1 and 2) and the value of the axial deformation(ϵ_z) or tangential (ϵ_θ) which can be obtained directly through the application of strain gauges(ϵ_{SG}).

Depending on how the gauge is positioned on the container, it is measured: parallel to the axis of the vessel, the value of ϵ_z is measured and if it is placed circumferential, ϵ_θ is obtained.

$$P = \epsilon_\theta E \frac{2e}{D} \tag{6}$$

Measures the deformation in tangential direction.

$$P = \epsilon_z E \frac{4e}{D} \tag{7}$$

Measures of axial deformation.

In this work we intend to evaluate the progress of the internal pressure of the fire extinguisher, taking into account the ambient temperature, which directly affects the measure. While it is true that inside buildings the temperature remains constant, this situation is quite different for outside equipment which are exposed to the elements, and since the containers are made of metal they are much more affected by the action of temperature, which causes thermal expansion (TE), it generates a new deformation (ϵ_{TE}) in the vessel, as well as in the gauge and is seriously affected by measurement error. We focused the problem in the small variations of temperature inside the buildings ($\triangle T < 5^{\circ}$).

The deformations caused by the increase in temperature is expressed in equation [8], and since the extinguishers are made by isotropic materials, we can find the same deformation in any direction. Since our system is also capable of measuring temperature and the material is known, temperature deformation can be determined, and is of equal magnitude both in the axial direction and tangential direction.

$$\epsilon_{TE}^{\theta} = \epsilon_{TE}^{Z} = \alpha(\triangle T) \tag{8}$$

α, coefficient of thermal expansion, (microns/ $^{\circ}$C)

$\triangle T$, increase in temperature ($^{\circ}$C)

thus introducing into the calculation of the pressure [6], [7] the correction, we will obtain the effects due exclusively to the pressure.

$$\epsilon^{\theta,Z} = \epsilon_{SG}^{\theta,Z} - \epsilon_{TE}^{\theta,Z} \tag{9}$$

Finally, to avoid errors in the gauge measurement due to the temperature, the gauge configuration was changed. In previous work, [4] a full-bridge configuration was used to connect the sensor to the DAS, where the sensor was mounted with three 120 ohms calibrated resistors: tolerance 3% and a thermal coefficient lower than 50 ppm. On this occasion one resistor was replaced by a free gauge (without connecting it to anything), as we can see in Fig. 2.

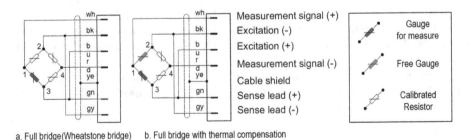

a. Full bridge(Wheatstone bridge)   b. Full bridge with thermal compensation

Fig. 2. Wheatstone bridge configuration

3.2   The Integrated Device

This section details the SmartFire integrated device architecture, the description of the prototype and the software architecture that allows us to apply the algorithm for calculating the pressure of a fire extinguisher.

One of the objectives of this work was to develop an economically viable platform, or the cheapest one able to record the pressure data of the extinguisher. Other requirements were: the size factor, low consumption, temperature record, movement detection, communications, etc.

Since the device has reduced dimensions, low energy consumption and low budget, the option of using a microcontroller was considered. A microcontroller like Arduino allows us to have a wide variety of components available, which are also at low cost.

The architecture of the device consists of an input signal capture system and output wireless communication, managed by a control system. It is composed of a microcontroller Arduino which has a Wemos for WiFi connection and also Bluetooth. These wireless communications are very useful and the system is coupled to the fire extinguisher and should allow its use of free form without algurno cable. Similarly, the device must be able to communicate independently and therefore the power is provided by a battery whose status is also monitored by the software system.

The device consists of a WEMOS D1 ESP-WROOM-02 motherboard with 10-bit digital and analog I/O, so an amplifier (HX711 Load Cell Amplifier Module) is used, providing 12 bits. The ESP32 Dev Module microcontroller that has a WiFi module (ESP8266 Mini Wifi Nodemcu Module) built inside the board and the power system is an 18650 BATTERY HOLDER. The microcontroller is programmable using the Arduino software development kit (SDK) and takes measurement of the sensor encoded in it in JSON format and transmits it. This process happens once every second. The connections and installation of the prototype can be seen in the Fig. 3.

To evaluate the correct functioning of the device, HBM equipment (Quantum MX840A) has been used, which has allowed the proposed prototype to be calibrated with high precision. It is a DAS (Data Acquisition System) and it takes a calibrated pattern, since this device is a calibrated commercial system. The process of how this is done is fully described in a published article [4].

3.3   MQTT and Web Server

Message Queuing Telemetry Transport (MQTT) is a protocol that lets devices to connect and share information in a named topic. One of the main advantages of MQTT is that it lets the devices connect and stay connected as long as possible, in contrast to other protocols like HTTP which needs to create a connection each time it sends or receives information. The Server is running a Mosquitto server, which is a MQTT server implementation and also has a MQTT client developed by us using Python and paho package for python. Once the client receives the message it decodes it from the JSON format and recodes it in SQL to store it

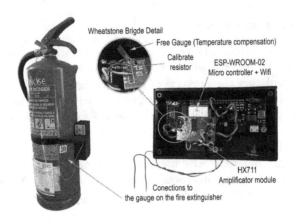

Fig. 3. Prototype device.

in a PostgreSQL database. Since it is the easiest way to create software and to be sure of working in multiple devices and multiple operating systems using a HTTP server, we developed a control panel using a Laravel framework in Php language and mounted it over a nginx web server.

The interface has 2 data displays, the first one is a gauge display which lets us see the current state of the Extinguishers. This display is auto-refreshing once every second, so the user does not need to refresh the browser to continue getting the current state of the extinguishers. The second display is the history display, it shows the history of every extinguisher, one chart for each extinguisher. This chart also has an auto-refresh feature, but in this case, to avoid overloading the browser of the client and the client performance (which may or may not occur depending on the clients machine), the refresh rate of the history graph is once every 30 s.

4   Case Study

The objective is to develop a controlled parameter prototype in order to validate the proposed model. Once manufactured, pressure would be applied and redundant measures would be taken to verify that they all showed the same value, so that the recognized methods will validate ours.

Since the theory of cylinders has been sufficiently tested and its use for metallic materials has been proven, a calibrated specimen made of metal was constructed.

In our case, a pressure vessel was manufactured with steel St 37 − 2 whose properties are shown in Table 1 and the dimensions are shown in Table 2 as a controlled pattern.

The dimensions of this test specimen (pressure vessel) are mainly determined by the pressure limitations of the test laboratory and although it is possible to access higher pressure levels, this is not necessary since the results are perfectly extrapolated.

Table 1. Steel St 37 – 2 mechanical properties

Propertie	Value	Unit
Mechanical		
Ultimate Strength	425	Mpa
Yield Strength	333	Mpa
Young's modulus	205	GPa
Poisson's ratio	0.29	
Thermal		
Thermal expansion coefficient	11.5	µstrain/ºC

Like in previous work [4], firstly pressure is applied just to validate the pressure measurements and secondly, it is done the same for calibrating the gauge measurements. All this experiment will validate the measurements of the prototype against DAS. On this occasion the variations of temperature are taken into account. If both measurements are equal or almost equal with a negligible difference it can be guaranteed that the prototype can be used for commercial and professional use.

The temperature was measured by a T- Thermocouple: Range $(-30...+199,9)$ ºC, Resolution 0,1 ºC, Accuracy $\pm0,5\,°C$

Table 2. Dimensions of the fire extinguisher (Cylindrical part)

Dimension	Magnitude
Diameter (d_i)	170 mm
Length	450 mm
Thickness	1.5 mm

5 Results

To validated the case study it is necessary to compare the results obtained by the PLC (pressure measure) system and the SmartFire prototype (deformation measurements) vs the calibrated pattern (DAS) to evaluate the accuracy of calculations. The PLC pressure results are compared vs the different manometers inserted in the pressure circuit (serial) and the DAS. Manometers are used as redundant measures and DAS is taken as the main reference.

Table 3. Longitudinal deformation measurement (in microns) by different techniques vs Pressure. ε_z^{th}, Theoretical values, ε_z^{Ard} Smartfire and ε_z^{DAS}, Data Acquisition system.

Pressure (bar)	ε_z^{th}	ε_z^{Ard}	ε_z^{DAS}	$\varepsilon_z^{\Delta T}$
1.17	15.79	15.55	17.94	−4.31
2.10	28.29	28.60	30.31	−4.03
3.02	40.75	41.49	42.30	−3.11
3.68	49.61	50.19	49.07	1.08
4.07	54.94	56.06	54.16	1.56
4.53	61.15	62.25	59.72	2.85
5.06	68.22	69.49	65.72	4.99
5.58	75.22	76.00	72.19	6.06
6.63	89.45	89.12	85.91	7.09
7.23	97.49	96.22	93.05	8.89

The pressure measured from the PLC match perfectly with the obtained values from the DAS (average error lower than 0.2%), to highlight that the PLC measurements were much more accurate than those we obtained from the redundant manometers present in the circuit.

Related to the deformation measure, the prototype was compare vs DAS (it was used one more time as pattern), and the error between the two curves showed an average error of 3.5%.

Taking into account that the input data (geometry, material and pressure) are known, the theoretical value of deformation is calculated. DAS results were compared vs the theoretical values (Table 3), the maximum error between the two curves was 2.8%. Once the proposed correction is applied the average error goes down to 1%. During the essay the ΔT was about 1ºC, It can be observed (Fig. 4) that the Δ $(\varepsilon_z^{\Delta T})$ measured is 13.19 vs the theoretical value of 11.5 predicted for this material. The difference can be due to the inaccuracy of the coefficient of thermal expansion of the material or the range of the temperature, which is too low.

All the values correspond to the longitudinal deformations (ε_z) included in Table 3, and are expressed in microns. Notice that the longitudinal axis is used as a reference for the deformations, whereas the transversal axis is used for validating the DAS measurements.

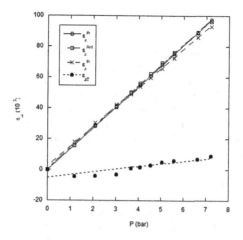

Fig. 4. Comparison chart of the measurements obtained: Theoretical values (ε_z^{th}), Smartfire (ε_z^{Ard}) and Data Acquisition system (ε_z^{DAS}).

6   Conclusions

This article has presented a platform which by means of basic sensorization allows us to monitor the state of pressure of fire extinguishers. The platform enables us to know the status of any fire extinguisher in real time that is connected to the platform through the sensorization described. The use of an agent system allows communication between the prototype and the monitoring platform. The platform registers the data of the conditions of each fire extinguisher and enables us to notify a responsible person when these conditions change.

Future work is intended to incorporate techniques of Machine and Deep Learning to the platform, so that thanks to the large amount of data collected the platform can anticipate the change of conditions of a fire extinguisher. The inclusion of these techniques would allow us to replace the fire extinguishers at the end of their useful life (out of range), resulting in greater safety and economic savings. In addition, the possibility of developing a similar system for CO_2 fire extinguishers will be evaluated, as it is a more complex case. For improving the accuracy of the results, the thickness of the metal sheet in the gauge localization has to be measured by the appropriate method (i.e. ultrasound), because depending on where the gauge is placed the theoretical values change due to the non-uniformity of the metal sheet. Also, an essay must be performed using a large range of temperatures to assure the reliability of the method for outdoor fire extinguishers.

Acknowledgments. This work was financed by ERDF funds through the V Sudoe Interreg program within the framework of the COMPRESSer project, Ref. SOE2/P1/E0643.

References

1. Bolton, W.: Instrumentation and Control Systems. Elsevier (2015)
2. Chase, O.A., Teles, M.B., De Jesus dos Santos Rodrigues, M., De Almeida, J.F.S., Macêdo, W.N., Da Costa Junior, C.T.: A low-cost, stand-alone sensory platform for monitoring extreme solar overirradiance events. Sensors 18(8), 2685 (2018). https://doi.org/10.3390/s18082685, http://www.mdpi.com/1424-8220/18/8/2685
3. Choi, Y., et al.: Numerical and experimental study of a plate-stiffened prismatic pressure vessel. Ocean Eng. 164, 367–376 (2018). https://doi.org/10.1016/j.oceaneng.2018.06.022
4. Garcia-Martin, R., González-Briones, A., Corchado, J.M.: Smartfire: intelligent platform for monitoring fire extinguishers and their building environment. Sensors 19(10), 2390 (2019)
5. Gere, J.M., Goodno, B.J.: Mechanics of Materials. Cengage Learning (2012)
6. Marin, I., et al.: i-light–intelligent luminaire based platform for home monitoring and assisted living. Electronics 7(10), 220 (2018). https://doi.org/10.3390/electronics7100220, http://www.mdpi.com/2079-9292/7/10/220
7. P.MARTORELL - SISTEMAS CONTRAINCENDIO SEVILLA: Tecnología: extintores monitoreados electrónicamente - p.martorell. https://www.pmartorell.com/tecnologia-extintores-monitoreados-electronicamente/
8. Vullo, V.: Circular Cylinders and Pressure Vessels. SSSSM, vol. 3. Springer, Cham (2014). https://doi.org/10.1007/978-3-319-00690-1
9. Zhai, L., Jiang, W.: Intelligent environment monitoring system for university laboratories. Future Internet 10(11), 110 (2018). https://doi.org/10.3390/fi10110110, http://www.mdpi.com/1999-5903/10/11/110

Edge Computing Driven Smart Personal Protective System Deployed on NVIDIA Jetson and Integrated with ROS

Sergio Márquez Sánchez[1](✉), Francisco Lecumberri[1], Vishwani Sati[5],
Ashish Arora[6], Niloufar Shoeibi[1], Sara Rodríguez[1](✉),
and Juan M. Corchado Rodríguez[1,2,3,4]

[1] Bisite Research Group, University of Salamanca, Calle Espejo 2,
37007 Salamanca, Spain
{smarquez,fcolecumberri,Niloufar.shoeibi,srg,corchado}@usal.es
[2] Air Institute, IoT Digital Innovation Hub (Spain),
37188 Salamanca, Spain
[3] Department of Electronics, Information and Communication,
Faculty of Engineering, Osaka Institute of Technology, Osaka 535-8585, Japan
[4] Pusat Komputeran dan Informatik, Universiti Malaysia Kelantan,
Karung Berkunci 36, Pengkaan Chepa, 16100 Kota Bharu, Kelantan, Malaysia
[5] Amity School of Engineering and Technology, Noida, India
vishwanisati@gmail.com
[6] Indian Institute of Technology, Dharwad, India
ashish555@gmail.com

Abstract. The industrial sector is the key driver of the society's economic and social development. However, it is necessary for workers in this sector to have knowledge of and comply with the safety standards of the industry, designed to ensure their safety at work. Companies take different measures to reduce the rate of accidents; they use Internet of Things and Industry 4.0 technologies to detect and give notifications of anomalies detected in the work environment. This article proposes the design of an architecture using Personal Protective Equipment (PPE), where the collected information is processed by Artificial Intelligence (AI) techniques through Edge Computing and the implementation of Multi Agent System and ROS technology. The proposed system is to be embedded in the PPE worn by workers, guaranteeing their safety and integrity through the prediction and notification of anomalies detected in their environment with no need for internet give that in some cases there is internet connection is not possible.

Keywords: e-Health · Context modelling · Condition monitoring

1 Introduction

Wearable technologies are becoming a profitable way to monitor a person's health statistics, such as heart rate and physical activity. The use of Smart PPE is

© Springer Nature Switzerland AG 2020
F. De La Prieta et al. (Eds.): PAAMS 2020 Workshops, CCIS 1233, pp. 385–393, 2020.
https://doi.org/10.1007/978-3-030-51999-5_32

becoming increasingly common and it has become a very useful tool, used by many on a daily basis. Thanks to PPE, information about the worker's environment can be extracted in order to reduce the rate of accidents and occupational diseases, leading to a significant improvement. The worker and their environment can be monitored in real-time, through devices as smartwatch, helmet, belt, bracelet or suit, which alarm the worker by emitting sounds, images or vibrations. Normally the obtained information is transmitted to a server which responsible for collecting and processing information. Subsequently, Machine Learning techniques may be applied.

Currently, the accident rate among workers is high in all types of industries, especially because of the technological transformation within the working environment. Thus, it is necessary to improve the field of Job Safety Analysis (JSA). Different researches have aimed to design new tools and solutions for the protection of people in their working environment, developing technology capable of real-time monitoring, to improve safety and health in the workplace. In addition, some researches have focused on taking advantage of the benefits of smart data and AI, to obtain a support system in the performance of tasks at work, capable of evolving and learning. This proposal involves the use of Edge computing technology, it integrates the NVIDIA Jetson board and a Robotics Operating System (ROS) required for system management. Through ROS we can manage different software frameworks, which are independent of each other. ROS facilitates the implementation of a multiagent system, increasing the speed of software development and its redistribution. In the present scenario, ROS is implemented in different domains: Healthcare, industry, medicine and automotive electronics. The healthcare sector is growing rapidly and its approach is optimal as it introduces robotics operations [17,18] in daily activities.

2   Related Work

Over the last decade, wearable devices have captured the attention of industries and of the academic community. This interest has been manifested in the growing tendency of organizations to research and develop such products-. They can be useful in multiple fields: sports, security, health and entertainment.

A study of the different regulations and manuals of Occupational Risk Prevention "ORP" has been carried out on the basis of the content provided in the book [1]. The purpose of this study was to learn about the risks that may be captured thanks to their compatibility with the tools/devices. To this end, the situations that present a greater incidence in different scenarios, grouped by activity/sector, have been identified. This study makes it possible to build models for the detection of emerging risks and to create ontologies for the association of actions and risks.

For example, fall statistics show that the most serious consequences could be solved with early attention, sometimes the injury or contusion causes a loss of consciousness or the inability to call for help. Thus, an automatic warning system could lead to a significant improvement in the safety of the workers. There is a relationship between the time the a worker spends lying on the ground and the severity of the fall. In addition, the fear of falling leads to a significant decline in the quality of life of as people grow older; reducing their outings, their social life, their independence. In older workers fear may increase the risk of falling [2,3]. In recent years, numerous systems based on information technologies have been designed to solve those problems. However, their use is not widespread. Hawley-Hague et al. [4] have conducted a systematic review of studies on the people's perception of technology for fall prevention or detection. These authors conclude that there are a number of intrinsic and extrinsic factors, motivating people to use those technologies and adopt them permanently. Among the intrinsic factors: 1) User control to cancel false alarms or disarm the system at certain times. 2) The independence gained with the system to move without fear. 3) The user's self-perception about their risk of falling. Some of the PPE that we can use as book [5] suggests are Protective helmets for industry, Eye and face protectors, Ear protectors, Protectors of the respiratory tract, Protective gloves, Safety shoes and boots, Protective clothing, Life jackets for industry, Fall protectors. PPE is designed to protect workers from injury and illness within the work space resulting from contact with chemical, radiological, physical, electrical, mechanical and other hazards. Research has been carried out on equipment and auxiliary systems for the detection, warning and identification of hazards, which can be integrated in the system, ensuring that workers' meet the safety requirements [6–10]. To this end, an analysis will be made of the possibilities of adapting, developing and optimising existing technologies of: Measurement of anthropometric parameters, real-time location systems and sensor networks. The anthropometric parameters will serve to establish estimates of the worker's state in real time, understanding state to be the situation in which a given set of biometric measurements is within pre-determined thresholds. In this sense, it will be investigated what metrics can be obtained by means of sensors (bio-electromagnetism, temperature, heart rate, skin moisture and conductance, level of ionizing radiation, etc.) and what level of failure and accuracy they produce.

This analysis includes the definition of the specifications for the different communication subsystems, the actors that will participate in the network and a system of priorities between the sensors, worker and environment of visualization of the alerts. The possibilities of wireless sensor networks with technologies such as Wi-Fi, Bluetooth and radio frequency will be analysed.

Research will be carried out on the emergence of risks and ontologies will be created for the association of actions and risks. The aim is to prevent and protect the worker as well as to eliminate the risk whenever possible. To do this, it is essential to have context information to model the worker's environment, so that the system learns to identify patterns and the risks faced by the worker, predicting them before they occur. For this reason, the implementation of a sensor network in the work environment will be studied, which will help complement the information obtained by the PPE (ambient temperature, humidity, gases, artificial vision...) regarding the conditions of the worker's environment, facilitating the identification of risks (electricity, gas inhalation...) [11–14].

Thanks to extensive research in the fields of IoT and Machine Learning, NVIDIA's Jetson Nano, the latest addition to the Jetson family of embedded computing boards, is being used as an edge computing platform for ML inferencing. Vittorio Mazzia et al. [15] have worked on real-time detection of apples to estimate the apple yields and therefore, manage the apple supplies. Researchers had also worked previously on proposing a machine vision system for yield estimation. Unfortunately, those algorithms required high computational power, utilized intensive hardware setup, and had weight and power constraints, making them unsuitable for real-time apple detection. Regarding machine learning algorithms, Mazzia et al. used Jetson Nano that contributed to accelerating complex machine learning tasks. The light weight, low power consumption and form factor significantly made the goal of yield estimation plausible.

Siddhartha S. Srinivasa et al. [16] have devised MuSHR, an economic robotic race car, an open source platform to advance research and education in the field of robotics. The hardware architecture of the robotic car comprises of Nvidia's Jetson Nano, on which the computations are performed. Srinivasa et al. mention that the ability of Nano to be loaded with the desired operating system and program through an SD card has been the primary reason for its inclusion in the hardware architecture of MuSHR.

In the present world, Internet of Things (IoT) has emerged as one of the fields where ROS has been implemented. In this context, a novel concept, Internet of Robotic Things (IoRT) was given by [18]. It is a paradigm that shares certain aspects with the Internet of Things and Robotics. The architecture described in [19] has 5 layers: hardware layer, network layer, internet layer, infrastructure layer, and application layer. One of the key benefits associated with this idea is the processing of the computationally heavy tasks can be done on the cloud instead of doing it on the local server. However, the task of deciding on the processes that should be performed in the cloud is still not clear.

In another notable work [20], a novel protocol, ROSLink, is defined. It is a communication bridge between ROS and Cloud Robotics. In ROS, there is no functionality of controlling robots over the internet. Although the ROS master can be deployed at the workstation, making it possible to control the robot remotely, this approach is not scalable and is only limited to a Local Area Network (LAN). This inspired the authors to come up with a communication protocol that can be equipped with ROS. ROSLink protocol is based on a 3-tier architecture. In this protocol, there is a proxy server running at the ground station and a client interacts with the robot with the help of this protocol through the proxy server.

3   Proposed Method

The concentrator node consists of a NVIDIA Jetson Nano, which mounts Ubuntu Mate as its operating system. The objective of this node is to collect the measurements sent by the different devices, store them and route them to a display mechanism. To enable communication between the measurement devices and the concentrator, the latter provides the system with a Mosquitto server, which implements the MQTT communication protocol. The MQTT protocol has been chosen because it adapts to the volume of data that needs to be transmitted and also provides native security standards, such as Transport Layer Security (TSL) and Secure Sockets Layer (SSL). The data will be sent between the device microcontrollers and the concentrator in JSON format (Fig. 1).

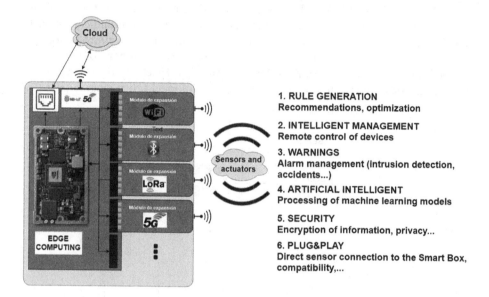

Fig. 1. Gateway edge computing

The data received in the concentrator will be collected by a software developed in Python 3. This software is in charge of carrying out the storage tasks and sending the data to the visualization dashboard. For the storage, a database implemented in "MongoDB" is used, where the data received by the MQTT protocol are stored. MongoDB has been used because it is a document-oriented database, in which the received JSON can be stored without previous transformations. The processing of the data stored in MongoDB is done from a software developed in Python 3 in a remote machine, more powerful than a Raspberry Pi. Phyton's SKLearn library (Scikit-learn) is used to process data. This library is focused on the processing of large blocks of data, including classification algorithms, regression and group analysis. Through the analysis of these data, it is intended to find behaviour patterns that allow to predict anomalous situations. The Gateway Edge Computing System for industrial machines is capable of receiving data from different types of wireless sensors (via Wi-Fi, LoraWan, Bluetooth, Zigbee,. . .) and at the same time it must receive data from the machine cycle so that they can be linked to the sensor data. The Gateway will also be connected to the Cloud, making it possible to send data to the server and to analyse those that need a higher level of computation and do not require low latency. This data will be used to train a neural network capable of controlling the process. At the same time, the process will be controlled using other machine learning strategies, such as logistic regression. The sensors must obtain the measurements that the machine controller is not able to obtain by itself. The range of variables measured by the sensors can differ depending on the machine in question and its application. Examples of the parameters measured include vibration, temperature, pressure, gases, infrared or even cameras. Integration with the platform and its security framework, testing of the nodes and secure communication with the platform. The choice of a reliable and robust communication protocol for the industrial environment and the development around this standard of a communication mechanism that optimizes data transmission (packetized data, relevant and significant data transmission for the capacity of local processing...) (Fig. 2).

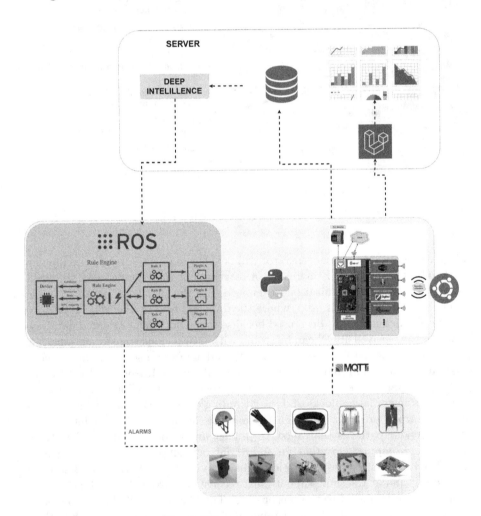

Fig. 2. Diagram of the system

For data capture, devices developed in different projects; their characteristics and connectivity meet the requirements the proposed system and can therefore be integrated in it [21,22]. The following Fig. 3 shows some of them.

DEVICE	USE	SENSORS	RISK FACTORS
HELMET	Protection for impacts and state detecting work environment	Light sensor, moisture, gas sensor, accelerometers, sensitive force resistors, etc.	Lack of adequate lighting, Temperature, Air Quality, movement,
BELT	Fall detection	Accelerometer and noise sensor	Falls and noise inside the workplace
BRACELET	Worker health condition	Temperature, rate pulse sensor and accelerometer	Falls, low and high body temperature and pulse inappropriate
POSTURAL CORRECTOR	Correction of back posture	IMU's	Back and neck problems
ENVIRONMENTAL MODULE	Environment status	Gas, temperature, humidity and light	Risk Environmental condition
ELECTRIC MODULE	Electric and magnetic field	Hall sensor	Electric and magnetic condition
INTRUSION MODULE	Detect intrusion workspace	PIR sensor	Detect when someone enter inside de workspace

Fig. 3. Devices that can be integrated in the system

4   Conclusions and Future Work

In a future work we are going to focus on the implementation of the system proposed in this article. For this purpose, real devices will be selected to improve security in different industries and through Gateway Edge Computing and the architecture presented in the article, AI algorithms, Multiagent Systems and ROS will be implemented [9,12,14,23–27]. Thanks to them, the most important risks will be determined, trying to suppress or minimize them as much as possible.

Acknowledgments. This work was supported by the Spanish Junta de Castilla y León, Consejería de empleo. Project: UPPER, aUgmented reality and smart personal protective equipment (PPE) for intelligent pRevention of occupational hazards and accessibility INVESTUN/18/SA/0001.

References

1. Espeso, J.A., Fernandez, F., Rodriguez, A., Menendez, F., Vasquez, I.: Manual para la Formación de Técnicos de Prevención de Riesgos Laborales. Editorial Lex Nova (2006)
2. Noury, N., Rumeau, P., Bourke, A.K., O'Laighin, G., Lundy, J.E.: A proposal for the classification and evaluation of fall detectors. IRBM **29**(6), 340–349 (2008)
3. Bianchi, F., Redmond, S.J., Narayanan, M.R., Cerutti, S., Lovell, N.H.: Barometric pressure and triaxial accelerometry-based falls event detection. IEEE Trans. Neural Syst. Rehabil. Eng. **18**(6), 619–627 (2010)
4. Hawley-Hague, H., Boulton, E., Hall, A., Pfeiffer, K., Todd, C.: Older adults' perceptions of technologies aimed at falls prevention, detection or monitoring: a systematic review. Int. J. Med. Inform. **83**(6), 416–426 (2014)
5. Zúñiga, A.H.: Seguridad e Higiene Industrial. Editorial Limusa (2003)
6. Wang, X., Tarrío, P., Bernardos, A.M., Metola, E., Casar, J.R.: User-independent accelerometer-based gesture recognition for mobile devices. ADCAIJ **1**(3) (2012). ISSN 2255-2863
7. Oliveira, T., Neves, J., Novais, P.: Guideline formalization and knowledge representation for clinical decision support. ADCAIJ **1**(2) (2012). ISSN 2255-2863
8. Coria, J.A.G., Castellanos-Garzón, J.A., Corchado, J.M.: Intelligent business processes composition based on multi-agent systems. Expert Syst. Appl. **41**(4), 1189–1205 (2014)
9. Tapia, D.I., Fraile, J.A., Rodríguez, S., Alonso, R.S., Corchado, J.M.: Integrating hardware agents into an enhanced multi-agent architecture for Ambient Intelligence systems. Inf. Sci. **222**, 47–65 (2013)
10. Nihan, C.E.: Healthier? More efficient? Fairer? An overview of the main ethical issues raised by the use of Ubicomp in the workplace. ADCAIJ **2**(1) (2013). ISSN 2255-2863
11. Macek, K., Rojicek, J., Kontes, G., Rovas, D.V.: Black-box optimization for buildings and its enhancement by advanced communication infrastructure. ADCAIJ **2**(2) (2013). ISSN 2255-2863
12. Casado-Vara, R., Martin-del Rey, A., Affes, S., Prieto, J., Corchado, J.M.: IoT network slicing on virtual layers of homogeneous data for improved algorithm operation in smart buildings. Future Gener. Comput. Syst. **102**, 965–977 (2020)
13. Satoh, I.: Bio-inspired self-adaptive agents in distributed systems. ADCAIJ **1**(2) (2012). ISSN 2255-2863
14. Tapia, D.I., Corchado, J.M.: An ambient intelligence based multi-agent system for Alzheimer health care. IJACI **1**(1), 15–26 (2009)
15. Mazzia, V., Khaliq, A., Salvetti, F., Chiaberge, M.: Real-time apple detection system using embedded systems with hardware accelerators: an edge AI application (2020)
16. Srinivasa, S.S., et al.: MuSHR: a low-cost, open-source robotic racecar for education and research (2019)
17. Noori, F.M., Portugal, D., Rocha, R.P., Couceiro, M.S.: On 3D simulators for multi-robot systems in ROS: MORSE or Gazebo? In: 2017 IEEE International Symposium on Safety, Security and Rescue Robotics (SSRR), pp. 19–24. IEEE (2017)
18. Araújo, A., Portugal, D., Couceiro, M.S., Rocha, R.P.: Integrating Arduino-based educational mobile robots in ROS. J. Intell. Robot. Syst. **77**(2), 281–298 (2015)

19. Ray, P.P.: Internet of robotic things: concept, technologies, and challenges. IEEE Access **4**, 9489–9500 (2016)
20. Koubaa, A., Alajlan, M., Qureshi, B.: ROSLink: bridging ROS with the Internet-of-Things for cloud robotics. In: Koubaa, A. (ed.) Robot Operating System (ROS). SCI, vol. 707, pp. 265–283. Springer, Cham (2017). https://doi.org/10.1007/978-3-319-54927-9_8
21. Sánchez, S.M.: Electronic textiles for intelligent prevention of occupational hazards. In: Herrera-Viedma, E., Vale, Z., Nielsen, P., Martin Del Rey, A., Casado Vara, R. (eds.) DCAI 2019. AISC, vol. 1004, pp. 217–220. Springer, Cham (2020). https://doi.org/10.1007/978-3-030-23946-6_29
22. Sánchez, S.M., Vara, R.C., Criado, F.J.G., González, S.R., Tejedor, J.P., Corchado, J.M.: Smart PPE and CPE platform for electric industry workforce. In: Martínez Álvarez, F., Troncoso Lora, A., Sáez Muñoz, J.A., Quintián, H., Corchado, E. (eds.) SOCO 2019. AISC, vol. 950, pp. 422–431. Springer, Cham (2020). https://doi.org/10.1007/978-3-030-20055-8_40
23. Li, T., Sun, S., Corchado, J.M., Siyau, M.F.: A particle dyeing approach for track continuity for the SMC-PHD filter. In: 17th International Conference on Information Fusion (FUSION), pp. 1–8. IEEE, July 2014
24. Fdez-Riverola, F., Iglesias, E.L., Díaz, F., Méndez, J.R., Corchado, J.M.: SpamHunting: an instance-based reasoning system for spam labelling and filtering. Decis. Support Syst. **43**(3), 722–736 (2007)
25. Corchado, J.M., Fyfe, C.: Unsupervised neural method for temperature forecasting. Artif. Intell. Eng. **13**(4), 351–357 (1999)
26. Trindade, N., Antunes, L.: An architecture for agent's risk perception. ADCAIJ **2**(2) (2013). ISSN 2255-2863
27. Oliver, M., Molina, J.P., Fernández-Caballero, A., González, P.: Collaborative computer-assisted cognitive rehabilitation system. ADCAIJ **6**(3) (2017). ISSN 2255-2863

Load Generators for Automatic Simulation of Urban Fleets

Pasqual Martí$^{(\boxtimes)}$, Jaume Jordán®, Javier Palanca®, and Vicente Julian®

Valencian Research Institute for Artificial Intelligence (VRAIN),
Universitat Politècnica de València, Camino de Vera s/n, 46022 Valencia, Spain
pasmargi@inf.upv.es, {jjordan,jpalanca,vinglada}@dsic.upv.es
http://vrain.upv.es/

Abstract. To ensure cities sustainability, we must deal with, among other challenges, traffic congestion, and its associated carbon emissions. We can approach such a problem from two perspectives: the transition to electric vehicles, which implies the need for charging station infrastructure, and the optimization of traffic flow. However, cities are complex systems, so it is helpful to test changes on them in controlled environments like the ones provided by simulators. In our work, we use Sim-Fleet, an agent-based fleet simulator. Nevertheless, SimFleet does not provide tools for easily setting up big experiments, neither to simulate the realistic movement of its agents inside a city. Aiming to solve that, we enhanced SimFleet introducing two fully configurable generators that automatize the creation of experiments. First, the charging stations generator, which allocates a given amount of charging stations following a certain distribution, enabling to simulate how transports would charge and compare distributions. Second, the load generator, which populates the experiment with a given number of agents of a given type, introducing them dynamically in the simulation, and assigns them a movement that can be either random or based on real city data. The generators proved to be useful for comparing different distributions of charging stations as well as different agent behaviors over the same complex setup.

Keywords: Multi-agent system · Simulation · Transportation · Electric vehicle · Smart city · Urban fleets

1 Introduction

With more than half of the world's population living in cities, the list of challenges for keeping them sustainable has grown. "A smart sustainable city is an innovative city that uses ICTs (Information and Communication Technologies) to improve quality of life, the efficiency of urban operations and services and competitiveness while ensuring that it meets the needs of present and future generations concerning economic, social, environmental and cultural aspects"[1]. In

---

[1] This definition was provided by the International Telecommunication Union (ITU) and United Nations Economic Commission for Europe (UNECE) in 2015.

© Springer Nature Switzerland AG 2020
F. De La Prieta et al. (Eds.): PAAMS 2020 Workshops, CCIS 1233, pp. 394–405, 2020.
https://doi.org/10.1007/978-3-030-51999-5_33

this paper, we focus on one of these challenges, traffic congestion (and its associated carbon emissions), from two different approaches. The first is the transition to electric vehicles (EV), which would greatly reduce the carbon emissions generated by cities. The main problem that users encounter to switch to EV is the insecurity they feel towards access to EV charging stations [2,6]. The allocation and installation of EV charging stations inside a city is not a trivial problem and it entails a great disbursement of money for municipalities. As for the second approach, it is based on traffic flow optimization. Improving this requires accurate data. One way of researching how to deal with such challenges is through the use of simulators [4]. With them, we can see the effect some of the changes would have over the city after defining them. However, cities are very complex systems, so it is necessary to have a complete simulator that allows experimentation with big, complex configurations for both charging station allocation and traffic inside the city. The more realistic the simulator, the more accurate and useful experiments would be for real-world applications.

In this work, we use SimFleet simulator [5], which is able to place different varieties of agents with custom behaviors over real-world cities to develop and test any type of strategies. Nevertheless, there is an important flaw in SimFleet to prepare simulations with a significant number of agents, and also to have an appropriate representation of the traffic of a city. Therefore, in this paper, we propose a significant improvement for SimFleet: the inclusion of two generators at different levels. On the one hand, a charging stations generator to create several distributions of these infrastructures, and to be able to make comparisons and simulations with well-informed charging stations emplacing systems such as the one in [3], which uses several data sources to feed a genetic algorithm that obtains solutions. On the other hand, a load generator of agents on the move in a city such as urban fleets of taxis, private vehicles, delivery transports, buses, etc.; and customers of taxis or packages. Furthermore, this load generator can consider real data of the city, which implies a more informed approach to generate the real traffic of a city to be used in dynamic simulations.

These generators will allow SimFleet users to create realistic scenarios easily without having to write long configuration files, and more importantly, to generate load representing real traffic of the specific city by using available data such as population, traffic, and tweets, from open data portals[2], or gathered with other tools such as [7].

The rest of this paper is structured as follows. Section 2 presents the fleet simulator SimFleet, in which this work is built upon, and its main flaw. Then, Sect. 3 explains the two main generators proposed in this work, that is, the charging stations simulator and the load generator of urban fleets. Section 4 presents some experimental results using the generators in SimFleet. Finally, the conclusions of this work are presented in Sect. 5.

---

[2] http://gobiernoabierto.valencia.es/en/data/.

2 SimFleet Description

SimFleet [5] is an agent-based fleet simulator to test strategies. Each simulation counts with a series of customers, transports and a fleet manager. Customer agents represent people (or packages) that need to be transported from their origin location to their destination in the city. For doing so, each Customer agent requests a single transport service, provided by a Transport agent. Finally, the FleetManager agent is responsible for putting in contact the customers in need of a transport service, and the transports that may be available to offer these services. In short, the FleetManager agent acts like a transport call center or directory facilitator [1], accepting the incoming requests from customers and forwarding these requests to the appropriate transports.

For the movement of Transport agents around the city, SimFleet makes use of OSRM[3], a routing engine for finding shortest paths in road networks. Querying an OSRM server specifying the service *route* and passing origin and destination points returns the shortest route between those two points.

The behavior of each agent and the way they get to agreements is determined by its strategy. In our work, however, we set aside the aspect of implementation and testing of strategies to focus on the creation of simulations, a feature in which SimFleet has weaknesses.

2.1 The SimFleet Flaw

To understand the weaknesses SimFleet presents in relation to simulation creation we must first explain how the experiments are described. SimFleet uses a configuration file in JSON format to load the agents of a simulation. The agents and their features are the relevant part of the configuration for our line of work. There are four types of agents: fleets, transports, customers and stations. Each agent, depending on its type, has a certain amount of attributes that must be indicated for their creation.

Currently, the only way of filling the configuration file is to manually create each agent, giving values to their attributes. This is inconvenient to create scenarios with a great number of vehicles, customers or packages. Besides that, it is likely that users employ SimFleet for reproducing the mobility around a city in a simulated environment. This task involves the dynamic input of agents in the simulation as well as their informed movement around the environment based on real data from the city. Additionally, the introduction of randomly generated agents that interfere with the main simulated task could be useful for building a more realistic trial as well as testing different distributions of charging stations or simply evaluating new strategies. Our work aims to fulfill those needs by the introduction of Generators that automatize the creation of simulation configurations.

---

[3] http://project-osrm.org/.

3   Generators

We will now introduce our work, which consists of generators to facilitate the setup of bigger and more realistic simulations with SimFleet. It includes a charging stations generator, which populates the simulation area with a given number of charging stations following a determined pattern; and a load generator, which populates the simulation space with different types of agents with an associated movement that can be pseudo-random or informed (provided we have access to real-world data). Besides that, fully random versions of both generators were also implemented so as to compare informed versions against them.

A simulation on SimFleet is defined by its configuration file. To automatically create experiments means to generate new configuration files or fill a previous one with data according to some parameters. For this, all generators include the option to get as input a configuration file and they are prepared to leave the present objects of such file unchanged while including the ones generated. Besides that, each generator works with a GeoJSON file that defines the area of the real world where our simulation will take place and thus they have to populate. We will call this file the **city map**, since, usually, simulations are performed within the borders of a city. Since it represents a real-world location, all geometries defined in the city map are indicated with latitude-longitude points; to manipulate them we will use the Python Shapely library[4].

3.1   Charging Stations Generator

The charging stations generator is used in order to test different distributions of charging (or petrol) stations of any kind over an area. The generator has many parameters; we will only present the relevant ones: n charging stations to distribute; p charging poles of the distribution; and distribution type, $\{random, uniform, radial\}$, that affects how stations are positioned inside the area.

Each station may have several charging poles. The allocation of charging poles between stations will be discussed further on. The generator outputs a file in GeoJSON format which indicates the type and position of each station. Such a position, however, can not be any point inside the city map but rather a valid point: a point belonging to a street or road. For obtaining valid positions, we make use of the function *getValidPoint*, which given a point returns the nearest valid point to it. This function uses the service *nearest* of OSRM, which returns the nearest point belonging to a street or road with respect to the specified coordinates.

Random Distribution. In this type of distribution, n valid points are generated within the city map. Each of the points indicates the position of a charging station. For the generation of points, the bounds of the polygon that defines the city map are used: $x_{min}, y_{min}, x_{max}, y_{max}$. Using these values, random x and y coordinates are generated for each point. Then, the corresponding valid point

---

[4] https://pypi.org/project/Shapely/.

is obtained. If the point is contained in the city map, it is stored as a station location; otherwise, it is discarded. This process is repeated until there are as many stored points as the number of stations.

A random distribution is interesting from the experimentation perspective to compare other more informed distributions against it.

Uniform Distribution. This distribution divides uniformly[5] the city map (see Fig. 1a) into equal size cells, generally with rectangular shape. To do so, it creates a wider working area, the *grid* (Fig. 1b), defined from the bounds of the polygon representing the city map. If such bounds are x_{min}, y_{min}, x_{max}, y_{max}, the grid is the four vertex polygon defined by the points $\{(x_{min}, y_{min}), (x_{min}, y_{max}), (x_{max}, y_{max}), (x_{max}, y_{min})\}$.

The number of rows and columns of the grid is determined by the number of stations (n) and its width and height, following the criteria shown in Eq. (1). If the number of stations is a perfect square, i.e., its square root is a positive integer, the grid will have the same amount of rows and columns, obtaining exactly n cells. However, in general, the number of rows and columns will depend on whether the grid is wider or higher, having one more column than the number of rows (or vice versa) accordingly.

$$\begin{cases} rows = cols = \sqrt{n} & n \text{ is perfect square} \\ rows = \lfloor \sqrt{n} \rfloor, \, cols = \lceil \sqrt{n} \rceil & height < width \\ rows = \lceil \sqrt{n} \rceil, \, cols = \lfloor \sqrt{n} \rfloor & otherwise \end{cases} \quad (1)$$

Once the grid is split, we trim each of the cells against the city map, which causes cells outside of it to disappear and those laying over its borders to get an irregular shape (see Fig. 1c). These final cells are stored in a list of valid polygons where stations can be placed.

Next, an iterative process begins to allocate every station. The list of valid polygons is traversed and a station is placed in the closest valid point (using the *getValidPoint* function) to the centroid of the polygon. This process finishes once every polygon has one station in it or all stations have been allocated. After this, if there were still stations to allocate, the rest are positioned in a random valid point of a randomly chosen valid polygon (Fig. 1d shows a possible outcome).

Besides this, we also implemented a random version of this distribution in which the city map is divided in the same way emplacing, however, each station in a random valid point within a randomly selected cell.

Radial Distribution. This distribution was inspired by the radial distribution of activity within certain cities, which presents a higher rate towards its core and decreases as it gets closer to the peripheries. It requires an additional parameter c, which indicates the number of circles that will be used to divide the city map.

---

[5] The name "Uniform distribution" does not refer to a probability distribution but to how stations are divided in the city map.

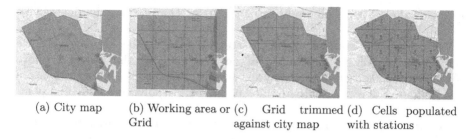

(a) City map   (b) Working area or (c)   Grid   trimmed (d) Cells populated
                    Grid   against city map   with stations

Fig. 1. Uniform distribution of stations process

The division process begins by defining two copies of a wider working area, created as described for the uniform distribution. One of those copies will be divided into a series of triangles, 8 by default as can be seen in Fig. 2a, by joining every vertex and sides' middle point with the centroid of the original city map. As for the other, it will be divided by c concentric circles with an initial radius r calculated taking into account the map dimensions. To avoid circle overlap, each circle is trimmed against the one created before it, starting by the last (and biggest) created. This obtains an area with a middle circle and many rings around it, as can be seen in Fig. 2b. Take into account that from now on when we mention circles we will also be referring to the rings. Next, the two aforementioned areas are intersected with each other, dividing each circle into 8 polygons, and trimmed against the city map, obtaining a division of it as shown in Fig. 2c.

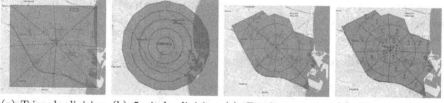

(a) Triangle division (b) 5 circle division (c) Final city map (d) 20 stations be-
of working area   of working area   division   tween 5 circles

Fig. 2. Radial city map division

Each station is then allocated in the closest valid point to the centroid of one of the polygons. The number of stations per circle (n/c), as well as the amount of polygons a circle has, is taken into account to allocate the stations as uniformly as possible within the city map and each circle. The algorithm populates each triangle starting from the inner circle and moving towards the outer. Once all polygons of a triangle have a station assigned, the algorithm will select the next triangle according to the number of stations and the total number of polygons to divide the stations uniformly within a circle. The final distribution can be seen in Fig. 2d.

The number of stations may be greater than the number of polygons since the number of circles is determined by the user. The algorithm described above places only one station in each polygon. In this case, the rest of the stations are assigned a random position by randomly choosing a polygon and a valid point within it.

We also implemented a fully random version of this distribution that divides the city map in the same way, takes into account the number of stations per circle, but chooses randomly the polygons within a circle as well as a valid point within them.

Charging Poles Allocation. The amount of charging poles (spots for a vehicle to charge) we want in our configuration is one of the parameters of the station generator. There must be at least one charging pole in each station. After this, if there are more charging poles to be distributed they will be allocated according to one of the following methods:

The first one distributes the points evenly by traversing the list of stations, adding one point to each until all points have been allocated. Then, the list of stations is shuffled, so as not to benefit stations that are traversed first. In this way, the stations will have either p/n or $p/n - 1$ charging poles.

The alternative is a pseudo-random distribution of the remaining points that works choosing a random amount of points and a random station to which assign them. To avoid a too uneven distribution of poles, such a random amount can be limited by a parameter that indicates the maximum percentage of the total charging poles that a single station can have. For instance, using a maximum percentage of 30%, we ensure that no station will have more than $0.3 \cdot p$ charging poles.

3.2   Load Generator of Movements in a City

The load generator is used to create either a random or informed load on the simulation. Such load can be adapted to any of the agent types that SimFleet offers: electric vehicles, taxi fleets, customers for taxis, delivery vehicles, packages, etc. The relevant parameters of this generator are: agent type t; amount of agents n; minimum distance min_dist in meters; starting delay d in seconds; amount of agents per batch $agents\_per\_batch$.

The generator aims to create a movement of at least min_dist meters of n agents of t type within the borders of a given city map. The delay parameter d determines at what time of the simulation the generated agents will start running; by default, it is 0. The amount of agents per batch is introduced to give different delays to sets of $agents\_per\_batch$ agents, which will begin its execution at the same time. This may be useful when generating a large number of agents. If indicated, the first batch of agents will have a delay of d; the second, a delay of $2d$, and so on. As we mentioned above, all generators are prepared to receive an existing SimFleet configuration file as input and fill it with agent data. This enables the use of the load generator to introduce, in the same simulation, different types of agents in various amounts, with different delays and batch sizes, to create a complex system.

Random Movement Generator. The random load is created by choosing a random route (random origin and destination points) for the agent to perform. Both random origin and destination points must be valid points of the area, and they must be at least *min_dist* apart from one another. This process is repeated to create n agents of type t. The origin point will determine where in the area the agent will spawn, whereas the destination point indicates where it will finish its execution. If the agent type is customer or package, the movement is performed by the corresponding transport vehicle that carries it after it gets picked up.

Informed Movement Generator. The informed version of the load generator aims to reproduce more realistic movements around the city map. For this, it is necessary to provide the generator with relevant data from which to ground the routes of the agents. This data can be obtained from diverse sources; often open data platforms that the government of a city or country makes accessible for its citizens. For our generator, we used the following data:

- **Population information**: It shows the amount of people that live in different zones of a city. The population information (P) is defined as: $P = \{(C_1, p_1), (C_2, p_2), \ldots, (C_n, p_n)\}$, where C_i is a closed polygon representing a zone in the city together with its population p_i.
- **Traffic information**: It shows the number of vehicles moving around a certain area. The traffic information (T) is defined as: $T = \{(R_1, t_1), (R_2, t_2), \ldots, (R_n, t_n)\}$, where R_i is a polyline that follows a street or road indicating the volume of traffic t_i.
- **Twitter activity**: Information about the amount of geo-located tweets, from the social network Twitter, tweeted from a certain location. This information can be used to determine where a representative percentage of the population is spending their time. The Twitter activity (A) is defined as: $A = \{(Q_1, a_1), (Q_2, a_2), \ldots, (Q_n, a_n)\}$, where Q_i is a point represented as a latitude-longitude tuple and a_i the number of tweets in such coordinates.

The information is used to create a probability distribution among the available points of the area. The selection of the origin and destination points will be performed according to such distribution. For this, we begin by creating a set of available points. The city map (M) is divided as if it was a grid similarly as explained in Sect. 3.1 for the uniform distribution, obtaining $M = \{(G_1, O_1), (G_2, O_2), \ldots, (G_n, O_n)\}$; where G_i is a closed polygon and O_i the nearest valid point to the centroid of G_i. The number of rows and columns of the grid is a configurable parameter and it determines the granularity of the system. A higher amount implies more cells in the grid which directly translates

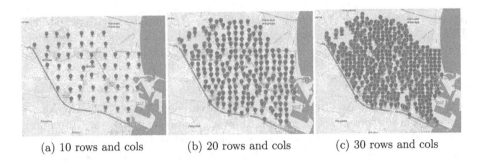

(a) 10 rows and cols   (b) 20 rows and cols   (c) 30 rows and cols

Fig. 3. Number of available points according to map division granularity

into more available points, as it can be seen in Fig. 3. The more points, the more distributed will be the probability.

By merging the city data with M, we join, for every polygon G_i, the population, traffic and Twitter activity amounts that take place within its area: $M = \{(G_1, O_1, \{p_1, t_1, a_1\}), (G_2, O_2, \{p_2, t_2, a_2\}), \ldots, (G_n, O_n, \{p_n, t_n, a_n\})\}$ and calculate the probability associated to each point O_i as in Eq. (2):

$$prob(O_i) = w_p \cdot \frac{p_i}{\sum_{j=1}^{N} p_j} + w_t \cdot \frac{t_i}{\sum_{j=1}^{N} t_j} + w_a \cdot \frac{a_i}{\sum_{j=1}^{N} a_j}; \text{ with } w_p + w_t + w_a = 1 \quad (2)$$

where w_p, w_t and w_a are weights that control the influence of each of the factors over the probability. Finally, the generator takes into account the set of available points (S) and their corresponding probability: $S = \{(O_1, p(O_1)), (O_2, p(O_2)), \ldots, (O_n, p(O_n))\}$ to generate the routes.

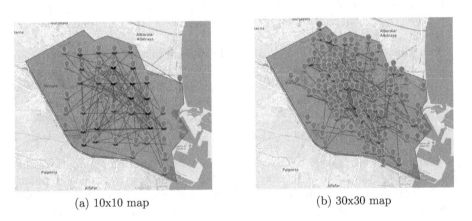

(a) 10x10 map   (b) 30x30 map

Fig. 4. 100 routes examples

Once every point in S has its probability assigned, a process to create the n routes begins (see examples of Fig. 4). This process is very similar to the one used in the random load generator, but this time the origin and destination points are chosen from S according to the probability distribution and ensuring the *min_dist* between both points.

4   Experimental Results

To present experimental results for our generators, we define and set up a simulation and then execute it in SimFleet with two different strategies.

4.1   Setup

The experiment defined takes place over the main area of the city of Valencia, Spain. We generated 20 electric charging stations distributed uniformly in the area. As for the load, we used the informed load generator to create a fleet of 30 electric taxis and 30 customers with a granularity of 30. Taxis were created with random values for their autonomy so that some of the taxis would be forced to charge in one of the stations. For the customers, the weights of Eq. (2) were $w_p = 5/12$, $w_t = 1/4$, $w_a = 1/3$, increasing the impact of population and Twitter activity. The routes of the customers were defined by points that were at least 700 meters apart. For the taxis creation, the weights of Eq. (2) were $w_p = 1/3$, $w_t = 5/12$, $w_a = 1/4$, giving more importance to traffic and population. Figure 5 shows the described experiment in SimFleet.

(a) Experiment setup   (b) Experiment running

Fig. 5. Experiment shown in SimFleet

We executed this setup using two different strategies for the FleetManager and Transport agents. The first strategy is the *default* one provided by SimFleet: All customers send their transport service requests to the FleetManager which, in turn, forwards them to every taxi in the fleet, ignoring their state. Taxi agents, if available, will accept the request of a random customer, taking into account that it may have already another taxi assigned. As for charging, taxis choose a random available station. In contrast, the *modified*, more informed strategy works in the following way: Customers still send their requests to the FleetManager but the latter will just inform the nearest taxi to the customer among the available taxis. Taxis will then attend requests of the customers closer to them, which will reduce the customers' waiting time. Also, if the taxi needed to charge, it would not go to a random station but the closest one to it.

4.2   Results

The metrics that SimFleet offers to evaluate simulations are the average waiting time of the customers until their assigned transport picks them up, the average total time the customer waits for their transport service to be completed, and the simulation time. Since the modified strategy aims to reduce customer waiting time and total time, we will use them as the metrics to improve.

Table 1. Time (seconds) for the tested strategies

Strategy	Avg. waiting time	Avg. total time	Avg. simulation time
Default	21.06	25.28	50.38
Modified	**11.50**	15.72	43.14
Improvement	45.39%	37.82%	14.37%

The results presented in Table 1 are an average of 5 different executions, since the agent behavior is not deterministic for neither of the strategies. As can be seen, the modified strategy achieves an average waiting time of 11.50, which implies an improvement of 45.39% over the time achieved by the default strategy. The generators achieve their objective of facilitating the configuration of experiments and the comparison of agent strategies in different simulations. Some video demonstrations of the generator setups in SimFleet are available online: strategy comparison[6], delay start and batches[7], and ecar fleet[8].

5   Conclusions

In this work, we have identified the need for enhancing SimFleet simulation potential and presented two tools to do so: the charging stations generator and the load generator. Knowing that one of SimFleet's purposes is the implementation and comparison of agent strategies, the generators are effective to help in the research of solutions for traffic congestion or any other type of challenge derived

---

[6] https://viewsync.net/watch?v=XNRLQTUIL-Y&t=0&v=QesxSMdEFLI&t=0.

[7] https://youtu.be/90gUOVmz4co.

[8] https://youtu.be/EokHXBAzlL4.

from city sustainability. Provided we have access to city data, with the use of the informed load generator, we can test different driver behaviors over realistic settings to identify problem sources and look for appropriate solutions.

As for the EV charging stations infrastructure, thanks to both generators we can simulate different distributions over a city and, using its real city data, recreate movement within it to analyze the performance of each distribution. This information can be of use for municipalities or other entities in charge of infrastructure creation.

The placement of a charging station should take into account current traffic trends but one must keep in mind that it may as well have an impact on traffic once the station is working. In future work, we aim to develop coordination strategies among transport and station agents in order to find ways of optimizing traffic and achieving a maximum global utility. Such strategies may be the basis for autonomous EV in the smart cities of the future.

Acknowledgments. This work was partially supported by MINECO/FEDER RTI2018-095390-B-C31 project of the Spanish government. Pasqual Martí and Jaume Jordán are funded by UPV PAID-06-18 project. Jaume Jordán is also funded by grant APOSTD/2018/010 of Generalitat Valenciana - Fondo Social Europeo.

References

1. Campo, C.: Directory facilitator and service discovery agent. FIPA Document Repository (2002)
2. Dong, J., Liu, C., Lin, Z.: Charging infrastructure planning for promoting battery electric vehicles: an activity-based approach using multiday travel data. Transp. Res. Part C: Emerg. Technol. **38**, 44–55 (2014)
3. Jordán, J., Palanca, J., Del Val, E., Julian, V., Botti, V.: A multi-agent system for the dynamic emplacement of electric vehicle charging stations. Appl. Sci. **8**(2), 313 (2018)
4. Noori, H.: Realistic urban traffic simulation as vehicular Ad-hoc network (VANET) via Veins framework. In: 2012 12th Conference of Open Innovations Association (FRUCT), pp. 1–7. IEEE (2012)
5. Palanca, J., Terrasa, A., Carrascosa, C., Julián, V.: SimFleet: a new transport fleet simulator based on MAS. In: De La Prieta, F., et al. (eds.) PAAMS 2019. CCIS, vol. 1047, pp. 257–264. Springer, Cham (2019). https://doi.org/10.1007/978-3-030-24299-2_22
6. Skippon, S., Garwood, M.: Responses to battery electric vehicles: UK consumer attitudes and attributions of symbolic meaning following direct experience to reduce psychological distance. Transp. Res. Part D: Transp. Environ. **16**(7), 525–531 (2011)
7. del Val, E., Palanca, J., Rebollo, M.: U-tool: a urban-toolkit for enhancing city maps through citizens' activity. In: Demazeau, Y., Ito, T., Bajo, J., Escalona, M.J. (eds.) PAAMS 2016. LNCS (LNAI), vol. 9662, pp. 243–246. Springer, Cham (2016). https://doi.org/10.1007/978-3-319-39324-7_22

Towards a Dynamic Edge AI Framework Applied to Autonomous Driving Cars

G. Muratore[2]($\boxtimes$), J. A. Rincon[1], V. Julian[1], C. Carrascosa[1], G. Greco[2], and G. Fortino[3]

[1] VRAIN, Valencian Research Institute for Artificial Intelligence,
Universitat Politècnica de València, Valencia, Spain
{jrincon,vinglada,carrasco}@dsic.upv.es
[2] Department of Mathematics and Computer Science (DeMaCS),
University of Calabria, Via P. Bucci, 87036 Rende, CS, Italy
mrtgpp921011063v@studenti.unical.it, gianluigi.greco@unical.it
[3] Department of Informatics, Modeling, Electronics and Systems (DIMES),
University of Calabria, Via P. Bucci, 87036 Rende, CS, Italy
g.fortino@unical.it

Abstract. This work proposes an innovative solution in the field of Edge AI in order to efficiently exploit new hardware components available on the market at low cost. Edge AI means that algorithms are processed locally on a hardware device. The algorithms use data (sensor data or signals) that are created on the own device. The idea of this paper focuses on demonstrating the validity of the proposed solution by implementing an autonomous driving system that exploits communication between intelligent agents. In this case, our self-driving cars are equipped with a low-cost device that allows you to recognise objects along the way and consequently take actions by running a machine learning model. The presence of a machine learning model also allows the developer to modify it by extending the flexibility and application possibilities of the proposed solution.

Keywords: Autonomous driving · Internet of Things · Edge AI · Intelligent agents

1 Introduction

In the last decade we have been able to observe how Artificial Intelligence (AI) has advanced continuously, playing an important role in different areas of knowledge such as medicine [1], robotics [2], or autonomous cars [3], among others. In all these applications were necessary large computing units, high-performance servers, capable of executing millions of calculations per second. Some examples are Cloud services such as *Amazon Web Services (AWS)*[1] (that introduced its *Elastic Compute Cloud* and was the first public Cloud Computing service available), *Microsoft Azure*[2] (that was announced as *Azure*) and *Google Cloud*

---

[1] https://aws.amazon.com/es/.
[2] https://azure.microsoft.com/es-es/.

© Springer Nature Switzerland AG 2020
F. De La Prieta et al. (Eds.): PAAMS 2020 Workshops, CCIS 1233, pp. 406–415, 2020.
https://doi.org/10.1007/978-3-030-51999-5_34

Platform[3]. However, so much computing power has some drawbacks, such as the space they need and their high energy consumption.

At the same time as AI evolved, electronics and microelectronics evolved as well. This evolution has made it possible to create smaller and more powerful devices capable of accessing sensors, actuators and being connected to the Internet. This is what we now call the Internet of Things (IoT) [4,5], which allows almost any everyday element (refrigerators, lights, televisions, etc.) to be connected to the Internet. However, there are still some cases in which complex processes are required in which it is necessary to use some AI tools. Therefore, these devices are seen in the need to use the cloud as an AI computing tool and return to the device the results obtained. This process in some cases is too costly, due to the time required to send such data. It is for this reason that some of these devices have evolved to what we know today as EDGE Computing [5–8]. Edge Computing allows all data generated by IoT devices to be processed where they have been generated, thus avoiding sending data from point A (fridge) to a farther B point (cloud or data centre). This means that the refrigerator collects and processes the data at its place of origin, thus avoiding the massive sending of information to the cloud. According to Cisco, some 50 billion IoT devices will be connected by 2020, but all these volumes of data are passive if they cannot be analysed or interpreted.

This data processing in most cases, are used to perform simple actions on the systems. However, some of these actions could be performed within each of the devices, to do this it is necessary that these devices have the ability to use AI techniques such as machine learning models. These models would help detect patterns in the lower layers of the system, thus avoiding the massive sending of information to higher layers. This would decrease response times, as well as, the massive sending of information to the same point.

These devices capable of performing these actions at a low level is what we know today as *Edge AI*. Edge AI enables the creation of intelligent solutions in real-time using deep learning techniques. These solutions must have a number of key features, such as energy efficiency, low-cost and a balance between precision and energy consumption. Currently, deep learning techniques are conventionally deployed in centralised computing environments. However, these applications have some limitations such as costs generated by energy consumption, and latency in the network due to massive data sending. To address these limitations, Edge Computing, often referred to as *Artificial Edge Intelligence*, has been introduced in which calculations are performed locally from data acquired from various devices or sensors. The challenges of meeting the requirements for implementing Edge AI are to ensure high accuracy of the algorithms while having low power consumption. However, this would not be possible without the latest hardware innovations, including central processing units (CPUs), graphics processing units (GPUs), application-specific integrated circuits (ASICs) and system-on-a-chip (SoC) accelerators, which have made Edge AI possible. Thanks to these

---

[3] https://cloud.google.com/.

advances there are applications such as the one presented by [9], in which they detect apples in real-time using Edge AI or Smart Parking using Edge AI [10].

This article presents a tool based on Edge AI, which incorporates deep learning techniques, allowing the user to modify the models online.

2   System Description

This section describes the framework developed, which enables interaction between intelligent entities and Edge AI devices. This framework provides the developer with a series of tools that allow him to train models of deep learning, dynamic change of learned models and communication between intelligent entities. One of the most important characteristics of the framework presented in this article is the ability to dynamically modify learned models. Allowing the developer to deploy the system anywhere and through a WiFi network send the new model. This dynamism makes this framework an ideal tool for applications in smart homes, smart cities, health care, among others. Another important feature is the ability to be used in different low cost and energy consumption devices such as Rasberry Pi[4], Beagle Bone[5] and any device that incorporates Linux.

The Fig. 1 shows the diagram of the proposed framework. Which incorporates two types of intelligent entities or agents. The first is the edge agent, this agent is located within the environment, then we have the manager agent, this agent is in charge of the actions at high level as the training of the models. Each of the agents presented in this framework was carried out using the SPADE platform and these are explained below.

2.1   Manager Agent

The manager agent is the one in charge of performing the actions at a high level, that is, he is in charge of performing the tasks that require high computational performance. Such as the training of the different deep learning models and the transmission of those models to the Edge Agents. This agent is composed by a two-state machine (Fig. 2, in the first state it takes a set of data to learn.

It is in this state, where the agent performs the image pre-processing tasks, the resizing and the division of the data set in three: training, validation and testing. Once this is done, the agent starts the training process of the Mobilenet network, the result of this training is a model. To which a series of transformations must be made, so that it can be embedded inside the Edge device. These transformations consist in converting from a *.h5 file to a *.kmodel file. For this it is necessary to perform intermediate transformations such as *.h5 to *.pb and then from *.pb to *.tflite and this last one to *.kmodel as can be seen in the Fig. 3.

---

[4] https://www.raspberrypi.org/.
[5] https://beagleboard.org/bone.

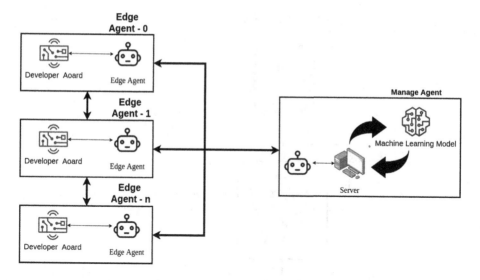

Fig. 1. Framework diagram

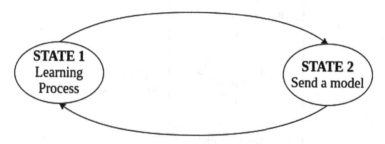

Fig. 2. State machine of manager agent.

Once the model is obtained the agent manager goes to state two, in this state the agent waits for a request from the edge agents. If in this state the agent receives a request from an edge agent, it sends the new model to the agent.

2.2 Edge Agent

The Edge agent is located within the environment, it is in charge of interacting with the environment. This interaction is done using sensors or actuators, which are connected to the system. The sensors allow the agent to introduce information to the machine learning model. the results provided by the model are used by the actuators to interact in the environment.

Image Database

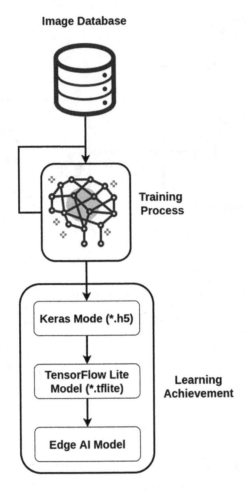

Fig. 3. Process to get the learning achievement.

This agent is composed by a state machine with two states (Fig. 4). The first state is the main process, in this state the agent executes the actions. These actions will be determined by the application in which it is being used. It is in this state where the agent is perceiving the information of the environment, using the different sensors connected to it. This information is then used by the machine learning model, the result obtained from this model will serve the agent to interact with the environment.

The second state of the edge agent is in charge of making the requests to the agent manager, in order to know if there is a new model available. If there is a new model, the Edge Agent receives a message containing a URL. This URL allows the agent to download the model and the labels associated to this model. Once the template has been downloaded, Edge Agent can now use the new template.

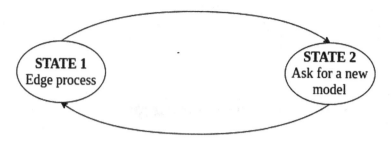

Fig. 4. Edge agent state machine

3   Case Study

This section describes a case study, in which we will use the system proposed above. The case study focuses on the use of autonomous cars, capable of dynamically modifying the learning models. This dynamism will allow the car to identify objects within the road, acting according to the results delivered by the model.

The Edge agents are built using a Raspberry Pi 3 - Model B and a Grove AI Hat for Edge Computing. Each car is equipped with 2 different cameras one for the Raspberry Pi and the other for the Edge device. The camera used by the Raspberry is in charge of performing the autonomous driving, performing a line tracking. The second camera is in charge of classifying the objects within the environment and sends the processed information to the Raspberry. This information contains the probabilities of the objects to be classified, extracting the maximum probability and associated index. Once these two elements are in place the Raspberry can know which object is being classified and acts according to the programmed behavior. This action can be to completely stop the car, reduce the speed or increase the speed.

The figure shows in more detail the main objective of the case study. In this case we have an edge agent represented by a car, which has as its initial model the detection of a horse on the road. Once the edge device detects the horse, it sends the information to the Raspberri and this causes the car to stop. Spend a time (t), the model changes and now the object to be classified is an other car, once Edge device detects the police car the Edge Agent reduces its speed.

To train the neural network of the proposal presented, the first thing is to build a dataset. In a first approach it was decided to perform this task automatically, our system will be given the class names and the system will download the images from Google. After several tests, we decided to give up this idea because too many images were not suitable for classification tasks and the network performance was very low. For this reason, we decided to use part of the WSID-100 [11] data set. The Manage Agent uses the data set to train the network, to perform such training the agnete manager divides the data set into a proportion of 80% for training, 10% for testing and 10% for validation. As a result of this training process, a machine learning model and a firmware suitable for cars are

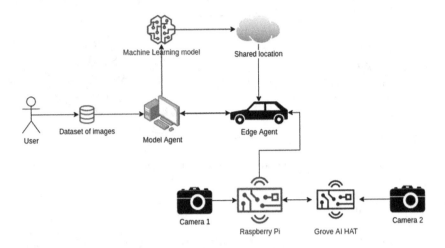

Fig. 5. Case study diagram

obtained. Once you have the trained model, the Agent manager loads this model into a shared resource so that it is available for Edge Agents (cars) (Fig. 6).

The Fig. 7 shows the accuracy of our training process, it can be seen that in these two graphs the accuracy is very high, which indicates that the classification process is good.

After the evaluation of the model the agent starts a series of transformation on it to make it suitable for EdgeAI devices. In particular the first transformation convert our *H5* model in a *TensorFlow Lite* model [12]. However this conversion is not yet sufficient in fact the agent has to convert the obtained *TensorFlow Lite* model in a *Kmodel* file through *nncase*[6], a neural network compiler for Kendryte K210 AI accelerators[7]. To flash the model in an EdgeAI device we need also a custom firmware. The agent create the firmware *bin* file exploiting the Kendryte K210 standalone SDK[8]. To do this process is needed to provide the *Kmodel* file and to put some information in the *C* source file of the firmware.

An important information needed is the memory location where is located the machine learning model. To flash properly the firmware and the *Kmodel* file into the EdgeAI device is needed *Kflash*[9], a Python-based Kendryte K210 UART ISP utility. In order to do this we need a *Json* file that reports the details and the size of the two files in a standardised way. The agent then packs the bin, the *Kmodel* and the *Json* files in a *kfkpg* file.

Once obtained a file ready to be flashed in the EdgeAI device, the agent uploads it on a shared resource reachable from Edge Agent then it goes into *State 2*. Now, Car Agent can request for a new model to the Model Agent. If the

---

[6] https://github.com/kendryte/nncase.
[7] https://kendryte.com/.
[8] https://github.com/kendryte/kendryte-standalone-sdk.
[9] https://github.com/kendryte/kflash.py.

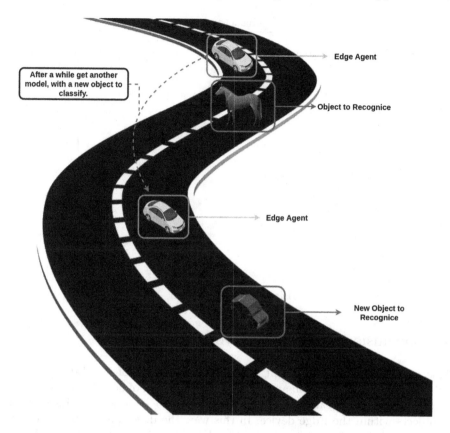

After a while get another model, with a new object to classify.

Edge Agent

Object to Recognice

Edge Agent

New Object to Recognice

Fig. 6. Case study approach

Model Agent has calculated a new model it sends an URL and a list of labels to the car. The car stops driving to download and burn the model in the HAT. When it finishes to burn the model returns to the driving mode. If a new model is not available the car returns to drive without the burning process. If this is the case the Edge Agent receives a message containing an URL to the *kfpkg* file and a list of labels.

The *kfpkg* file contains three files.

1. A *Bin* file – This file is the firmware of the IOT device and comes from the compilation of source code in the Kendryte K210 standalone SDK
2. A *Kmodel* file – This is the file of the Machine Learning model in the special format *Kmodel*.
3. A *Json* file – This is a file in which are listed in a formatted way the file that the tool has to flash and the location of memory where to flash each file. We noticed that the device arise errors when the file are not burned in an aligned way so the address are calculated in a proper way.

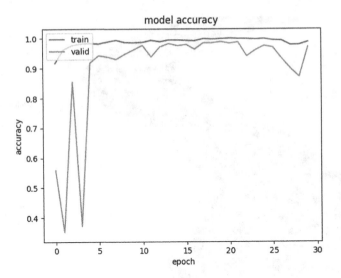

Fig. 7. Accuracy graph

4   Conclusions and Future Work

This article presents a tool that allows the integration of two Edge AI technologies for the classification and dynamic modification of deep learning models. This dynamic modification of models, allows us to perform the classification of objects within the Edge device. In this way, the developed system does not need to send the information obtained to the servers for analysis, thus reducing the latency in obtaining answers. Our system was built using a low cost and low energy consumption development system. As future work, tests are being carried out that will allow us to use our tool in other scenarios, as well as the possibility that the systems can learn other types of input data, such as sounds or sensor signals.

Acknowledgements. This work was partly supported by: ERASMUS+ Programme, KA1 Istruzione Superiore, Carta Erasmus+: 29388-EPP-1-2014-1-IT-EPPKA3-ECHE, ACCORDO PER LA MOBILITÀ ERASMUS PER STUDIO - a.a. 2019/2020, Progetto n° 2019-1-IT02-KA103-061203 - CUP: H25J19000080006, Generalitat Valenciana (PROMETEO/2018/002). Universitat Politecnica de Valencia Research Grant PAID-10-19.

References

1. Chang, A.: The role of artificial intelligence in digital health. In: Wulfovich, S., Meyers, A. (eds.) Digital Health Entrepreneurship. HI, pp. 71–81. Springer, Cham (2020). https://doi.org/10.1007/978-3-030-12719-0_7

2. Yang, L., Henthorne, T.L., George, B.: Artificial intelligence and robotics technology in the hospitality industry: current applications and future trends. In: George, B., Paul, J. (eds.) Digital Transformation in Business and Society, pp. 211–228. Springer, Cham (2020). https://doi.org/10.1007/978-3-030-08277-2_13

3. Khayyam, H., Javadi, B., Jalili, M., Jazar, R.N.: Artificial intelligence and internet of things for autonomous vehicles. In: Jazar, R.N., Dai, L. (eds.) Nonlinear Approaches in Engineering Applications, pp. 39–68. Springer, Cham (2020). https://doi.org/10.1007/978-3-030-18963-1_2

4. Li, H., Ota, K., Dong, M.: Learning iot in edge: deep learning for the internet of things with edge computing. IEEE Netw. **32**(1), 96–101 (2018)

5. Alonso, R.S., Sittón-Candanedo, I., Rodríguez-González, S., García, Ó., Prieto, J.: A survey on software-defined networks and edge computing over IoT. In: De La Prieta, F., et al. (eds.) PAAMS 2019. CCIS, vol. 1047, pp. 289–301. Springer, Cham (2019). https://doi.org/10.1007/978-3-030-24299-2_25

6. Wang, T., Mei, Y., Jia, W., Zheng, X., Wang, G., Xie, M.: Edge-based differential privacy computing for sensor-cloud systems. J. Parallel Distrib. Comput. **136**, 75–85 (2020)

7. Zhou, Z., Chen, X., Li, E., Zeng, L., Luo, K., Zhang, J.: Edge intelligence: paving the last mile of artificial intelligence with edge computing. arXiv preprint arXiv:1905.10083 (2019)

8. Sittón-Candanedo, I., Alonso, R.S., Corchado, J.M., Rodríguez-González, S., Casado-Vara, R.: A review of edge computing reference architectures and a new global edge proposal. Future Gener. Comput. Syst. **99**, 278–294 (2019)

9. Ke, R., Zhuang, Y., Pu, Z., Wang, Y.: A smart, efficient, and reliable parking surveillance system with edge artificial intelligence on IoT devices. arXiv preprint arXiv:2001.00269 (2020)

10. Mazzia, V., Khaliq, A., Salvetti, F., Chiaberge, M.: Real-time apple detection system using embedded systems with hardware accelerators: an edge AI application. IEEE Access **8**, 9102–9114 (2020)

11. Howard, A.G., et al.: Mobilenets: efficient convolutional neural networks for mobile vision applications. CoRR, abs/1704.04861 (2017)

12. Abadi, M., et al.: TensorFlow: Large-scale machine learning on heterogeneous systems (2015). Software available from tensorflow.org

Author Index

Printed in the United States
By Bookmasters